A HISTORY OF vIOLENCE

A HISTORY OF VIOLENCE

From the End of the Middle Ages to the Present

ROBERT MUCHEMBLED

Translated by Jean Birrell

polity

First published in French as *Une histoire de la violence* © Editions du Seuil, 2008

This English edition © Polity Press, 2012
Reprinted in 2012

Polity Press
65 Bridge Street
Cambridge CB2 1UR, UK

Polity Press
350 Main Street
Malden, MA 02148, USA

ISBN-13: 978-0-7456-4746-3
ISBN-13: 978-0-7456-4747-0 (pb)

A catalogue record for this book is available from the British Library.

Typeset in 10 on 11.5 pt Sabon
by Toppan Best-set Premedia Limited
Printed and bound in the USA by Edwards Brothers, Inc.

The publisher has used its best endeavours to ensure that the URLs for external websites referred to in this book are correct and active at the time of going to press. However, the publisher has no responsibility for the websites and can make no guarantee that a site will remain live or that the content is or will remain appropriate.

Every effort has been made to trace all copyright holders, but if any have been inadvertently overlooked the publisher will be pleased to include any necessary credits in any subsequent reprint or edition.

For further information on Polity, visit our website: www.politybooks.com

Liberté • Égalité • Fraternité
RÉPUBLIQUE FRANÇAISE

This book is supported by the French Ministry of Foreign Affairs as part of the Burgess Programme run by the Cultural Department of the French Embassy in London. www.politybooks.com

CONTENTS

Introduction   1

Chapter 1   What is violence?   7

             Is violence innate?   9
             Violence and manliness   12
             Semen and blood: a history of honour   23

Chapter 2   Violence: seven centuries of
             spectacular decline   31

             The reliability of the crime figures   31
             Seven centuries of decline   38
             The 'making' of young men   40

Chapter 3   The youth festivals of violence (thirteenth
             to seventeenth centuries)   45

             A culture of violence   46
             Violent festivities and brutal games   52
             Youth violence   67

Chapter 4   The urban peace at the end of
             the Middle Ages   82

             The pacificatory towns   83
             Controlling the young   93
             Violence costs dear   100

**Chapter 5   Cain and Medea: homicide and the
construction of sexed genders (1500–1650)   119**

A judicial revolution   121
In pursuit of the ungrateful son: the spread of
   the blood taboo   131
Medea, the guilty mother   147

**Chapter 6   The noble duel and popular revolt:
the metamorphoses of violence   161**

The duel, a French exception   164
Noble youths sharpen their swords   170
Popular violence and the frustrations of youth   182

Chapter 7   Violence tamed (1650–1960)   197

Murder is forbidden   200
The civilizing town   211
Violence and changing concepts of honour in
   the countryside   225

**Chapter 8   Mortal thrills and crime fiction (sixteenth to
twentieth centuries)   243**

The devil, assuredly: the birth of crime fiction   244
From bloodthirsty murderer to well-loved bandit   251
Blood and ink   262

**Chapter 9   The return of the gangs: contemporary
adolescence and violence   274**

Death in paradise   276
Juvenile delinquency   283
'Rebel without a cause', or 'eternal recurrence'   288

Is the end of violence possible?   301

Notes   306

Select bibliography   339

Index   361

INTRODUCTION

From the thirteenth to the twenty-first century, physical violence and brutality in human relationships were on a downward trajectory all over Western Europe. This is shown by the curve of homicides recorded in the judicial archives. The very high level of seven centuries ago first fell, by roughly half, in the years 1600–50. This was followed by a spectacular fall over the next three centuries, up to the 1960s, in which the number of cases dropped to a tenth of what it had been; subsequent decades have seen a slight but clear increase.[1] Yet, throughout this period, age and sex patterns in the case of murder have remained remarkably constant, which raises many questions. Women are rarely involved, accounting for about 10 per cent of murderers today, which is the same, with only slight variations, as it has been since the end of the Middle Ages. Most murders are committed by young males of between twenty and thirty years of age. Up to the nineteenth century, murder was more frequent in the southern states of Europe than in the countries of the north. Today, an invisible frontier separates the Western world from the former Soviet bloc, principally Russia, where the murder rate reached 28.4 per 100,000 inhabitants in 2000, whereas it ranged between 1.9 and 0.7 in the European Community before its enlargement.[2]

The only conclusion on which the majority of contemporary experts are agreed is that the Old Continent has seen the emergence of an effective model for the management of male, and especially juvenile, violence. If we exclude wars, which require a different type of analysis, man has become increasingly less openly a wolf to man during this period – at least until the last third of the twentieth century. The changes observed since then may indicate a disturbing reversal of the trend.

How did the European 'factory' succeed in controlling and shaping individual aggression? For some specialists in the social sciences, aggression is a purely biological fact. A historical approach distinguishes this

1

notion from that of violence, which is its ethical shaping by a civilizat-ion.[3] The fact that the variables of sex and age with regard to homicide have changed little over seven centuries in the West seems, at first sight, to confirm the thesis that human beings are predatory and murderous by nature. However, the secular decline in the curve of homicide is essent-ially the result of a slow cultural evolution. It is due primarily to a decrease in the number of fights between young males, both among the elites, who had frequently killed each other in duels, and among ordinary people, who had engaged in frequent manly confrontations and knife fights in public places. The explanation is to be found in the radical change in the masculine notion of honour and in the pacification of human relations, first in public places and then, more slowly, within the family, in the course of what Norbert Elias called the 'civilizing process'.[4]

Male aggression, though a biological reality, is also strongly influenced by society, religion and the state. The relatively rare appearance of women in this context is due to two factors. They do not often kill or injure each other, and when they are struck by men, it tends to be with a degree of moderation, as the latter often avoid sustained attacks on their faces, bellies or reproductive organs. This phenomenon may be explained by a natural inhibiting mechanism, which is useful for the survival of the species. However, it was also a result of imperative cult-ural models which required the daughters of Eve to demonstrate a gentle-ness specific to their sex, refrain from brutality and never carry a weapon. Until our own day, the culture of violence has been essentially masculine in our world. I hope to show in this book that it was transformed, nev-ertheless, between 1300 and 2000. Under pressure from the legal system, its status gradually changed from that of a normal collective language, which had created social ties, and helped to validate the hierarchies of power and the relations between generations and sexes in the core com-munities, to that of major taboo. The West invented adolescence by way of a stronger symbolic tutelage over unmarried young men. This process complemented the efforts of a new educational system intended to keep under much closer supervision an age group seen by the established authorities and adults as particularly turbulent, insubordinate and dan-gerous. This is an aspect of the 'civilizing process' that has so far been little analysed. It was designed to limit the 'natural' aggression of the new male generations by imposing the prohibition of murder, with the increasing approval of the adults of their localities.

The principal change came around 1650, when, everywhere in a Europe ravaged by interminable wars, a strong hostility developed to the sight of blood. From this time on, the Western 'factory' reshaped individ-ual behaviour, which was habitually violent, especially among the young, by a system of norms and rules of politeness which devalued armed confrontations, codes of personal vengeance, excessively harsh hierarchical relationships and relations between the sexes and age groups. This resulted, over the centuries, in a veritable transformation of the collective sensibility with regard to homicide, which culminated, during the industrial age, in its becoming a powerful taboo.

This change was not painless, except for many townspeople, who were much less hostile to being 'disarmed'. This was because the 'urban peace' had already, by the end of the Middle Ages, lessened the violence of the inhabitants of towns more effectively than elsewhere. A system based on graded fines and sanctions had curbed the aggression of the local youths by giving them a precocious sense of self-control, while the dangerous young bachelors born outside the cities had been branded and then banished – as it were, sent to kill elsewhere. Other social groups put up a stubborn resistance. In the first place, the nobles demanded the right to kill in the name of the point of honour. Their culture of the duel, established in the sixteenth century, assured the transition from the law of bloody vengeance to the state monopoly of violence, because it encoded aristocratic aggression. This made it easier for it to be reoriented towards the armed service of the prince and then the nation. The peasant world, to which the vast majority of the population belonged up to the nineteenth century, fought long and hard against the erosion of its manly founding traditions, as is shown by a long series of armed revolts, some of them extremely serious. Nevertheless, in the end, though very slowly, it accepted the prohibition on blood, which provided the adults with new ways of curbing the hot-headedness of the young, impatient to get their place in the sun. More recently, the sudden emergence at the end of the twentieth century of the problems posed by the young rioters of the inner cities gives the impression that there has been a return of the repressed. Is the process going into reverse? Are we seeing a 'de-civilizing process'?

For me, the time to attempt a synthesis of a major phenomenon for the understanding of contemporary Europe seemed to have come, after some forty years of personal research and after supervising many theses. The patient method of the historian, capable of spending long hours seeking evidence in the archives, needed to be broadened out and confronted with that of other specialists in the social sciences. The specific facts, local or regional, reveal their full significance only when collated with each other, before being tested against more general explanations. Comparisons between the various countries for which sufficient accessible works exist, and a change of scale, to give a long-term view, proved equally necessary, so as to avoid documentary myopia and national prejudices. The construction of historical meaning is not a science guided by infallible laws. Rather, it is an artisanal 'bricolage' of concepts, techniques, often imported from elsewhere, and laboriously assembled information. Thus, in the pages that follow, I will try to compose a panorama stretching across the centuries, made up of innumerable fragments of past reality, which come into their own only when related one to the other. The county of Artois, on which I have worked for several decades, served as testing-ground for my attempt to penetrate the enigma posed by the permanence, over seven centuries, of the structures of homicidal violence in Western Europe, in the context of a spectacular reduction in the number of criminal acts recorded by the law. My discovery of the principal paradigm linking the phenomenon primarily to young men was only possible as a result of this approach. It is well known to specialists in the industrial age, but it has almost always been ignored or neglected by those who study earlier periods. It did not seem crucial to me in the 1980s, when I wrote my thesis on violence in Artois. To interpret it correctly, it was necessary to leave the narrowly criminal sphere and enlarge my perspective to the global procedures used by a society to assure its continuity, faced with the formidable challenge posed by the passing of the baton to the new generations by the ageing adults. Gradually, the working hypothesis that became my central thesis, the idea that the management of masculine violence was introduced at the end of the Middle Ages in order to resolve this problem in a new way, became clearer. Even more than that of incest, the prohibition on male violence slowly turned into an obsession.

This prohibition was imposed, nevertheless, without completely inhibiting the aggressive potential of the young men, which was necessary to the 'just' wars of a civilization increasingly interested in conquest after the Great Discoveries. It deflected it and confined and controlled it through morality and religion, making it useful rather than destructive. Yet the system frequently broke down. This happened not in times of generalized conflict, which thinned out the ranks of young men, but in times of peace and strong population growth, which made it increasingly difficult for the young to integrate. In France, this was particularly the case around 1520, 1610, 1789, 1910 and, more recently, in 2005, in the banlieues, or deprived housing estates on the outskirts of the big cities. Conditions can vary, obviously, from one country, or even more one region or locality, to another, which makes it impossible to formulate a categorical explanation. But it seems, at least, that there has been since the end of the Middle Ages a strong general correlation between outbreaks of juvenile violence and a disruption, for one reason or another, of the procedures for managing the replacement of the generations on European soil.

The first chapter defines the very complex notion of violence while the second offers a panoramic overview of its spectacular decline during the last seven centuries, particularly visible in the case of murder. The remaining seven chapters adopt a more chronological approach, not without some overlap, as the old, outdated traditions often continued to coexist with the new. Chapter 3 is devoted to the juvenile festivals of violence, from their origins in traditional agrarian civilization to the time when, in the seventeenth century, they were called into question. They gave ground only slowly, however, and still today influence customs that are now seen as savage. This was already the case in the most powerful towns in the fourteenth and fifteenth centuries, where there was a sort of municipalization of aggression, assured by a system of fines, which provided an original urban peace. I describe this in chapter 4. Its effectiveness declined, however, in the age of Luther and Calvin, under the combined impact of triumphant monarchs and fiercely antagonistic churches.

In chapter 5, I trace the growth, between 1500 and 1650, of a new sensibility promoted by these powerful forces. All over Europe, the attention of the criminal justice system was focused on homicide and infanticide, as is shown by the increasing number of death sentences passed on the perpetrators. The latter came largely from the young of both sexes. The Western 'factory' thus began both to construct the two genders in a radically new way and to insist on an increased respect for human life. This met with powerful resistance. Chapter 6 examines two of its fiercest forms, those of the nobility and the peasantry. The former imposed a new culture of violence by inventing the rules of the duel. This was tolerated by the bellicose states then dominant, because this type of cruel confrontation allowed a ruthless selection of the best officers. However, the rebellious peasantry, who sought to preserve their manly traditions, were subjected to a relentless campaign of repression.

A period of tamed violence, which began about 1650 and lasted until the 1950s, is the subject of chapter 7. With the exception of periods of war, European societies were now governed by a powerful blood taboo, which sharply distinguished them from the United States. Only a tiny 'residue' of youths, described as villainous, savage and barbarous, resisted. The majority of young males meekly accepted the prohibition on killing. The young women who broke this taboo by getting rid of their foetus or newborn child were gradually treated more leniently by judges, juries and public opinion, as they came increasingly to be regarded as victims of society. Civilization has many ways of imposing on the new generations its ethical and moral messages, or prolonging them in the form of conditioned reflexes.

Chapter 8 is devoted to the *récit noir* and the detective story from the sixteenth to the mid twentieth century. It shows how the taste for blood passed from reality to the imaginary and became a fantasy, designed to pacify the behaviour of its readers, while at the same time giving them the outlet of mortal thrills. More ambiguously, this chameleon genre also made it possible to dream of violence, to have a personal oneiric experience of it, and to keep it alive so that it could be reactivated and made to serve to the community in time of need. The literary glorification of murder, an internal contradiction in our culture, as seen in Fantômas, shortly before the First World War, found permissible outlets in 'just' and patriotic conflicts. Juvenile aggression was thus confined and deflected rather than eradicated. It resurfaces whenever the procedures for containing it are weakened and conflicts between age groups intensify.

Chapter 9, which discusses the worrying return of youth gangs since 1945, reminds us that contemporary adolescence remains associated with violence. This is especially so on its poorly integrated margins, but perhaps also more widely, as is shown by the fights between the supporters of different football clubs. In our own period, disquieting fractures are revealed by the increasing ineffectiveness of the procedures for the handing on of the social torch to the young by the old, whose life expectancy is much longer than in the past, and who are often tempted to cling interminably to power. The main explanation for the recent explosions of destructive brutality in the inner cities probably lies less in any alleged 'de-civilizing process' than in the greater difficulties faced by the most deprived, in particular the new generations of both sexes, in getting access to their share of the social cake in a period marked by large-scale unemployment and fear of the future. May the Western cycle for controlling juvenile aggression, introduced some five hundred years ago, be coming to an end before our very eyes?

— 1 —

WHAT IS VIOLENCE?

The word 'violence', which comes from the Latin *vis*, meaning 'force' or 'vigour', appeared in French at the beginning of the thirteenth century, and characterized a quick-tempered and brutal person. It also described a power relationship aimed at subjecting or constraining another person. In the centuries that followed, Western civilization gave violence a fundamental role. On the one hand, it fiercely denounced the excesses of violence and declared it illegitimate, recalling that divine law forbade the killing of another person; on the other, it gave violence an elevated, positive role and declared it legitimate, to validate the action of the knight who shed blood in defence of widows and orphans, and to defend the 'just' wars waged by Christian kings against the Infidel, troublemakers and the enemies of the prince. Until the middle of the twentieth century, the continent lived amidst violence. Not only did it enable the continent to respond to the challenges of its rival, Islam, in particular the Turkish threat, but violence frequently governed relations between monarchs and lords, great and small. Internal wars between states and, from the sixteenth century, between antagonistic Christian religions were waged for more than half a millennium; they spread to the rest of the world in the eighteenth century and culminated in the terrible world wars of the first half of the twentieth century. The generations born since 1945 are the first to have seen war disappear from the West, although certain eastern frontiers of the continent have continued to suffer its ravages, or at least remain under its threat. The European Union has in recent times been an oasis in this regard. It is also the only large grouping of nations in the world to have abolished the death penalty on its soil for all crimes, including mortal violence. It has slowly and painfully exorcized the problem, and now regards human life as sacred and homicide as a major taboo.

It is my aim in this book to try to understand how Western culture has managed, in seven centuries, to stamp out a multiform murderous violence that was still, only recently, deeply embedded in its fabric. It may even, at certain periods, have been crueller and more destructive than in other civilizations. For the formidable warriors produced on its soil spread fire and the sword to other peoples during the crusades and during the conquest of America by the conquistadors in the sixteenth century, and to the rest of the world in the age of colonization, before passing the torch to the United States in the twentieth century. A true 'culture of war' has presided from its origins over the development of the West, even intensifying with the Great Discoveries.

That is not my subject here. Western culture was fertile territory for other types of violence because it was based on a manly ethic which elevated brute force into a model of behaviour, particularly in the profoundly unequal societies of the Middle Ages and the *ancien régime*. The second sex was left with little more than the role of weak, unarmed women, necessarily dependent, protected by males who derived pleasure from them and demanded they provide them with sons to continue the lineage. Nobles or commoners, powerful or weak, all men were educated in the context of a 'culture of violence' based on the need to defend masculine honour against rivals. The brutality of human relations was a universal social language, considered normal and necessary in the West until at least the seventeenth century. Until its slow monopolization by the state and the nation, violence shaped the masculine personality according to the noble model of manliness and the mastery of the use of weapons demanded of every aristocrat; it thus created, in opposition, the model of the weak woman. Until the disarmament of the ordinary population, which was slowly and painfully achieved on princely orders from the seventeenth century, the lowest male shared this ethic and wielded a knife or a sword with ease and without much respect for human life. From the Age of Enlightenment, the efforts of the civil and religious authorities to devalue this attitude began to bear fruit. The great armed peasant revolts that set whole regions ablaze became fewer, and the number of homicides prosecuted by the courts declined everywhere, not least in France, England, the Low Countries and Sweden. A new culture of the taboo on blood and the rejection of violence gradually came to prevail on the continent, not without some savage resurgences, or significant chronological and geographical variations.

The social sciences, those remarkable products of the Western genius in the nineteenth century, have recently turned their attention to the question of homicidal violence. Their common discourse of devaluation with regard to this 'criminal' phenomenon usually ignores its socially structuring aspects and the positive forms it could assume in the eyes of both actors and governments in the Middle Ages and the sixteenth century. We need to go back to this fact if we are to achieve a proper understanding of the problem and reveal the causes of the massive changes of the last five hundred years. We may begin by asking if violence is innate or a cultural construction, before trying to explain its close relationship to manliness in the history of the West; this will lead us to a discussion of the symbolic link forged between semen and blood to define masculine honour in our culture.

Is violence innate?

In legal terms, violence designates crimes against persons, including homicide, assault and rape. The classification of these phenomena is not the same in all countries and at all periods, which complicates the historian's task. Specialists in the *ancien régime* generally omit infanticide, on the grounds that it is particularly under-recorded. Offences against property form a separate category today, although some robberies are accompanied by aggravated, even lethal, violence. The statistics for the anglophone countries, both recent and old, clearly distinguish two types of homicide, premeditated and unpremeditated, the latter designated as manslaughter. Such a lack of standardization illustrates wide differences in the way homicide has been perceived in the various countries, and even more the various periods, considered here.

The general characteristics of homicide pose a major puzzle. The profile of the typical offender has changed very little since the thirteenth century, in spite of the considerable decline in recorded numbers observed all over in Europe. Women are in a tiny minority. The majority of murderers are young men aged between twenty and twenty-nine. Under the *ancien régime*, their victims often resembled them in age and sex and the murderous confrontations usually revolved round issues of rights, precedence and honour. Members of the wealthiest and most privileged groups were no less involved than others. The marked decline in lethal violence from the seventeenth century seems to be linked both to the general pacification of public space and to the abandonment by young men of good families of this type of confrontation; they turned instead to duels, until these were, in due course, criminalized.[1] Most lethal violence continues today to be committed by young men who are poorly qualified and come largely from working-class or poor backgrounds.[2] This reveals not only an economic and social divide, but a major cultural difference: violent behaviour has been more quickly and more easily eradicated by education, morality and pervading pressures among young men from the upper social ranks.

9

These observations suggest that violence is not a purely innate phenomenon. It can be distinguished from aggression, which is a potentiality for violence, whose destructive power can be inhibited by civilizations – if they decide to do this, and if there is sufficient acceptance among those affected for their views to be imposed. At the beginning of the twenty-first century, for example, young men from poor backgrounds have much less to lose than sons of good families, whose reputations and future careers can be ruined if they are prosecuted for wounding or killing someone. In the case of the former, on the other hand, a sense of injustice or deep frustration weakens the moral and ethical constraints regarding the shedding of human blood, which are inculcated into all alike by the socializing institutions.

Our civilization has resolved this major contradiction by adopting a very fluid semantic use of the concept of violence. It has, at the same time, imposed a blanket prohibition on it. Specialists distinguish two antagonistic meanings of the term. The first identifies the violence at the heart of life: all living creatures are driven to predatory or defensive behaviour when threatened. But man is not an ordinary animal, it is argued, and he is without a conscious desire to destroy his fellows. This humanist vision, inherited both from Christianity and from the philosophic Enlightenment, is not accepted by all scholars. Psychoanalysts, psychologists and ethologists identify a specific aggression in humans. Freud developed this notion by opposing the death impulse (Thanatos) and the life impulse (Eros). He based his ideas on the Oedipus complex linked to the fantasy of the 'murder' of the father. Erich Fromm, for his part, put the forms of human violence into two groups, one normal, the other pathological. Among the former are those which are expressed in play or are directed at preserving life, out of fear, frustration, envy or jealousy, but also, with a dose of pathology, out of a desire for revenge or a loss of hope. The second group, oriented by death impulses, includes compensatory violence 'in individuals afflicted by powerlessness', sadism and an 'archaic' bloodlust, producing murderous rage. He is unequivocal in claiming that man is the sole primate capable of killing and torturing members of his own species for no good reason, purely for pleasure. Our fellow men can 'play at being violent and slaughtering each other', added Daniel Sibony. The neurologist, psychiatrist and ethologist Boris Cyrulnik argues that there is a violence specific to humans, because they, unlike the animals, can picture imaginary worlds, which sometimes leads them to commit genocides, when they identify 'inferior races' to be destroyed.[3]

Certain ethological theories derived from the observation of animal behaviour have proved controversial when applied to humans. In the footsteps of Konrad Lorenz, they link the aggression mechanisms to the defence of the 'territory' of the individual or the group.[4] These have been strongly rebutted by scholars who do not believe that the aggressive instinct is the organizing principal of human societies; in which case it would have led to a biological cul-de-sac and caused the species to disappear. The essential characteristics of the latter are, on the contrary, cooperation and solidarity. The two positions derive from irreconcilable philosophies. They oppose the heirs of Thomas Hobbes,[5] for whom 'man is a wolf to man', so should put his trust in an absolute state, alone capable of protecting him, and those who believe in the natural goodness of man, represented by Rousseau and the *philosophes* of the Enlightenment. Between these two extremes come the heirs of a pessimistic theology of human nature as being strongly marked by aggression, who can see its salvation only in faith: 'Religion invariably strives to subdue violence, to keep it from running wild'; it 'instructs men as to *what they must and must not do* to prevent a recurrence of destructive violence', and it drives a community in crisis to choose a 'surrogate victim' whose sacrifice makes it possible to restore the order that has been disturbed.[6]

A debate of this type is neither the business of historians nor within their competence. At most, they may note that past centuries have bequeathed us a double conception of violence: legitimate when employed by institutions, such as states when they wage war, or churches when they persecute 'heretics'; illegitimate when committed by individuals in opposition to the law or morality. This fundamental ambiguity stems from the fact that human violence is both biological and cultural. The search for sexual dominance, necessary to the propagation of the species, may unconsciously and automatically condition the 'age-old aggressive reflex', but it is generally deflected or repressed by parental and social rules and prohibitions. These, imposed on us all from infancy, produce automatic reflexes that assure the survival and protection of the community.[7] Such a theory has the virtue of defining murder not as an absolute intangible but as the transgression by an individual of the norms decreed by his culture, in conditions which depend on the chances of success it offers that individual. An abnormal blockage, which is particularly intolerable for young men, can thus reactivate aggression, inasmuch as this stems from an unconscious survival mechanism of the organism faced with dangers or hostile signals emanating from its environment. The notion of 'territory' can be used with caution, because, though man is not an animal, neither is he pure mind. The consciousness of a threat comes from worrying situations such as the overpopulation of a town, the density of a crowd or the disquieting approach of a man who is armed or whose attitude appears strange. The regulation of distance – that is, the safety zone within which an individual does not allow an enemy to penetrate – is biological in origin, but plastic and culturally

11

modified according to period, place and the prevailing values in a society, and it plays an important role in aggressive interactions.[8]

Psychological approaches, too, can make a useful contribution. Violence is activated by frustrations or narcissistic injuries in the sphere of *amour propre* and self-esteem. The intensity of the brutal response seems to be greater when the insults or disparaging remarks come from an admired person or authority figure, such as a teacher or policeman.[9] It is even more pronounced in a group, as Gustav Le Bon showed in relation to the crowd.[10] In this situation, individuals lose their inhibitions and experience a sense of impunity linked to anonymity, as we see in the case of the gangs of hooded rioters from the inner cities at the beginning of the twenty-first century. Empirical studies have also demonstrated that a high population density, for example in a nursery school, increases aggressive behaviour, each child seeming to defend its own territory.[11]

Violence and manliness

Psychological and psychoanalytical theories cannot wholly explain violence. This is because it is in a complex relationship with other things, with the victim, in the first place, and then with all the institutions which need to consider its forms and its consequences to assess its impact and repress it. Every society seeks to control the dangers that might threaten its survival and establishes its own threshold of tolerance for violence. It does this theoretically, through the prevailing values and the law, and more concretely through the exercise of criminal justice. Luís Fróis, a Portuguese Jesuit who lived in Japan, described, in 1585, the main differences between the customs of that country and Portugal in the case of aggression, homicide and its punishment:

4. With us, it is an insult to tell to someone to their face that they are lying; the Japanese laugh and take this as a compliment.

5. We do not kill without authority or jurisdiction; in Japan, anyone can kill in their own house.

6. With us, it is surprising to kill a man, but not to kill cows, chickens or dogs; the Japanese are surprised to see us kill animals, but kill men as a matter of course.

7. In Europe, we do not kill for theft, at least up to a certain sum; in Japan, they do it for the most trifling theft.

8. With us, if a man kills another, if it is in self-defence, he is exonerated by the law; in Japan, he who has killed must die in his turn, and if he managed to flee, another is killed in his place...

12

24. With us, to kill flies with the hands is regarded as dirty; in Japan, the princes and the lords do it by pulling off their wings before throwing them away...

58. We often succumb to anger and rarely master our impatience; they, strange to say, remain always in this very moderate and restrained.[12]

The perception of the phenomenon also varies within a civilization, especially according to social and age groups and gender. True cultures of violence prosper, even in the long term, when living conditions are hard and the law difficult to apply, as, for example, among the pioneers of the American western frontier in the nineteenth century. Though remarkably pacified since then, our own Western world is still familiar with violence: youth gangs in the inner cities, elite military units, certain sportsmen and women, the prison world, the lower classes confronted with the harshness of their living conditions, among others.[13]

Yet destructive aggression is a male affair. In contemporary Europe, only 10 per cent of murderers are women, which was also the case in thirteenth-century England. The variations recorded in the seven centuries since have been slight. In France, women accounted for 14 per cent of all crimes and offences committed in 2002, and for 5 per cent of the prison population.[14] In China, between 1736 and 1903, just over 2 per cent of the 22,553 known murderers were women, but women accounted for 11 per cent of the victims.[15] It is tempting to relate these facts to invariants of human nature, feminine gentleness as opposed to masculine brutality. But explanations which invoke the male hormones particularly activated by the climate, especially heat, are quickly disproved. Those which cite the predatory aggression induced by the need to assure the survival of the species, and inscribed in the genes of the male hunter, driving him to destroy his rivals and impregnate as many partners as possible, are peremptory assertions it is impossible for the historian to verify.[16] For the latter, it is the construction of human beings by their culture that is important. The essential link is not that between violence and masculinity, because this is a biological given. It is that established with manliness, a notion defined by each society in the context of the determination of the sexual 'genders' whose existence it recognizes. Until quite recently, the West accepted only two, and established a powerful functional inequality between them.

The same was true of imperial China, where the subjection of women was even more flagrant. But such similarities conceal very different treatments of homicide. In the autocratic and conservative society of the Middle Empire, the social order was based on the supremacy of the old. The fundamental taboo with regard to violence, whether fatal or not, was applied to parricide, which constituted the 'absolute familial, social,

13

physical and metaphysical evil'. This taboo extended to the murder of grandparents, superiors and older persons, and to that of a husband by a wife, even if the act had only been attempted or the son or wife had played only a minor role. Nor was the insane parricide spared, so terrible was the crime. It represented the most extreme transgression against paternal authority, 'conceived both as the basis and reflection of the celestial order rising in judiciously graded stages to the emperor'. The murder of a father or mother was in practice extremely rare: it was imputed to only fifty-eight of the 22,162 men, and only seven of the 491 women, guilty of homicide in almost two centuries. Masculine familial murder accounted for 17 per cent of the total and, with the exception of the wife, who was the victim in 844 cases, it primarily involved distant or very distant relatives. By contrast, 66 per cent of the small number of female murderers had killed their spouse, and 15 per cent another member of their family. The Chinese system was based on the definition of society as an extension of the family, and its identity was rooted in a 'paternal metaphor'. Inculcated by the laws of morality and the cult of ancestors, it seems to have been very effectively protected by the judicial system. Executions for parricide were rare, and made a spectacle out of the absolute evil and its punishment. 'It was as if the judges felt the need, at regular intervals, to provide the social body with the representation of the supreme danger and its eradication.' The crime that is most feared, like paedophilia in France today, is the one that represents an intolerable threat to the collective values on which the permanence of a civilization is based. In which case, the punishment far exceeds the crime, so as to allow a general repair of the torn social and cultural fabric.[17]

The Chinese example makes it easier to grasp the relativity of the notion of crime, which is always shaped by societies according to the basic principles they wish to defend. Some have practised the killing of newborn babies or ritual incest between brother and sister, which suggests that the universality of the taboos in these spheres may essentially be an absolute invented by the social sciences within the context of the promotion of our own culture. The Biblical prohibition 'Thou shalt not kill' has not always been observed on European soil. Its real acceptance can even be dated to the age of the absolute monarchs, when a massive theoretical and judicial effort was made to 'discipline' populations appalled by the terrible Wars of Religion between 1562 and 1648. With the restoration of order, at different dates in different countries, male homicide and female infanticide were made inexpiable crimes. The death penalty was employed much more frequently than in the past for these offences, and it performed a symbolic function by defining the supreme danger, and eradicating it. This has echoes of imperial China, but the essential objectives were different.

14

To enhance the sacrality of sovereigns and of great men, several of whom had been assassinated, like Henri III and Henri IV in France, and William of Orange, who had aspired to a crown in the Low Countries, European lawyers developed the concept of lese-majesty. It was applied first to regicide, then extended to other crimes committed against monarchic or religious authority, such as forging currency, military desertion, treason and satanic witchcraft. The torture of the regicide Ravaillac, torn apart alive by four horses in 1610, served as a model to define the absolute horror of this act. This crime without parallel was closely linked to that of parricide, the most serious homicide after the assassination of a prince, and punished by mutilation, such as the severing of a hand, before execution. The proliferation of tortures described by Michel Foucault formed a chain of meaning which linked assaults on the royal person to those on fathers and, more generally, to the act of shedding human blood.[18] Unlike in imperial China, the aim was to impose a new state system, by demonstrating its efficiency in protecting subjects against all the dangers they had experienced during the previous troubled decades. One of the most visible signs of its success was its progress, however gradual, in disarming populations, curtailing the excesses of the noble duel and punishing the most dangerous criminals. The system provided a growing sense of security. The spectacle of the agonies of a regicide was exceptional, and the torture of homosexuals and burning of witches relatively rare, except in the latter case in the Germanic territories; the principal targets were those who had committed acts of lethal aggression or infanticide.

The number of homicides fell sharply in Western Europe in the first half of the seventeenth century, whereas the number of death penalties for this crime greatly increased.[19] Whereas murder and the killing of newborn babies had previously been regarded as fairly banal occurrences, only half-heartedly and not very effectively pursued by the courts, these now assumed the status of major crimes and became closely bound up with the concept of lese-majesty. In the eighteenth century, the priorities shifted once again, in the direction of crimes against property, at a time of strong economic and commercial growth. In both England and France, the two great rivals on the European and world stage, robbery became, in its turn, the most unacceptable of crimes. Death sentences were increasingly often passed on those guilty of it, especially in London and Paris, the two greatest commercial centres in Europe.[20]

The thesis that there was a shift 'from violence to theft' between the end of the Middle Ages and the Age of Enlightenment is no longer generally accepted. The real change was not a transformation of the criminal realities, but rather an evolution of the repressive gaze.[21] Western culture has been adapting to new developments for some five hundred years.

The emergence of a new type of serious crime and, in its wake, a harsher repression of associated transgressions is a consequence of a change in the basic values underpinning this culture. At the beginning of the twenty-first century, the judicial focus in the West has shifted again. The worst crimes are now linked to the preservation of the lives and sexual innocence of children. At a time when the death penalty has been abolished in Europe, it is symptomatic that those who talk of possible exceptions refer to this threat to children, now designated as the most unspeakable crime that a human being can commit.

The relativity of the notion of criminality suggests the need to draw a clear distinction between, on the one hand, the individual pathology operating in the transition to the act of murder and, on the other, the definitions of transgression or illegal forms of behaviour constructed by the state, the law and the various institutions of control in the community in question. Insanity, for example, lies behind only a tiny proportion of murders. A more common explanation is that the act of murder originates in the frustrations created by contradictions between the individual desires of the perpetrators and the future opportunities they are offered by society. This particular criminological discourse works better for the contemporary period than for earlier centuries. The eighth observation of the Jesuit Luís Fróis reminds us of the banality of homicide in Europe and refers to the mechanism of the princely pardon in cases of self-defence. By contrast, the Japanese were ruthless in such affairs, as, indeed, was increasingly the case with many Western judges in the eighteenth century. Eastern empires, Japanese or Chinese, and absolute monarchies in the West were alike, ultimately, in demonstrating the illegitimacy of the individual violence that led to the killing of a fellow creature. By brandishing the threat of the death penalty for those who dared to kill, they strengthened their control over their subjects. This had not been the case in the European societies of the immediately preceding centuries. Then less strictly controlled by the state, they had allowed more latitude to the local and regarded the death of a human being with a degree of indifference, in the context of a culture in which male violence was the norm.

In these circumstances, aggression had a positive value. It was better, obviously, if it did not lead to the death of an adversary, in accord with Christian morality. Such misfortunes did not, however, though frequent, lead to the marginalization of the guilty party. Readily pardoned by the king, in return for a fine, he also made financial reparation to the victim's family in the form of a *paix du sang* ('blood peace'), before resuming an honourable place in the community. Male murderers were treated even more leniently if they were young, because the adults of their locality tolerated their displays of violence in the belief that youth must have its fling. It is because of this acceptance that it was young men aged between twenty and twenty-nine who were most likely to commit murder. During their long wait for marriage, both in the countryside and in the towns, young men in this age group adopted a culture of bachelor gangs. These were based on competition between peers to enhance their value in the eyes of the girls and to compensate for the frustrations associated with this uncomfortable state, between childhood and full adulthood. Their principal concern was to extol a manliness which made them exist in the eyes of others. They carried weapons, in particular knives or swords, and used them freely in fights intended to demonstrate their valour, inflicting or receiving wounds which infection and the inadequacies of contemporary medicine often rendered fatal.[22] Young noblemen, trained for combat and imbued with an equally manly warrior ethic, were not fundamentally different in this regard from the peasantry, before their isolation after the invention of the rules of the aristocratic duel in the sixteenth century.

Not all unmarried men were killers. Only a tiny minority committed murder. The highest homicide rate recorded for the thirteenth century is a little over 100 murders for every 100,000 inhabitants. Given that women were rarely involved, we may deduce a maximum of 100 murderers for every 50,000 men, all ages included, that is, about 0.2 per cent of the contingent. Young unmarried men probably accounted for scarcely more than a fifth of the male population in the demographic conditions of the time and provided less than half this total. In other words, at most one young man in a thousand committed murder. To kill one of one's peers was by no means the norm, even if happened a hundred times more often than in our own day. The manly masculine code which caused this also led to a much larger number of confrontations which, though violent, did not have such serious consequences. Homicide was the tip of the iceberg of a system of rivalry between peers which was usually settled simply by blows, even more often by displays of bravado between young 'bloods'. It is an indicator of changes in this culture of masculine violence, revealing its occasional fatal flaws.

The homicide rate fell on average to 10 per 100,000 in the first half of the seventeenth century. The decline is spectacular. There was a tenfold decline in the number of young male murderers, a sign of the retreat of the culture of manly violence in the face of the advance of a new intolerance, conveyed by many other means than the law alone. The Western 'factory' was inventing adolescence as a dangerous age, which must be closely controlled so as to prevent its lethal excesses. After that, the trend speeded up, to produce a rate of around 1 per cent in the middle of the twentieth century, a hundred times lower than in the Middle Ages. This implies an equivalent reduction in juvenile murderous violence, as the

17

principal actors remained the same. In the England of the early twenty-first century, homicide is primarily a male affair. The murderer and his victim usually know each other, or are even related, and, in nearly half of all cases, they have quarrelled. They are mostly aged between sixteen and thirty-five. The most common weapon, used in 28 per cent of cases, is a sharp implement.[23]

Homicide is a social construction. In our own day, the authorities and the bodies charged with its repression have developed a precise definition and interpretation which emphasize some of its aspects and overlook others, such as deaths due to negligence or dangerous driving; this is even before a defendant has to face the legal processes which will decide on his guilt.[24] 'The criminal becomes the inverted double of the honest man', the judicial ritual allowing the state 'to affirm its authority in an emotional and symbolic manner'.[25] The principal target in the case of murder is the young male, impatiently waiting to reach maturity and accede to the advantages of adult life, who transgresses the most sacred codes by killing one of his peer group. On the one hand, society urges him to define himself by reference to an ethic of manliness; on the other, it exhorts him to keep his cool and learn the self-control necessary to avoid this inexpiable crime. It forbids him to engage in illegitimate physical violence, the latter defined in opposition to the violence decreed by the community and employed in its service, for example in the just war. War also serves to control the explosive potential of the new generations by binding them to the defence of the common good and the model of the respectable adult man. The rapid decline in homicide rates since the seventeenth century testifies to the increasing success of social control in this sphere. Murder has become a residual phenomenon in our societies. Less extreme forms of physical violence are also ranked as abnormal, defined as an impediment to the later social success of young men. So far has this gone that aggression is now primarily associated with society's marginals and losers. They are stigmatized both by the authorities – the police and the law – and by the modern media, who connive to heighten the anxieties of decent people, appalled by incomprehensible acts of savagery.

The distaste for blood and the taboo on violence have been the cornerstones of the Western system since it embarked on the conquest of the globe some five hundred years ago. Stamped with the seal of absolute illegitimacy in the internal relations of societies, these have enabled states to appropriate a monopoly of legitimate force, both in war and in the use of the death penalty, until its recent abolition. They have also helped to assure the least conflictual possible transmission between generations, by making the implicit contract forged between them dependent on the younger generation acquiring mechanisms for the pacification of their

18

behaviour. The management of the patrimony must continue to be assured on the previous model, by good family men, so that the hard core of murderers, often from poor backgrounds, can all the more justifiably be excluded from the 'normal' succession. When the young become too numerous, after a period of peace and demographic growth, intergenerational tensions increase and youth violence returns in a big way. In France, it produced the 'Apaches' of the *belle époque*, who rediscovered the temptation of the knife fight, and the *casseurs* ('rioters' – literally 'wreckers') of the banlieues in 2005.

The taming of manly aggression was part of a wider phenomenon, the social and cultural pact on which the state and the whole of Western civilization were based. This aggression, a biological reality, was strongly shaped and oriented by the dominant forces for cohesion, in order to produce an exemplary ordinary subject who was not constantly challenging the values or norms of his community, national or local. Europe achieved the feat of producing sociability on the basis of a particularly unstable element, the sexuality of young men.[26]

It has been argued that the repression of homicide was linked not only to the definition of masculinity, and the greater disciplining of the stronger sex, but to a reformulation of the male and female roles to the benefit of the former. In England, a new 'culture of sensibility', which emerged in the eighteenth century in sentimental works of fiction, depicted men as savage hunters and fishers, for whom women were the prey. It has been interpreted as an effort to force the man of chauvinist and brutal honour to transform himself into a sensible and prudent being.[27] In the nineteenth century, the stronger rejection of violence was closely linked to the desire to change the masculine model and make it more 'natural'. The tolerance extended to unpremeditated murder, or manslaughter, which was punished by at most a year's imprisonment, began to disappear, and the fatal accident no longer led systematically to acquittal. The number of men accused increased twice as fast as that of women between 1805 and 1842, a sign of a 'masculinization' of the crime and the punishments, part of a secular trend towards an increase in the discipline required of men.[28]

The modification of masculine roles, visible in the street, the workplace and the home, led to changes in feminine roles as well. The concept of 'hegemonic masculinity' has been developed by anglophone scholars to explain this chain of transformations, which extended to children, too. The pivot on which everything turned was manliness. Until the changes of the late twentieth century, the position of the male, whatever his social status, was strongly correlated with the assertion of his heterosexuality, but much less than before with the need to demonstrate it violently in the theatre of everyday life. Women, meanwhile, had to remain in their place so as to confirm the man as a man. The passivity required by the cultural norms constructed the woman as a gentle and helpless creature, normally incapable of murderous violence. A woman who behaved aggressively seemed abnormal, even totally Other. The mother who killed her own child was an extreme example of this, mad, unnatural or deeply disturbed by what had happened to her. Such a conception drew attention to this monstrous act and inexorably led to an increase in the recorded statistics. The child was now seen as innocent by nature. If one child killed another, that child was assumed to be profoundly evil or diabolic.[29] There were marked social differences, however, in practice, because the softening behaviour and the redefinition of masculine and feminine roles did not penetrate all social levels as deeply or at the same rate. In the industrial age, this only encouraged denunciations of the brutality and coarseness of the working classes and of the resistance of the peasantry to change. Judicial repression was, as a result, increasingly directed against these categories of the population.

Our civilization no longer wants to contemplate violence by women and probably underestimates the violence they suffer. It has for centuries preferred to focus on the 'civilizing woman', whose mission is to soften behaviour, turn men away from violence and restrain the brutality of their sexual desires. While it is clear that women play a fundamental role in cultural transmission, nothing proves that they have always conceived their role as that of docile and obedient sheep. In contemporary Greece, at Pouri, women frequently smack babies to make them be quiet and beat their sons up to the age of twelve, when they come under the authority of the father. They are reproducing the corporal punishments they experienced in childhood: hanging by the hands and feet from the main roof beam of the house, or upside down from a tree, sometimes under a fire meant to 'cure' an insufferable child; needles stuck into the palm of the hand; scalding hot boiled eggs crushed in armpits. They are eternal minors, still harassed as adults, particularly at the hands of their mother-in-law. A disrespectful or idle son may be driven out, under a hail of stones, by his father. The corporal punishments at Arnaia are less cruel but still harsh and slaps across the face are frequent, even if they are counterbalanced by gifts. In both places, daughters are brought up to respect the privileges of their brothers, who will inherit everything.[30]

In reality, women can be violent – cruel at executions under the *ancien régime*, brutal against each other or against men, scratching and biting, pulling hair, kicking or pummelling with their fists. Many documents testify to this, more often at the end of the Middle Ages and in the sixteenth century than since. The process that led to a reduction in female violence began very early in the towns,[31] but made slower progress in the villages. Until this change, which varied from one country and region to another, routine brutality was part of ordinary life. Contemporary Greece simply sheds a little light on a female violence that may have been more general before it was concealed or denied. It was probably less developed than that of men, in particular in its bloodier forms, if only because, unlike men up to the seventeenth century, women did not carry weapons. It was still part of a 'culture of violence' which extended to the whole of the population. Children were brought up both to suffer violence and to practise it. Little shepherd boys defended their territory against the flocks of other villages, using their crooks and slings, causing serious and sometimes fatal injuries to adversaries of their own age. Everybody was violent at the end of the Middle Ages and in early modern times.[32] Neither states nor the Church had the means, or indeed a real desire, to try to control at all rigorously the lethal violence of the population, especially as it played a structuring role in local societies, establishing hierarchies and contributing to the exchanges between the inhabitants. This is not to say that the law of the jungle prevailed; far from it. There were precise codes and rituals regulating the brutality of human relations. In this world of proximity, a strict sense of honour obliged men to avenge not only their own honour, which was based on the overt demonstration of their manliness, but that of their whole family group, while women were kept closely supervised to protect their sexual purity or their virtue. The more backward Mediterranean societies have retained this collective conception of honour, which was also the basis of the noble duel in the age of absolute monarchs.[33] In our own day, in Calabria, 'what characterizes [masculine] honour is nothing other than mastery of the penis and the knife. In fact, to be a real man, you must possess the sexual power which enables you to reproduce yourself, hence assure the posterity of your blood and your name, and you must know how to wield a knife, which helps to preserve the group.'[34]

The juvenile culture of violence in the fifteenth- and sixteenth-century West was based on identical rules. The sharp implement, sword or knife, was a symbolic representation of the individual, who endured an extended purgatory between childhood and marriage, and who had to prove that he was capable of acceding to manhood. Young men banded together into gangs in the evening after work and on Sundays and holidays. Their aggression was mainly directed against each other, as they were competitors in a tight marriage market. The rest of the time, they flirted with girls, often collectively. They went to great lengths to win their sexual favours. This was in spite of the close watch kept on young girls, not only by their fathers and brothers, but by the women of all ages who surrounded them whenever they were at risk, especially during the collective evening get-togethers or in the fields, at the wash-house or at the mill. The position of grown lads was an uncomfortable one; they represented a third population group, in relation to the dominant adult males and the weaker sex, as female sociability encompassed all ages and even included pre-pubescent boys. In this context, the injuries inflicted and murders committed by young men were treated indulgently by their elders, by the local authorities, by the law and by the king himself, who was free with his pardons.[35] This was probably a price that had to be paid to prevent bachelors, frustrated and kept in close tutelage, from more frequently turning on the established males who monopolized power and women. In any case it encouraged a regular cycle of extreme violence, ruled by the law of honour and the law of vengeance. The emergence of a strong state, from the sixteenth century, gradually threatened the equilibrium of this system by increasingly prohibiting youthful excesses and by raising the value of human life, under the threat of the death penalty for murderers.

The transition from private vengeance, based on the collective defence of honour, to the banning of homicide was neither quickly nor easily achieved. The first, and most rapid, stage, which took some two centuries, involved separating young men of good family from the common, violent cultural model. The invention of the meticulously codified duel helped to make this possible. A spontaneous creation, this type of combat illustrates the nobility's desire to preserve its eminent right to lethal brutality. However, the nobles were commanded by the monarchy, more or less firmly and rapidly depending on the country, to abandon a practice so wasteful of human life; instead, they were to devote their energies to the glory of the prince alone, risking their lives on the field of battle. The 'civilizing process' began with the 'curialization' – or making courtiers of – warriors at Versailles under Louis XIV, when the obligation to curb their aggression under the mask of politeness was forced on them.[36] The traditions of manly confrontation survived, however, and for a very long time, lower down the social scale, especially in southern Europe and in regions less firmly under central control, such as Auvergne and Gévaudan in France. Periods of crisis in the transmission of values, at times of juvenile overpopulation, led to their revival on a significant scale at fairly regular intervals. The members of inner-city gangs at the beginning of the twenty-first century are practising a concept of manly honour which has some echoes of that of the young men of earlier centuries, in that the destructive effects of their aggression are felt primarily by their peers. This can still be seen as a mechanism that allows some of it to be deflected away from adults, even though it is the latter who are primarily responsible for the strict controls imposed on these young men.

The judicial treatment of homicide thus reveals the progress of the softening of manners and control of manly aggression. The history of violence in the Old Continent is that of the toppling of a culture in which it had positive effects capable of regulating collective life, in favour of a culture in which it was indelibly marked with the seal of illegitimacy. Made a supreme taboo, it came to define the normative roles, according to sex, age and social status. Human beings were ranked on a scale of good and evil according to their 'nature': innocent in the case of the child, gentle in that of women, self-controlled but still manly in that of young unmarried men.

Semen and blood: a history of honour

Homicidal violence has become a residual phenomenon in Western Europe at the beginning of the twenty-first century. It continues to be much more important in the rest of the world, including the United States, Russia and the countries of the old Soviet bloc. Many theories have been advanced to explain this phenomenon, but they all take insufficient account of its chief characteristic, virtually unchanged for seven centuries: it is at its peak among young men aged between twenty and twenty-nine. A satisfactory explanation can only be found in the long term, and must give due weight to the problem of the transition to full adulthood.

Economic conditions have a role in determining levels of human aggression, but they are not, on their own, a sufficient explanation. The peaks of youth violence are not closely correlated with a general deterioration in living standards, but rather with situations of demographic surplus, against a backdrop of a malaise caused by particular difficulties in integrating, for example in the banlieues of Paris today. The short-term fluctuations in the curve of homicide in the industrial age are probably associated with effects of this type, as are the significant differences observable between countries, regions, towns and rural areas. Wars, which thin out the ranks of the young in particular, tend to have a calming effect. The exceptions are when they are followed by a major disorganization which encourages a criminality of crisis directed at property, with a use of force made easier by the weakening of moral codes and structures of control.

As social interpretations have revealed their limitations, specialists have turned to broader hypotheses. Many have been attracted by that of Norbert Elias regarding the slow 'civilizing process' operating in the West from the sixteenth century on. Elias identified a new model of the individual, increasingly less impulsive, controlled by the more effective disciplines put in place by churches and states, and capable of exercising greater self-control of his instincts. Two crucial forces, he argued, led to this transformation of the personality: the modern state and the market economy which developed in the big towns, such as London and Paris. On the one hand, the state claimed a monopoly of legal violence and demanded that behaviour be pacified, beginning with the noble warriors, who had to accept the refinement of etiquette and the obligations of a politeness which prohibited the overt expression of aggression. On the other, trade, then rapidly expanding, both led to and demanded a restriction of inter-personal violence; it could only prosper in conditions of freedom and security, said Enlightenment thinkers such as Adam Smith.[37] Attractive though it is, this theory has been seen as too general and inadequate by other historians, especially those who reject its over-simplifications with regard to the medieval period.[38] Many Scandinavian scholars have tried to verify its validity empirically, but it is mostly used today as only one explanatory factor amongst others.[39]

The argument that the decline in violence was linked to the increasing control imposed by the modern state goes back at least to the *Leviathan* of Thomas Hobbes. Whereas Elias placed it firmly within a larger spontaneous civilizing process, some historians have made it the sole explanation of the emergence of a more peaceful society, as a consequence of the strengthening of the law and the action of the authorities, seen in the increased use of the death penalty.[40] The weakness of this argument lies in the fact that the sharp decline in homicide is visible at the same time, in the first decades of the seventeenth century, in absolute states like Sweden and France and in states lacking centralized structures, such as the United Provinces and England. Nor can the growth of means of coercion really explain this phenomenon, as the Italian towns of the Renaissance, though equipped with large police forces, were unable to reduce significantly the high volume of everyday conflictuality.[41] It seems more pertinent to seek the cause in a higher level of acceptance by subjects of the legitimacy of the state, whatever its type. A strengthening of feelings of solidarity and mutual trust has been observed in the Protestant societies of the northern half of Europe and in New England, where the homicide rate also fell after 1630. By contrast, the Catholic Mediterranean countries remained true for a long time to the old model of lethal violence, probably as a result of the very different type of relationship established between the authorities and civil society.[42] Thus the growth of a Protestant ethic did more than pave the way for capitalism;[43] it made a major contribution to the decline in murderous behaviour, in particular among young men.

Given the inadequacy of the social and political explanations, including the stimulating theory of Norbert Elias, we need to add a cultural dimension, in the broad sense of the term. The true nature of the problem emerges only when we try to understand it in relation to the relevant civilization as a whole. Like death and the cemetery, violence was at the heart of life until its gradual criminalization from the seventeenth century on. England is a case apart. Its judicial system excluded torture and differed from those of the other European countries. Murder had been the exclusive business of the crown since the Norman Conquest. It appears in three forms: culpable homicide, punishable by death; excusable homicide, for which there could be a royal pardon; and justifiable homicide, tried by a jury, which could bring in a verdict of not guilty.[44]

Elsewhere, most notably in France, the Low Countries and Spain, the inquisitorial judicial system, written and secret, which developed from the sixteenth century, preserved the tradition of the princely pardon for the unpremeditated homicides which merited such indulgence. However, the courts still had no concept of mitigating circumstances. The death penalty could in theory be applied in case of accident, non-premeditation or complicity in such crimes. This encouraged those accused to seek a royal pardon, either after sentencing by a court or after fleeing in search of a safe haven and escape from judicial proceedings. Nevertheless, the development in France of the principle of arbitration by the higher judges sitting in the *parlements*, which enabled them to make a free choice of punishment, unlike the lesser magistrates, who had to stick to the letter of the law, produced changes in the sixteenth century. Its application led to greater severity, as death sentences for homicide increased in number under Henri III and Henri IV.[45] The repression became equally harsh in other countries at different dates, but mostly between the beginning of the Wars of Religion, in the 1560s, and the end of the Thirty Years War, in 1648. In parallel, private negotiations aimed at establishing a *paix de sang* between the perpetrator and the victim's family became less common.[46] The shift from the regulation of violence by families to a system controlled by states, and also churches, happened in the context of the growth of 'social discipline', which has been the subject of much debate among German historians of the Reformation.[47] The period is characterized by a spate of edicts designed to limit the occasions for sin, forbidding dissolute practices, dancing, attending many festivals and taverns during religious services, the abuse of alcoholic drinks, the carrying of weapons, etc. The supervision of behaviour, in particular of the excesses committed by young men, intensified in both Protestant and Catholic countries.[48] Its effects were clearly neither immediate nor complete, because there was strong resistance in the rural world and among the poorer citizens. The children of good family, targeted by the pedagogues of both camps and subject to stricter moral surveillance, felt the effects at an early stage. They were not only educated in a new way, but given a new type of training in relational life, through the codes of politeness which developed the model of the 'perfect gentleman', for example in France from the 1630s.[49]

Until then, youthful confrontations had been part of a very different system of relationships from our own, based on precise social codes. As in the animal kingdom, where fights between males rarely result in the death of one of the protagonists, they were more displays of manliness with consequences that proved fatal than battles to the death. They were essentially about the defence of honour. In a world where every individual – and not just the nobles – had his own, honour was directly linked to sex, status and age. It also expressed collective values, in contrast to the cultures of personal guilt of a later date. Everyone was closely supervised by their fellows and lost status in the eyes of all if they did not behave in the correct way. The law of shame ruled this world, where the regard of others mattered much more than self-regard. This resulted in a very dense network of norms and requirements, characteristic of a society of proximity and reciprocal surveillance. If dishonour fell on an individual, it contaminated all the members of his 'clan', his close family, relatives, neighbours, friends – even the whole of a village or urban district if an aggressor from another parish could later boast of having humiliated those of the first. Murderous violence was simply a reflection of the intensity of the collective feelings which bound an individual to his group, to the point where vengeance became a sacred obligation, essential to the restoration of the collective honour that had been besmirched.[50] Not only did the purity of the women have to be defended as a supreme value by all the men, but the men had to avoid losing face in public if their manliness was challenged, if they were the subject of insults, threats or even jokes. To give way before an aggressor, to be beaten or defamed, was dishonourable not only for the one directly concerned, but for all his relatives, who would force him to respond even if he had no wish to.

In this context, violence was both legitimate and obligatory in order to escape shame. It was not only a matter of the wishes of those immediately involved, because it set in motion exacting mechanisms that went well beyond them. There were some safeguards to halt the murderous escalation, in the form of the agreements known as the *paix à partie*. These were encouraged by respected villagers who occupied a neutral position as local *apaiseurs* ('conciliators'), often notables or the *curé*, and frequently sealed by a verbal agreement, publicly registered in the inn. Some were recorded in writing before notaries. They included financial and symbolic damages: the guilty party was required to utter public words of repentance to restore the honour he had slighted. The king regularly referred to them in his pardons, requiring that 'satisfaction be

26

made to the interested party' before they could take effect. The violence was also recognized by official justice, which strongly encouraged private agreements of this type. Where the accused had agreed to them, it reduced the fines prescribed by the law, as in fifteenth-century Arras and sixteenth-century Scandinavia.[51]

This use of public humiliation to smooth away conflicts and allow the reintegration of the culprit into the community was slow to disappear. The courts, especially the local courts, imposed harsher sentences than in the past to serve the interests of the state, but they also continued, in certain cases, to order penalties of 'reintegrative shame' intended to restore peace to a parish. Many victims of humble origins were less interested in ensuring that the offender was punished than in restoring their own position in the eyes of their fellow inhabitants. They appealed to the judges to assure the restoration of their honour by transferring the infamy onto the accused, who was obliged to humiliate himself in his turn.[52] Such strategies testify to a heightened awareness of the importance now assumed by criminal justice, but also to the capacity of the population to manipulate the innovations in their own interests, without wholly abandoning the traditions. Peasant litigants, in particular, began increasingly to have recourse to the law as a new form of pressure designed to force an adversary into a compromise he had refused. It is for this reason that a very large number of cases had no legal conclusion; they were abandoned by the plaintiffs when the opposing party, anxious to avoid excessive costs, finally accepted a private peace agreement.[53] The law courts continued for a long time to be used in this way by villagers to settle internal disputes and restore the social order that had been disrupted, as in Denmark in the nineteenth century.[54]

The old culture of a permissible violence, necessary to restore the honour of a group, did not disappear with the 'judicial revolution' of the seventeenth century. Rather, it adapted to the new prohibitions. In the countryside, the transition from the use of force to the complaint lodged before the courts as a way of obtaining redress was slow, which explains the long time-lag compared with the rest of society, even prolonged resistance in the Mediterranean world, where the vendetta is still sometimes operative today. The judicial acculturation of the towns happened more rapidly, because murderous violence disturbed public order and caused anxiety to respectable inhabitants. The new severity of the courts, the invention of the police in the Paris of Louis XIV and the shocking example of the many young people hanged for theft on the gibbets of Tyburn, in London, all helped to accustom subjects to the heavy-handed protection of the state. It was integrated into a new culture of personal guilt, which left less space than before to the collective sense of honour and the law of shame. The more vulnerable communities

27

retained their attachment to it, however, as did groups of young men with a strong collective identity. In the seventeenth century the university students of Uppsala, in Sweden, continued to attack the Guard, while those of Dorpat assaulted soldiers and those of Abo/Turku clashed with schoolboys; and in all three towns there were also more confrontations with the citizens.[55] The culture of youth violence similarly persisted among the apprentices of eighteenth-century London and in certain urban trades with a reputation for roughness, such as the butchers, the porters and the poor day-labourers. The use of the traditional sense of honour by these groups still strengthened their collective consciousness and helped them to claim from others respect for their social position, in a difficult, even hostile, environment. For the authorities, it was simply a totally illicit and excessive brutality, against which they fought hard. They took a similar view of the excesses of the soldiery, who also occupied an uneasy position in relation to the rest of the population, whose frequent hostility made them close ranks round an identical conception of honour and manliness.

The retreat of lethal violence in Europe started in the Protestant north – Scandinavia, England and the United Provinces – but also in France and the Catholic Low Countries, before spreading to the whole western part of the continent between the seventeenth and the nineteenth centuries. As the trend is initially visible in very different types of state, including countries with little centralization, it cannot be explained in the purely political terms of the rise of absolute monarchy. Nor was it specifically Protestant. The underlying ethic, based on the responsibility and guilt of the individual, to the detriment of the law of shame and of collective honour, was also found in Catholic France and in the Spanish Low Countries, the latter characterized by an even more demanding form of Baroque Catholicism. Nor is the phenomenon specifically associated with urbanization, as the Scandinavian towns were few and small. Lastly, inasmuch as it was the product of a softening of manners, it cannot wholly be explained by the theories of Norbert Elias. These assume that the French warrior, softened by contact with the etiquette of Versailles in the last decades of the seventeenth century, was imitated by the other social categories. But the marked decline in the homicide rate actually began some fifty years earlier, in the 1620s, or even the 1580s in France. Elias was right, however, about the importance of the nobility in initiating this process. It has been shown that the social elites had largely abandoned the 'culture of the knife fight' by the seventeenth century in Scandinavia, and in Amsterdam in the Age of Enlightenment, although they had actively shared it at the end of the Middle Ages, along with the rest of the population. This withdrawal by the privileged and the wealthy is, however, illusory. They abandoned practices that were now criminalized, and likely to cause grave problems for those involved and for their families, but they invented a nobler and crueller form of mortal combat, the duel, against which the authorities fought long and hard. In France, they had to accept a compromise and, the law and Christian morality notwithstanding, concede to the aristocrats the possibility of defending to the death the honour of their lineage. With almost only this exception, homicide became increasingly unacceptable in civil society. It was dissociated from a culture of lawful violence, now confined to the legal representatives of the prince and to the military in the context of wars, self-evidently always just.

In the end, the only common factor that can help us to understand the transformation over time of a collective right into a moral taboo, which could not be transgressed without harsh punishment by the authorities, is the age of the principal actors, young men awaiting full adulthood. The Europe of the Wars of Religion broke new ground by adopting a radically different attitude to these young men and by ceasing to tolerate their lethal excesses. The change was in reality even more far-reaching, because it concerned the status of masculine youth in general. As a consequence of increasing suspicion of the dangers represented by this age group, new forms of control and education were developed in order to curb their aggression and leave them with much less latitude than in the past for living between the worlds of childhood and adulthood. The traditional village relationships had been based on the power of mature men, while women had formed a group of their own, and pubescent boys had joined the 'kingdoms of youth'; these had made it easier for them to resist the demands of the adult men and to wait their turn to accede to a full life. This structure had allowed the replacement of the generations exactly as before. It had hardly been conducive, however, to the economic progress demanded by the towns, or to the changes required by kings and churches. The system was broken to be replaced by a new social pact. Young males had to abandon the violence linked to the code of collective honour in favour of a culture of personal guilt defined by the moral pressure of the age; this was necessary in order to alter the repetitive mechanism by which property and founding principles were transmitted to the new generations, on a continent where 80 per cent of the population were peasants. Thus the West invented adolescence, a stage of life that was more clearly defined and more supervised, in order to impose everywhere the new dynamism of the states, churches and towns, including on the rural masses deeply attached to traditions of social fixity. The aim was not only to prevent young men from endangering the peace of the communities, but also to teach them a new approach to life, respect for it, and the obedience due to the institutions proclaiming themselves guardians of legitimate violence.

The rapid fall in homicide rates since the seventeenth century does not express a totally objective reality, but an increasingly harsh attitude to the brutality governing social exchanges which had previously been ritually inculcated into young bachelors. The figures for murder need to be relocated within the context of a long political, religious and cultural offensive designed to pacify the manners of the young by devaluing the defence of honour. The latter had previously been the basis of the continuity of a European civilization dominated by great landlords, where the mass of the population had been peasants. It was a major change of direction, at the very time that Europe was embarking on world conquest. The internal balance of the continent shifted, beginning with the most dynamic regions, which embarked on their colonial adventures in the seventeenth century. As the interior was pacified, the violence of the young males, beginning with the sons of good families, was partially reoriented towards the exterior – except in the social groups where the old notion of honour, on which the code of deadly vengeance was based, survived, and except in periods of heightened tension due to population increase and the difficulty faced by the new generations in integrating. The smugglers of the eighteenth century and the famous highwaymen, Mandrin and Cartouche, belonged to this age group, as did the principal actors in the French Revolution...

— 2 —

VIOLENCE: SEVEN CENTURIES OF SPECTACULAR DECLINE

A comprehensive review of the figures assembled by historians and criminologists in connection with homicide and assaults against persons is necessary before we can proceed. However, we must be careful not to accord them an absolute value, but rather seek to understand what they say. One recent strand of thought would deny them all validity as indicators of the 'reality' of the crimes they record. It is true that they never capture the 'dark figure' of violent acts actually committed, but only reveal those that were the subject of formal charges, and their treatment by the police and the law. It has too often been forgotten, however, that their function is not and never has been to reveal the totality of the conflictual phenomena present in a society. Whether produced by institutions of control and repression, or simply deduced from official sources with other objectives than the systematic counting of offences, before the arrival of statistics in the eighteenth century, they offer not so much a picture of concrete criminal activity as a normative gaze directed at what contemporaries considered the worst threats. If we interpret them from this standpoint, in the context of a broad cultural and social history, it is possible to appreciate their full importance as indicators of the major shifts in the perception of violence against persons during the last seven centuries.

The reliability of the crime figures

Violence takes many forms and it is never captured in its entirety by the documents of repression, including in our own period. Its lesser manifestations, such as abuse and threats intended to terrorize an interlocutor, blows that leave no mark and, most of all, violence within the family,

31

generally go unrecorded. The exception is in the towns, which sometimes, as early as the Middle Ages, kept a record of fines for such
offences, even simple slaps across the face.[1] The best indicator is homicide, which has been considered a capital crime in Western Christian
civilization from its origins. In the present society of automated surveillance, and given scientific police techniques, it is difficult to conceal a
human corpse or the remains of a newborn child. Some recent and very
rapidly and highly publicized cases, following macabre discoveries in
dustbins or freezers, prove the point. Recent statistics are, in consequence, close to reality in this sphere, which has not always been the
case. Yet the gravity of murder in the eyes of the representatives of the
law and Christian morality means that it was never possible for it be
concealed as easily as more banal forms of violence. Only infanticide,
although it was criminalized by 1557 in France, was until quite recently
the subject of a powerful law of silence, within the locality and within
the family.[2] This is probably the chief reason why researchers working
on the pre-industrial period do not, as a general rule, include the figures
for infanticide in those for homicide, regarding them as having little
credibility.

It is true that the reliability of the figures for homicide also depends
on the effectiveness of punitive practices. Before the advent of crime
figures, an innovation signalling the recent prioritizing of repression,
justice was more formidable in appearance than in reality. Many offenders slipped easily through the gaping holes in a system only loosely
administered by the small number of officials responsible for maintaining
order.[3] At the end of the Middle Ages, and often still in the sixteenth
century, plenty of murderers fled without leaving any trace in the archives,
except, sometimes, in the well-managed towns where those it had been
possible to identify were condemned to death in absentia or sentenced
to formal banishment. It was also necessary for a complaint to have been
made or a rumour to have spread, as public action was not automatic.
Other indirect documents, such as the *levées de cadavres* ('collection of
corpses') from the public highways, show that homicides were significantly under-recorded. The pardons (*lettres de rémission, lettres de
rappel de ban* and *lettres de pardon*) granted by the king of France and
other great European princes, by virtue of their right of sovereign mercy,
differ from the classic judicial sources in that they prohibited any possible
action, even already embarked on, against the recipients, who were
authorized to return if they had been banished, and annulled any penalty
decreed by a court. These texts, which complement the documents of
repression, make it possible to measure the intensity and extent of real
violence, which was on a larger scale than suggested by the surviving
legal documents. It is estimated that more than 50,000 *lettres de rémis-*

sion were granted by the kings of France between 1304 and 1568, which was when the series ended, though not the practice, which continued up to the Revolution. Nearly 15,000 such *lettres* were issued under Charles VI, between 1380 and 1422. Another significant spate started in 1480. This went together with a systematic concentration on acts of violence which ended in homicide.[4] This had been the case, in 1525, with 208 of the 218 individuals pardoned by Francis I, that is, 95 per cent of the total.[5]

From 1386, the duke of Burgundy copied his French cousin and transmitted this mark of sovereignty to his successors, the kings of Spain, for the Low Countries and Franche-Comté. In this shifting ensemble, which lost the rebellious Protestant United Provinces in 1579, and which probably accounted for just over a tenth of the French population at that date, some 15,000 *lettres de rémission* are known to have been issued before 1660, of which 3,500 were for the county of Artois alone. With a population of some 170,000 in 1469, according to a precious census, Artois had about a dozen towns and a territory thickly scattered with nearly 800 nucleated villages. Heavily populated, and the granary of the Low Countries, it had an overall population density of 40 inhabitants per square kilometre. About 40,000 people, or 23.5 per cent, lived in towns, Arras, the capital, and Saint-Omer each having populations of between 10,000 and 12,000. Little is known about its later demographic profile, but it is unlikely that that there was sustained population growth before 1725 in this frontier region, marked by war and insecurity from the time of the dukes of Burgundy until its integration into the kingdom of France under Louis XIV. We may reasonably use the figures for 1469 as a rough guide, therefore, in an attempt to evaluate the impact of violence on society.

Like the rest of Europe at this period, however, Artois experienced sharp short-term fluctuations, expressed by the jagged curves of the demographers. Far from being immobile, this was a world characterized by a very high birth rate and probably an equally high death rate, due to war, disease and famine. In spite of a 'massacre of the innocents' which continued into adolescence (only one newborn child in two reached the age of twenty), and in spite of low life expectancy (at most another twenty years for the survivors), this was a society significantly more subject than our own to pressure from the new generations. The next generation was thinner on the ground and old people were fewer, even though some individuals survived to an advanced old age. In the absence of effective contraception, the chief mechanism regulating the population was an increasing delay in the age of marriage, which limited the number of children per woman. If Artois resembled the French model, girls probably married at about twenty, and boys at between twenty-four and

33

twenty-five, in the sixteenth century, but at about twenty-five and twenty-seven, respectively, in the second half of the seventeenth century. The average age of marriage was even higher in the towns. Tradition and moral pressure were stepped up in the second half of the sixteenth century, under the influence of the Catholic Counter-Reformation, which made the life of the unmarried young a 'matrimonial purgatory'. Their sexuality seems to have been increasingly constrained, as suggested by the decline in the number of illegitimate births as the seventeenth century progressed (about 1 per cent in the French countryside) and the rarity of pre-marital conceptions (barely 5 per cent, for example, in the north-west part of the Most Christian Kingdom).[6] The pressure weighed most heavily on the boys, in theory condemned to continence during their protracted wait for marriage. Following Jean-Louis Flandrin, some historians believe that frustrated young males found ways round this, by frequenting understanding widows or married women, by engaging in masturbation, especially heterosexual, with girls anxious to avoid pregnancy, or by devising ways of letting off steam. One of the most important of these was implementing a notably manly ethic of confrontation between gangs of unmarried youths, which was readily tolerated by the adults and the authorities. The injuries or homicides that resulted were regarded with great indulgence as the inevitable consequences of the irrepressible explosive temperament attributed to young bachelors.[7]

The *lettres de rémission* reflect these social and cultural phenomena with great precision. For Artois, between 1386 and 1660, 97 per cent of them, even nearly 99 per cent from the sixteenth century, concerned lethal violence perpetrated by men. Only fourteen of the murderers were women, that is, 0.36 per cent of the contingent, six of them in the fifteenth century. This was also the case in Castile between 1623 and 1699. The 'Good Friday pardons', which were much less common, were also largely devoted to homicides: 428 out of 434, or 98.6 per cent, were committed by men, five of the six women involved having been accomplices of a husband or lover (the sixth had smothered a young girl).[8]

The rate for the issue of princely pardons in Artois was slow, to begin with, in the fifteenth century. It then speeded up under Charles V or, to be more precise, between 1500 and 1555, before slowing down perceptibly in the reign of Philip II, from 1556 to 1598, when serious disturbances and religious wars culminated in splitting the Low Countries into two hostile entities. The increase in the rate of their issue was at its highest under the rule of the archdukes, from 1599 to 1634, before stagnating after the resumption of hostilities against France, followed by the conquest of Artois, between 1635 and 1660.[9] The number of murders recorded, 3,198 for the 275 years in question, an annual average of 11.6, was slightly lower than the total of persons pardoned for homicide, which sometimes included several accomplices in the same crime. Criminologists calculate a homicide rate of between 0.5 and 2 per 100,000 inhabitants for the various countries of Western Europe today. By the same criteria, and using the population estimates quoted above, the rate revealed by the *lettres de rémission* for Artois alone was 6.8 from 1386 to 1660. This conceals very great fluctuations: 1.2 in the fifteenth century (231 cases), 9.7 from 1500 to 1555 (927 cases), 7.3 from 1556 to 1598 (536 cases), 18.8 from 1599 to 1633 (1,158 cases) and 7.8 from 1635 to 1660 (346 cases). Between 1500 and 1660, the 2,967 known homicides pardoned represent an average rate of just under 11 per 100,000 inhabitants. Paradoxically expressed by the practice of the princely pardon, the sharpest growth in murderous violence came in the decade 1521–30, with a first peak of seventy-five for the single year 1523, that is, a record rate of 44 per 100,000, and then another between 1591 and 1640.[10] The first period corresponds to the height of a war with France, marked by terrible pillaging, price rises and epidemics in 1522–3, before the Peace of Cambrai (1529), which removed the county from French suzerainty. The second, in contrast, was an era of peace and prosperity, the 'golden age of the archdukes', from the death of Philip II in 1598 to the resumption of hostilities with France, especially after 1635. While disastrous combinations of circumstances could lead to a sharp increase in murders, this was not always the case, as the period of the worst disturbances, under Philip II, saw a sharp fall in pardons. It is possible that this reduction is evidence of a decline in princely tolerance of homicide, at a time of general revolt against the monarchy. More important is the fact that the long period of stability, and probably also of demographic growth, under the archdukes was accompanied by a terrible and prolonged outburst of murderous violence. This correlates with an increasingly strict moral and religious supervision of the population, in an attempt to extirpate Protestantism and frustrate the Calvinists of the northern provinces, who had become effectively independent. The witch hunt was then at its height and royal ordinances prohibiting dances, rigorously controlling festivals and taverns, dedicating Sundays to prayer and clearly differentiating the sacred from the profane proliferated. The traditional balance of the communities, especially the rural communities, was badly disrupted.

These sources reveal both the scale of lethal violence between males, which is under-represented in the classic judicial archives, and its very pronounced chronological and geographical fluctuations. The most intense conflictuality was not found along the frontier with the powerful kingdom of France, as might be expected. This wide southern strip, defined as the 'high country' and including the capital, Arras, produced only a quarter of the *lettres de rémissions*, although it contained 60 per cent of the population in 1469. It was the northern 'low country', adjoining Flanders and influenced by its customs, that provided the majority, three-quarters, with only 40 per cent of the inhabitants. The crucial issue, in a period of population growth, which was probably the case in the first third of the seventeenth century, was that of the division of inheritances. The problem was much more acute in the area influenced by Flemish law, by which no descendent could be disinherited, even a bastard.[11] A key factor in homicidal violence, though generally ignored or minimized for such periods, for lack of evidence, is the age of the protagonists. Though it is rarely revealed directly, it can be deduced from references to family situation, which become increasingly common in *lettres de rémissions* from the sixteenth century. Of 2,563 people guilty of homicide for whom we have such information, namely 66 per cent of the total for Artois, 1,514 were bachelors – that is, young men or men of marriageable age – as against 1,049 adults and married men with or without children; that is, a proportion of three to two. Excluding the fifteenth century, for which the evidence is inadequate, it emerges that young men are slightly less numerous than adults under Charles V, that they become more numerous under Philip II, and that they made up two-thirds of the contingent after 1600, a trend accentuated even further in the second third of the seventeenth century. Between 1601 and 1635, they account for 51 per cent of all those pardoned, compared with 25 per cent each of adults and those whose family situation is unknown. Similar information is provided for only one victim in three, a total of 1,086, which makes any argument here rather more risky. We may note, nevertheless, that three-quarters of them were single men, as against a quarter who were adult and married men.[12] The *lettres de rémissions* put the emphasis on a youthful turbulence which merits closer examination.[13]

The classic judicial sources suggest a much lower rate of homicidal violence. At Arras, capital of the county of Artois, with a population of between 10,000 and 12,000, 32 per cent of the 555 persons who appeared before the magistrates between 1528 and 1549, under Charles V, were accused of crimes against the person. Homicide, as in the *rémissions*, an almost exclusively masculine crime, was alleged against eighty-nine men and just one woman. Of the former, nine men of evil repute and deemed incorrigible were sentenced to the ultimate penalty, while fifteen were acquitted. The majority of the others, that is, fifty-eight, were banned in perpetuity, on pain of death if they returned. Only a few of them, a total of four, were present in person for their trial, the rest being judged in their absence. Fifty-four had fled, many of whom would probably later seek a royal pardon.[14] According to these documents deriving from judicial practice, the homicide rate in Arras was around 4 per 100,000 during the period under consideration, that is, a very much lower rate than the 9.7 revealed by the letters of pardon for the same period.

Contrary to a mistaken but commonly held idea, the town was no more inclined to criminality than the countryside. On the contrary, the princely pardons granted to citizens accounted for only 18.5 per cent of those granted for Artois, only 17.5 per cent if the fifteenth century is excluded, although the urban population represented 23.5 per cent of the total in 1469. One hundred and forty-three persons from Arras were pardoned between 1500 and 1660, and ninety-one from Saint-Omer, which had a population of comparable size. There were ninety-nine and ninety-three *rémissions*, respectively, during the same period for Béthune, with 4,000 inhabitants, and for Aire-sur-le-Lys, with fewer than 3,000.[15] If we take the period 1500–1660, during which the average number of homicides pardoned, as we have seen, was around eleven for the county, it was around fifteen at Béthune, none at Arras and five at Saint-Omer. Unlike the small towns close to Flanders, like Béthune and Aire, the larger cities were reducing lethal violence. Indeed it was much more closely controlled here than in the countryside, both by urban privileges[16] and by procedures for defending the collective peace. Further, by tradition, criminals who fled from Arras were threatened with a terrible fate: any man could claim immunity if he killed a fugitive sentenced to a fine of 60 *livres*, the usual rate for the crime of murder. Six of the accused men claimed this right between 1528 and 1549. At the same time, the town accounts record 163 fines punishing assaults, often trivial but including some murders, in particular when the perpetrators had deliberately fled the urban enceinte. These examples have to be added to those described in the criminal archives and the *lettres de rémissions*. The capital of Artois had many ways of repressing violence. It was not one of the authorities' main preoccupations, unlike theft, which was committed by 20 per cent of women and at least 22 per cent of unmarried men between 1528 and 1549. The fact that 90 per cent of those guilty of offences against property had been born outside Arras, and that the principal penalty, in 87 per cent of cases, was banishment, accompanied by shaming punishments, such as cutting off the ears, in 10 per cent of cases, suggests a desire to exclude strangers, especially rootless youths.[17]

The towns and the countryside did not deal with murder in the same way, which justifies separate discussions. In both cases, however, the prosecution of the culprits in the courts represented only a small part of the reality before the age of statistics. In Arras, the local judges dealt with two or three times fewer fatal combats than are contained in the *lettres de rémissions* granted to inhabitants of the town. Other documents contain information which does not appear in either of these sources, in particular the lists of urban fines, the reports of the *levées de cadavres* and the accounts of eyewitnesses and chroniclers. We may be sure that the 'dark figure' of homicides is many times higher than the figures extracted from judicial proceedings alone. Comparing the latter to the lists of inspections of corpses in Amsterdam from the end of the Middle Ages to the early modern period, one historian has estimated that the judicial record of violent deaths amounts to at most 10 per cent of those actually committed.[18] This has been seen as excessive by other historians, who have pointed to the need for comparative verifications.[19] Yet the Dutch order of magnitude seems plausible, if we take account of the letters of pardon, the many fugitives and the victims who disappeared without trace. There is today a general consensus regarding the great underestimation of the figures from before the nineteenth century if they are based solely on judicial documents. This only makes the seven-century-long decline in lethal violence in the West the more spectacular and interesting.

Seven centuries of decline

This decline was revealed by Ted Robert Gurr, in 1981, in the case of England from the thirteenth to the nineteenth centuries. He based his calculations on some thirty works by different authors, adding statistics for London from the beginning of the nineteenth century up to the date of his article.[20] The results took the form of an S-curve. The homicide rate was very high at the beginning of the period – around 20 per 100,000 inhabitants on average, with spikes of 110 in Oxford and nearly 45 in London; it then fell by half, to about 10, in 1600, before plummeting to settle at around 1 in the twentieth century; this was in spite of a perceptible rise in the last decades of his period. Gurr correctly perceived this as a major cultural shift in Western society, the result of a heightened sensitivity regarding violence and of the growth of internal and external methods for the control of aggression.[21] Various criticisms of his work soon followed, in particular in connection with the use of statistics based on material that is extremely diverse and variable according to period. These reservations are justified as regards the recording of the phenomenon, which has changed often and radically over seven centuries. They lose some of their validity, however, if we consider the various series as evidence of official attitudes to homicide, expressed by the judges in their practice, and treat them as indicators of the changes they reveal. They are a description not so much of the criminal reality as of changes in the repressive approach, linked to the success, over the long term, of a patient battle to strengthen social control in this sphere and to impose greater personal self-control over lethal violence.

Many empirical verifications carried out in various European countries have, in any case, validated this thesis, relocating the problem at the level of Western civilization as a whole. A complete series of indictments for homicide in the county of Kent between 1560 and 1985 has shown a sharp decline in the rate, from 3–6 to 0.3–0.7 per 100,000 in four centuries. In Amsterdam, the trend is even more spectacular, the index falling from 50 in the fifteenth century to 1 in the nineteenth century.[22] Lastly, a recent comparative study drawing on some ninety works dealing with ten countries has made it possible to establish 390 estimates of rates for the pre-industrial period and compare them with contemporary statistics for Sweden, England, Switzerland and Italy. It confirms the S-curve of Ted Robert Gurr.[23] The Middle Ages generally presents a very high level of murderous violence. The lowest rate recorded is 6 and the highest 150 per 100,000, with very marked variations according to region, but also significant differences between big cities, small towns and the countryside, as in the case of Artois. The recent discovery of the systematic under-recording of the phenomenon in the judicial sources suggests we should significantly sharpen Gurr's S-curve, which makes the turning points observed around 1620 and in the nineteenth century even more dramatic.

In the sixteenth and seventeenth centuries, major differences emerged between five groups of countries. In England, the rate per 100,000 fluctuated between 3 and 10. In the Low Countries and the United Provinces, the swings were even greater, from 40 to 4 in Amsterdam and from 10 to 4 or 5 in Brussels, before fluctuating between 0.7 and 3 in both states at the end of the eighteenth century. In Scandinavia, high rates were maintained until 1620, followed by a very sharp drop, to reach, in Sweden, the figure of 4 at the beginning of the eighteenth century, then 1.3 in 1754, date of the creation of national statistics for deaths. More discontinuous studies suggest a later decline in Italy. The rate around 1600 in Rome was between 30 and 70 homicides per 100,000 and in the duchy of Mantua between 35 and 55; in Sardinia it was 20 at the end of the eighteenth century. It was not until 1840 that the rate fell in Rome to 10. Less is known about the Holy Roman Empire and Switzerland, but the rates seem to lie somewhere between the northern and the Italian models.

By the nineteenth century, much more credible figures make it possible to distinguish an area characterized by a low homicide rate, from 0.5 to 2, including the more industrialized countries of the north, among them France and Germany, from the southern and eastern peripheries, where the rates exceeded 2 and sometimes even 5. In the latter region, violence was at its greatest in the rural areas, most of all in southern Italy. If we exclude the countries of the east, the homicide rate continued to plummet between 1880 and 1950, bringing the rates in the north and the south of the continent increasingly into line, and eventually stabilizing almost everywhere at 0.4–0.6 per 100,000 inhabitants, the lowest rate ever reached. The trend was the same for all types of violence against persons, including theft, which made Western Europe an oasis of peace in the world at the end of the Second World War. Homicide rates and those for lesser types of violence and theft have begun to climb again, however, since 1950.

The correlations that exist between many states at the same period make it possible to argue that homicidal violence has been treated in an identical manner in western and southern Europe since the thirteenth century. The chronological variations seem essentially to derive from local factors and differences in economic and social development. This was already the case in the sixteenth century. Three areas as different as France, England and Scandinavia experienced in parallel the same trend of a rapid rise in homicide rates between 1580 and 1610, followed by a continuous decline.[24] Before we examine the underlying causes of these phenomena, it needs to be emphasized that the principal changes are not linked to wars, except negatively – the excess of legal murder seemingly having served to sicken contemporaries and reduce the number of criminal murders. In France and England, the marked decline of the 1620s came after long and terrible religious conflicts, just as the survivors of the two world wars of the twentieth century helped to impose the age of security and peace which prevailed around 1950. A second observation concerns the northern model: England, Scandinavia and the United Provinces were Protestant from the sixteenth century and adopted an ethical model (described by Max Weber) which seems to have helped to raise the value of human life.[25] Thirdly, this ethic affected primarily the younger generations, in whom it was inculcated by the Churches and the various socializing institutions. The key to the problem is surely to be found, therefore, in young men, and in the way in which the European 'factory' taught them the meaning of life and respect for the life of others.

The 'making' of young men

Women rarely account for more than 15 per cent of the total number of those who commit murder. The average stands between 5 and 12 per cent and has remained remarkably stable since the thirteenth century. Murderous violence is a male crime, and essentially an affair of young men of marriageable age, as we have seen from the Artois *lettres de rémission*. Yet historians of pre-industrial centuries have rarely shown interest in this variable, even though it is one of the principal preoccupations of specialists in contemporary criminology, in particular in the United States; in New York between 1976 and 1995, the peak age for murder was twenty among males.[26] A comparison of studies of Mantua at the end of the sixteenth century, Amsterdam in the eighteenth century, the south of France at the end of the Age of Enlightenment and Alençon from 1741 to 1745, with some German statistics for the year 1908, reveals a startlingly similar model in all cases, with a concentration of between 35 and 45 per cent of murderers from the 20–29 age group. The curve takes the form of a slightly dissymmetric bell: the 10–19 age group accounts for between 5 and 20 per cent of the total, almost as many as the 40–49 age group; the 30–39 age group provides between 20 and 30 per cent of those accused, the percentage among the older groups being negligible.[27] Children and young persons up to the age of twenty form the largest population group, around 40 per cent in France in 1740, while those aged over sixty comprise only 10 per cent. The various age groups seem almost all to be represented in accord with their respective size, even though the figures for the youngest are a little on the low side and those for the group 30–39 a little high. The single exception, and a spectacular one, concerns those who have passed the fateful age of twenty. Under the *ancien régime*, only half of newborn babies survived to this age and prepared for a late marriage. If we look at the two groups on either side, we can observe the gradual rise of a culture of murderous violence, on emerging from childhood and during puberty, a veritable explosion, sustained for about a decade, which then remained at a fairly high level among young adults who had passed the age of thirty, and were by then usually married. The fluctuations recorded over the centuries seem to be primarily linked to changes in the status of this age, which would be called 'adolescence' in the industrial era, and in particular to factors associated with the difficulty of becoming a full adult, acceding to the married state and finding a valued place in society.

The principal explanatory hypothesis explored in this book relates to the mechanisms for the replacement of the masculine generations and the turbulence associated with periods marked by greater difficulties in achieving this transition. Homicidal violence is both an expression and a symptom of this, through judicial repression and against a backdrop of the imposition of greater social control and the growth of mechanisms of self-control among the vast majority, who avoided murderous brawls. From the seventeenth century, such clashes are primarily a sign of the limitations and failures of these collective cultural practices. The marked secular decline in murder thus demonstrates the increasing effectiveness of the management of young men by the European 'factory'. In the

41

beginning, the most extreme youth violence had been not only accepted, but actively encouraged, as a way of fostering a manly ethic among both the peasantry and, even more, the nobility, whose vocation was to become ruthless warriors. This is why murder was so common and so banal at all levels of society at the end of the Middle Ages and for a long time after.

Some historians believe that the pacification of the elites began in the sixteenth century in the Protestant north of the continent.[28] In fact, it started several centuries earlier, especially in the large towns of the Burgundian Low Countries, with the introduction of a rigorous system for the defence of the urban peace, which I will describe in a later chapter.[29] In France and in Finland, it was linked to a change of attitude on the part of the judges, who began increasingly to pass death sentences instead of the traditional punishments of fines and obligatory compensation for the family of the victim. In France, the change began in the last third of the sixteenth century, when the excessive laxity of the royal *lettres de rémission* was replaced by a new rigour on the part of the magistrates of the *parlement* of Paris. In Finland, a similar radical shift began to check the spiral of tolerated violence around 1620.[30] The trend was later in southern Europe and in regions resistant to central government, like the Auvergne, in France. Many historians associate it with the abandonment by the nobility of the easy resort to killing, under the influence of the 'civilizing process' described by Norbert Elias.[31]

The thesis is not entirely satisfactory. Certainly, it makes it possible to understand the transformation of noble values brought about by a new education, which imposed a firm 'discipline' on young aristocrats; this characterized the modern states which copied the forms of authority introduced by Louis XIV and by the Catholic and Protestant churches, all determined to moralize young people. It comes up against a major contradiction, however, since the abandonment of an ethic of violence might have had disastrous consequences by turning wolves into lambs, at the risk of weakening the power of the state, which was essentially based on the military capabilities of the nobility. This is probably why the sixteenth and seventeenth centuries saw the growth of a culture of the point of honour expressly reserved to the aristocracy. This served as a gradual transition between the culture of violence previously shared by all and that of the 'curialization' of warriors described by Elias. In spite of many official prohibitions, this modernized successor to the earlier right of vengeance made it possible to strengthen both the murderous capacities indispensable to officers in the face of the enemy and their sense of profound difference from the common people, by reason of the refined code supposed to govern these illegal but tacitly tolerated confrontations. The triumphal France of the seventeenth century was the true home of the duel, but it was later adopted by other bellicose countries, such as Prussia in the nineteenth century. This type of combat deserves to be discussed in some depth, as a specifically elitist adaptation of the prohibition on lethal violence, which was more ruthlessly imposed on young men from the lower social ranks. The criminalization of homicide did not advance at the same rate in every country or sector of the population.

In parallel, a culture of knife fights, the original model for the noble duel with swords, continued to thrive over the centuries. It was a typical expression of masculine honour. Though it was practised by all sectors of the population in the Middle Ages and the sixteenth century, it was particularly common among unmarried men. It was not normally meant to kill. Rather, it took the form of ritual challenges intended to establish a visible superiority, so as to increase value in a tight marriage market ruled by the laws of endogamy and homogamy. Three-quarters of spouses, and an even higher proportion in the villages, came from the same place and the same socio-professional group. Knives and swords were assertions of manliness between protagonists of the same age who usually knew each other well. In Artois, France, England, Sweden and Cologne, the typical quarrel flared after a visit to the tavern on a Sunday or a holiday, and between young bloods who were armed and anxious to shine in the eyes of all, or seduce a watching girl or avenge an affront.[32] The wounds, which were not usually mortal, became infected, although their essential function had often been to assert a victory or humiliate an adversary. Advances in surgery are partly responsible for the decline in homicide rates from the eighteenth century, by preventing these unintended disastrous consequences. But this was not the main reason for the decline. These manly games were denounced with increasing vigour by the authorities, who began to punish the offenders harshly, stepping up the number of death sentences. The fall in homicide rates is in large part testimony to the success of the offensive conducted against adolescents who were too ready to engage in knife fights. In Amsterdam, it was only young men from the lower classes who continued to resort to this type of combat at the end of the seventeenth century, and the practice had disappeared altogether a century later. It persisted longer in Italy, where the change came only at the end of the nineteenth century. It could also reappear: in Finland, strict laws passed in 1662 and 1682 succeeded in eradicating the noble duel, but the nineteenth century was, in the province of South Ostrobothnia, an 'era of knife fighters'.[33] The Parisian Apaches at the time of *Casque d'Or*, at the beginning of the twentieth century, the New York gangs made famous by *West Side Story*, in 1961, and some inner-city youths today have all rediscovered these same rituals based on the defence of the manly honour of young men.

The figures for repression do not simply reveal intangible crimes. Rather, they record the gradual penetration of the various levels of society by an increasingly fundamental taboo on homicide. Today, this crime is directly correlated with violence in all its forms, robbery and sexual assault.[34] There have been few studies of the subject for earlier centuries, often for lack of sources. Nevertheless, the relationship has been demonstrated for the small towns of Sweden in the sixteenth and seventeenth centuries: the curves of physical aggression and homicide are the same, both in their overall shape and in their fluctuations.[35] Such a correlation dates back to an old culture of youth violence, against which our civilization has fought fiercely for five hundred years, even though it had previously been part of the normal currency of daily, and above all festive, life all over Europe.

— 3 —

THE YOUTH FESTIVALS OF VIOLENCE
(THIRTEENTH TO SEVENTEENTH CENTURIES)

The perception of homicidal violence at the end of the Middle Ages and in the sixteenth and seventeenth centuries was very different from our own. Not only did violent death then seem very ordinary, but it was regarded as legitimate, even necessary, by contemporaries. Only its extreme forms, premeditated murder committed out of hatred or revenge and parricide, were in practice liable to a death sentence. The penal theories which emerged from the late twelfth century in various European countries advocated rigorous prosecution in these rare cases, known as *cas énormes* in France, *kwade feiten* in the Low Countries, *delictos atroces* in Castile and 'heinous crimes' in Scotland. Other types of murder, described as 'manslaughter' in England, were universally regarded with a high degree of indulgence and rarely brought to the attention of the judicial authorities. As a result, bloody cruelty was commonplace. To understand why, we need to relocate it in the normal context of human relationships. Life was steeped in brutality; not in a pathological way, except in exceptional circumstances, but in the ordinary way of things, and for both sexes, irrespective of social condition and age – babies were no more likely to escape it than old people. Deeply rooted in human life, violence was in no way a taboo at this period. On the contrary, it had a positive value, maintaining the hierarchies and regulating material and symbolic exchanges. Even more, it presided over the world of play and the world of work. Just as the cemetery was in the middle of the village, around the parish church, the taste for blood was at the heart of a culture of violence which shaped social and sexual roles. In societies where the king was a dominant male, imitated by the noble warriors, the essential norms were based on the expression of an exaggerated manliness. Despite the persistent efforts of the Churches, Catholic and then Protestant, to impose respect for the precepts of humility, peace and the defence of the weak, of widows and of orphans, masculine honour remained the absolute yardstick, from the princely court to the smallest village, until the eighteenth century – and even long after in certain regions and sectors of the population. It was transmitted from father to son, leaving softness to women, regarded as a natural weakness proper to their sex. Men in the making, pubescent boys were under great pressure to distance themselves from the feminine world by visible acts of great brutality, because they needed to demonstrate their capacity to replace, one day, their fathers. Relegated to the margins of the two worlds they valued most, those of power and sexuality, they vented their frustrations by demonstrating their physical power and their skills during festivals and games. It was a small step from ludic release to murder, especially as unmarried men frequently went about armed, as an act of bravado or defiance. It was to prove very difficult for the authorities to detach them from traditions which valorized honour and masculine strength, because they amounted to a veritable educational system which linked the proof of manliness to a constant festive confrontation between peers, so as to impress both the girls and the fathers.

A culture of violence

At the end of the Middle Ages, the development of the central state and of urban jurisdictions in a few regions where towns were particularly important – northern Italy, the Low Countries, the Holy Roman Empire and southern France – complicated an already confused situation as regards the punishment of homicide. In the duchy of Brabant, for example, only the murder described as *laid fait* was automatically prosecuted by an agent of the prince. If the act had been unintentional, that is, *beau fait*, several possibilities were open to the culprit. The simplest was to make a private peace, or *paix à partie*, with the relatives of the victim, for a consideration, so that they would not exercise their right of vengeance against him or his family. Alternatively, he could flee, find a safe haven, and then ask the sovereign for a *lettre de rémission*. Granted freely or accompanied by a fine, this document entailed compensating the victim's family, so that a return to the area would not trigger a spiral of vengeance. Another solution was for the culprit to submit to local justice, to 'compose' with it for blood money, assessed to reflect his financial situation, before proposing an amicable resolution to the heirs of the deceased.[1] Public action was of little importance compared with the need to keep the peace between the families concerned.

Sometimes, the murderer took no action at all, but continued to live as if nothing had happened, though at the risk of one day being attacked in his turn by an avenger with a long memory. Those who were feared for their cruelty or their skill with weapons, in particular nobles and soldiers, often relied on such fear to impose their presence, and re-offended without scruple. Violence did not of itself lead to social exclusion, unlike theft, which gave rise to more fear and contempt, especially in the towns. Fights, injuries and homicides were part of the landscape at the end of the Middle Ages, to the point where it has been possible to see them as characterizing the lifestyle of the citizen elites.[2]

Insults and acts of violence were common, but we know little about them, especially in the villages. However, a few rare documents enable us to assess their importance. The register of fines of the episcopal court of Arras from 7 March to 12 December 1328 records ninety-six 'big fines': thirty-four for usury, thirty-one for sexual offences (adultery, including by a *curé* with a married woman, concubinage, bigamy and relations with two sisters, considered to be incest), eighteen for assault and battery, ten for offences against ecclesiastical jurisdiction (marriage in secret or without publication of banns, false oath in confession), two cases of false witness and one of leaving an inn without paying.[3] The offenders included fourteen women, that is nearly 15 per cent, all accused of usury. The assaults had all been committed by men: three had beaten a woman and three a clergyman (plus one brawl between two clerics). These acts of brutality were not the main concern of the bishop's representatives, as they are in third place and amount to barely 19 per cent of the total, but they at least show a desire to contain a specifically masculine violence.

Like the religious authorities, lords tried to limit the all-pervasive violence by a similar system of fines. Only a few traces of this survive. They include the law granted on 6 January 1469 by the powerful abbot of Saint-Bertin to the village of Arques, in Artois, of which he was the lord, which enables us to get a good idea of what it was like. The text is inspired by the practices in use in the large towns of the county of Artois, Saint-Omer and Arras. The appointed magistrates had the right to investigate the most serious cases, including murder, although the sentence was determined by the superior court of the bailiff of Saint-Bertin. For a 'casual', unpremeditated homicide, the offender was required to make a *paix à partie* with the relatives of the deceased, that is, compensate them, and then pay a fine to the lord. A person who severed the limb of another was to lose a hand or pay a very heavy fine of 60 *livres* to the lord, as well as compensate the victim. If the act had been casual, unpremeditated or in self-defence, a 'private peace' was still necessary, but the price paid was twenty times less, that is, 60 *sous*. The carrying of weapons was forbidden, except for the lord's officials; offenders paid a fine of 60 *sous*, or 6 *livres* if the weapon had been drawn, even if no one was wounded, and 60 *livres*, or the loss of a hand, as well as compensation to the family, in case of injury, including if inflicted with the large knife used for cutting bread and 'usually carried to serve oneself at table'. For a blow with a sword not resulting in death or mutilation, the same penalties applied; the weapon was also confiscated and the medical costs had to be paid. Striking with a stick brought 30 *sous* to the lord, plus another 30 to the injured party if he made a complaint, plus payment of medical expenses in case of injury, or if care proved necessary. A fight with the fists or feet that shed blood cost 20 *sous* to the lord, with another 20 *sous* to the victim if he instituted proceedings. Tearing the clothes off someone was punished by the same fine, doubled if the offender was convicted of having started the fight, not forgetting damages to the injured party in both cases. Lying in wait for someone with a bow or crossbow at the ready yielded 20 *sous* to the lord, doubled if an arrow was fired without hitting its target. Every insult cost 20 *sous*, two of which went to the injured party and two to the denouncer. A man who beat or abused his wife paid a fine of 60 *sous*. No doubt from a Christian concern for equality, the same applied if the wife was the aggressor. Anyone who had been attacked and acted in self-defence was not liable to any financial compensation, unless he was carrying a prohibited weapon, in which case he was fined as above. Lastly, the guilty party who failed to provide a security or guarantee of payment of what was owed within a fortnight could be detained, though not in a *vilaine prison*. The insolvent pauper with a bad reputation, or 'a bad lot', was simply put in the pillory, then released.[4]

The meticulousness of the stipulations with regard to a wide range of threats and acts of violence, both verbal and actual, testifies to the existence of very brutal everyday relationships. The lord reserved the most serious offences, premeditated murders, which were punished by death and the confiscation of property. In all other cases, we may wonder whether the systematic reliance on fines did much to dissuade offenders. The system trivialized bloodshed by integrating it into a dense network of financial transactions with the authorities and the individual concerned. The price of life was not, in the end, very high, especially as those who proved bad payers were simply threatened with prison, and the poor of bad reputation escaped with public exposure in the pillory. It is doubtful whether threats such as these could succeed in eradicating the culture of large-scale and general violence revealed by other sources from all over Europe.

England is exceptionally well documented on the subject for the thirteenth century. 'Culpable' homicide, which was distinguished from 'excusable' or 'justified' homicide, was a capital crime and, like several others described as 'felonies', fell within the competence of the royal courts. Like the *laid fait* of the Low Countries, it carried the death penalty. The records of the sessions of the royal justices in eyre are well preserved up to the beginning of the fourteenth century, when they cease until the organization of professional police forces in the nineteenth century.[5] The justices received remarkable accounts of homicides which are without equivalent in any other country. These make it possible to estimate homicide rates per 100,000 inhabitants, which varied enormously, between a maximum of sixty-four for the session held at Warwick in 1232 and a minimum of four for each of the two sessions held at Bristol in 1227 and 1248. The fate of the accused was equally varied. Only 1,251, a little more than a third, appeared before the court; 1,441 others, or 41 per cent, who had prudently taken flight, were declared outlaws, which entailed the confiscation of their property to the benefit of the king and summary execution in case of capture. Those who appeared were generally treated leniently: 970 were acquitted while 274 were condemned to death, that is, 28 and 7 per cent respectively of all the accused, and a ratio of four to one in favour of the release of those attending the sessions. To which should be added fifty-six royal pardons, which we may compare with the unhappy fate of twenty murderers slain without benefit of trial.[6] Though a uniform law encouraged severity, the evident restraint of the juries reveals a practice tending to leniency in the prevailing culture of violence. The sentences were particularly light if the deceased had been killed by a group and not in a one-to-one fight. Two-thirds of cases involved at least one accomplice, and a tenth of cases more than ten. The impression given is that the local juries saw the use of force as a normal way of settling certain conflicts, especially when carried out collectively, in view of the obligations created by such ties between the individuals. They refused to criminalize these acts as the law prescribed, in blanket fashion, offering only a choice between the ultimate punishment and acquittal, including for accomplices. Jury practice ultimately led, in a statute of 1390, to a distinction being made between murder, intentional homicide committed out of malice and justified manslaughter, especially in self-defence, to escape a mortal danger.[7]

A duty of violence existed. Thus the students of the Norman nation at the university of Paris summoned their members, at the beginning of the fourteenth century, to ask whether they should take up arms and attack the members of another nation. After a vote in favour, the ensuing battle left one clerk wounded and another dead. The strength of familial solidarities is shown by the very small number of murders of relatives: 159, or less than 0.5 per cent of the total, according to the thirteenth-century eyre rolls; they included sixty-four wives and thirty-two husbands murdered by their spouse, and twenty-seven brothers who had killed each other. Parricide, matricide and infanticide were extremely rare

49

according to these sources, as were instances of masters killing servants.[8] This is probably not a true reflection of reality, as brutality within the family was common; we may doubt, in particular, whether there were only ten cases of infanticide in thirteenth-century England. Such silences are primarily an expression of the strength of the taboos and the effectiveness of the law of silence within the community in these matters; mortal violence was generally regarded as banal, except when it happened within the family, when it was unspeakable because it ruptured essential ties and brought shame on the whole household.

This was true of female violence, too. Homicide was overwhelmingly masculine: 91 per cent of the accused were men, as were 80 per cent of the victims recorded in the eyre rolls. Women provided one victim in five but fewer than one in ten of those accused. This under-representation has been a constant in our culture, still visible today, and in the same proportions. It reflects a powerful social prohibition, the unacceptability of female violence. Not only were women not taught to use violence to resolve a conflict, unlike men, but they did not carry weapons and were not trained in their use. The female murderer was considered an anomaly in the thirteenth century. Those who appeared in person before English juries were acquitted in the same proportion as men, but as many as a third of them, 41 out of 123, were condemned to death, as opposed to less than a fifth of men, that is, 206 out of 1,128. The judicial alchemy tended to minimize the responsibility of men but maximize the guilt of women, which led to one woman being sent to the scaffold for every four men. Further, their crimes differed in certain respects. The men had killed someone not related to them in 96 per cent of cases and when, as in half the cases, they had not acted alone, they had been assisted by someone unrelated to them in 84 per cent of cases. In contrast, 19 per cent of female murderers had attacked a relative and 53 per cent had acted together with a relative, parent, child, sibling or, most often, husband or lover (47 per cent of cases).[9]

English society was steeped in violence in the thirteenth century, in which it was in no way exceptional in Europe. But this aggression was controlled by imperative codes. It was gendered, specifically masculine, and more intense in the countryside than in the towns. Contrary to received opinion, the big cities, although they were home to extremely unstable populations, had some considerable success in containing the problem. London had much lower homicide rates than most places in the country, and Bristol had the lowest rates recorded.[10] In this turbulent world, the family offered a haven of relative peace. Powerful taboos seem to have protected the life of its members, in particular the father and the other males. Blows were certainly common within the home, but they must not result in a death. Destructive fury was both inhibited between

50

close relatives and oriented towards the outside, to fall on persons who were not unknown to their aggressor, but who were not bound to them by ties of blood or marriage. The women who broke the unwritten rules forbidding them to kill or injure were treated very harshly and, if they had attacked a male from their own household, above all their husband, they were regarded as doubly abnormal. Only if they had assisted a relative against an assailant could they expect any leniency. However, the brutality of relationships within the home, where women occupied a subject position, led some of them to rebel, even to try to eliminate the source of their miseries. As for women victims, usually killed by an aggressor of the opposite sex, 17 per cent had suffered at the hands of a relative, compared with only 4 per cent of men. The difference is a sign of the obvious dominance of the stronger over the weaker sex.

Blows also formed a veritable relational language between men. They demonstrated their manliness and were used to assert their social position if it was challenged. Many men carried a weapon, if only the knife they used to cut their bread. The little information provided about types of injuries suggests that most were inflicted with a knife, axes taking second place. The education of boys was based on the exaltation of physical force and it accustomed children to endure it, through the corporal punishment inflicted by parents on children, by masters on apprentices and by teachers on pupils. Character was also built by rough games, tournaments for the nobility, friendly fights with neighbours and trials of physical strength between teams from different villages on feast days. In short, everything combined to make violence acceptable, and even seen as satisfying a need, according to Given.[11] In the absence of information, he seems not to have attempted to assess the part played by young men of marriageable age. Yet it was fundamental. The judicial construction of the problem revealed by the eyre rolls was the result of a compromise between the law, which prescribed the death penalty for murder in Christian territory, and the rules of the community, in which violence was a way of regulating relationships. It was forbidden to women, who were expected simply to endure it, but it served to develop and reveal manliness, and to position every protagonist on the social scene. To learn how to fight with a knife was a duty, an injury inflicted or received was an honour and a homicide that resulted was a feat of arms, even if it was condemned by the law and the church. It was only to be expected, therefore, that unmarried men would be the most violent, because they tried to match up to the masculine ideal defined by the society in which they longed to assume a place, even though they were kept on the sidelines by the adults, to postpone the day of their own replacement. This marginalization was also a way of deflecting away from the household and the family the youthful violence that was intensified by the need to

51

demonstrate a masterful strength. Thus, homicide was primarily part of the rituals of competition between young men vying with each other in the same tight marriage market. It was closely associated with festive sociability and it put into action the tacit contract existing between the masculine generations. The young bloods accepted a deferred share in the riches and a delayed access to full sexuality because they were confident of one day taking their parents' place, and because their parents tolerated their excesses of murderous brutality.

Violent festivities and brutal games

The Europeans of the late Middle Ages inhabited a world deeply marked by two great traditions: the Christian heritage, established for a thousand years, and the even more ancient peasant customs, observed by at least four-fifths of the population and also strongly influencing the urban minority. The agro-liturgical calendar which resulted was an attempt to reconcile sometimes contradictory phenomena. The church tried to impose meditation and prayer on people who lived in often difficult conditions and who demanded the right to festivities whose excesses were found unacceptable, even subversive, by the authorities. Until the middle of the sixteenth century, villagers and citizens regularly turned the world upside down, drinking, eating, dancing and indulging in every imaginable extravagance so that they could forget their everyday cares and lay aside, for a while, the seriousness that was demanded of them.[12]

There were plenty of occasions for this. A large number of festivals punctuated the liturgical year. Like Sundays, when it was forbidden to work on pain of a fine, they were devoted to religious practice, but also celebrated in a notably profane fashion, before, after and even during the ceremonies. Though varying according to country, region and parish, these festive interludes, Sundays included, added up to well over a hundred a year. The liturgical calendar began with Advent, a long period of fasting, sexual continence and penance, followed by twelve days of rejoicing beginning with Christmas. The anniversary of the Massacre of the Innocents on the orders of King Herod, 28 December, was dedicated to a particularly colourful festival of inversion, known as the Feast of Fools in France, Spain and the Germanic countries and as the Festival of the Boy Bishop in England. Young clerics celebrated boisterous parodic rites in the churches, after which they ran through the streets beating any women they encountered in order to ensure their fertility, and also that of the fields, in a distant echo of the wild Roman Saturnalia of the winter solstice.

In Venice, Carnival started early, on 26 December. Elsewhere, it began on various dates, from Kings' Day (6 January) to Candlemas (2 February), culminating on Shrove Tuesday in a great festival of abundance. On Ash Wednesday, the first day of Lent, which lasted till Easter, and might fall as early as 5 February or as late as 10 March, an effigy of St Pansard, personifying Carnival, was burnt in public. In his *The Fight Between Carnival and Lent* (1559), Pieter Bruegel the Elder admirably portrayed the transition from the most riotous merrymaking to penance, fasting, continence and the prohibition of all pleasure for the next forty days, until the liberation marked by the festival of Easter. Other festivities punctuated the Easter cycle or commemorated the holy patron of the parish. In May, at the end of a long winter of evening gatherings, the life of relationships became increasingly intense. Many marriages were celebrated, bringing additional occasions for dancing, eating, drinking at the inn and playing games of every type.

A month of youth and courting began on 1 May. Gangs of boys planted shrubs, 'mays', in front of the houses of nubile girls. The qualities or failings of the girl in question were celebrated in a symbolic language that everyone could understand, while brothers watched over the purity of her in whom resided the honour of the whole family. Excesses were frequent, nevertheless. As a result, in the second half of the sixteenth century, the Catholic Church dedicated the month of May to the Virgin, in an attempt to prevent the proliferation of marriages and their unremitting disorder; one should not marry, it said, in the month of Mary. Another great fertility festival followed, on St John's Night (24 June), when great bonfires were lit. Couples anxious to marry, or to have children that year, joined hands and jumped over the bonfires, then took ashes or brands to use in magic acts of healing or protection, in particular to ward off evil spells. This was the night of witches. Only barely Christianized, it perpetuated a feast of fire, at the time of the summer solstice. In some regions, flaming wheels were rolled down hillsides.

In Artois, July was dedicated to a large number of parish festivals, the *ducasses*, called *kermesses* in the Catholic Flemish-speaking countries, which commemorated the anniversary of the dedication of the local church. The heavy agricultural labour of early August limited the number of occasions for enjoyment until the harvest festivals of arable areas, which made 15 August, the date of the Assumption, a day of feasting and sexual release. Wine-growing areas had similar festivals at the end of the grape harvest. All Saints' Day and All Souls' Day, 1 and 2 November, ended the year. They were not only commemorative, as they were organized round joyful traditions linking the dead to the living. Before the prohibitions imposed in the second half of the sixteenth century, dances, feasting and games took place in the cemeteries, where people went to eat over the tomb of their dead ancestors, as if the dead could share this meal. The young men were charged with conducting a symbolic dialogue with the dead by ringing the bells throughout the night of 1 November. The representatives of the new generations held out a hand, as it were, to their ancestors, so as to assure the future of the community, guaranteed both by their own virility and by the fertility of the land in which the deceased lay buried. The wheel of time then began to turn once more, immutable, alternating times of toil and times of joy, times of privation and times of festive abundance.[13]

Young people always played a major part in the festivals, in particular the most important and most unbridled of them: All Saints' Day, the long period of Carnival, the month of May, St John's Day and the merrymaking marking the end of the agricultural year. The young embodied the hopes of the parish, its chances of survival in a hostile world deeply scarred by famine, war and epidemics.[14] Every European village was an entity with a stable core but shifting contours, and much energy was put into preventing external dangers from threatening its collective existence. Economic and matrimonial exchanges with other parishes were closely supervised to ensure that they did not have a worryingly weakening effect. The dominant model of marriage, therefore, was fundamentally endogamous and homogenous, as more than three-quarters of the rural population married someone from the same place and the same social rank. Villagers were trained from a tender age to defend their territory and their rights against any encroachment.

Once freed from their mother's apron strings, at around seven, little boys were sent to watch over the flocks on the borders of their territory. There, they met boys of similar age from neighbouring villages and together they learned the hard rules of life, by means of crook or sling, to prevent 'strangers' from setting foot on their territory. An injury received or inflicted was a source of pride. Any watching adults, such as women collecting wood or washing linen in the river, encouraged the combatants, exhorting them not to let themselves be beaten by someone smaller than them. At the age of around fourteen, pubescent boys passed through a ritual stage by leaving behind the second childhood which had been spent under the thumb of their father. They discovered their virility, in the strict sense of the word. At Sacy in Burgundy, Restif de la Bretonne, aged about seven, which dates the episode to around 1741, watched a dozen young lads 'who were twice my age, that is, who were at the age of puberty', showing off in the sunshine in a way he describes in a note in Latin: 'All of them, without shame, exposing their penis, played at who could retract their foreskin the furthest. Did they go so far as to eject their semen? I was unable, because of my age, to tell; but I observed that no one blushed.' The fact that he could not approach the group

54

indicates its specificity, its members keeping their distance from the other inhabitants. All the more so as they were now regarded with deep distrust by the girls, despite bumping into them on numerous occasions, at church, in the village square or in the fields, because they threatened their chastity and thus the honour of the men of the family. Fathers and brothers in particular kept a close watch on the virtue of young girls, helping to keep the young roosters well clear of the hen run. As their own parents sent them out to work during the day and encouraged them to spend as little time as possible within the house, world of the very young and site of adult sexuality, they were forced to invent their own sociability.

This took the novel form of structured groups like that described at Sacy. The boys of marriageable age formed themselves into 'kingdoms of youth'. These groups existed all over France, under various names: 'youth abbeys' in the Midi, Burgundy and the Dauphiné, *bachelleries* in Poitou and the Vendée. With the exception, it seems, of England, they are documented all over Europe, including Switzerland, Germany, Italy, Hungary, Romania and Spain. Emerging in the twelfth century, perhaps even earlier, they developed until the eighteenth century, before disappearing at various dates in various regions under pressure from the moralists who denounced their excesses. They were a response to the increasingly late age of marriage in Western Europe, regarded by demographers as the principal mechanism for population control in the absence of widespread and effective contraception, as it reduces the number of children conceived per couple. In France, the age of marriage for men was between twenty-eight and thirty on the eve of the Revolution, whereas it had been more like twenty-three at the end of the Middle Ages. Thus pubescent boys were forced to undergo a very long period of waiting before they could accede to full adulthood and a legitimate sexual life. For a decade at least, even for some fifteen years around 1789, a combination of religious prohibitions and, even more, the strict supervision of daughters by their families prevented them from easily obeying their instincts.

Historians no longer believe that the mass of young unmarried men opted for continence. Illegitimate births may have been less than 1 per cent in French villages in the seventeenth century, but plenty of outlets existed. These ranged from masturbation, as at Sacy, which was also sometimes heterosexual, as in seventeenth-century England, to furtive embraces with married women and widows, by way of prostitution, rape – then not really considered criminal – and even bestiality.[15] It remains the case that these young men had to spend more than a third of their life in an uncomfortable situation, on the margins of a community that was distrustful of their explosive potential. Girls, for their part, were kept under the tutelage of parents and other women, in order to preserve the treasure of their virginity. They did not form structured groups of adolescents, which would have been an obvious target for the males. Feminine sociability was a mix of all age groups and it operated on hierarchical lines, especially in the evening gatherings and at the oven or the mill. The 'old ladies' protected the 'innocents' from the assaults of men, even if the latter's advances were not always unwelcome to the recipients.

The youth groups, kingdoms of manliness, encompassed all the boys of the parish, but split into smaller groups according to the occasion and to affinities, perhaps sometimes also in line with social status. In the typical village, with a population of a few hundred, the boys might form a single band, a dozen or more strong. In big parishes, and especially in the towns, there might be many groups, organized by district. A 'king', a 'prince' or an 'abbot', that is, a leader, was appointed each year, at a major festival, usually after a trial of strength or skill from which he had emerged the victor. A new member, who could hardly refuse to join on reaching puberty, paid his dues in the form of money or drink. He began by learning the traditions, acting as lookout for his elders, carrying their cloaks or weapons, undergoing initiation rites which marked the abandonment of childhood for the state of young man. His fellows might include some married men, especially in the first year of their conjugal life when they were still without children, sign of full transition to the adult state.

The principal activities of the members took place in festive periods and places. In the evening after work, at night, on holidays or on Sundays, they assembled to go to the tavern, organize games and dances in the square or pay collective court to the girls, serenading them beneath their windows with musicians. The members patrolled the streets and felt powerful enough to venture as a group to the borders of their territory so as to provoke similar gangs from other villages, with whom they might already have clashed when they were watching over the flocks. The challenges and battles which followed seemed perfectly normal to contemporaries, including to princes, who were quite prepared to grant pardons if someone got killed. These events had a positive value for the competitors, clearly delineating their exclusive rights to a territory or to the matrimonial opportunities existing within it. For the kingdoms of youth were driven by a fierce spirit of competition with other similar groups. Their members frequented the festivals of other parishes, to join in the dancing and to try to impress the girls, who were jealously guarded by the local lads. Any sign of weakness, any failure, had major consequences for the community as a whole, which was mocked by the neighbours, humiliated and weakened, because the victors might come to claim the spoils of victory.

56

The kingdoms of youth played an important role in the village. Although they were a product of the long marginalization of the bachelors and led to mortal combats between them, they were an effective way of strengthening social cohesion. They were guardians of tradition, especially in the sphere which was a particular obsession of their members, gaining access to women. They were not, in general, hostile to the adult men responsible for their long banishment from the legitimate pleasures of the flesh, except when a period of strong population growth unbalanced the system by making the waiting more painful and more uncertain. The murder of adults by adolescents was rare, as long as the frustration was not exacerbated by the difficulties of inheriting in an overpopulated world, when patrimonies shrank due to the large number of children. The power of the established adults was all the less likely to be challenged in that the pubescent sons looked forward to exercising it themselves, in their turn, in exactly the same way, and to enjoying the fruits of the marriage for which they had waited so long.

In fact, they were allowed great latitude in policing the normality of the matrimonial system, as it was practised by their fellow inhabitants. They kept a close watch not only on their own rights, but on those of others, with general consent, to the point where a stranger who married into the parish had to pay a high price or risk injury, even death. They levied a tax on all new unions, demanding gifts in money or kind, such as the *plat du trancheur* in Artois. During the wedding night, they brought the new couple a *chaudeau* or a *rôtie*, an aphrodisiac mixture destined to give them extra vigour. Presented in a rather unsavoury manner, with many a smutty or scatological joke, the offering served as a pretext for inspecting the sheets of the nuptial bed to verify the virginity of the bride. The majority of the group's activities were organized round courtship, which culminated in the month of May. Supervising the behaviour of married couples of all ages was part of this. The young men paraded cuckolded husbands naked, sitting backwards on a donkey, to teach them not to permit an infidelity that was everybody's business, as it demonstrated a feminine power in the very place where the man should be sole master. They laid defaming paths between the houses of adulterers and held charivaris aimed at ill-assorted couples. Particular targets were elderly widowers who had married a young girl, thereby depriving the young men of an opportunity in what was already a very tight marriage market.[16]

The kingdoms of youth were not simply assemblies of frustrated young men who found some compensation by engaging in acts of violence and various excesses. This harsh view of them, held by moralists eager to see them disappear, fails to appreciate their deep rootedness in the society which produced them. They were the result of a tacit accord between masculine age groups, and designed to provide the best possible preparation for the passing of the baton to new generations, in a context of increasingly delayed marriage and of sexual frustration exacerbated by strict local prohibitions. The repressive activities of the religious and civil authorities from the mid sixteenth century only made the situation worse. In exchange for their acceptance of an immutable social order, synonymous for them with a very long wait, these young bachelors got the right to engage in ritualized violence, even if it involved fatalities, and to exercise strict supervision over the sexuality of everyone else. The imperative norms of village society obliged them to demonstrate their emerging virile capacity. Forged in childhood, brought to a peak within the restrictive context of the abbeys of youth, their culture of male power had only a single objective: to prove that they were equipped to replace fathers and impregnate women, even though access to the latter was officially forbidden before marriage. The brutality they engaged in was not solely compensatory. It was an imperative rule of life, indispensable if they were to exist in the eyes of others and, in due course, lead a full life and be respected in their turn, as fathers who imposed their will on all around.

The village of their birth was the centre of their world. At the heart of the economic and matrimonial region in which most of life was led, it was vigorously defended against potential enemies. A formidable xenophobia was practised against strangers, vagrants and soldiers, including those of the prince, because they pillaged and raped without scruple. The same defence mechanism was deployed against near neighbours, though more nuanced due to the need to maintain relations with these 'false strangers', especially if they lived within a radius of four or five kilometres. In fact, they exchanged property with them, and also land, produce, services and women. One spouse in four or five came from within this distance, no more than a day's walk away, at a time when it was exceptional to venture further than a dozen kilometres to marry – courtship being a long and assiduous business inhibited by distance. The most adventurous sometimes found a partner by frequenting the festivals of these 'enemy friends', who themselves did exactly the same. In Somain (Nord), at Michaelmas (29 September), the young lads made a bouquet of little wax flowers to give to 'the most beautiful girl from outside'. The aim was to attract potential brides from neighbouring parishes and the prize was also awarded in the form of a 'rose or other jewel'. The practice was abolished in 1531, on the orders of the abbot of Cysoing, lord of the village, in order to avoid the 'disagreements, fights and deaths' to which it had led.[17]

The ecclesiastical prohibitions directed against consanguinity made this sort of openness to the outside world necessary, especially in the case of tiny communities where the available girls were few. But there was still fierce rivalry between the inhabitants of neighbouring villages, though known and familiar, to ensure that the exchange was not too unequal or likely to weaken a place that was poorly protected. The use of insulting nicknames and the permanent competition between the young men in question testify to this. Custom decreed that the marriage ceremony should take place in the parish of the bride, so the animosity between the local bachelors, deprived of a prospective partner, and the friends of the bridegroom from outside was frequently expressed, usually in a playful manner, but sometimes roughly enough to lead to a tragedy, even the death of the new husband before his wedding night.[18] The very strong sense of identity of the rural communities was based on this culture of violence, sustained by the young men. Beyond ten, and even more twenty, kilometres, the frontiers of a little *pays* with common cohesive features, lay a world which provoked not so much aggression as fear in those who ventured into it. Homicides committed far from a native parish, in a town, for example, among strangers, usually involved other factors such as urban contempt for country-dwellers, provocation, attempted theft or needs to be assuaged.

The concentration of hopes and desires within such a small area meant that all relationships were potentially explosive. In a world where everyone knew everyone else, and where it was difficult to avoid prying eyes, sociability could easily become conflictual. Overlapping ties of family, neighbourhood and friendship constituted dense networks which protected the individual, but also imposed obligations, such as that to intervene in support or defence of one of its members. Thus every individual carried many others on his shoulders. A quarrel about a child, an animal or a right risked degenerating into a petty war, gradually involving two factions or two neighbouring communities intent on fighting with whatever weapon lay to hand. A regulatory system usually prevented things deteriorating far enough to endanger the survival of the group. The culture of violence was not simply a law of force. It was based on imperative rules which marginalized those who transgressed. Everyone was aware of these limits, which they generally observed so as not to lose face in the general opinion or find themselves the subject of the dreaded rumour mill, which could lead to their exclusion from normal exchanges. Life was a stage on which everyone had to demonstrate their normality, according to their sex, age and position within the community.[19]

Such precepts regulated the distribution of space. The house was regarded as an inviolable sanctuary, especially at night. An attack on it merited unanimous disapproval and was enough to excuse a homicide committed in its defence. 'Leave that man in peace in his own home. He's not doing anything to you. He ought to be safe in his own house', shouted a spectator to an assailant at Laventie, in Artois, on 20 May 1525. It was unacceptable to enter a house without permission, or even stray within its safety zone, sometimes marked by a hedge, more often invisible, though still known to everyone. The bachelors who went to pay court to a girl were well aware of this; they never went too close without permission, let alone entered the house itself without the express consent of the father.

All other space was common to varying degrees, subject to traditions which had the force of law. Men gathered at the forge, a specifically masculine world. They rarely risked disturbing the women at the mill or the washing place or where they gathered to spin, fearing their wrath, expressed in insults and humiliating gestures. The washerwomen on the banks of the Seine were famous for their vulgar mockery of boat passengers, not hesitating to 'moon' at them as a sign of contempt and derision. The winter evening gatherings were largely a female sphere. The older women kept a close watch on the young girls, tempted by the bands of young bloods who hung around this treasure beyond their reach; the older women reprimanded any girls who were too forward and scolded the young Casanovas who were too bold. The fields, the paths and the woods were not neutral zones, even if everybody frequented them and some spent time there. Only the unmarried men dared to go there in a group at night. Girls had to be careful not to be found there on their own, even in daytime, or on the roads, where they ought to be accompanied by male guardians, especially on the way home from festivals; otherwise they risked irrevocably compromising their reputation.

The busiest places, such as the village square, the church, the cemetery and the tavern, were also those where violence was most likely to break out, and from which it was hardest to flee in the face of the hostile intentions of an enemy met by chance. Although they were governed by minutely detailed rules and obligatory codes of behaviour designed to assure the routine safety of the inhabitants, they were the scene of many flare-ups. They were parade grounds on which everyone had to display their personality so as to get others to recognize it. A humiliation was even more serious if it was public. It led to an escalation of violence in full view of spectators, who took sides, intervened, even joined in the fight.

The square was both a thoroughfare and a meeting place, especially after the mass; it was the scene of games and dancing at festivals and weddings, of music, and of spectacle when a pedlar or a doctor or a dentist temporarily set up shop; it was also a marketplace and where a range of negotiations, such as the hiring of harvest workers or domestic servants, was conducted . The inhabitants jealously defended their rights to this vital space, where everyone met everyone else and exchanges took place with 'strangers'. The members of the local kingdom of youth demanded a glass of wine or beer from their peers from a neighbouring village if they came to join the festivities. The square was an important showground, where conflicts were numerous but closely controlled, because everything happened in full view and it was essential to abide by the norms of honour so as to avoid a shame that would reflect on one's family and friends. It was conducive to crime, but less than one might expect, because the cases which appear in the judicial sources conceal the much larger number of incidents which did not end in bloodshed, or were simply settled by a symbolic victory. Animosities could be damped down there, especially as the many manly games dissipated some of the surplus bellicosity by awarding the competitors the public victories for which they yearned – like sport at the highest level today.

The church and the cemetery played a similar role. By definition sacred, they were nevertheless used for many profane pursuits until, from the end of the sixteenth century, the Churches insisted they be treated with more respect. Until then, the house of God had played host to many secular activities, including financial transactions. By age-old tradition, boys gathered to flirt with the girls at the entrance, which was also the scene of frequent disputes between lords over precedence. Around the building itself, the parish cemetery, rarely closed, was frequented by people and animals and served as a sanctuary for criminals pursued by the courts; it was a scene of constant activity, in particular on All Souls' Day, when people danced there, had fun and gorged themselves. Marriageable girls liked to stroll there at night, which meant that many disputes and murders took place among the tombs, or even inside the church. On the evening of Sunday 9 August 1523, a dozen inhabitants of La Couture, in Artois, erected a table in the cemetery of the neighbouring village of Locon, where they ate and drank for a solid four hours, while laying siege to their enemies, natives of the parish, who had taken refuge in the church and who rang the bells to appeal for assistance. Cemeteries and churches were also the scene of many ambushes and duels; some fifty such cases involving nobles have been noted in France between 1470 and 1660.[20]

Violence was employed here, as in the village squares, to make the act clearly visible and highly memorable, so as to enhance the honour of the perpetrator and his family, even if he was a simple peasant farmer. This sort of behaviour had been common since the Middle Ages, if we are to go by the repeated synodal statutes forbidding the spilling of blood or semen in these sacred places. The fact that one could not worship there or bury the dead until the place had been re-consecrated seems not to have worried the murderers unduly. They were a tiny minority, however, compared with the vast majority who frequented these places peacefully. Such spectacular murders were transgressions of rules that the majority observed. Churches and cemeteries were not exempt from homicidal conflicts because nowhere where people came together at that period was exempt. We should not see the recorded incidents as evidence of a universal bloodthirsty madness, however, but rather as exceptions. In fact, aggression was subject to a degree of control in all public places, lay or consecrated. The collective peace-keeping mechanisms prevented a large number of potential or actual conflicts from ending tragically.

This was so in the case of the taverns. They seem, at first sight, to be schools for crime, so many murders were committed inside or just outside them. This is to forget that, for every incident that led to a death, there were hundreds of entirely peaceful visits and countless instances of a quarrel that was confined to provocation, insults and blows, without going to such extremes or leaving any trace in the archives. The black legend of the tavern was born in the second half of the sixteenth century, when prohibitions on drinking there during church services, or on Sundays or festivals, proliferated, together with regulations limiting opening hours to daytime on working days. Until then, these establishments had actually played an important peace-keeping role, by defining rules of behaviour that amounted to a sort of popular 'good manners', designed to limit the eruptions of violence encouraged by the masculine code of honour.

The inn was often in the centre of the village, as in Bruegel's *Kermesse at Hoboken*, an engraving of 1559. He shows people playing a variety of games in the village square, while some boys and girls dance in a circle in front of an inn, opposite the cemetery; a procession arrives at the church, filing past the spectators at an open-air theatre, where the stage is mounted on massive barrels. In the foreground, dancers accompanied by a musician emerge from another inn, packed with customers; a man is relieving himself against one of its walls. Recognizable by their colourful signs, eloquent for the many who were illiterate, taverns also welcomed women and children, and performed a number of functions. Commercial, community and family business was conducted there. Written contracts were drawn up, hiring labour, buying or selling land, arranging a marriage or restoring the peace between visceral enemies. More often than not, the negotiations were verbal, before witnesses, sealed by a drink. Matchmakers and conciliators charged with defusing some imminent bloody vengeance went to the inn to oil the wheels of human relations. Story-tellers, musicians and men able to elucidate an edict or a point of law visited the tavern in passing. Ecclesiastics and nobles mingled with the rest of the population before the chilling moral austerity of the seventeenth century, joining in the entertainments and jokes. Children learned hard lessons there; one little five-year-old boy whose father was teaching him to drink like a man vomited several times before falling dead drunk to the ground at La Cauchie, in Artois, in April 1616.[21]

The tavern, principal site of village sociability, was a microcosm ruled by strict norms. Its 'politeness' was not that of the 'civilizing process' described by Norbert Elias. The codes in operation there may seem crude, but they were effective enough to allow individuals who were armed, extremely touchy about their honour and increasingly quarrelsome as the drink flowed to spend long hours, even whole days, in each other's company. Convention demanded that a new arrival greet the company, wait till he was invited before sitting down with anyone, and leave his most formidable weapons propped up against a wall; they were in any case difficult to manage within such a restricted and often overcrowded space. Yet people were rarely separated from the knife they used to cut their bread, which was one of the last resorts, with heavy pots, in case of attack. For reasons of security, metal pots often had a glass base and bread knives were often put down in front of their owners, where they could quickly be seized if the need arose. The fact that space had to be shared did not mean that people crowded each other. Everyone had to keep to his own place, that is, the space assigned to an individual or a group, separated from that of others by invisible but very real barriers. Entering or leaving the tavern, even to satisfy a call of nature, had its risks. If you passed close to someone it was important to signify the absence of hostility by a word or a gesture, so that they did not feel threatened. Leaving the inn was particularly dangerous, as an enemy might seize the occasion to bar the way, lie in wait outside or claim he had been jostled or challenged. Once over the threshold, the tacit guarantees of non-aggression associated with the collective gaze, which imposed peace and accepted the validity of a conflict only if certain conventions had been observed, no longer applied.

Drinking together was a strong mark of solidarity. In Artois, one spoke of 'drinking and making peace' to settle a difference. The imperative norms that surrounded this moment of obligatory conviviality make its importance clear. A new arrival offered a '*bien venue*' on joining a group, and a '*bien allée*' on leaving, in both cases a sign of peace. The ritual prolonged that of the laying down of weapons and framed two uneasy moments, because a seated man was in a weak position in case of sudden assault by a person on his feet. If you walked past someone sitting at table, without lingering, it was prudent to defuse the tension by some friendly expression. In return, those greeted offered the newcomer a drink, which he accepted, before moving on. The reciprocal greeting was a statement of non-hostility. A refusal to conform to these conventions

63

signified the contrary. It meant a quarrel had to be picked subtly, later, on a pretext that would be found acceptable by others, after a demonstration of normality through the obligatory relational ceremony.

To start a quarrel in these circumstances was a whole art. The moment of paying the collective bill was a good opportunity, if you could show that the cost had not been fairly shared. Another tactic was to drink someone's health. The common mug was then passed to the person in question, who had to reciprocate. A refusal was considered an intolerable insult. It was possible cleverly to exploit the codes by loading your actions with veiled pejorative undertones calculated to provoke the ire of another. Sending a present of food or drink to a table, a common sign of friendship or respect, could conceal a challenge if the symbolic language employed was disparaging. The same applied, in Artois, if you put some elder as a May branch in front of the house of a nubile young woman, as this shrub signified a stink in the local culture. To steal a personal item, especially a weapon, or a hat or a feather, was guaranteed to enrage the victim. The more direct challenges which began in the form of a joke were hard to take if they impugned the victim's honour. To pull someone's beard was an intolerable insult, because this hirsute adornment was evidence of its owner's virility. Worse still were the jokers who urinated from an upper room on to a table below, or into someone's hat, or onto their feet, well aware of how deeply offensive their act was. In marking their territory in this way and in announcing that their masculinity was superior to that of their victim, they initiated a trial of strength which quickly lost its playful dimension. It was rare, however, to utter in public the supreme insults, those which concerned the purity of the women of the enemy's family, above all his mother. As in the French banlieues of the twenty-first century, to tell a young man to go screw his mother left him with no alternative other than a violent response to avenge the insult.

There are many examples of nobles joining in the festivals, dances and games and frequenting the inn. Before marriage, they, too, shared the culture of the kingdoms of youth, though they sometimes formed socially homogeneous groups. The distancing from the peasantry recorded from the seventeenth century on was not acceptable in earlier times. In 1529, monsieur de Charnacé, lord of Gué d'Argent, and his son, riding through a village, had the contents of a chamber pot emptied over their heads. On the following Sunday, leaving high mass, they had to listen to a song gleefully commemorating this event. That same year, Gilles de Montfort and his cousin René Darmoyens, who lived at Esvres (Indre-et-Loire), arrived early one morning at an inn and breakfasted there; then they twice went to 'play a game of real tennis for wine', before returning to drink their winnings, and continuing, without a pause, to drink until evening. In 1536, a group of four or five nobles led by François de Kergonnonaon and Alain Le Mesguen, in what looks very much like a youth band, went on an extended pub crawl from an unspecified starting point to La Chapelle Saint-Yves, on the invitation of a certain Jean Prigent, before going their separate ways. They were no doubt Bretons, like Julien de la Couldre, gentleman, who lived at Noyal (Morbihan). One day, after dinner, in 1551, he paraded through the streets of the town of Limerzel with some friends, behind a man shaking a tambourine. When they were refused entry to an inn by the landlord, who called them 'lechers, thieves and brigands', they climbed in through a window. In 1552, Guillaume de Montamat, lieutenant of the château of Penne in the *sénéchaussées* of Agenais, was told that a lay brother from the locality had been holed up for three days with a whore. With some friends, he laid siege to the house. The monk fled through a window. Caught by the little band, who were on their way to find some musicians, he was stripped of his clothes and tied to the girl, on whose head they had placed his hood; he was then led back to the convent in this state, through the main street, 'to an accompaniment of frying pans and pots'.

As in the previous cases, these practices were typical of the kingdoms of youth, who swarmed over the neighbourhood, to the accompaniment of musicians, on the evenings of festivals. The last example describes the equivalent of a charivari, usually destined for ill-assorted couples. Despite his official title, de Montamat was not claiming to be acting with the sanction of the law. Rather he was stigmatizing a sexual misdemeanour in the traditional fashion, in this case committed by a man who had made a vow of chastity. It was also in the name of the eminent rights of bachelors to police the morals of the parish that Guillaume Blanc, baron de Montagu, in Rouergue, acted, or so he claimed, in 1552, when he and some companions went to the market town of Vabre in search of a 'public whore' called Jehanne Boissonne, who was 'lustfully kept' by a certain Loys Ozeil. They broke the window of her house, led the naked girl to a meadow nearby, and then 'having made her put her clothes on took her home and enjoyed her'.[22]

Mattinata in Italy, *vito* in Andalusia, 'rough music' in England, *ketel-musik* in Flemish-speaking regions, *Katzenmuzik* in Germany, the charivari, or 'doing the cat' in Burgundy – they all evoke the fundamental right to supervise morals devolved on young males in European peasant societies until the Reformation and Counter-Reformation imposed the new social discipline. This custom reveals the function assigned them in exchange for their acceptance of the social norms and constraints: to act as the conscience of the community and periodically to rebind the ties between it and the nourishing earth. Under cover of Christianity, the young males perpetuated fertility rites. It was their task to assure the future of the group by warding off dangers. In accord with a thinking still deeply imbued with sympathetic magic, it was they who were best placed to attract forces identical to those by which they were driven, as shown by their constant demonstrations of their virility. In return, their elders allowed them periodically to turn the world upside down, during Carnival and numerous other festivals of inversion at which the non-established, for a while, ruled the community.

They then experienced a sort of apprenticeship in the future, tasting pleasures normally forbidden to their age group, while at the same time concentrating on the village territory the vital energy that was theirs, for the greater good of all. As their sexual power was impossible to suppress without producing serious tensions, village society channelled it to put it at the service of the community. The bachelors benefited in that they enjoyed very great latitude at the many carnivalesque festivals held during the year. Modern sport had not yet been invented, but a wide range of tough physical competitions helped to use up their surplus energy while at the same time reassuring the adult spectators of the capacity of their progeny to confront the future.

Among the expressions of parish vitality incarnated by the young men were violent entertainments directly linked to the agricultural cycle. This 'deep play', to use the expression of Clifford Geertz, reveals the vision society as a whole had of itself, just as the Balinese cockfight throws light on the whole of the local culture.[23] All over Europe, the young men of two villages, or, in a town, those of a parish, competed with the married men in sporting contests of great brutality focused on a ball that was closely contested for hours on end over the whole of a territory. In England and France, injuries were far from rare, and there was even the occasional fatality in the course of furious mêlées in which there was only one rule: to win. The game of *soule,* highly appreciated in Picardy, Normandy and Brittany, called *choule* in Artois, was played at festivals announced by the ringing of bells, during Carnival and at the feast of Brandons ('Torches'). The victors believed that a good harvest would follow, an interpretation which suggests an ancient fertility rite designed to ask, in the depths of winter, for the return of the sun, represented by the ball. At the feast of Brandons, with the same aim and according to the same symbolism of fertilizing light, young men beat the trunks of trees with flaming torches. During the games of *soule*, the ferocity of the combat, equally visible in the Italian ball games of the *calcio* of Florence and the *pallone* of Siena, highlights the intense competition between neighbouring communities to prevent any reduction of their vital space or intrusion into their marriage market. Victory was a sign of collective strength and success. This was why boxing so enthused the crowds in eighteenth-century England. Similarly, the great Italian cities promoted

66

rivalry between districts by organizing nautical jousts or ritual battles for control of a bridge, modelled on those between the fishermen of Venice and the workers in the Arsenal in the sixteenth century.[24]

These events, hymns to manly strength, culminated in the fights between animals and the games which culminated in their death. The correlation established between human male strength and the blood which flowed onto the earth replaced the sacrifices forbidden by Christianity to assure symbolically the fertility of the women and the fields. In Elizabethan England, dogs were pitted against a bull, a bear or a badger in widely enjoyed spectacles. In Spain, bulls might be treated in the same way, but the most popular form, before the eighteenth century, was the *corrida*, in which mounted aristocrats tried to kill the bull with thrusts of a lance, dismounting to finish it off with a sword only if it was wounded. The *toro de fuego*, sent running into the night with flames between its horns, is even more strongly reminiscent of a fertility rite.[25] In other regions, smaller creatures were the subject of violent festive traditions. The goose was sacrificed in Champagne, Birmingham, Rome and Toledo, at different times of year. Live cats were thrown from the belfry at Ypres on the second Wednesday in Lent. In Paris, until the eighteenth century, cats were suspended in a sack over the St John's bonfire, dedicated to fertility. At Beaumetz-les-Loges, near Arras, sickles were thrown at a pig to kill it, a practice recorded by 1414, which gave the village the nickname of 'Beaumetz Pourchelet'. The slaughtering of an exposed animal by throwing stones, sticks or knives at it is frequently referred to throughout an area comprising Champagne, Picardy and the modern *département* of Nord, where some of these popular entertainments were reinvented at the end of the twentieth century.[26]

Youth violence

On Sunday 19 May 1624, the feast of the confraternity of the *jeu d'armes* was celebrated at La Bassée (Nord), in order to choose a new king of youth for the next year. David Leturcq, the incumbent, attended mass with the companions. They then all went into the town hall, where the banquet preceding the competition to award the title was to be held. David fell out with the others because he wanted to move straight to the competition, which they refused, in accord with the custom which decreed they should eat together first. In the face of his 'anger and fury', they left. He did the same and bumped into Fremin Pollet, one of the companions, who was unaware of what had happened. 'Come on, let's go eat', he said. David, beside himself with rage, shouted: 'So you want to eat, do you, you so-and-so? Yet you weren't at mass', before drawing his sword and striking Fremin on the head. The young man died of his injuries a few days later. In his defence, David spoke of a disappointment in love. Having been unable 'to marry a certain girl he loved', he had fallen into despair and debauchery, drinking day and night to the point where he was 'lost in mind and spirit'.[27]

His vexation was surely more than simply amorous in origin. It seems obvious that David was finding it difficult to come to terms with the loss of the prestige attached to his title. For a year he had ruled over a group recognized by the municipal authorities. In the great towns of the Burgundian and then Spanish Low Countries, the confraternities were authorized to bear arms for the defence of the country, as a way of controlling youthful excess. The sovereign was free with his pardons for acts of violence, in this as in other contexts. The *lettres de rémission* requested by David Leturcq from the emperor Charles V put the emphasis on the rage which had overwhelmed David and on his drunkenness. Other applicants spoke of the 'stupidity' of youth. Guilbert Racine of Pontarlier (Doubs) explained the theft of turkeys from a prosecutor, performed with accomplices, 'as a way of passing the time, being then in adolescence', for which he had been banished for six years from Franche-Comté in January 1620. It was generally accepted that boys would behave brutally, impelled by the 'folly of youth'. The expression is used in the request for a pardon made by Jaspard Baillon: 'a young man of means', when living in the suburbs of Valenciennes in the house of his father, in April 1641, he had heard his father complain about a neighbour who had just abused him in the street and threatened him with death. 'Boiling...and in the folly of youth (*ex calore iracundie*), in those first moments when nature does not allow one to be master of oneself', Jaspard had seized his gun, approached the man and hit him in the shoulder with a bullet. His victim had survived without being crippled, argued Jaspard, and they 'had made it up and sworn harmony and inviolable union for the sake of heaven and their mutual pacification'. The ten years' banishment imposed on him by the courts was annulled without difficulty.[28]

This very tolerant image of the young unmarried man as incapable of self-control is in marked contrast to an extremely negative contemporary moral definition which emphasized the many sins committed at this 'dark' and 'dangerous age'. Five of these were peculiar to it and caused it to attain the peak of human depravity: pride, sensual pleasures, mocking and scoffing at religious men and things, rashness and wantonness.[29] The lawyers who drew up requests for pardon on behalf of murderers, in the Low Countries as in France, did not subscribe to this. They reflected a very relaxed attitude on the part of the authorities, at least until the upheavals of the sixteenth and seventeenth centuries. This vision accorded with that of ordinary people, who saw youthful violence as perfectly normal and excusable, as long as it did not break with the established traditions, and who made allowances for the surplus vitality which caused it, made worse by youthful lack of self-control; boys will be boys, they said!

Quarrels, challenges and duels were by no means confined to the nobility. They were, as everybody knew, part and parcel of ordinary life for unmarried young men. On the first Sunday in July, early in the seventeenth century, a large group of them gathered to pass the time in a yard next to the church of Noyelles-Godault (Pas-de-Calais). They were approached by three young men from Dourges, a neighbouring village. 'Who goes there?' said one of the locals. 'What's it to you?' replied Philippe Guilbaut, servant of the miller of Dourges, who then started throwing stones, one of which hit a certain Jacques Breton on the head. 'Inflamed with anger and annoyance', the local lads flung themselves on the aggressors. Guilbaut was beaten on the head and back with sticks, the presence of which in their hands was justified by the culprits by explaining that they served as props...He died of his wounds some three weeks later – only because he hadn't been properly looked after, claimed the accused. At Neuf-Berquin (Nord), on Sunday 5 September 1604, Paul Dufort and his brother-in-law met Mathieu Choix and his brother-in-law in the road. They first greeted each other in the normal way, then one of the second pair exclaimed: 'What fine fellows we have here', adding, speaking directly to Paul, 'How handsome you are!' 'As handsome as you', came the retort. Then, taunted by Mathieu, who asked him: 'Which of us would you like?', Paul replied, 'If it came to it, I'd just as soon have one as the other.' Mathieu drew his sword and, brandishing a knife in the other hand, attacked Paul. They were both restrained by some onlookers but managed to free themselves and fought. Wounded in the back by a knife, Mathieu died within the hour. The murderer was a married man and a father but he had retained the habits of his youth. He explained that he had made peace with the 'interested party', before asking for, and receiving, his pardon.

A quarrel could break out without any apparent real cause. Even if concealed hatreds were at the bottom of it, it seemed acceptable to the prince and to the lawyers to grant a pardon for an act committed after a challenge. For, beyond the avowed motive which can seem trivial, there was always the need for the culprit to defend his honour and not to lose face in public. In Lille, in the tavern of the Sickles, in March 1605, a master surgeon got into a protracted quarrel with a man who had taken his hat ribbon, which was adorned with a medal. On the way out, drunk and angry, he struck him in the chest with the 'little knife he was carrying', so seriously that his victim died soon after.

An orphaned foundling of Tournai (Belgium), who had become a parish clerk in the town, Jean Boury, threatened to beat a young girl who attended the school he ran, because she had jeered at him in the streets. She complained to her father and a fight followed. Jean hit the father in the shoulder with the little knife he used for trimming quill-pens. The wounded man died three weeks later. At Quienville – modern Hondeghem – in French Flanders (Nord), on 22 July 1609, the feast of St Mary Magdalene, Pierre Bazeur, aged nineteen, from Sainte-Marie-Cappel, near Cassel, left the inn to walk a girl home. As he didn't have a weapon to assure their safety, he took the sword of Jacques de Quick, a boy of the same age, without his knowledge. Jacques was told about it by a cousin. When he got back, Pierre heard him say: 'You must be very proud of yourself, taking my sword to fight the young lads.' He handed the weapon back to its owner saying that he had done him no wrong, but asked who had told him. Jacques pointed to his cousin, who received a mighty blow which knocked him off the bench. Jacques came to his defence and, in the ensuing brawl, was wounded in the left side. Having taken to his bed for four weeks, he died five or six months later, 'having often pardoned the said Bazeur'.[30]

The *lettres de rémission* from which these stories are taken were granted in large numbers by the kings of Spain for the southern Low Countries until 1660, and by the kings of France until the Revolution. They allow us to get close to the phenomenon of murderous violence and they reveal its youthful element.[31] They show that, in Artois, more than two in three of the culprits fled after their crime. Of these, 4 per cent became soldiers, which meant they enjoyed judicial immunity as long as they were in arms. Only 12 per cent were imprisoned. The fate of the others is unknown, which means that they cannot have been captured. This massive indifference on the part of the law was not only due to lack of means. It reveals a high degree of tolerance towards those who killed another human being. As the act was unacceptable in law and liable to a death sentence, those who compiled the requests for a pardon, lawyers well versed in the legal subtleties, wrapped the raw facts of the story provided by the culprit in absolutory excuses. The *lettres* reflect not so much what had actually happened as the conception in the minds of the authorities of the ideal subject, unlucky enough to have been caught up in a disastrous chain of events which had lacked a criminal dimension, and which could therefore be pardoned.

Each supplicant provided on average two justifications. The most common was a positive opinion on the part of officials or protectors, followed, in descending order of frequency, by the culprit's unblemished reputation, an evocation of Christ's passion, in commemoration of which the prince might be moved to spare the sinner, and the plea of legitimate 'self-defence'. Numerous other arguments were put forward on occasion, for example that the murderer was the sole support of his family or parents, who would starve without him. This plea, which was offered 156 times, became much more common in the seventeenth century, when it was joined by a dozen references to sons of widows. Drunkenness was cited only twenty-three times, because royal edicts made this an aggravating circumstance. Yet it is clear from the stories that drink was a major factor. Given that the officials must have been as well able to spot this as the historian, it shows how the pardons had to observe established codes in which every fact appeared in a specific place. Internal contradictions in the story seem not to have worried those whose responsibility it was to verify the document. They were not seeking total coherence, but rather to establish whether there had been lies regarding the lethal blows, so as to identify acts committed out of hatred or after an ambush, which were not in principle pardonable.

In Artois, between 1400 and 1660, over 80 per cent of homicides were committed in villages. The zone of highest crime was not the 'high country', bordering a hostile France, but the southern 'low country', adjacent to Flanders, which had only 40 per cent of the total population around 1469. A violent crescent extended from Saint-Omer to the region of Lalleu, by way of Béthune, along the modern border between the *départements* of Pas-de-Calais and Nord: this region had 726 homicides in 37 rural parishes during the period in question. Yet some of these places were far from large, like Laventie, where 61 homicides were pardoned. The explanation for the big difference between the two regions lies in the customs and lifestyles. The south, strongly community-minded and a region of small, nucleated villages and few towns, put a high value on marriage and awarded the land to those children who wished to stay on it, thanks to the right of parents to prefer some over others. The north, which attached great importance to lineage, under the direct influence of the law of neighbouring Flanders, had the greatest number of lethal brawls; it was more urbanized, its villages were larger and its inheritance practices favoured equality between the children of all marriages, no child being a bastard through the mother. It seems likely that the acute problem of diminishing patrimonies as a result of demographic pressure contributed to the higher level of violence in this area. It has been observed that the great peasant revolts of the end of the Middle Ages were more common in countries of precocious egalitarianism such as Flanders and Normandy. It has also been noted that, in Brittany, equal inheritance led to fierce and incessant rivalry between heirs.[32] To which should be added cultural factors, including the difference of language, because Flemish was spoken in the north of the county of Artois, near Saint-Omer. The position of women in society was also very different; the witch hunt flourished in Flanders, whereas in southern Artois it never really got under way. The case of the *pays* of Lalleu, which included Laventie, is exceptional: deep in Flemish territory, it nevertheless had customs close to those of the south, which may have created additional tensions in the effort to preserve them. The situation of sons of marriageable age was very different in two such separate worlds. Youthful aggression, already highly developed by the traditions of the age, was also a response to anxiety in an egalitarian region where, if there were too many brothers and sisters, and the inheritance was steadily shrinking, the harsh prospect loomed of acceding to a status markedly lower than that of the father. The later age of marriage in the seventeenth century made the situation even more explosive by postponing access to legitimate sexuality, just when the moral constraints of the Counter-Reformation were being stepped up. The ferocity of the confrontations shows that the traditional mechanisms of ritual juvenile violence were coming under pressure from an increasing number of negative factors, which sometimes resulted in homicidal rage.

This was not, however, the norm. Acts of murderous violence followed a strict seasonal timetable, dictated by the showing-off of young Romeos seeking to shine in front of the girls. In the first half of the sixteenth century, violence was at its peak in Artois during the warm season, that is, the months of May, June and July; in the second half of the century, it peaked in May, and in the first third of the seventeenth century, in June and July. These high points were the direct result of an intensification of sociability. At the end of the cold season, during which violence tailed off, aggression picked up during Carnival, and especially after Easter. This was the beginning of the season of love, when unmarried males had to prove their manliness so as to enhance their value in the marriage market. The hormone surge was added to a culture of competitiveness between young men, at a time of year when there were more occasions for encounters. May was the month of the codified amorous pursuit carried out as a group, July was the month of the *ducasses*.

In spite of the lack of detail in many cases, it seems that at least 42 per cent of homicides happened on a Sunday or day of festival, though they together accounted for only just over a quarter of the year, and especially, in descending order of frequency, in the evening, at night or in the afternoon. Dusk, 'between dog and wolf', when the bells rang for vespers, was a particularly dangerous time. The village square, the marketplace, the church and the cemetery were places for display and bravado, but mortal combats were rare. They were more common on the roads, and most of them were linked to drink, to the tavern or to leaving it. Nearly one homicide in two took place during or after a long session in an inn, including in the seventeenth century, just when edicts against frequenting such places were proliferating. Both blood and beer flowed freely in this indispensable space of conviviality, theatre of life and of death.

The stories recounted by the accused usually passed over in a prudent silence any circumstances that might have led to a pardon being refused. They are not entirely reliable, therefore, with regard to the number of individuals involved in these mortal combats. Fights between two individuals seem to have been most common, 54 per cent of the assailants and 62 per cent of the victims suggesting that they had been alone. Only 22 per cent of the former had acted with an accomplice, only 18 per cent of the latter. It was less common for there to have been a larger number of protagonists, on either side, but 8 per cent of the murderers and 9 per cent of the deceased had been part of large brawls in which they had been supported by more than four others. The frequency of one-to-one fights increased in the second half of the sixteenth century, whereas the number of confused scuffles, which had been very high in the fifteenth century, fell by half in the second third of the seventeenth century. This was after a royal edict decreeing that the participants in a fatal brawl should be punished as harshly as the culprits. It is by no means certain, therefore, in either case, that this represented a real change, as the petitioners may have omitted to mention accomplices so as to prevent proceedings against parents or friends.

The social origin of the protagonists is known for only half the accused and 29 per cent of the victims. All we can do, therefore, is suggest general trends. Men of the church were no less violent than the rest: they provided 1.5 per cent of the aggressors, which is roughly in line with their numerical weight, but 7 per cent of the victims. The nobles, in contrast, were the killers in more than 7 per cent of the confrontations and victims in 3 per cent, though they were hardly more numerous than ecclesiastics in contemporary society. The rural world accounted for the biggest single group, with 59 per cent of the aggressors and 49 per cent of the victims. City-dwellers were under-represented, at 13 per cent and 17 per cent respectively. Lastly, soldiers, a conspicuous presence in a frontier province frequently at war, provided 17 per cent of the murderers and 20 per cent of the deceased. Their military culture encouraged them to get into fights, with each other but also with townspeople and country-dwellers, in which they were more often the victims than the aggressors. No sector of the population was immune to violence, though some came out of it better than others, suggesting a familiarity with weapons and fighting. This was the case, as one would expect, with the nobles. But the peasantry was in no way behind, in particular the richest, the *laboureurs*, and the poorest, the landless labourers. The figures show that it was not only with other peasants that they fought and that they were more often the victors than the vanquished when they confronted a city-dweller, a soldier or even, on occasion, a nobleman. One in every two of the fights involving the latter was with a commoner, whom they often defeated. The murderous brutality of the nobility was at its height in the fifteenth century, when it accounted for more than a third of cases, but it subsequently diminished, to settle at about 4 per cent in the middle of the seventeenth century. By this time, the pardons were almost all for gentlemen of minor importance, often soldiers. Everything indicates that the aristocracy withdrew on a massive scale from ordinary sociability in favour of cultivating their pride and redirecting their violence into the fighting of codified duels.[33]

Women, who were required by contemporary mores to shun violence, and who frequently tried to separate the combatants, at risk to their lives, were more often the losers than the winners in a fight, as were some other masculine groups. However, with the possible exception of ecclesiastics, this was not because of any lesser capacity to use force and weapons, but because they were exposed to many more conflicts due to their occupation: rural servants, shepherds and cowherds, innkeepers and the universally detested soldiers. The risk was everywhere and spared no one, especially in the countryside, where death was a familiar presence.

The danger increased for those who were leaving childhood, at around 14, when the first signs of puberty appeared. Overall, we have information for two-thirds of those accused of homicide. Of these, 59 per cent were 'young men' or 'sons' without establishments and 41 per cent were married. Of the very few cases where precise age is recorded, that is, for one culprit in fourteen, 60 per cent were between seventeen and twenty-four, which is the age-range of the members of the kingdoms of youth. We may note a change over time. During the first half of the sixteenth century, slightly fewer unmarried than married men were involved. The proportion of the former increased slightly in the second half of the century, rising to 70 per cent in the first third of the seventeenth century, and even higher during the next three decades. This phenomenon certainly reflects the increasing leniency of the prince towards the very young, but also a powerful surge of lethal juvenile violence. The tolerance of the sovereign is to be explained by a maelstrom of brutality which is a sign of an increasing malaise among the young men of the villages and a disequilibrium in the traditional procedures for the transition to the adult state. For, throughout the period, of the victims for whom we have information, that is, one in every three, three-quarters were unmarried, with a peak of 80 per cent in the second half of the sixteenth century. The correlation is made even clearer by the fact that 879 *lettres de rémission*, more than a quarter of the entire corpus, relate to mortal combats between young unmarried men. This figure rises to 38 per cent of recorded cases in the first third of the seventeenth century. In contrast, homicides between neighbours were very rare, only twenty-five in all, and criminality within the family remained infrequent, with 209 examples, including a single parricide arising from a hunting accident, twenty-two fratricides, seven wife-killings and forty-one murders of a brother-in-law. This brings out, paradoxically, the strength of family solidarities and their sacredness in the eyes of the authorities who granted the pardons. A degree of fragility is suggested in marriage, but we should perhaps conclude that the brother-in-law without an establishment could also be a rival in the virility stakes. Tensions in the marriage market also encouraged animosity between young men and adults. Fights between a bachelor and a married man are never very common in our sources, but they rose from 43 in the sixteenth century to 111 between 1601 and 1660, a sign of the increasing frustration experienced by young males. The desire for a public revenge is emphasized by the fact that the confrontation ended in victory for the younger man in 60 per cent of cases.

The culture of youth violence was a constantly repeated demonstration of manliness. The participants wanted to prove theirs in the eyes of all. They might be hoping to make a good match, but might equally be aiming to raise their status in the eyes of the girls and have sexual relations outside marriage, even though this was increasingly stridently forbidden by the church.

In neighbouring Flanders, religious control in the sexual sphere was significantly tightened in the period leading to the 1670s, and at its most effective from then until the 1760s. In the seventeenth century, however, it did not prevent some young bachelors from being sexually active, increasingly so as they aged, their activities peaking between the ages of twenty and twenty-nine, when the prenuptial conception rate rose to 12 per cent.[34] In other words, physical relations outside marriage were not impossible. Nevertheless, they were much more difficult to achieve than in the nineteenth century, when the prenuptial conception rate among young Flemings in the 15–19 age group reached 40 per cent or more. It was essential to shine in this tight market if one was to escape the unmarried lot. To do this, young men had to make their masculine power clearly visible by symbols that were easy to decipher.

The ritual battles among the young men of Artois were not aimed at doing their competitors to death. Their purpose was rather to demonstrate the superiority of the victor. This explains why they usually involved the knife, that penis substitute. Only a few men, victims included, did not ostentatiously carry this extension of the self. We have information in four out of five cases: knives, daggers or swords were used in 61 per cent of them over the period as a whole. Next came shafted weapons, such as the spear, the lance or the halberd, used in 9 per cent of cases. Sticks, with or without a metal tip, were involved in a similar number of cases, firearms of some sort in less than 6 per cent. Otherwise, a mixed bag of weapons was used, including many tools in everyday use and a few dozen bows, shepherds' crooks, hatchets or weapons of war. The sixteenth century was above all the age of the sword, usually wide and short, mentioned 631 times, together with daggers and estocs or 'tucks'; long, four-edged *verduns* and slender, fragile rapiers were less common. Knives are referred to 232 times, without further qualification; they were probably similar to the broad-bladed bread knives which the peasants painted by Bruegel carried in their belts. The popularity of the sword at all social levels is a sign of the insecurity of a period of war, but also of the pride universally attached to its possession. It became rarer between 1611 and 1661, superseded by the knife, with 366 mentions as against 259 of swords and 80 of daggers or poniards. In fact, there is only a slight difference between the short, broad-bladed sword carried by all contemporaries and the long knife whose points Philip II ordered to be broken to render them less lethal. It was largely a matter of the extra prestige attached to the possession of a fine weapon used to cut (in a downwards action) rather than to thrust, like the rapier. In the seventeenth century, the prohibitions on carrying a sword in peacetime, and the fact that the nobility, at a time when it was increasingly isolating itself from the ordinary world, made this a distinctive sign, helped to make it less common. Its role in murder became almost negligible between 1651 and 1660: a mere three examples as compared with seventy injuries inflicted by knives and forty-one by firearms. The rarity of the latter before the decade 1631–40, marked by a return of war, is explained by their cost and by very strict edicts. In 1614 pistols of less than 32 inches, which were easy to conceal, were forbidden on pain of a very heavy fine and perpetual banishment. Further, anyone who shot at another person, even if he missed, with any sort of 'powder weapon', incurred the death penalty.

Some light is thrown on the precise purpose of the aggressors by an analysis of the wounds inflicted, which is possible for a little over four victims in five. The blow that proved lethal had been aimed at the head in nearly 46 per cent of cases, at the body or the chest in 21 per cent, the limbs or thighs in 10 per cent, the groin or abdomen in 8 per cent and the back or shoulders in 7 per cent of cases. These locations generally rule out a clear intent to kill. Those involving the head include more dangerous attacks on the throat or the eyes, but a very tiny proportion as compared with the cranium. The head, almost invariably covered by a hat or cap, in a society where decency required one to hide one's hair, was usually hit from above, with a knife or a sword, a shafted weapon or a stick. If the cranium was hit or cut open, the injured man rarely died on the spot. He often succumbed to an infection or other after-effects, sometimes after a formidable surgical trepanation, which rarely healed its victim. The delay between the fight and death, known for 87 per cent of the deceased, is telling: 9 per cent died on the spot and 29 per cent during the following night. The rest survived longer, 26 per cent for between one and three weeks, 6 per cent for between one and three months, fourteen hardy specimens even longer than this.

The intention was not usually to kill. The combatants were well aware that to hit someone in the belly or the chest with a thrust with a sharp implement or a shot from a gun, or to strike someone between the shoulders, an event rarely mentioned because it implied an unacceptable treachery, had much more serious consequences than a blow to the head. A connoisseur and skilled technician, thanks to his occupation, Antoine Levriendt, a sergeant of Tournai, told how, making his rounds on the evening of 27 August, probably in 1623 or 1624, he came across a man who was drunk, and tried to take away his sword. Meeting with some resistance, he drew his own, 'meaning to hit the hat brim of the said aggressor, named Jean Vanicquier, to give him something to remember him by, hit him on the forehead, and as he was injured he was trepanned, which trepanning led to his death'.[35] Young bachelors who fell out with someone usually wanted to hit him on the head, not send him to his grave, in which case they would be forced to go into exile to escape justice; they wanted to 'give him one' (a wound) and then boast that they had got the better of him.

The head was for them the symbolic centre of manliness. It was the same with the nobles, who fought wearing elaborate and feathered helmets intended to terrorize their adversary. Like the shameful member, as it was then called, the head ought in normal circumstances to be kept hidden, while expressing in various ways the unbending power of its owner. This is why serious quarrels could break out when someone pulled the hair, even worse, the beard, of another, even in jest. A young lad from Saint-Omer who wanted to take the principal position in a dance, on 26 August 1608, was heard to say 'that to go into the middle you needed to have a beard'. The ecclesiastical authorities of the Counter-Reformation prohibited priests from wearing a beard, so as to give greater visibility to the chastity demanded of the clergy by the Council of Trent. Further, the headdress made the man, as noted above in the case of the theft of the hat ribbon decorated with a medal belonging to a surgeon of Lille. The seventy-nine inhabitants of Artois who died for stealing items of headgear only confirm this. It was an act of bravado to go out proudly sporting a feather in one's cap as a symbol of manly strength and challenge to any possible rivals. There is no need to force the interpretation to draw this conclusion. It was plain during a bitter-sweet verbal exchange at Dickebush, in Flanders, on Sunday 31 May 1615. A shepherd asked a bachelor 'if his member wasn't stiff'. He was heard to reply that that would be the case with a 'dedicated fighter', that is, someone in the habit of picking quarrels at the *ducasses*. The shepherd then went one better, still in jocular mode, by telling him that, for that, he would need to have 'a feather on his head as high as this lime tree', indicated by a gesture. A third young ruffian then arrived. More threat-eningly, he provoked the shepherd by saying that if he didn't have a feather just then, he did sometimes wear one. 'And if I had one, you wouldn't have the nerve to take it off me.' At these words, the two men came to blows.[36]

The young men of Artois had short fuses and they walked the streets carrying a blade to challenge anyone who might be around. Like all European males of the period, they wore their masculine honour proudly, on their faces, under their hats and on the blade of their sword or knife. They had more to prove than their elders, so they strutted about more ostentatiously to demonstrate their manliness in every way they could. The innumerable brawls which were the result posed no danger to the social fabric. On the contrary, they made visible the normative codes of sociability and solidarity, which were imposed on them as well as on the adults and the young girls of marriageable age, at whom these constant skirmishes were principally aimed.

Yet this world of festive violence did not exist in isolation. In spite of some resistance, the new values imposed from outside gradually eroded the old practices during the course of the seventeenth century. Tolerance for the ritual homicide committed by young men waned after the 1630s, in Artois as in many other countries in Europe.[37] In France, an identical but earlier trend for its criminalization, pioneered by the *parlement* of Paris in the 1580s, resulted in an increasing number of death penalties for homicide.[38] The decline of princely tolerance seems to have begun under Francis I, perhaps even earlier. In 1525, while Charles V granted 56 *lettres de rémission* to his subjects in Artois, Francis I – or rather the royal chancellery, the king himself being a prisoner in Spain after the battle of Pavia – issued 218 for a kingdom with a population of between sixteen million and eighteen million inhabitants, that is, a hundred times larger than the county of Artois. The characteristics of the cases were nevertheless similar. In France, too, the violence extended to all social groups, with an over-representation of nobles, soldiers and inhabitants of Paris, at that time probably the largest city in Europe, which provided nineteen of the murderers. Lethal violence was almost exclusively mas-culine – 99 per cent – and primarily the act of young unmarried men.

Age is recorded or can be deduced in 52 per cent of cases, as it was considered an absolutory excuse; killers in the 14–30 age group provided four-fifths of the total and 37 per cent of the explicit mentions. Two pronounced seasonal peaks, in June and October, suggest a rural sociability slightly different from that in Artois, and less murderous in May, July and August, probably due to stricter control of the youth rituals of spring and the height of the harvest. By contrast, the towns, Paris in particular, saw eruptions of violence during Carnival and in July, August and November. It is almost as if they preserved the traditions better than in the countryside, 'turning the world upside down' to relax a moral strait-jacket that was at other times more effective than in the villages. The fights involved bladed weapons in two-thirds of cases, a broad sword more often than a knife. The victim had been wounded in the head or neck in one in three confrontations. The accused, too, also wounded in just under a third of cases, had head injuries in nearly half the cases. The victim died on the spot, or at the latest on the following day, in only a fifth of cases. More than three-quarters of the murderers took refuge in a sanctuary where they were out of reach of the courts.[39]

A man's honour was concentrated in his head. This was the most common target in Picardy under Francis I, too, and in Aquitaine in the seventeenth century.[40] The usual pattern of the aggression, as it is revealed in the *lettres de rémission*, was for a gradation of gestures and words between young bachelors, armed with a sword or a knife, who knew each other, often resembled each other in almost every way and were in competition for the local girls. There seems often to have been no open animosity to begin with. Many encounters began with cordial exchanges, in the tavern or elsewhere. Then, one of the two became heated over some usually trivial pretext, some drunken utterance, words taken exception to, a not very subtle joke cracked by the other... Conviviality turned to conflict, initially verbal, but with the threat of blows ever-present in the background. Things escalated if a humiliating gesture was added to the words. A slap across the face, for example, could not go unpunished without throwing into doubt the manliness of its recipient. It brought to an end the first phase of ritual exchanges, aimed at demonstrating a superiority expressed through the intimidation of the adversary. Things often stopped there, if the troublemaker was content with having inflicted a minor loss of face on his interlocutor, or if the latter feared he would come off worse in a fight. But a brawl developed under the influence of alcohol, or when the young antagonists got their hackles up and each was convinced he would be the victor. Any physical contact, clumsy or deliberate, made it impossible for them to back down. The challenge had to be taken up. The one who had his hat knocked off or his beard pulled, or who was jostled or approached too close, that is, the one whose bodily space suffered an intrusion, responded with greater force. Sometimes he tried to defuse the situation by sending out pacificatory signals, ready to be satisfied with a limited revenge. They both knew that there was a risk of passing the point of no return, with all the disastrous consequences that would ensue for both, that is, injury, death or flight to avoid justice. The roles were interchangeable, in that each of them embarked on the fight convinced of being in the right. In the end, the culprit was the one whose opponent died, even long afterwards. This, in theory, exposed him to capital punishment, unless, that is, he obtained a royal pardon or died, in his turn, from his injuries. More dramatic threats, verbal or even more gestural, such as putting one's hand on one's knife or sword, or drawing it, or angrily advancing on the enemy, all still left open the possibility of stopping the murderous escalation. The intervention of friends, especially women, to restrain the protagonists also allowed them, at this late stage, to walk away with head up. On the other hand, incitement by friends or family not to let himself be pushed around, which was equally common, encouraged a young man to pass the point of no return. Those who felt they had supporters, which was commoner among those seeking a pardon than among their victims, as we have seen, believed they would have the advantage. Controlled ritual violence then gave way to an armed confrontation in which the risks were high, even if it was not primarily directed at killing the enemy, as is shown by the position of the wounds and the small number of those who died on the spot. In reality, the main aim of each protagonist was to inflict an injury on the other, so that he could boast about his prowess in the future. It was the ineffectiveness of medicine that turned many of these young bloods into murderers forced to flee justice and the vengeance of the opposing party.

The knife fight and the sword fight were part of the symbolic language of youth, intended to demonstrate the manliness of the protagonists. Despite accidents, exceptions and madness, it was not, in general, an art of killing. It was aimed rather at humiliating, by hitting the most highly valued part of the human being, the head. In Artois, the number of blows to the head diminished a little, from 41 per cent of cases between 1598 and 1630 to 31 per cent between 1631 and 1660. The blows were increasingly often aimed at the body, in particular the lower abdomen or groin, and the number of those delivered from behind became significant. These changes were the result both of the new use of firearms and of new ways of using a knife; the latter was now mentioned much more frequently than the sword, and more often used to thrust than before, against a vital spot. The delay before the injured person died also diminished: 14 per cent died on the spot and 34 per cent in the next few hours, whereas medical progress reduced the proportion of those who succumbed to infection in the next few weeks.

It seems that the lust to kill became more common at this period, a sign of the crisis being experienced by the culture of youth violence. The authorities examined the circumstances and the descriptions of the injuries with a new attention, because the criminalization of homicide happening all over Europe in the 1620s meant that they reacted with greater severity. The defence of honour and vengeance, which had motivated more than half the aggressors in Artois in the fifteenth century, slowly became less common, settling at a third of the total in the period 1630–60. To be more precise, the high level of princely leniency in such matters was reduced in this period in the Spanish Low Countries, as the law, modernized by royal edicts of 1570, created an increasingly negative image of homicide within society. At the same time, rural traditions were being eroded by the decline of festive activities, under pressure from a restrictive new morality and a legislation directed against profane entertainments, dances, the carrying of weapons, drunkenness and all the liberties allowed to young men, in particular that of walking around in armed groups at night and on holidays. A new world was slowly emerging in the countryside, that of self-control and the 'civilizing process'. It did not derive only from the court model by way of the legacy of the Italian Renaissance. It was articulated in 1530 by Erasmus, the great humanist of Rotterdam, in his *On Good Manners for Boys*, and it had taken firm root in the large towns, in particular in the Low Countries. Since the end of the Middle Ages, they had been reducing lethal violence by carefully controlling it.

— 4 —

THE URBAN PEACE AT THE END
OF THE MIDDLE AGES

The European society of the late Middle Ages was characterized by a very high level of violence. The peace of God, which the church had tried to establish in the eleventh century, had proved ineffective. The central state was as yet neither equipped nor anxious to intervene effectively in this sphere. Indeed, it was itself based on a cult of war, legitimated by the mission incumbent on the king and the knights to defend the faith, although this was in practice frequently diverted into a struggle for power between the strong and the ambitious. The princely *lettres de rémission* only reinforced the validity of such principles in the general opinion, even among the most lowly, so that homicide was seen as a fairly humdrum act if it was committed by a young man in defence of his own honour or that of his family. Like the noble duel at a later date, combat, whether single or not, was in this context a sign of normality rather than of criminal deviance.

The only social space in Western Europe where different values prevailed was the city. This had probably been the case from the beginning, as towns had revived, long centuries after the fall of the Roman Empire and urban model, by claiming privileges and by slowly establishing a third way between the dominant world of the aristocracy and the world of the peasantry. The urban renaissance had begun in Italy, with the cultural movement of that name. In the fifteenth century, it was still a minority phenomenon, except in a few regions of the continent marked by the imprint of Rome, such as northern Italy, or by exceptional urban growth, such as the shores of the North Sea, the Rhineland and southern Germany. A dense network of communications and exchanges connected these two regions, by way of Lyon. Set apart from these interchanges, Paris, the largest European agglomeration, possibly with Naples, was an exception, both medieval and modern, traditional and innovative, essential without being the most important before the Bourbons.

The most dynamic urban world was that of economic relations. It was not immune to the oppressive influence of the society in which it functioned. Lethal violence was at a high level. In Italy and Flanders alike, pavements often ran with blood. Swords and knives were constantly bringing lives – famous and obscure – to a sudden end. This happened even in churches, where a duke of Milan was assassinated, and where Lorenzo de Medici, 'the Magnificent', narrowly escaped the same fate. But a wind of change was blowing in these worlds, in which peace was more necessary than elsewhere. This was not simply for moral reasons, but rather to make the town attractive and wealthy, assuring the safety of those who worked there or came there to conduct their business. Places of exchanges, by definition, the public square and the tavern could not be the scene of ritual confrontations, as they were in the countryside, without ruining the city's reputation. The maintenance of order was an absolute priority. Many strangers, merchants but also workers, had to be accepted, even though xenophobic reflexes were as powerful in the town as in the village if the new arrivals took the places or jobs of the natives, or even married and settled down. True 'republics' administered by a patriciate, even if they were under the tutelage of a prince, the towns experienced their golden age up to the 1520s. After this, there was a dramatic escalation in the demands of stronger centralized states, in a context disrupted by the challenges of the religious reformers. In the space of a few generations, the towns invented specific forms for the pacification of the manners of their citizens and achieved a spectacular reduction in violence. This was done using very different techniques from the public spectacle of torture later employed by the absolute kings. The towns acted simultaneously on three fronts: prohibitions to limit the occasions for brawls; the organization and supervision of population groups, in particular turbulent masculine youth; and systematic punishment, but by fines, and only rarely by physical punishments.

The pacificatory towns

Towns did not foster crime. On the contrary, they were always trying to soften the rough manners of their inhabitants, who were protected by the town walls, watch and guard and by its reassuring legislation. An optical illusion has allowed some historians to assert the contrary, because the judicial sources are few and laconic for the countryside, with the exception of the *lettres de rémission*, but abundant for the towns, which gives the impression of an explosion of lethal violence.[1] Much also

83

depends on the date and the type of document used. The archives of repression kept by the magistrates, who ruled the municipality and judged their fellow citizens, account only for a small part of the phenomenon. They are concerned only with the individuals who represented the greatest threat to the local peace. Many other cases appear in the fiscal records, in particular in the lists of fines, which are closer to reality because these were the most common form of urban punishment, followed by judicial pilgrimage.[2] A third category, which is difficult to measure, frequently eludes us, because it was a part of the private practices for halting the mechanism of vengeance: *fourjurement* ('forswearing'), *asseurement* ('assurance') and the *trêve* ('truce'), or compensation for the damage through peace agreements. These various measures were supervised by official representatives of the civic body, the *apaiseurs* or *paiseurs* ('conciliators'), frequently mentioned in the Low Countries. They might result from agreements freely negotiated between the parties, or they might be obligatory, like the judicial truces imposed by a legal court or the *fourjurement* required by some municipalities when the culprit had fled. In the last two examples, the family of the murderer renounced him, thus escaping the vengeance of the opposing lineage, whereas *asseurement* was a promise by the family of the victim not to harass the family of the assassin. The truce temporarily interrupted hostilities so that a final agreement could be worked out, which might be registered as a private contract before the magistrates or a notary.[3] Private peace and financial composition also existed in the countryside, but in a much less coordinated and controlled way. The towns damped down violence by checking the traditional spiral of events that led to vengeance. It was, however, a slow process.

The fourteenth century seems often still to have been a period of high levels of conflictuality. For Antwerp, a complete set of records for the accounting years 1372–87 lists a total of 1,501 cases punished by the magistrates, that is, around a hundred a year. Those sentenced included 119 murderers and accomplices, that is, 8 per cent of the total. Insults, blows, threats and woundings accounted for 43 per cent. Seventeen per cent of sentences were for offences against authority (false oaths, refusal to testify, disobeying public ordinances, returning from banishment, etc.), of which 2 per cent were for breaches of the peace. Theft and receiving accounted for 13 per cent of cases, and another 10 per cent were financial offences, confiscations of pledges, defaults of payment and usury. Offences against morality and religion were very rare, at only 1 per cent, including a single case of witchcraft. The eighty-four death sentences, just over five per year, suggest a high degree of severity, which was unusual in towns at this period. Secondary corporal punishments were rare – a mere three ears were cut off.[4]

In fourteenth-century Ghent, many offences of all types never came before the courts because they were settled by a private agreement. Death penalties and mutilations were rare. The main sanctions employed were fines, exile and expiatory pilgrimage, which might be redeemed, in addition to compositions with the victims or their family imposed by the courts. Violence, it has been claimed, was above all a phenomenon of the upper ranks of the patriciate, especially the young. This was not only because these privileged persons had the time to walk the streets and frequent taverns and markets, but because they regarded violent confrontations as a normal part of their lifestyle and because they had the means to pay the price, which was set at a high level by the authorities.[5]

The absence of the lower classes seems suspicious, because numerous studies have shown that they were equally violent. It is probably a consequence of the partial nature of the sources, such as the criminal register of the Châtelet of Paris for the years 1389–92, which records the execution of 87 per cent of the accused it mentions, but chooses only the most serious cases. This was probably the work of the provost of the capital, seeking to respond to royal injunctions urging the authorities to greater severity. In any case, there were many courts operating in Paris. Some could impose the death penalty, like the lordship of Saint-Martin-des-Champs. Its archives mention more than 300 offenders prosecuted between 1332 and 1353, only seventeen of whom were condemned to death. Of the 357 individuals arrested by the sergeants of the Châtelet in July 1488, fewer than one in three was eventually sentenced. Of the 111 who appeared, only one was executed, four were banished, two after being whipped, six were birched in public and all the others released, often within twenty-four hours, after paying a fine or even, in some cases, without.[6]

What we need to retain from these partial records is the fact that violence existed in towns, but that they were relatively protected islands in a sea of great brutality. Some fragments from the criminal register of the *parlement* of Paris for the years 1319–50 give us some idea of its scale. They describe bands of robber knights in Périgord, Vermandois and on the frontiers of the empire, men who revelled in cruelty, throwing a prisoner to the dogs, killing women and children and burning at will, confident of the support of their kin. Vendettas and premeditated murders were ten-a-penny but hardly energetically prosecuted by the judges. The count of Forez refused to condemn one murderer to death on the grounds that he was young and had acted on the orders of his master. Similarly, the sergeant of the prior of Anet, arrested for having killed his master, was sentenced only to the pillory after having a hand severed. He avoided this last penalty by claiming that his honour and his rights had been gravely impugned, because the prior had taken his son to make him a monk without his permission.[7]

85

Within the shelter of its walls, the city managed to check some violence from outside and to limit that of its citizens, not least that of the unmarried men. On the one hand it screened, on the other it softened manners. Unable to shut itself off completely, which would have spelled its doom, it kept a close watch on new arrivals and sorted them according to the danger they represented and the benefits they might bring. Arras was a substantial town of 12,000 inhabitants and the centre for the production of the famous tapestries sold by the name of *arazzi* in Italy. Its ordinances of police survive from 1405 and at once reveal the principal urban fears. The question of security dominates. Checks on the fortifications and detailed instructions in case of fire rub shoulders with the frequently repeated obligation on keepers of lodging-houses to declare the names of foreign visitors and to accept no one without knowing their identity. The owners of stews, the public baths, were not allowed to take lodgers. Prostitutes, who were supervised by a municipal official, the *roi des Ribauds* ('king of the Ribalds'), were also closely regulated. Prohibitions on going out at night without a light or visiting the stews with girls were issued on occasion, as on 15 June 1437. In case of danger or epidemic, as on 18 April 1438, impoverished vagrants were required to leave and pigs were driven out to avoid 'corrupting' the air. Around 1444, the fear of strangers, linked to that of a surprise invasion, resurfaced. This led the magistrates to grant the burgesses the right to band together against them; in other words, defend themselves by force if necessary. The prohibition on carrying weapons was frequently repeated after 1456, the year when games of *choule* (a ball game), *boules* and archery were prohibited at Michaelmas; reference was also made to *trêves* made between enemies under municipal supervision, which had to be renewed and published on the eve of All Saints' by the magistrates leaving office. In 1464, it was ordained that any banished person who returned to the city was to be handed over to justice, even if he had caused no trouble. On 22 December 1470, the game of dice was prohibited on Christmas night and Christmas day and restricted to specific locations on the following days. The principal ordinances were regularly republished on the first Sunday after All Saints' Day, then just before the night of the feast of St John Baptist. They reiterated, in particular, the regulations regarding strangers, persons of ill repute, the game of dice, going out at night without a light or sleeping with girls in the stews, carrying arms and the closure of the gates after the last bell. On 5 April 1474, as strangers and *caïmans* ('beggars') were looking for trouble in the town, all those of no fixed abode or without visible means of support were instructed to leave, on pain of whipping and banishment. Dances were forbidden on 8 July 1478. Prostitutes were supervised even more closely: on 28 July 1484, it was forbidden to anyone, hotel-keepers included, to give them lodgings and they could no longer ply their 'wicked trade' on the walls. On 20 January 1486, the 'great scandal' created by the women who frequented places of ill repute, in particular the Petit Marché, at night, after the ringing of the first bell, called *carrefour*, was denounced. Anyone who gave them accommodation was also threatened with banishment. On 29 December 1493, in a period of anxiety and fear of a surprise enemy attack, the supervision of the stews and prostitutes was stepped up even further; keepers of lodging-houses were instructed to disarm their customers, and young bachelors and servants were to assemble behind their father, friends or masters in case of alarm, and not to 'form bands and gather separately'.[8]

With the exception of some ordinances that were regularly repeated, concerning night-time, pleasure-houses, stews and hostelries, strangers, vagrants and prostitutes who flooded the town in the evening, this legislation lacks a sustained character. It primarily reveals waves of strong anxiety when enemies came close, epidemics raged or threatened or life became, for some reason, harder. The principal fears of the municipal magistrates emerge, nevertheless, with some clarity. They were concerned above all to prevent the formation of any stable criminal associations within the walls. Procurers, *caïmans*, thieves, bandits and beggars were expelled. They tried to settle on the other side of the walls, where there were many makeshift taverns, which did a roaring trade because local taxes did not apply to them. Public women haunted these places, too, and solicited for custom on both sides of the walls as well as in the city centres, or set themselves up in the stews. The magistrates tried in vain to confine them to a red light district, under the supervision of the *roi des Ribauds*, by preventing them from circulating at night. The magistrates also periodically tried to prohibit games, dances and the activities of the youth bands, especially when the collective security was threatened, as in 1493.

Large numbers of marginals, thieves, *caïmans*, 'houliers', 'goliards' and bandits passed through the towns or tried to settle there permanently, attaching themselves to the world of prostitution. The towns were terrified they would form a criminal society. They were kept under close supervision and expelled without further ado as soon as they constituted a threat. Neither in the Low Countries nor in France was a 'court of miracles' allowed to form. Only its phantasm existed, testifying to one of the deepest fears of the citizens. The band of the Coquillards of Dijon, to which François Villon belonged, was perhaps one of the rare exceptions; or it might have been one of the turbulent youth groups described above. It was only really possible for organized banditry to flourish in the countryside and on the roads. At the end of the fifteenth century and in the first decades of the sixteenth century, it became the principal target

87

of the brutal repression conducted by a new mounted military police force, the *Maréchaussée*, established in the Low Countries by Charles the Rash, and then in France in 1520 by Francis I. The provost marshals were at first charged solely with punishing deserters from the army, but their responsibilities were soon extended to include all offences committed by those of no fixed abode on the highways, and also to robberies carried out there. The emergence of this punitive princely force is a sign of crisis in the citizen model of harmony, after a period of rapid population growth which culminated around 1520. A rising tide of disreputable characters and rootless and hopeless peasants banged on the doors of the cities. The mass rejection by the latter of all those they refused to assimilate, and of the native sons banished for various crimes, threw hordes of 'useless people' onto the roads. They tried their luck in one place after another, settling temporarily outside the walls if they were allowed to. This dangerous marginal world was the target of the *Maréchaussée*. Between 1500 and 1513, the provost responsible for the county of Artois sentenced 106 persons to death, 30 to fines and 54 to other penalties. Between 1518 and 1527, when marginality became a huge social problem throughout Europe, the same provost had 222 persons executed, imposed fines on 142 others and sentenced 21 to other punishments. In comparison, Arras applied the death penalty on average just once a year between 1528 and 1549, the only period for which we have information. The *gouvernance* of Arras, a royal court primarily concerned with the surrounding countryside, also passed one death sentence a year. In this same period, the prince pardoned two murderers for the whole county. It looks very much as if the provosts of the marshals had been given the job of clearing the stretches of uninhabited waste ground where large numbers of those excluded from the urban peace took refuge. In Artois, their victims, identifiable in a third of cases, fall into four equal groups: those who had committed homicide, often of bad reputation and guilty of other offences; highway robbers, who occasionally murdered; thieves apparently not acting in gangs; and those accused of other types of serious crime, such as vagrancy, witchcraft, forged currency, and treason to the benefit of the enemy.[9]

The rarity of capital punishment in the urban courts was not, therefore, a sign of weakness. The late medieval towns, or at least those which prospered, as in Italy or Burgundy, had no need of the spectacle of torture to achieve calm. It was enough for them to prevent individuals from forming dangerous minorities by controlling them closely. This was done through repeated ordinances, but even more by means of the dense networks of ordinary sociability. The crafts and the population groups supervised their own members and proved impenetrable to all those they would not accept as one of them. The city was, accordingly, a world

hostile to strangers, as it was to all who refused to adhere to the normative values of their group of reference. Even the prostitutes constituted
a tightly controlled population group, under the leadership of the *roi des
Ribauds*, who was also responsible for the supervision of gaming tables
and the venal nocturnal world. An explicit contract linked this infernal
world to the municipality, which accepted its presence and drew significant revenues from it, while at the same time limiting its disorder and
excess. The introduction of a special mark, attested as early as 1423 in
Arras, was meant to differentiate the 'women of joyous life offering love
for sale' from the virtuous and respectable female inhabitants. It also
distinguished them from those who sold their charms in the streets and
from the *curatières* who attracted married men to their own homes and
became kept women. On pain of a fine, half of which went to the sergeant and half to the *roi des Ribauds*, they had to wear 'on their left
arm, between the shoulder and the side, a piece of scarlet cloth the width
of two fingers and half a quarter long, or thereabout, sown onto their
dress', or the same in white if they hit on the idea of appearing in a
scarlet dress. When they wore a coat, they had to sow the strip of cloth
on sideways so that it was clearly visible. In Lille, in 1430, a 'ban on
wild women' repeated the obligation to wear an identical mark. The
management of prostitution began to change, however, at the end of the
fifteenth century, due to the spread of the 'Naples sickness', that is,
syphilis. In 1492, in Arras, the proprietors of four stews, le Soleil, le
Paon, le Gaugier and l'Image de Saint-Michel, were instructed to devote
their premises in future to other uses and, if they accepted guests, lodge
them 'without keeping a brothel'; this was to be done within a fortnight,
on pain of an exorbitant fine of 100 *livres*. Le Soleil and le Paon were
still stews in 1504, and the owners of the 'brothel of the Sun' were punished in 1533 and ordered to close down the establishment for good. In
1550, the stews of le Glay had to cease their activities for a fortnight for
'having admitted young men with the girls on Good Friday during the
holy divine service'. Two prostitutes were banished for a year and the
two young clients found with them birched behind closed doors.[10]

The town was a machine for producing social consensus. It coped with
the misdemeanours of some of its members by branding them with a seal
of infamy, which made them more visible and easier to control. This was
the case with prostitutes, often from outside, who were necessary to the
collective health and also a financial godsend. Male vagrants were not
so lucky. Admittedly, an ordinance aimed at them by Philip the Good,
in 1459, was not strictly enforced, especially in Brussels and Antwerp,
but it inaugurated a period of increasing severity by providing for the
unemployed to be imprisoned, sent to the galleys or banished after
having a hand or an ear cut off. The cities were often content simply

with summary expulsion, sometimes after cutting off the ears of thieves, which made it possible to recognize re-offenders. The atmosphere suddenly changed around 1510–20, when the increase in the numbers of beggars, coming from an overpopulated rural world, began to cause great unease. The authorities reacted by differentiating the poor who had homes, who wore a sign authorizing them to beg for alms, from the rest, who were thrown out en masse, for example at Mons and Ypres in 1525 and at Lille in 1527. The assistance of the state was soon necessary given the hordes of poor who were causing disturbances in the towns. In 1531, an edict of Charles V prohibited begging and denied residence to unemployed strangers. Only the native 'honest poor', selected by the authorities, and on condition they did not frequent taverns, had the right to receive support from a 'common purse', which was introduced everywhere on a common model.[11]

Urban stability came at a price, that is, the exclusion of those without jobs or homes. Many people wanted to settle in the cities, in particular many rootless young men driven out of the countryside by demographic pressure. Only a few, however, were permitted to penetrate the local networks of solidarity and share in the collective peace. Outside the gates, they mingled with the throng of locals banished for having broken the law. Towns would not accept those who were dangerous. On the contrary, their existence was based on a systematic rejection of those who did not share their values, even if this was for lack of material means. They were scarcely more welcoming to the peasants who sought refuge within their walls in time of war, or to any animals that threatened the security of the population: in Arras, a municipal dog-killer, paid per capita, had the job of eliminating stray canines, including those whose owners let them roam free at night. As we have seen, pigs might also be banished during epidemics. Beyond the walls, the immediate periphery was a crowded world, home of the excluded, the banished, robbers who preyed on travellers, dealers of every type, pimps and women of easy virtue.

The chief difference between the world on the other side of the walls was cultural. The 'suburb', that is, the external space where urban power was exercised, was far from constituting a lawless zone. It was a refuge for those who could not be assimilated, and it acted as a sort of safety valve, with the express permission of the authorities. They kept a close watch on everything that happened and even had the makeshift shacks erected there razed to the ground when there was an imminent threat from an enemy, so as to create a security zone. Only here was it possible for a sort of court of miracles to exist, closely supervised, roughly dealt with as soon as the slightest problem surfaced. Drink, sex and violence were its essential characteristics, whereas inside the walls a more policed urbanity was to prevail. By their words, their gestures and their behaviour, the citizens were invited to demonstrate their membership of a privileged and pacified world. Town air softened. At least, it obliged everyone to master their impulses and desires so as to avoid being relegated to the other side of the walls, to join those who did not know how, or did not wish, to exercise a similar self-control or display the signs.

The 'civilizing process' was not born only in the Italian courts of the Renaissance. It also derived from a growing need for civility, in other words, a desire to soften even further the mechanisms of social relations in the powerful and prosperous citizen worlds of Italy and the north-west of the continent. The famous thesis of Norbert Elias linking the civilizing process to the abandonment of individual violence in return for greater protection, assured by the state as it became the sole repository of legal violence, makes insufficient allowance for the earlier existence of a comparable phenomenon in the 'urban republics' of the fifteenth century.[12] This was the case in the Burgundian Low Countries. During the golden age of the cities, up to 1520, the construction of a culture of pacification was achieved here through the definition of a new type of personality, an individual who restrained his brutality, preferred compromise to bloody vengeance and gave proof of his normality in every sphere. This citizen of the new wave, an advocate of the prudent management of the passions and of the happy medium, probably took his model from the old Western monastic tradition of asceticism and continence, adapted to a world of exchanges and expansion. Nevertheless, the religious element lost ground to a morality of success. It was not by chance that later, in the sixteenth century, many northern towns, Antwerp in particular, were open to the temptations of Calvinism. Their most active citizens recognized in it cultural forms and an ethic favourable to commercial capitalism that suited their needs.[13]

In 1530 the great humanist Erasmus, an advocate of a more austere faith, though without going so far as to break with Catholicism, produced the bible of the disciplined citizen, *On Good Manners for Boys*. This short work, written in Latin, is too often presented simply as an aristocratic manual intended to educate a young prince of Burgundy. It was inspired both by the monastic model and by its author's own observation of the northern cities that he knew well, having been born in Rotterdam, in one of the most urbanized and dynamic regions of Europe. The rules of propriety and modesty set out in this book were opposed to those of the peasantry, but also to those of the nobility, so often motivated by the sense of honour and vengeance. This was true of the Burgundian court, even though it was one of the most refined of its day. In the name of 'nature' and 'reason', Erasmus advised the child to be moderate in all things and to exercise restraint in eating, in working and even more in physical bearing. His aim was not to form a warrior but a person well versed in the codes of human relations, a 'citizen' in the Latin meaning of the word, that is, a person polished by the world in which he lived. Do not fold your arms, he says, because that makes you look like an idler and a thief. Whether standing or seated, avoid putting one hand on another, a posture which some deem to be elegant, but which gives 'a soldierly bearing'. Remember that 'everything that pleases fools is not necessarily wise'. Do not uncover the parts of the body that natural modesty requires to be hidden, even if there is no one to see. Remember that what is most agreeable in a child is 'modesty, that companion and guardian of good manners'. Walk neither too slowly nor too quickly and avoid gestures intended to demonstrate manliness, such as 'reeling', because this 'foolish semihalting gait' should be left 'to Swiss soldiers' and those who like to 'sport feathers in their caps'.[14]

Good manners, whose principal utility was to defuse aggression, were born in an urban context much earlier than Elias claimed. They were already strongly developed in the Italian cities of the thirteenth century. They are visible in the pedagogic work of Hugh of Saint Victor, an Augustinian canon who died in 1141. However, Erasmus, who had read Hugh, was concerned not so much with providing an inspiration to sanctity for the benefit of a monk as with a method for living with others in the overpopulated and potentially dangerous spaces of the northern cities. He put so much emphasis on the notion of the happy medium because he wished to urge introspection and self-control on his readers.[15] To keep a watch on one's tongue, one's dress and one's gestures, on the shifting stage of the theatre of daily life, was a necessity if one was to avoid pointless conflicts and so save one's time, one's blood and one's money; and one's semen, too, because success meant no longer wasting bodily fluids as well as no longer wasting material goods. The thrifty spirit, that active stimulus to nascent capitalism, also encouraged strict control of sexual excesses.[16]

The fierce repression of the pleasures of the flesh that was decreed by many sixteenth-century monarchs had begun much earlier in certain towns. The prosperous and powerful city of Bruges was relentlessly prosecuting the 'unmentionable sin' of sodomy by the end of the fourteenth century. From 1385 to 1515, according to the registers of the comital officials, ninety individuals were burnt for this crime, three were sentenced to fines and nine others to corporal punishments. Other sources, which do not overlap with the former and exist only from the end of the fifteenth century, the confessions and sentences recorded by the municipality, put sodomy in second place, with 15 per cent of cases, after theft (46 per cent) but before homicide (9 per cent), in the period 1490–1515. Of the twenty-one persons found guilty of sodomy, sixteen were condemned to death, as were all twelve murderers and thirty of the sixty-three thieves. The judges were more severe on people born outside Bruges, as the latter provided forty-two of the seventy-four people executed, all crimes lumped together, including twenty-two of the thirty thieves, eight of the twelve murderers and four of the six rapists. Everything suggests a desire to instil terror in those who engaged in these three reprehensible activities, whereas natives accused of the same crimes were much less often and less harshly punished. Only sodomy presents a reverse profile, as ten of the sixteen people punished were natives of Bruges. In the classic context of a two-tier justice, almost invariably more merciful to the locals, sodomy appeared both as the principal internal threat and as a 'tool for disciplining society', at a time of social instability marked by a huge increase in the number of marginals attracted by its reputation for wealth.[17]

Controlling the young

In the eyes of the municipal authorities at this period, violence and rape were often seen as normal activities of young men who remained unmarried. As a general rule, the urban sources say little about homosexuality. Paradoxically, this may be a sign of great leniency in this sphere, as was the case in Florence before the promulgation of an extremely harsh law in 1542.[18] The precocity of the battle against sodomy in Bruges, and its focus on offenders born inside the town, marks the emergence of a taboo that may have been intended to define manly culture in exclusively heterosexual terms, although the members of the bachelor bands were probably as tempted to engage in homosexual behaviour as those of the great Italian towns. Was it perhaps a sign that the local authorities were taking closer control of the youth companies?

These organizations proliferated at the end of the Middle Ages, under the close supervision of the city in question. From Dijon to Arles, every town in south-east France had one or even two 'abbeys of youth', festive confraternities that were recognized, elected their abbot and their dignitaries in the presence of the magistrates, and received money and authorizations from them for their activities. They were federative structures, which brought together males of all social conditions, married and unmarried, between the ages of 16–18 and 35–40. They sometimes merged with shooting confraternities, or even with neighbourhood groups, but they were very different from the little gangs of between three and five young men, usually aged between eighteen and twenty-four, who behaved with extreme violence at this same period and committed many collective rapes: 125 assaults of this type were reported to the authorities in Dijon between 1436 and 1486, ninety of which involved a total of over 400 perpetrators and accomplices.[19]

The abbeys helped to calm the traditional juvenile violence which, in the cities, took the pathological form of frequent rapes born of frustration. It seems probable that the loosening of solidarities and weakening of the law of vengeance in these milieus encouraged a powerful loss of sexual inhibition, impossible on such a scale in a village. The immediate remedy was to punish, which has left documents, but also to promote as an antidote confederated abbeys that were permitted to levy fines on ill-assorted marriages. In case of refusal, they resorted to charivaris and donkey-rides, though without excessive brutality. The first abbeys are documented at the end of the fourteenth century in the south-east, and references to them become frequent around 1450. Their activities, oriented towards extolling a tempered manliness, turned into the right to heavy drinking and feasting, contributed to the maintenance of the urban peace. They took over, in a more moderate fashion, that control of the sexual morals of all of the inhabitants that had devolved on the juvenile bands, and they inherited procedures for the socialization of masculine youth, whose excesses they tried to moderate by mingling married and unmarried, and rich and poor. In Dijon, between 1450 and 1540, their calming role was particularly visible in the month of May, when the number of gang rapes fell, in favour of organized festive occasions for the letting off of steam, involving the coronation of a king of love, banquets and a variety of games.[20]

In 1454, the duke of Burgundy confirmed the privileges of the 'Mère folle' (Mother Fool) of Dijon. This festive company was later to have more than five hundred members of all social conditions; they included the prince of Condé, received in 1626, and the bishop of Langres, the date of whose reception is unknown. Until it was abolished by royal edict in 1630, the 'Mère folle' or 'Gaillardon' had been at its most active during Carnival, with processions of floats and people disguised as winegrowers. Although they were far from popular with the Church, bodies of this type celebrated the Feast of Fools in churches between Christmas and Epiphany and distinguished themselves on various other festive occasions, under the leadership of the prince of Love at Lille, or the abbot of the Conards at Rouen. Lyon, the largest city in France after Paris, had a score of festive abbots. These associations, which were ruled by adults, and which had to reckon with occupational groups and neighbourhood solidarities, had as their main role the maintenance of harmony and peace in the town, whether it be Lyon, Turin or Rome. The festivities could go badly wrong. It was not uncommon for there to be criticism of the authorities or the powerful. The farce of the Parisian Basoche in 1516, for example, mocked the young king by showing that Mère Sotte

(Mother Fool) ruled at court. And the jollity could turn into mob aggression if the circumstances were right. The Carnival degenerated into a bloody riot at Udine in 1511, at Berne in 1513 and at Romans in 1580; in London, the Shrove Tuesday celebrations ended in a revolt on twenty-four occasions in the first half of the seventeenth century. In Dijon, in 1630, the masquerade provided the occasion for an anti-tax protest, a pretext for the suppression of the company of the Mère folle, which had been involved.[21]

Before their rapid ossification after the middle of the sixteenth century, the festive abbeys had been a part of the urban triumphs. They showed a considerable capacity to adapt to very varied social and economic conditions, assimilating elements likely to destroy the necessary consensus. They developed soon after a period of great tension, at the beginning of the fourteenth century, when the violence of the little bands of young males could scarcely be contained; and their golden age preceded the period when control of the collective destiny was assumed by increasingly powerful princes and Churches. In this interim phase, between 1450 and 1520, security was essentially a local matter and adolescence one of the main concerns of the magistrates. Turning the explosive energies of turbulent young men into activities that were coordinated by adults, and using them to demonstrate the power of the city, was a way of limiting the number of homicides and violent quarrels in favour of events and spectacles that were enjoyed by the inhabitants as a whole. The cities of the Burgundian Low Countries practised to perfection this art of federating energies by means of festivals, organizing brilliant and spectacular ludic competitions with their peers from all over the region.

In 1437, in Arras, the abbot of Liesse (Joy) and a number of journeymen rhetoricians were given money to cover the cost of the reception offered with 'great reverence to the abbé de L'Escache-Profit [Abbot Money-pockets] of Cambrai'. In 1455, the solemn entry of the duke of Burgundy provided an opportunity to represent the history of Gideon 'with signs and other entertainments'. Several festive confraternities received a cash subvention on this occasion: those of the abbot of Liesse, the most important, the abbot of Bon Vouloir ('Goodwill'), the king of Lours ('Leisure'), the confraternities of Saint-Jacques, the prince of Glay, the king of the Loquebeaux ('Sticks'), the prince of la *Testée* and the Young People of the church of Saint-Géry.

An even more sumptuous spectacle was held on 5 February 1494. A month before, outsiders intending to come to the Dimanche Gras ('Carnival Sunday', that before Ash Wednesday) festivities were instructed to leave their weapons and armour in their lodgings. Festive associations from elsewhere were expected, and were to be welcomed with great pomp according to a precise ceremonial, on pain of an arbitrary fine in case of transgression. The companies ruled by the abbot of Liesse, the prince of Bon Vouloir and the prince of Saint-Jacques, in good order behind their leader, were to go to meet those of Cambrai, Douai, Saint-Pol, the episcopal city of Arras (distinct from the town), Béthune and Lille. On 4 February 1494, Aire-sur-la-Lys, a little town in the east of the county, organized water jousts with its neighbours of Thérouanne, who sent the king of the Grises Barbes ('Greybeards'), the abbot of Youth and the legate of Outre l'Eau ('Over the Water') 'to frolic' with the abbot of Liesse and the prince of Youth of Aire, who had themselves received the king of Fortune of Blaringhem the week before.

A document drawn up in 1533 states that the abbot of Liesse of Arras helped to 'maintain the ancient and good friendships with the nearby towns and the communications of the merchants and other worthy people who frequented this town'. The responsibility was ruinous, as the office-holder had to pay for his robes, pages, lackeys, trumpets and drums, as well as the cost of journeys to Douai and Cambrai; the municipality confined itself to paying for the dinner in honour of the Lundi Gras (Shrove Monday). In 1534 the arrival at the mass for this festival was meticulously regulated to avoid hitches and arguments. The festive procession turned the world upside down: the first to enter were the dignitaries regarded as the least important, that is, the provosts of the Coquins ('Knaves') of Cambrai and of Arras, together. They were followed, alternately, by outsiders and citizens of Arras, according to a detailed protocol. Cambrai sent six representatives, the chief of whom, the abbot of l'Escache-Profit, took the next-to-last position, preceding the master of ceremonies, the prestigious abbot of Liesse of Arras, who entered the church last. Douai sent two representatives, including the Capitaine Pignon, who entered immediately before the pair just mentioned, and the episcopal city sent one, the prince of Franche Volonté ('Free Will'), who preceded Pignon and followed the delegate of Hénin-Liétard. The citizens of Arras were represented, in rising order of prestige, by the prince of the Bas d'Argent ('Silver Stockings'), the admiral of Malleduchon ('Misbehaviour'), the mayor of the Hideux ('Hideous') and prince of Youth, the prince of the Butchers, the prince of Saint-Jacques, the prince of Honour delegated by the drapers, the king of Lours and the abbot of Liesse. Following a quarrel over precedence, one defection is noted, that of the prince of Love of Tournai, who had wanted to take the place of the capitaine Pignon of Douai, but been assigned an inferior position by the magistrates.[22]

Urban cohesion was not an empty phrase in the Low Countries of the fifteenth century. Each town promoted it systematically, to make it a conditioned reflex on the part of the inhabitants. The network of sociability was so dense that it prevented undesirable, dangerous or violent strangers from establishing themselves. The old xenophobia, which had assured the cohesion of rural parishes, operated even more strongly here. However, if the rejection of outsiders was carried to extremes it risked impoverishing the community in every way. The northern towns of the duchy of Burgundy devised a powerful antidote by providing further opportunities for economic exchanges not only through markets and fairs, but through festivals. Whereas the Italian towns were wearing each other out in incessant military conflicts, this region developed a strong sense of belonging to a common state because it was left with many liberties and privileges. The alliance forged between the modern monarchy of the grand dukes of the West and the flourishing cities assured the latter a concrete independence under the remote control of the central power. This original civic system reached its apogee around 1490–1510, benefiting from the political space opened up by the long and confused interregnum following the death of Charles the Rash, which lasted until the accession of Charles of Spain, in 1516. A veritable urban confederation existed thanks to the festivals, which were a great stimulus to the local economy. Contemporaries were well aware of this, as is made explicit in the accounts of the treasurers of Lille, a powerful cloth town with a population of some 40,000 persons. In 1547, they allocated a large sum to the prince of Love, 'in consideration of the fact that this festival had been beautiful, honourable and well-conducted, to the honour of that town, and that by reason of the multitude of people who had come to the said festival, both from neighbouring towns and further afield, the said town had benefited hugely in *assis* and *maltôtes* [taxes] on wine, *cervoises* and *keutes* [beers] and otherwise and similarly on the peasants and inhabitants of that town'.[23]

The festivals boosted the local economy. The councillors were sufficiently conscious of this to award subsidies in money or kind and also prestigious prizes to the winners of the numerous competitions. This made them even more attractive to the crowds of visitors, some of whom came from far away. These were occasions when the turbulent young were encouraged to let off steam, to eat and drink hugely and to compete in games of strength and skill, in an atmosphere of great jollity. This was under the discreet but firm control of their festive princes and abbots, who were later either recompensed or reprimanded by the magistrates. Religion and morality were not entirely absent, but liberties were taken with both, before the little ice age in festive behaviour was imposed from above from the mid sixteenth century. The mysteries presented at the church doors, even the Way of the Cross, sometimes turned to burlesque, on the model of the Feast of Fools and Feast of the Innocents and the long, boisterous period of Carnival. In the Lille processions of 1536, the crafts represented the life of Christ. His circumcision was portrayed by

97

the barrel-makers and the sharing of the loaves and the fishes by the fullers; the man who played the role was then given a slap on the face by the goldsmiths. Next, the coppersmiths mimed the removal of the crown of Darius by his concubine, who also boxed his ears for good measure. Led before Anne, Christ was slapped once more, this time by the shearers. Judas finally betrayed him under the aegis of the second-hand clothes dealers.[24] Mischievous gestures, like the slaps, did not seem in any way blasphemous in these circumstances. Signs of a relaxation of inhibitions, they were laughed at heartily by citizens who had been educated by fines into refraining from these small acts of violence.[25] The whole performance was an act of authorized and controlled licence, which helped to release tensions. It took some of the heat out of the aggression, while at the same time obliging the locals to mix with many strangers, so accustoming them to engage in fruitful exchanges.

> Go to the festivals, to Tournai
> To those of Arras and of Lille,
> Of Amiens, of Douai and of Cambrai,
> Of Valenciennes and of Abbeville,
> Where you will see ten thousand times
> More people than in the forest of Torfolz,
> Who serve, in halls and towns,
> Your God the prince of Fools.

This description, drawn from Martin Franc's *Le champion des dames*, written around 1440–2, brings out the festive reputation of the cities under Burgundian rule. They had managed to harness the peasant traditions of the kingdoms of youth and the Feasts of Fools in the interests of their own prosperity. From 1495 to 1510, the prince of Fools of Lille was the town's principal ambassador. He visited the other towns and himself received, with great pomp, his brethren of Armentières, Arras, Béthune, Cambrai, Courtrai, Douai, Hesdin, Lannoy, Orchies, Saint-Omer, Tournai and Valenciennes. The burlesque official made responsible for this task might change according to circumstances. The prince of Saint-Jacques played the role in 1506; in 1547, it was the prince of Love, after the Feast of Fools had been prohibited by the emperor Charles V in 1540. The most frequent exchanges were with Tournai, Arras, Cambrai and Douai; they, in their turn, received regular visits from the companies of Lille for their own festivals, for example during those of the Fools at Tournai in 1509 and 1510. The processions were sumptuous. When the prince of l'Estrille ('the Currycomb') of Lille set out for Valenciennes, he was accompanied by forty-one persons, including seventeen brethren, as well as trumpeters, heralds and pages, all mounted on fine horses and clothed in sumptuous robes. They were usually also accompanied by the organized crafts, such as the butchers and the *sayetteurs* ('cloth workers') of Lille, occasionally by the 'sworn companies' of the archers, the cross-bowmen or the gunners. In yet another way of managing the young, drawing on their fascination with weapons, these last groups gave demonstrations – which frequently resulted in fatal accidents.

The ideal urban festival was active and merry but closely supervised. Weddings are a good example. They were frequently the subject of police ordinances, especially at times of disturbance or famine, to prevent the eruption of lethal brawls between young men; as, for example, when they came from the local parish or district to claim rights in kind and cash, as happened in the villages. At Lille, after 1524, limitations were increasingly imposed on the number of guests, eventually settling at forty, that is, 'ten pairs of married people and heads of household on each side', which excluded, in principle, the bachelors...At a later stage, it was specified whether this included married persons or not, and musicians, servants and waiters were excluded from the total.[26] In spite of such stipulations, wedding celebrations continued to be occasions for very large gatherings, especially when there were dances, much to the displeasure of the councillors because it was then difficult to maintain order.

The chief aim of the authorities, as far as the young were concerned, was to divide and rule. The non-established males were distributed between several types of institution, which controlled their potential violence by educational regulations, with fines in case of uncivil behaviour. In the crafts, the apprentices and the journeymen were under the supervision of the masters. They obeyed adults in the 'sworn bands' of the shooting games and in the festive abbeys. These bands consisted of a few dozen individuals, that is, were differently structured from the little gangs of aggressive rapists recorded in Dijon. A town as big as Lille had a large number of them, forty-seven between 1500 and 1510, at the height of the phenomenon. The most active, throughout the century, were those of the duke of the Lake, followed by the prince of Lovers, the king of Scots, the lord of Peu d'Argent ('Lord Hard-Up'), the king of the Coeurs Aventureux ('Boldhearts'), the seigneur de Petit Fret, the prince of Saint-Martin, the emperor of Youth (mentioned as early as 1499), l'abbé A Qui Tout Faut and the pope of the Guingans. Each band had its own territory, which it defended against all encroachment, the magistrates settling disputes if all else failed. In 1526, count Lyderic claimed jurisdiction over the garden behind the market, which was contested by the abbot of the Sotte Tresque; the duke of the Lake ruled the street of Saint-Sauveur, the prince of Lovers the Place des Reigneaux, the lord of Peu d'Argent the parish of Saint-Pierre, and so on. The localization mattered because the leader of the company was authorized to levy taxes on the inhabitants for the fraternity's running costs and probably for its activities and banquets. The prince of Le Puy was a bigwig, a magistrate, a nobleman or an abbot, who ruled over a group of rhetoricians. They attended the festivals of 1499 and 1503, and competed in literary culture. A real ecclesiastic was the prelate of a group of Fools who called themselves the Clerks of Saint-Pierre, after a local church. They took part in processions and festivals between 1501 and 1527. A bishop of the Innocents, a clerk or choirboy, is mentioned in 1501 and again in 1503. He ruled throughout the day of 28 December, dedicated to inversion, and he also led his troop when it performed morality plays or foolish games during other entertainments.[27]

Youth could not, of course, be completely controlled. Its confinement by the local authorities, stubbornly pursued, and taken a stage further in the second half of the sixteenth century with the development of both Catholic and Protestant educational structures throughout Europe, was more of a fantasy than a daily reality. The city was in the process of inventing adolescence. The young men were allowed a considerable festive latitude, as long as they moderated the excesses that were dangerous to the reputation and hence prosperity of the city. The hard cases, the knuckleheads, were punished in proportion to their acts and their financial circumstances. The aim was to put them back on track by teaching them to practise the middle way, to exercise the self-control that alone could save them from trouble and impoverishment. The morality taught was primarily practical and personal, not as religious as it later became under the rule of the absolute monarchs: anger cost you dear, it said, and violence led to exclusion from the urban paradise.

Violence costs dear

According to a well-established historical tradition, 'the right of vengeance could not successfully resist the progress of princely authority', even if it coexisted for a long time with the exercise of public repression. Such a view allows too much importance to the central state, in particular in the nineteenth century; the scholars in question were well aware of the existence of the mechanisms for achieving an urban peace, designed to 'protect against the indiscriminate blows of familial vengeance those who had not personally contributed to provoking it'.[28] A more careful study of the various forms of power in Europe at the end of the Middle Ages enables us to identify a very different political system, present in particular in the towns of Flanders and Italy. These medium-sized civic republics organized their security in concentric circles, from their rural hinterland or *contado* to the monumental centre, by way of the ring of

100

walls, in close proximity to which lurked dangers, temptations and pleasures. They divided social space into cells, as in a beehive, which generally limited the scale of eruptions of violence. Nevertheless, exceptional
events could still cause the whole to implode, for example during a festival that turned to tragedy, a great popular internal revolt or a sudden
challenge to princely power. Majestic town halls, sumptuous market-
places, belfries and even processional giants, like Monsieur Gayant at
Douai, all attest to their strong sense of themselves, like the skyscrapers
of New York at a much later date. The patriciate that ruled these towns
constituted a powerful hereditary oligarchy. It was freeing itself from the
bombastic and brutal culture of the conquering princes and nobles, preferring a culture of the happy medium, oriented towards the quest, as
discreet as it was obsessive, for profit and power. It had to find a way
of avoiding unrest, which was always contrary to its interests, whether
it derived from the nobility or the people. Thrift was its passion, ostentatious profusion its enemy. Ascetic Calvinist ideas were very attractive,
consequently, to many of its heirs. Towns that were inspired by a sense
of moderation in all things were ready to receive these ideas. The first
of these was an apprenticeship in the moderation of everyday gestures.
This was necessary in a teeming world, where the sharing of territory
was more difficult than elsewhere and risked leading to innumerable
conflicts, aggravated by what survived of the right of vengeance. The
policing of the body – God taking care of the soul – was thus a priority
as economic success swelled the ranks of the population.

Town air softened manners. It did it in its own way, without visible
extreme repression, which gave some earlier scholars the false impression
that the town was a lax world where crimes were numerous and unpunished. The chroniclers of the fifteenth century made a major contribution
to the growth of such ideas by constantly bemoaning the lack of security
in cities. One of them, Jacques du Clercq, born between 1420 and 1424,
who settled in Arras in the middle of the century, has left his memoirs
for the period 1448–67, a time marked by war and disorder. A bad-
tempered moralist, he never stops complaining.[29] No one escapes their
quota of criticism. He accuses the princes, churchmen as a whole and
married men in general of lustfulness. He delights in seeing them punished by God, like the aged canon, reputed to have a concubine and to
commit incest, who met a sudden death on the tomb of one of his fellows.
For Jacques, there was 'no justice' in Artois or Picardy. In obsessive
detail, he conjures up the spectre of no fewer than 187 criminals who
roamed the county of Artois between 1455 and 1467, 89 of them in the
low country and 98 in Arras, not counting the many other shadowy
delinquents he refers to on occasion. His principal fears related to cases
of murder, which rose to 70 per cent, in the countryside and in the towns.

The insecurity of the roads was then very bad due to one of the many revolts of Ghent against the duke and to the proliferation of robber gangs. Nor did the city seem to Jacques any more tranquil. He denounced the misdeeds of gangs who raped, killed and plundered without fear of prosecution by a corrupt and inefficient justice, which harshly punished with heavy fines, he grumbled, only the defenceless poor. Yet he mentions only a dozen death sentences, that is, one a year, the usual rate for an urban jurisdiction at that period: three homosexuals, one man convicted of bestiality with his heifer (and burned together with it), a rapist, a female infanticide, four thieves and two murderers. Unlike Jacques du Clercq, the judges did not see murder as a threat to the social order. The only individuals executed on this account had both committed particularly horrible crimes: one had smashed the skull of his eighteen-year-old wife with a lead mallet, the other had cruelly murdered the son of a miller. As in Bruges, internal danger was associated with a perverted and non-impregnating sexuality, since all the sodomites punished were from Arras itself. In contrast, the death sentences passed on robbers suggest a severity directed against delinquent outsiders, which is corroborated by other heavy punishments imposed on young thieves also born outside the town.

Jacques du Clercq was a believer in strong ducal power. His jeremiads grew fewer after 1465, when Charles the Rash imposed firm rule. Jacques' criticisms were directed at a style of urban peace of which he disapproved. He showed no interest in the pacification procedures that he must have observed. However, he enjoyed describing the great festivals, especially princely or episcopal entries, such as that of the king of France, Louis XI, when he passed through Arras in 1464. Jacques also briefly noted, without appreciating its significance, the jousting at festivals involving delegates from Amiens, Le Quesnoy, Saint-Omer and Utrecht. Fascinated by bloodshed, he often described it in detail, perhaps to relieve his own anxieties, without ever referring to anything he himself had directly experienced. The military and noble practice of vengeance attracted his particular attention. He tells how a captain in the service of the count of Saint-Pol went to the festival of Avesnes-le-Comte, on 1 May 1459, with twenty-four former companions in war, in search of a certain soldier. When they found him, they wounded him seventeen or eighteen times in his face, head, arms and legs, but without killing him; with every blow they struck, they told him that the count their master wished to be remembered to him. Eight years earlier, the victim and some others had beaten up the bailiff and sergeants of the town of Saint-Pol. Some of the soldier's companions had already been executed, others 'cut' like him and, rumour had it, observes our narrator, none would escape a cruel punishment. In August 1458, the lord of Romcq, husband of the illegitimate sister of the count of Saint-Pol, had ordered a rival in love to be seized; he then had 'his genitals and member cut off, then his stomach slit open and his guts taken out and slashed in two, and in this way he died'. At bottom, the work is a record of the chief fantasies of its author. His fear of violence was probably heightened by unease at his own advancing years. In 1464, when he had reached fifty or a little over, he wrote that many men, most of them young, had left on foot for Rome since Easter, in groups of ten, twenty or forty, leaderless and unarmed. There were said to be more than 20,000 of them, all from the ducal states, and there were fears of 'a problem' if they gathered together. In fact, he was recording a general malaise due to increasing demographic pressure. He later notes that no one had ever seen as many marriages in Artois or Picardy as between Easter and mid August 1466. Old people, he adds, claimed they had never seen anything like it. In 1467, the world had a younger feel to it, because fashions were changing. Women, he marvelled, no longer wore trains to their gowns and sported round caps with a bourrelet and streamers down to the ground. Men wore their hair long in the neck and in front of their eyes, long shoes with points, padded shoulders and short clothes, so tight, he lamented, that you could see their 'humanity', that is, their sexual organs.

The aging annalist was not alone in wishing to restrain the new generations. Urban justice had invented an ingenious system for educating the brutish of all ages and for training the undisciplined young; that is, the fine. Together with corporal punishment and the death penalty, both used in moderation, the tax on crime affected a very large number of people. It punished, but it also reintegrated after payment, and it left offenders with the painful memory of a heavy financial loss associated with a failure of self-control. It thus instilled conditioned reflexes, each individual learning, at his own cost, that a high price had to be paid for succumbing to anger. The fine was sometimes accompanied by judicial pilgrimages or additional shaming punishments, such as whipping, public exposure or honourable atonement stripped to the shirt, which served as warnings to the offender to halt his progress towards certain disaster. The hopeless cases were banished from the town for a fixed term, or for ever, in the latter case with the threat of execution if they dared to return.

All the Burgundian cities had at their disposal this arsenal of measures that were more dissuasive than punitive. Arras obtained hers by a comital charter of 1194. A fine of five *sous*, handed in its entirety to the victim, punished insults. No trace of this survives because nothing went to the prince, which meant that nothing was recorded in the accounts for his county. One can only imagine the interest of such a list if one had miraculously been drawn up. Slapping someone's face, striking them with a fist or dragging them by the hair merited a fine of thirty *sous*, half of which went to the victim. A blow with a stick that did not shed blood was taxed at ten *livres*, of which three went to the plaintiff. Dragging someone by the hair after knocking them down meant a fine of eleven and a half *livres*, of which the victim received only fifteen *sous*, as for a slap on the face. Lastly, a very heavy fine of sixty *livres*, all of which went to the sovereign, was demanded for more serious but non-fatal offences: carrying prohibited weapons, armed pursuit of an inhabitant, theft, irreverence before the judge-magistrates and *plaie à banlieu*, also called *plaie ouverte et sang coulant*, that is, an open wound where the victim survived for the next thirty days. In case of death before this time limit, the offence counted as premeditated homicide and was dealt with as such. The names of those who fled without paying the sixty *livres* fine are recorded. Like those formally banished for murder, they were in future in a state of civil death; they could be killed by anyone, without legal repercussions, if they reappeared within the boundaries of the judicial zone of Arras.

The lists of fines in Arras survive for fifty-five fiscal years in the fifteenth century and for a further twenty-five between 1500 and 1534, the date of a new, radical reform of the repressive system, which involved a move to much harsher penalties. At the end of the Middle Ages, the reliance on financial penalties for violence encouraged individuals to prefer recourse to the intermediary of the law to private vengeance. The lure of gain cleverly encouraged this behavioural change, because the compensation received by the injured party was far from negligible. Denunciation of the culprit initiated a swift punitive process, which progressed rapidly from prison to judgement. Happily for the historian, lists of those detained in Arras have survived for thirty complete years, from 1407 to 1414 and from 1427 to 1450.[30] The reason for their compilation was once again financial, because the prisoners were obliged to pay fees to the ducal officers. At the minimum, they paid twelve *deniers*, that is, one *sou*, a day, which gave them the right to a loaf of bread, which cost one *denier* in 1407. Those wishing to take advantage of the greater comfort of the *belle garde* had to pay five *sous* a day. At these rates, the fifteen *sous* paid to the victim of a slap across the face would have covered the cost of a fortnight in the ordinary prison or bought 180 loaves of bread.

The prisons of Arras were overpopulated: 4,640 people passed through them during the thirty years in question. About a fifth were there for unpaid debts and their stay could not exceed seven nights. Of the others, 4 per cent of those sentenced were totally insolvent, so suffered an alternative penalty of incarceration and ate the 'lord's bread' before being freed for poverty; typical of these was a certain Jehan Le Bon, released after 179 days because he was unable to pay the sixty *livres* demanded.

The rest, that is, almost three-quarters of the contingent, spent only a very short time in prison, awaiting judgement: 87 per cent of them were detained for less than a week, half of them emerging at the latest on the third day. Neither age nor offence is specified in these sources, but the figures agree with those of the lists of fines which essentially concerned acts of violence. The 3,342 people incarcerated, an average of 110 per year, probably had the same characteristics as those pardoned for homicide in Artois. They had acted according to a similar calendar: a slack period from January to March, an increase in April, a peak between May and August, especially the last two months, a slight decline in September, a sharp fall in October, even more marked in November, the quietest time of the year, and a significant increase in December. Advent, Carnival and Lent seem to have been better supervised in the towns than in the countryside, but the feasts associated with Christmas, the month of May and the summer were equally conducive to crime, which suggests that those involved were primarily unmarried men. Some of them were drunk or thugs picked up at night and locked up for a few hours until they calmed down. Women accounted for only 10 per cent of the total. With the exception of the prostitutes, they had often been arrested in the company of men, a husband or a master, sometimes also in large mixed groups, like the ten men and five women imprisoned on 20 August 1428, or the eleven men and ten women brought in together on 20 September 1442. The occupations recorded are primarily those of the working-class urban world. The executioner himself was locked up on two occasions, in 1435 and 1443. His manservant and a sergeant were also imprisoned, once each, but not a single nobleman, burgess or personage of importance appears.

The Arras prison was not a mass school for crime, given the brevity of the time spent there and the scarcity of major criminals passing through. Between 1407 and 1414, 1,059 mostly male defendants, that is, more than 150 a year, spent some time there awaiting a judicial verdict. At this rate, a good part of the town's ordinary male population, and probably the majority of its unmarried men, with the apparent exception of those of good family, may have been involved in the space of a generation. The circulation was rapid, and it was even possible to leave, with a promise to return, if the process dragged on too long. Prison society was organized, with its hierarchies, its bosses, its rich and its poor. It is doubtful whether a short spell in such a place meant social disgrace. Rather, it was an opportunity to ponder the fact of an inability to control one's violence, and it thus became a step on the road to a degree of wisdom by making the negative consequences of a violent act both concrete and painful. Not only did it mean paying the price, which was very high for an ordinary worker, but the price was made much greater by the substantial costs of imprisonment, the loss of income and the obligation to offer the other prisoners a *marmouse*, or 'welcome'.

The flood dried up a little between 1427 and 1437, with an average of 110 cases per year, then fell to about 80 a year between 1437 and 1447, before dropping to 40 during the last three years of the period in question. This stepped decline was only partly linked to calamities, wars, epidemics and famines likely to have reduced the population. The period 1440–53, for example, was not particularly hard. Price trends were once again similar to those of the years 1380–1414, which had been characterized by a relative well-being. It seems rather to be a sign of the success, after many decades of trying, of the municipal policy of limiting violence and systematic recourse to fines, preceded by a short period of imprisonment. Incarceration was rarely punitive, but played a primarily preventative role. It acted as sort of threshold, producing a perception of anomie in those who resorted too readily to force. Unpleasant memories of it, associated more with the heavy financial sanctions than with the conditions of incarceration, lingered.

The prime target of the authorities was everyday, routine violence. They tried to dissuade because they lacked effective means to repress. To control the 12,000 inhabitants of their city they normally had the services of only a dozen 'town' sergeants, with four sergeants of the castellan, rising to six in 1449, assigned to supervise the prisoners. Financial penalties were central to their project to regulate social relations. The fifty-five lists which survive for the fifteenth century record 2,615 fines.[31] The annual average was forty-seven, compared with twenty-seven in the twenty-five registers which survive for the period 1500–34. The proportion of women, only 10 per cent in the fifteenth century, was exactly the same as that of female prisoners; it then fell by half during the first third of the sixteenth century. Taking both sexes together, the highest levels were reached between 1401 and 1410, with an average of 80, a minimum of 61 and a maximum of 122. The curve then declines, in spite of a few blips between 1467 and 1471, 1502 and 1504, and 1512 and 1524. This is evidence of an original urban system whose golden age came to an end around 1520. Nearly 8,000 fines were recorded in Brussels during the fifteenth century, and more than 4,000 between 1423 and 1498 at Nivelles, a small town in Brabant with only half the population of Arras; they included 2,121 for violence and 1,585 for theft.[32]

A tendency to judge this mechanism harshly, by the yardstick of the judicial statist 'modernity' that replaced it, has prevented a proper appreciation of its success in imposing calm and in creating a more civilized way of living together. It may have proved unable, at a later stage, to resolve the new problems posed by the religious conflicts subsequent to the Reformation. However, before that, it had shaped an original urban mind-set by replacing the law of vengeance with that of personal interest. Far from a sign of disorder, the very large number of pecuniary punishments for violence testifies to changes that were symptomatic of human relations in a busy world. The increase in the number of fines in Arras in the first decade of the fifteenth century came after a long period of prosperity and demographic growth. The rises in the curve also correspond to times when the number of young people and of marriages rose: for example in 1467, according to the lamentations of the chronicler Jacques du Clercq on this theme, and around 1520, when the rural exodus and the problem of marginals became social fears that resulted in increasingly repressive royal legislation.

The pedagogic zeal of the magistrates was more intense between 1401 and 1463 than later. It was primarily aimed at punishing those who struck a fellow citizen: 62 per cent of the fines recorded were for a hard *buffe* ('slap') or sometimes a blow with the fist; they had been administered by a total of 873 men and 136 women to 645 men and 342 women (a few cases not specified). The blow struck in anger, by both men and women, was aimed at someone of the same sex in nearly four out of five cases, mostly by one man at another. Only a minority of both men and women attacked someone of the opposite sex. The rarity of references to occupations, which are recorded for barely a fifth of the accused and even fewer of the victims, is unfortunate, as is the lack of indications of age. Among the hundred or so trades mentioned, almost all were of low social status. The few merchants or drapers recorded only make more striking the absence of the patriciate and the elites, an absence we have already observed in the case of imprisonment. Perhaps they were already exercising greater self-control than the rest? In any case, if they failed to turn the other cheek, as taught by the church, and obeyed their impulses, we may be sure that they were treated with special leniency by the judges, their peers, and would escape a spell in prison and the usual fine.

The fines reveal the existence of trades whose members were quicker to resort to violence than others: butchers, bakers, fishmongers, fullers, masons, shoemakers, carpenters and innkeepers. Among those who frequently got themselves hit were ecclesiastics, wine-sellers, barbers, merchants and, above all, male domestic servants, who provided twenty-two victims but only five aggressors. Sergeants, prostitutes and owners of stews were equally represented in both groups, revealing both the extent to which their occupations exposed them to fights and their readiness to defend themselves. It seems to have been rare for people to assault total strangers, as only twenty-three of the attackers and twenty-three of the victims were from outside the town. Everything suggests that the magistrates were chiefly concerned with the natives and that they had little interest in the others. However, it may also be that the latter, if they were the aggressors, chose to flee rather than pay the fine demanded. When they were the victims, it was very rare for them to claim the financial compensation they were due, even though its value was far from negligible.

At the beginning of the fifteenth century, a fine of thirty *sous* was equivalent to ten days' work on the part of a mason or twenty by a carpenter's labourer, that is, nearly a month's wages for the latter, allowing for holidays. It was always demanded in full, unlike other fines which could be 'compounded', that is, adjusted according to the offender's ability to pay. A fifth of those sentenced went into exile because they were unable to pay, which reveals the precarious condition of those involved, members of the lower ranks of the urban poor. They probably included many unmarried young men. Some of the formidable and thuggish repeat offenders may have belonged to this turbulent age group.

Between 1401 and 1408, Geffrin Chaullois landed a *buffe* on six different men, including his brother Henry, while only once claiming that he had been on the receiving end of a blow. Henry Chaullois, the brother in question, assaulted five persons and came off worse twice, including the one occasion involving his brother Geffrin, between 1402 and 1411. Between 1416 and 1432, Jacot Belin, known as Poullier or Poullallier, attacked nine persons, including two women, and was himself struck four times between 1416 and 1420, the last time at the hands of Willemet Gouffroy, called Chavet, son of Jean, whose blow he returned. The profile emerges in each case of a ruffian who began by receiving blows but then cultivated his own aggressive powers. These adversaries had first experienced the law of the strongest before imposing their own, never again suffering a similar assault, if the fiscal records are to be believed. Chavet had started out by receiving a *buffe* from the formidable Henry Chaullois in 1407. After the exchange of blows with Jacot Belin, in 1420, he appears only as the attacker of two other men. Disreputable characters like these two roamed the streets of the town, dealing blows right, left and centre: the fishmonger Jacotin le Conte, the potter Hanotin le Flament, the shoemaker Jehan Joli, called Joliet...Less common are the men who seem to have got on with their work for weeks while putting up with the violence of others, such as Pieret Poullier, servant of Jacquemart Poullier, who was struck five times between 1427 and 1433 without ever himself being fined for a similar offence.

The hard cases who dealt and received blows on numerous occasions perhaps came from youth groups attached to the manly traditions, like those which engaged in collective rapes in Dijon at about this time. Various signs – nicknames, links revealed, signs of reciprocal hostility, phrases like 'son of' – suggest this was the case. It did not stop them from seeking judicial protection in case of need, like the Chaullois brothers, who denounced each other. They were then caught up in the web of surveillance spun by the authorities. Their continued presence in the accounts over long periods of time shows that the objectives of the latter had been achieved, because they were still alive. The traditional escalation from a challenge to an insult to a blow, and then, lastly, to a knife or sword fight, was halted before tragedy ensued by a short spell in prison followed by a heavy financial penalty. For these survivors, urban mediation broke the infernal cycle which, in the villages, continued to produce a very large number of homicides pardoned by the prince.

The under-representation of the cities of Artois among those pardoned was due to a better management of relational aggression between males, which is known to be at its greatest intensity among the unmarried. The majority of those sentenced to a fine of thirty *sous* for acts of violence learned how to break the spiral of conflict before it became lethal. The Chaullois brothers and others like them gained years of life by paying fines that were, in the end, a good deal less than the price of blood. A large number of small fires broke out but were damped down before becoming major conflagrations. While relieving the feelings of their perpetrators, the large number of slaps on cheeks made it possible to avoid an equal number of murderous brawls. The defence of the honour concentrated in this prestigious part of the person was now assured by the judges, who succeeded in limiting the extremes of the law of the strongest and the law of vengeance. The fine was only the visible part of a massive programme of civic education. The courts offered their protection to the weakest and slowly accustomed all citizens to accept, with a better or worse grace, their mediation in matters of personal security. The small number of outsiders in the lists of defendants reveals the limits of their activity and, in the longer term, the weakness of a system whose effectiveness ceased on the other side of the city walls.

The aim was to calm down disputes between members of the community and oblige the most violent to avoid these of their own accord. Setting prices for blows also acted as a solemn warning, that is, to be content with a financial and symbolic redress for wounded honour, because to press a conflict further on the city streets would have disastrous consequences. The tariff increased at an exorbitant rate for those who struck with an implement without causing an injury, or who knocked their adversary to the ground and continued to strike or kick him, or for women who dragged another woman by the hair. The sum demanded was seven or eight times higher than for a slap, ten *livres* or eleven and a half *livres*, that is, equivalent to seven or eight months' wages for a carpenter's labourer, allowing for holidays. Fines at this level were less frequent: respectively 246 and 51 for the whole century, compared with 1,244 fines of thirty *sous* and 1,073 of sixty *livres*. The higher fines effectively served as a final warning, because half of those sentenced had to leave the town because they were unable to pay. This was in spite of the fact that the authorities accepted significant 'mitigations' in three cases out of four for those why tried to pay, because of their relative poverty. On average, these culprits paid just over fifty *sous*. They belonged to the lower social ranks but often from a little higher up than those sentenced for a slap. The system thus made it possible to separate the chaff from the wheat among the lower ranks of the urban world. It drove half the culprits into an exile synonymous with extreme difficulties of survival, given their insolvency. Most of the others were impoverished, made vulnerable and put under judicial surveillance, in compensation for the negotiation they had been forced to conduct with the magistrates in order to remain in the town. Any repeat offence risked ending in disaster. It is likely that this sword of Damocles made more than one man hesitate before giving full rein to a brutal temperament.

The fines of ten *livres* were distributed between the sexes in exactly the same way as those of thirty *sous*. They may have applied to more local neighbourhood quarrels between adults than the latter, to go by the indications of trades and the implements used to strike the adversary when the attacker was not content with feet and fists. The masculine weapon of choice, the stick, was most common. A range of everyday utensils are also mentioned: skittle, candlestick, harness, grill pan, stone and pot for the men, broomstick, wooden patten, distaff and bunch of keys for the women. The street seems to have been where most fights involving women took place, and when they attacked someone it was usually another woman. The accounts for 1415–16, for example, refer to a certain Jehenne, wife of Jehan de Prouvins, who had used a wooden patten against Julienne la Carpentière, *'femme de vie'* ('loose woman'), and paid 40 *sous* after mitigation; her opponent had hit back, also with a patten, before fleeing to avoid paying the fine.

Anger cost both these women dear. However, whereas the judicial system drove the poor into voluntary exile, the better-off were simply left to ponder a salutary lesson as they faced a relative impoverishment. The majority of female victims were prostitutes, and they had usually been assaulted by someone of the opposite sex, which brings out the precariousness of their situation. Men got into fights in the street, but in other places, too: they were often carrying sticks, suggesting encounters outside the home, while objects such as pewter pots reveal visits to the tavern. The most frequently mentioned are the cloth, food and building trades. The privileged, the rich and strangers are all rare. So are the very poorest, especially male domestic servants, often plaintiffs in the lists of fines of 30 *sous*, and repeat offenders, equally numerous in the same lists. Only a few individuals appear in both series, as victims hoping to get their share of the fine of 10 *livres*; they included that formidable dealer of blows Jacot Belin, called Poullier, in 1416. Everything suggests that the two worlds of violence were not the same. Fines on slaps seem essentially to have been aimed at the impulsive, perhaps primarily young men, in the hope of educating them into a less conflictual social life than in the villages. The fines on blows that did not leave an open wound affected mainly better-established adult males, together with the world of prostitution.

The list of fines of eleven and a half *livres* shares some features with that of fines of ten *livres*, namely social characteristics, absence of habitual offenders and flight due to inability to pay in half the cases. The heavier and less common of the two fines, which was in rapid decline from the mid fifteenth century, was the one most women had to pay. They provided ten of the nineteen accused and seventeen of the twenty-nine victims between 1401 and 1436, including nine cases of one-to-one fights. Most of the time, only feet and fists were used. The men who came out victorious went on kicking their victim once he was on the ground, whereas female victors in the same situation generally dragged their victim along by the hair. The punishment reflected an unacceptable level of ferocity and the loss of dignity suffered by a person knocked to the ground. The 'civilizing process' was already being inculcated by a symbolic management of the body of the citizen. The aim was always to repair wounded honour so as to prevent a murderous escalation, which risked being followed in its turn by an act of vengeance. The urban imaginary had developed a graded geography of the body, which sustained self-esteem. A slap involved a lesser loss of face than a blow, with or without a weapon. Worse for a man was the fact of being trampled underfoot, and for a woman of being thrown to the ground by another member of her own sex and then dragged along by her hair. In the latter case, the punishments were imposed primarily on prostitutes and women servants, a way of policing them, as far as this was possible, by putting them under the threat of a penalty that would mean ruin and exile.

The increasing rarity of the fine of eleven and a half *livres* in the second half of the fifteenth century stemmed less from its success in dissuading potential offenders than from the paucity of the financial return it brought to the town. It got a mere five *sous*, as against three *livres* in the case of fines of ten *livres*, which was a strong incentive to classify acts in the latter category. The behaviour in question had not been eradicated. In 1466–7, in one of the very rare cases involving the privileged rich, the lady Jehanne le Borgne, wife of Guillaume de Monbertault, composed for the highest sum in the series, four *livres*, for having beaten lady Ysabelle de Beaumont, widow of Guérart de Bailly, 'with knees, feet and fists'. The system also protected the weakest, especially prostitutes,

111

who were increasingly regulated at this period and who by this time rarely appeared in the lists of persons incurring a fine of eleven and a half *livres*. In 1469–70, Ambroise Millon was sentenced to pay such a fine because he 'had beaten with his fist, knocked to the ground, dragged along and kicked a whore'. Boudin Rumet was similarly punished in 1474–5 for having 'in the stews of Lille Adam dragged from a bed a whore called Boutilette, who was sleeping with a gentleman, and beaten her with sticks'.

The years 1401–11 were, in every respect, the most conflictual recorded in an overpopulated town: 288 'blood' fines of sixty *livres*, 425 of thirty *sous*, 39 of ten *livres* and 15 of eleven and a half *livres*. The number of fines in the first category subsequently fell spectacularly, after 1405, when fines of thirty *sous* became more numerous. Then they in their turn were overtaken, indeed left far behind, by fines of sixty *livres*, between 1450 and 1534. This double scissors movement illustrates both the intensity of daily brutality at the beginning of the fifteenth century and the uneven progress within the social body of a 'civilizing process' promoted by financial penalties. At the beginning, the fining of a large number of people for a slap was not yet preventing the fights from turning into murderous brawls. However, the desired effect was rapidly achieved, because many people were literally no longer able to afford a simple exchange of blows, even though a small number of hardened habitual offenders continued to take the risk.

The golden age of the slap, up to 1436, was a time when the spiral of conflictuality was slowed down by a mechanical effect and fear of impoverishment more than by the definitive internalization of new relational values. Demographic pressure and the loss of the purchasing power of the *livre* probably then helped to reduce the effectiveness of the process. This was not, however, the crucial factor. From the middle of the fifteenth century, the new generations seem to have been more successful in assimilating the lesson of self-control. The slap fell out of use, in what was probably a sign of a further pacification of the most ordinary aggressive behaviour, especially among young unmarried men. It did not, of course, disappear. There was a sharp rise in 'blood' fines between 1461 and 1475, and another, slightly less pronounced, in the first third of the sixteenth century. However, the general trend for the curve to decline from the 1450s allows us to conclude that the effort put into controlling the most impetuous behaviour, which could easily lead to a lethal combat, had become a priority of the magistrates and had been partly successful. Its impact here had been less, however, than in the case of petty violence without repercussions, which was almost eradicated, if we are to go by the gradual disappearance of fines of thirty *sous*. The disjuncture between these two types of behaviour was a real advance, due to the practices of

112

the urban peace. It prefigured the battle fought by the central state in the sixteenth century to criminalize homicide, taking advantage of the pacificatory techniques previously introduced in the towns.

The final stage of violence, when blood was spilled, spelled certain ruin for those who could not afford to pay its heavy price. In 1400, sixty *livres* was equivalent to several years' wages for an ordinary worker and more than a year's income for a craftsman in one of the better trades. The fine was so heavy that it was almost never paid in full. Only six of the 533 persons sentenced were in a position to do this between 1401 and 1436. The number of unpaid fines reached 53 per cent, besides five individuals exempted in full because of absolute poverty. Of the rest, the men paid on average five and a half *livres*, the women five *livres*. The repression was aimed at a wide range of offences. Woundings, threats followed by blows with a weapon and the carrying of arms accounted together for 64 per cent. To these should be added attacks on houses (10 per cent), offences against the authorities and prison escapes (nearly 11 per cent), and various much less common acts, such as abuse of authority, flight with one's property and non-payment of a bill at the tavern. The order of magnitude remained the same from 1441 to 1475, with 72 per cent woundings, blows and carrying of arms and 9 per cent attacks on houses.

It all amounted to a major effort to clamp down on what were then perceived as the worst assaults on the safety of persons and property. This mainly meant masculine violence, as that of women figured in only a third of the accusations in the first third of the century, closely followed by attacks on houses; it had in any case become almost negligible by 1441. Among those whose social situation is known, prostitutes are the most prominent. They were particularly exposed to the brutality of their clients, and developed a special capacity to resist in order to survive. Jacquette de Brelle appears ten times in the lists of fines, between 1405 and 1425: she paid three fines of thirty *sous* plus one of sixty *livres* reduced to forty *sous*, and she was six times the victim of aggression, four taxed at thirty *sous* and two at sixty *livres*.

The occupations of the men are known in a third of cases, which limits the significance of any conclusions. The privileged, merchants and well-off citizens are rare, though slightly more numerous than those of their peers who paid fines of thirty *sous* for a slap. A dozen are recorded for the first third of the century, to which we may add those rich enough to compound for at least eight *livres* of the fine. Together they represent about 20 per cent of the accused. The typical aggressor thus came from the common people, but differed in some respects from those fined for slaps: the food and transport trades are less well represented, the textile trade, the principal local activity, better represented: fullers, furriers and workers in a variety of specialized trades, *parmentiers*, *hautellisseurs*, *pourpointiers*, *caucheteurs*, *sayetteurs*, etc. Male domestic servants, themselves often humiliated and slapped, provided many of the attackers who caused injuries. They included many employed by powerful persons, apparently imitating the swaggering manners of their masters. Although they were so few in number in the town, sergeants and officials provided a quarter of those sentenced and 40 per cent of the victims whose occupation is known. This suggests a particular world, swift to resort to force to settle frequent conflictual situations, which often involved the police auxiliaries and servants of great men.

Cloth workers displayed a readiness to spill blood which resulted both from a specific culture of violence and from tensions in the labour market. The most brutal of all were the fullers. Doomed to hard and unpleasant work, these *ongles bleues* – literally 'blue nails' – were often the leaders of the great revolts in the textile towns of Flanders and Italy at the end of the Middle Ages.[33] They were energetic defenders of their rights, as a comparison between documents shows. Although the fines of sixty *livres* give the impression that most of the fights punished were between two individuals, some rare criminal fragments qualify this picture. For example, a fuller was sentenced to a cash fine in 1427–8 because he had crippled a fellow fuller, from Douai. It emerges from a different source, however, that this was actually a fight between four members of the same trade, including two born in Tournai. The most violent of them were often leaders of gangs, and probably young men, if we go by the complaints of Jacques du Clercq and other indications. Between 1410 and 1430, Pieret Warnier was a victim four times and the aggressor four times, always in connection with members of the Chevalier family, which suggests either the violence of youth or a spiral of familial vengeance. Bernard Bainart, *hautellisseur*, was sentenced on three occasions after 1406–7, once with three accomplices. He attacked a sergeant to liberate another *hautellisseur* in 1415–16, and had his arm broken in a fight in 1431–2. Hanotin Filloeul fled four times to avoid paying the fine between 1403 and 1416.

Alongside these violent recidivists, we can identify two other types of person punished by the authorities: occasional offenders who committed only one violent assault, and much more aggressive individuals who usually acted with accomplices and were also prominent among those fined thirty *sous* for slaps. Among the latter was Geffrin Chaullois, who wounded one adversary on two occasions and was himself once beaten by four assailants, between 1402 and 1408. Jehan Joli, called Joliet, a shoemaker, an accomplice of Geffrin Chaullois in 1402, was seriously injured in 1407, then escaped from prison in 1416. Another individual free with his fists, Willemet Gouffroy, was a sworn enemy of Geffrin and recorded as an attacker in 1416 and as injured in 1426. Unlike these men, some of those who paid several fines of thirty *sous* do not appear in the lists of 'blood' fines. One such was Jacot Belin, called Poullier, though he had been slapped in the face in 1420, by either Willemet Gouffroy or Robin Panot, and beaten up by Pierre Aoustin, called Porrus, sergeant of the castellan, whom he had slapped.

The documents cannot give the historian more than they contain. However, they make it possible to identify different types of response on the part of individuals in the face of the clear determination of the authorities to pacify manners. Some hard cases refused to bow beneath the yoke. They included workers in hard and competitive trades such as fulling, young men in bands enacting the traditional rituals of violence, and prostitutes, always a dangerously exposed group. Others occasionally gave in to anger or seized a weapon, but avoided ruin or exile by limiting the number of their fights and the violence of their exchanges. This would appear to indicate that they were more often trying to control themselves, out of a clearly perceived self-interest. Others confined their fights to slaps across the face, probably a sign of a relative internalization of the prohibitions, because they knew what the cost would be if they hit harder. Some seem to have enjoyed a small amount of transgression, demonstrating their manliness, but without going too far, like Jacot Belin. Many other inhabitants of Arras make no appearances in the sources at all. They may have been better able to master their aggression, even though occasions for anger were numerous in the urban world.

The high level of attention paid by the magistrates to the most trivial acts of violence, which were immediately punished, recalls the 'broken window' theory of today, found especially in the United States, which advocates an immediate response to the least sign of an increase in danger. The hundreds of punishments of slaps, like those for insults, for which we sadly have no lists, testify to an original urban practice which consisted of responding to the slightest indication of tension to prevent it from sparking a chain of violence culminating in the excesses of private vengeance.

A similar system to that in Arras existed in all the towns under the rule of the duke of Burgundy, and it was probably also found, if in slightly different forms, in Italy and other countries. It was based on constant surveillance and the use of graduated fines that led to the increasing impoverishment of those who stubbornly refused to conform to the established rules. It was not perfect, admittedly, because those who wanted to slip through the net could easily do so. To have the right to return, it was necessary to pay a financial composition negotiated with the magistrates, which was done by 38 out of the 170 who fled after being sentenced to a fine of sixty *livres* in the first decade of the fifteenth century. The insolvent tried to survive outside the law. Many settled close to the walls, sometimes in ecclesiastical enclaves or other 'franchises' where they could not legally be seized. However, the hordes of the banished had to avoid entering the territory of the 'suburb', because custom decreed that, if they were liable to a fine of sixty *livres*, they could be killed with impunity by anyone. The town, as we have seen, was able to use to its own advantage the mechanisms of private vengeance, though it was also trying to undermine them, legitimizing them in this one instance alone. It similarly closed its eyes to the furtive return of offenders, perhaps precisely because it hoped that their enemies would rid the community of them. Some hardened offenders managed to survive in these circumstances, since they appear several times in succession as having fines of sixty *livres* unpaid. This was the case on three occasions with Bernard Bainart, and twice with Hanotin Filloeul. Joliot, mentioned seven times in the registers for various fines, failed to pay a fine of sixty *livres* in 1402 and another of the same amount in 1416, the date on which he escaped from prison.

The large number of the banished who remained in the vicinity, hoping for a pardon on the occasion of a princely entry, posed problems of security. Those who had been condemned in the past or who had gone into voluntary exile were joined, between 1401 and 1411, by a contingent equivalent to almost 1 per cent of the population of Arras. The insecurity of the roads grew worse and business suffered. When shady characters and even those who constituted a danger in sudden periods of unrest, were also expelled, this stretch of land became a no-go area, given the disquieting profile of many of the exiles. As the other towns followed identical policies, and as the villages were hostile to strangers, the security imposed within town walls had as its counterpart the growth of a flourishing criminality in the uninhabited spaces, in particular on the roads leading to prosperous localities. This was the price that had to be paid for breaking the traditional spiral culminating in private vengeance, when there was little use of the death penalty. Internal stability was assured by graduated punishments and the expulsion of disruptive elements or their voluntary exile. The rarity of secondary corporal punishments, such as cutting off the ears of thieves, characterizes a justice that had little inclination to punish bodies, unlike the monarchic states of the future.

In the Burgundian 'urban republics' the social pact was based on the acceptance of internal peace and on each individual's control of their aggression. The deviants were punished quickly but with moderation, primarily by being hit in their pockets. The hard cases were driven out, abandoned to the insecurity and dangers of an unprotected life. It was for the sovereign to see to the pacification of the marginal zones teeming

116

with deviants and the poor! Though a sort of egoism, this approach produced a fairly effective public order, in spite of major popular revolts due to deteriorating conditions. Each city also equipped itself with the means to check on arrivals by requesting its neighbours in Burgundian territory for precise details of the expelled criminals. Those who were banished from Arras for murder or an unpaid fine of sixty *livres* had few options. Not only did they risk death if they returned to the town, but it was difficult for them to settle anywhere else, as Béthune and Saint-Omer in Artois, and Bruges and Ypres in Flanders, worked on the same principle and kept each other informed on the subject of gallows birds and various other perils.

The towns were defusers of crises, and they applied their principles in all spheres. At the end of the Middle Ages, they produced an original sort of 'criminal economy' by inventing a requirement for self-control on the part of individuals, primarily directed at the young males and prostitutes whose excesses were too disruptive of the collective peace. To moderate the passions and to rein in aggression became a necessity for anyone who wanted to survive and prosper in this context. Well before the 'curialization of warriors' at the court of Louis XIV, the 'municipalization' of violence helped to damp down aggression. It was repressed, supervised and turned into a source of income, thus made, at least in part, to serve the community. It is likely that the great Italian metropolises, the imperial towns, especially those of the Hanse, and others, such as Paris, had similar regulatory systems to compensate for the weakness of police forces.

Why, it may now be asked, were these little-known – because little-studied – practices replaced by the 'spectacle of torture' imposed by the great monarchies from the sixteenth century on? The explanation probably does not lie in possible crises, because the cities had demonstrated their capacity to adapt in the preceding centuries. It probably lies primarily in the progress of the new, centralized, repressive model, which offered better control of the neglected intermediate spaces. In creating the provost-marshals with the task of pacifying the main highways, Charles the Rash in Burgundy and Francis I in France relieved the towns of the pressure of the large numbers of banned persons and vagrants massed at their gates. Pragmatic as ever, the towns grasped the value of this system in increasing their own security, synonymous with their prosperity. They often agreed, therefore, though not without reservations, to relinquish some of their proud autonomy in return for these significant advantages. With the exception of the most powerful Italian urban republics, such as Venice and Genoa, and of the towns of the United Provinces, which banded together in a federative contract and repudiated the authority of the Spanish sovereign in 1579, the majority of towns accepted the leadership of the princes because it brought more gains than losses. Some of the proudest, like Antwerp, Ghent and Lyon, still stubbornly clung to their independence. Until they were forcibly incorporated into the sphere of statist modernity, they offered the Protestant reformers a world prepared to listen to their discourse of harmony and close supervision of morals and manners, because they had been applying such principles for many generations.

— 5 —

CAIN AND MEDEA: HOMICIDE AND THE CONSTRUCTION OF SEXED GENDERS (1500–1650)

In the Middle Ages the adults in the communities were as relaxed as the central authorities in their attitude towards the excesses of brutal young men, whose constant ritual battles closely followed the rhythm of Sundays and the festive calendars.[1] Such specifically youthful violence still dominates the European and American crime statistics, but it is now no longer found acceptable.[2]

This fundamental shift in perception began in the sixteenth century. It was originally a product of the radical change in judicial practice in Western Europe between 1550 and 1650. As the Renaissance gave way to Baroque civilization, the modern state, everywhere based on a single church claiming a monopoly of the care of souls, experimented with more effective methods of social control so it could best fulfil the missions devolved on the prince: to defend the true faith, to keep the peace, to impose the law and to promote the collective good. To make the monarch wholly credible in the eyes of his people, by providing them with the 'good policing' necessary to the common good and the safety of persons, the lawyers proceeded actively to criminalize certain types of deviance.[3] This 'invention of the penal' is well known to specialists, but its true significance has not always been appreciated. The spectacular tortures inflicted on regicides, homosexuals, witches and those who contested the dogmas of the established religion have monopolized attention. This has obscured major phenomena, commonplace but crucial: the surveillance of bodies and souls was increased not so much through fear of public execution and exposure of the shameful remains as by the construction of a new type of relationship between the spectators and the sovereign power. In other words, the role expected of subjects, and also the role they accepted, acquired a quite different dimension. Specialists today no longer discuss the modern state in terms of the cold

119

monster once presented by Michel Foucault.[4] They prefer to speak of a central power capable of listening to the complaints and prayers of the governed, which was the only way to appear a just and Christian authority, and not a tyranny. These specialists believe that the legal and moral rules that the state defended were not only prescribed but 'acclimatized', as they circulated between the top and the bottom of the social pyramid, under the influence of those who asked for them and those who oversaw their implementation. State power may have intensified or, to be more precise, become denser, but the mass of individuals affected, from humble supplicants to the intermediaries who put the innovations into practice locally, derived benefits from their contact, however fleeting and perfunctory, with what has been called a 'domination desirous of being accepted'.[5]

Though a salutary reaction to the extreme interpretations of the 1970s, which emphasized the state as Leviathan, the new historiographical trend goes too far when it forgets the notions of subjection and subordination; this was an age of far more hierarchical power relations than before and of massive intolerance. The trend has drawn attention, however, to an obvious fact that is too rarely taken into account: every power needs a minimum of consensus regarding the theories and practices it seeks to get accepted. Modern justice was not simply imposed on the masses. It seemed to many of them to have advantages, not least the city-dwellers who had long called for a security that was not constantly challenged by the law of vengeance, leading to a lethal violence that was too readily accepted.[6]

It is for this reason that homicide and infanticide were literally invented as inexpiable crimes from the first third of the sixteenth century, during a veritable 'judicial revolution'. They were part of a new pact sealed between the modern monarchies and the 'better sort' among the inhabitants; in other words, the adult males from the local elites who dominated and controlled the urban and rural communities. They were alike in wishing to consolidate social control in order to promote a greater sense of security in a period of serious unrest and conflict. The legal proceedings in the case of homicide and infanticide, though they varied in detail, were remarkably similar in all the principal Western countries. The very spectacular and elaborate staging of the corporal punishments designed to punish murderers, a majority of whom were young unmarried men, defined both one of the worst imaginable deviancies and the opposite normative figure of the young man who was obedient to God, the king, his father and his master, curbed his aggression and no longer carried a weapon. Only the aristocrats, in principle dedicated to war, claimed this last right as an exclusive monopoly. The execution of women who concealed their pregnancy or killed their baby, most of whom were unmarried, revealed the only two antagonistic options open to the daughters of Eve, namely to opt for the devil, like the witches or like Medea, unnatural parent who exterminated her progeny, or be a good, gentle, timid and submissive mother.

For both sexes, the court was a formidable theatre in which it was necessary to know how to play the social role assigned to have a chance of escaping execution. The latter was a sign not so much of the greater ferocity of the representatives of a supposedly pitiless state as of the desire to monopolize the inflicting of death in order to make this act less ordinary than it generally was at that time. As there was no easy way of detaching people from their longstanding taste for violence and bloodletting, the legal spectacle distanced physical suffering from the huge crowds it attracted and firmly associated it with the royal, God-given, sole right to punish. The trend towards less horrific forms of public execution visible everywhere in Europe from the mid seventeenth century, a hundred years before the criticisms of the *philosophes* of the Enlightenment, marked a new acceleration in the process of controlling murderous brutality. Through the changing forms of public judicial punishment, the central authorities, local intermediaries and populations engaged in a constant dialogue on the subject of the value that should be accorded to human life. Together they invented ways of controlling the explosive murderous potential of young men and of limiting the disastrous effects of feminine lustfulness outside marriage.

A judicial revolution

The metaphor of the theatre of judicial cruelty is not new. To restore it to its full importance, however, we need first to clear away the false ideas surrounding it. The phenomenon was neither medieval nor linked to the ecclesiastical Inquisition. It was the product of a remarkable standardization on the continent, some time by the first third of the sixteenth century, of the battle against the threats regarded by governments as the most serious. In statistical terms, these were homicide, infanticide and violence of every type. Robbery might be as frequent as assaults against persons in the records of some law courts, but, unlike them, it was only exceptionally punished by death. Severity was largely reserved for robbery on the highway or for acts accompanied by aggravating circumstances, such as murderous brutality and sacrilege.[7] Spectacular though these may be in the eyes of the historian, like the quartering of the regicide Damiens in 1757, all the other offences accounted for only a minority, even minuscule percentages, of those that were tried.

At the end of the nineteenth century, Durkheim claimed that a decline in the number of murders distinguished the civilized countries from the rest, and that their persistence characterized the remote areas, the rural world and the Catholic regions. For him, 'the supreme immoral acts are murder and theft'.[8] This ethical position, which is surprising today in the social sciences, nevertheless opens the way to a fruitful interpretation, if we accept that the main aim of the law is to draw a moral boundary by defining the norm by means of the spectacle of the punishment of deviances. From 1550 to 1650, all states, Catholic or Protestant, identified homicide and infanticide as two major and particularly dangerous forms of extreme turpitude. Theft assumed this role in the eighteenth century. In all three cases, the punishments prescribed, including the death sentence, were applied largely to the young: unmarried male murderers, pregnant girls who killed their baby or failed to declare their pregnancy, adolescents of both sexes who resorted to theft in huge metropolises such as London and Paris. The identifiable common denominator in the repression of these capital offences is not the 'absolutist' form of the state, or the evolution of economic structures towards commercial capitalism, or the overly vague 'civilizing process'. It is essentially cultural, that is, a massive Western effort, after the Renaissance, to impose an authoritarian control on the new masculine and feminine generations. The process was dependent, obviously, on the advance of the state, the desire for greater personal security and the need to soften highly conflictual human relations in order to transform societies dominated by the law of private vengeance. Its centre of gravity, however, lay elsewhere. It was the result of a fierce permanent negotiation between the central powers and the adult males who ruled the communities, aimed at defining effective means and methods capable of 'fabricating' a docile youth, in the form of theoretical prohibitions, but also of activity at the local level. Given that the objectives of the two parties did not always coincide, criminal justice and the scaffold became the principal symbolic sites for the quest for a consensus as delicate as it was shifting. Adolescence was slowly invented as an age that was disruptive of internal peace, and which must be closely supervised so as to channel its unsettling energy.

Such transformations were the result of a major change of scale in European civilization, an expansion of its perspectives after the discovery of America and the spread of the Italian Renaissance. Murderous violence had until then been part of the masculine rituals for learning about life and the adult role. It had been a private act, but essentially part of a communitarian management of the problem, and it had left young men with great latitude to demonstrate their manliness by wounding, even killing, each other. In the last resort, it was in the interests of fathers to tolerate a practice that deflected the aggression of their sons, as they waited in the wings, away from them and primarily against their peers.

The docility of the young before the local worthies, who treated their offspring like servants to be exploited at will before marriage, was achieved at the cost of blood.

The powerful feudal seigneurs of the late Middle Ages, the dukes of Burgundy, Lorraine and Brittany, and even more the great sovereigns such as the kings of France, England and Portugal, tried, nevertheless, to introduce a more repressive judicial system. A Christian prince had a mission to keep the peace between his subjects and to ensure that they observed the Biblical commandment not to kill another human being. The princes proceeded to claim as their own the divine right of life and death. They granted, therefore, an increasing number of pardons in the form of *lettres de rémission*. Though without challenging the mechanism of the private peace, which was still an obligation towards the family of a victim, these documents established a general monarchical case law. From the fifteenth century, they gradually linked the pardon to the accidental, unpremeditated character of a homicide, which made it possible little by little to distinguish this act from deliberate murder. The latter was made a royal case, called a felony in England, and punished much more severely. This process accelerated in the sixteenth century. To take the life of another then truly became a crime, perceived as such all over Europe by jurists whose works, in translation, disseminated everywhere the same definitions. One of the most famous, Josse de Damhouder of Bruges, spoke of 'the second crime which appeared on earth' after that of Adam and Eve. The terminology gradually became fixed, differentiating two forms of the phenomenon, one simple, called *homicide* in French, *totschlag* in German and 'manslaughter' in English, the other called *meurtre et assassinat* or 'murder'.[9]

Although it was neither uniform nor complete, the criminalization of homicide was generally achieved by the mid seventeenth century in most European countries. The Bernese, once masters of the Pays de Vaud, had by 1549 created an imperial court responsible for punishing acts of violence and premeditated murder. In the Low Countries, Philip II issued criminal ordinances inspired by Damhouder in 1570 and embarked on a vigorous campaign against the 'large number of homicides which are committed daily'. In France, the royal jurists advised that the excuse of legitimate self-defence should no longer be so readily accepted, and that torture should be used in doubtful cases. There were even some who argued that, as malicious intent was presumed in such an act, it was not for the prosecution to provide proof but for the defence to show that it had been an accident or a lawful desire to save a life under threat. They did not yet claim that whoever killed deserved death, like Muyart de Vouglans in the eighteenth century, but they urged a major tightening-up of practice. So, in the *parlement* of Bordeaux between 1510 and 1565, the desire to instil fear inspired an increasingly pitiless procedure which strictly limited the rights of the defence.[10] The same was true of the *parlement* of Paris between 1575 and 1604.[11] The French Criminal Ordinance of 1670 confirmed these changes by expressly confining *lettres de rémission* to unpremeditated acts or acts 'committed in the necessity of a legitimate defence of life'. From 1590, repression was greatly stepped up in the Swedish towns, a process that culminated in the following decades. The subsequent marked decline in the number of homicides prosecuted, also observed in Finland under Swedish rule, seems to have been primarily due to a decline in the number committed by members of the upper social ranks.[12] In Castile, the trend was later, but similar, as shown by a sudden upsurge in death sentences in Madrid in the second half of the seventeenth century, followed by a sharp decline until the middle of the next century. The night-time violence of bands of young men aged under twenty-nine was the principal target and it was pursued with equal zeal in the rural areas, which led to a sharp drop in the statistics for murder by the beginning of the eighteenth century.[13]

Everywhere, the role of the criminal courts changed. It was no longer their principal objective to reconcile the adversaries, but rather to instil guilt in and punish harshly those who committed homicide. The reasons usually advanced to explain this change, as radical as it was rapid, after a millennium of great tolerance, are hardly satisfactory. They highlight the escalation of cruelty at the time of the Wars of Religion, the progress of Roman law throughout the continent, and technical developments in weaponry which made it possible to kill at a distance and often made the injuries inflicted more serious. Yet the seventeenth century saw significant advances in surgery and treatment, which helped to make the consequences of such injuries less disastrous.[14] If we want to understand why such an ancient system suddenly became obsolete in the space of a few generations, we need to identify the needs of the people, as without the underlying agreement of at least some of them, the changes proposed by the authorities would have been impossible to apply for any length of time or in any depth.

There seems, at this period, to have been a deep desire for effective action by governments to remedy a situation that had become a source of major anxiety, in terrible times marked by instability, insecurity and a variety of conflicts. It was only with the active support of the populations that this could happen. No plaintiffs, no justice! Furthermore, far from being paralysed by the legal innovations imposed, ordinary people, and in particular the peasantry, were well able to select what suited them, adapt it to their own traditions and devise subtle strategies.[15] Thus certain capital crimes, such as rape and bestiality, were very rarely denounced in villages, although they were probably common. The local law of silence seems to have operated to spare the perpetrators a terrible fate, given that no one could be unaware of the severity of the magistrates: the *parlement* of Paris ordered fifty-five executions for the 104 cases of bestiality brought before it between 1564 and 1639. The culprits were mostly lads of peasant origin, aged between fourteen and twenty, almost all caught in the act.[16] The lack of denunciations, and even more of rumours, to initiate trials suggests a juvenile custom that was widespread but tacitly tolerated, as long as it was not performed openly and publicly. Similarly, non-aggravated theft continued, at least in the sixteenth century, to be treated leniently by the courts. Nor was it often prosecuted in the countryside, though it is abundantly attested by sources such as the ecclesiastical monitories. The magistrates' focus on homicide and infanticide, by contrast, resulted in their harsh repression, because the communities concerned were much readier to accept it and got something out if it. They incorporated the innovations into their traditional culture because they could benefit from them. The defence of honour remained a fundamental objective, but it was now equally well, or even better, assured by recourse to an intimidating justice than by a murderous fight. The law of vengeance was weakened as a result, and that of silence broken, when blood was shed. It was centuries before the same was true of arson, theft, incest or deviant sexual behaviour, which were still usually regulated by private agreement to avoid unnecessary cost and public humiliation.

The selective acceptance by the ordinary people of the towns and the countryside of this process of criminalization reveals both their self-interest and their perception of their own vulnerability, for which they needed the assistance of the authorities. The fact that they accepted in particular the challenge to the violence of young men and sexual freedom of unmarried girls suggests a wider malaise. The old were finding it increasingly difficult to transmit the customary values to the rising generations in a profoundly disturbed world. The centuries-old procedures for learning adult roles were still functioning, but the mechanism appeared to be breaking down. The tolerance in these matters seems to have lessened, a sign of muted unease among established adults in the face of young men and women who had as yet nothing, and whose demands they feared. The crisis, apparent all over Europe around 1520, coincided with a period of population pressure after a long period of reconstruction.[17] The rural exodus and the refusal of the towns to accept the impoverished crowds who pressed at their gates seemed to be spiralling. Marginality became a massive and deeply troubling phenomenon. The authorities tried without much success to fight against pauperism, which was on the increase because poverty forced rootless unemployed young people – many of them peasants – into begging and delinquency. The infernal cycle began with theft, so as to survive. It was followed by ear-cropping and expulsion, which led on to gang robbery, culminating, for those without hope, regarded as 'useless', on the gibbet. In parallel, the development of bitter religious conflicts, after Luther's stand in 1519, and the sudden outbreak of the great German peasant revolts, unleashed further waves of anxiety. In short, the West was shaken by a general crisis in the first decades of the sixteenth century. The strengthening of the powers of states and of the antagonistic Churches, and the development of a more effective criminal justice, were attempts to stem this tide. It was more than a century before a new equilibrium was established; it became visible only around 1650.

The new morality of the age of 'confessionalization' did not derive only from the choices of a few rulers advised by men of the church. It sprang, at a deeper level, from a need felt at the heart of every parish. Locally, the danger came from a variety of disruptive factors, including internal breakdown, pillaging by soldiers, opposing religious choices and outbursts of extreme violence. As the age of marriage began to be delayed, precisely when the law and religion were issuing stricter prohibitions on sexual relations outside marriage, the figure of the 'adolescent', male or female, began to emerge as yet one more source of anxiety. Relations between the generations became more strained in a context of increasing tension. It is for these reasons that the new judicial definitions of homicide and infanticide were favourably received. They offered an additional means of controlling the young, who were profoundly disturbed, even more vulnerable than the rest of the population, because it was they who felt the full force of the many prohibitions regarding the customary festive boisterousness, dancing and sex outside marriage. Faced with increasing tensions among the young, the communities found a way of strengthening the cohesion that was threatened by the 'innovations' imposed from outside. The constant popular revolts of the period had a cultural dimension in that they represented a collective defence of traditions.[18] Not enough attention has been paid to the fact that the acceptance of part of the new judicial system served identical ends, but more subtly. Without altogether repudiating the old pacificatory practices, the worried established adults protected themselves even more effectively by brandishing the threat of a judicial complaint – now more likely to succeed – against murderous young men or debauched girls. The adults thus deflected responsibility for the punishment onto the authorities who imposed respect for the law. The sword of Damocles suspended over the heads of young people, whose aggression was exacerbated by the spate of changes to their world, helped to reassure their fathers, without further endangering the already weakened cohesion of the local group.

A cultural history attentive to the reception of the norms – and not only to their production – makes it possible to understand why, from the sixteenth century, a radically different judicial system so quickly took root in Europe. It did not do this everywhere nor did it totally replace private methods of dispute-settlement and it only slowly substituted for the law of vengeance, which is sometimes still alive today, for example in the Mediterranean islands. But it slowly supplanted these ancient habits, helped by that fact that it was often seen as an additional way of reaching the classic compromise. In England, the initiative was wholly dependent on a private plaintiff. In Roman law countries like France, representatives of the king could begin an action, but the various costs involved greatly restricted the number of cases. More than 75 per cent of those dealt with by the *sénéchaussées* of Libourne and Bazas in the eighteenth century still originated in a private initiative. Further, the proceedings were often intended more to force the adversary into a settlement than to obtain a formal verdict against him. In fact, many accusers abandoned the case as soon as an agreement was reached. The same phenomenon can be seen in seventeenth-century Spain, in the *Montes* of Toledo, where over half the complaints resulted in a compromise without a judgement. Called *amistads* in Spanish, *paci e tregue* in Florence, *Sühnevertragen* in German and *accommodements* in France, these agreements often followed direct negotiations if the opponents were of equal social standing. When this was not the case, arbitrators, sometimes chosen from among the judges, continued, as in the Middle Ages, to offer their services in parallel with the development of the modern justice of the state.[19] The growing acceptance of the law visible everywhere in Europe until the end of the *ancien régime* thus presents an ambiguity. People accepted it not only under pressure from the central powers, but because they found it had advantages for them, in particular as an additional means of putting pressure on an adversary and as a protection against any subsequent vengeance from that quarter. As we have seen, those most favourable to it were the well-established adult males who dominated local life. In England these people of 'the middling sort' served on juries and filled the posts of constable, responsible for keeping public order. They were called 'elders' in Germany, or defined themselves as 'the better part' of the population, sitting on village assemblies in France and in the Spanish Low Countries.[20] Some were influenced by the moralization of behaviour associated with the 'civilizing process' coming from the courts and the towns. Others simply accepted what was most useful to them to strengthen their power in the parish, and make their enemies fear them and everyone obey them, especially their own children as they progressed towards adulthood.

This was no easier for them than it was for the supposedly absolute princes. The strengthening of authority was an obsession of the age, at all levels. However, the means for achieving it were limited. The cleverest way, adopted by the Churches and the monarchs, was to invoke the divine right to supervise closely both bodies and souls. However, this project was still dependent on the goodwill of the population, which made the bodies charged with the task of ensuring the effective supervision of morals in the localities even more important. This new responsibility devolved on Protestant consistories, churchwardens in England and Catholic priests hearing auricular confession. They were primarily concerned with supervising the 'weak', who must as a priority be given a Christian education, especially women, too easily taken in by the devil, and the young, 'virgin wax' on which sin so easily made its mark. To be effective, these intermediaries needed to work through the fathers of families. This inevitably enhanced their authority, which is why the most important of them quickly agreed to accept the 'judicial revolution' which confirmed their superiority, albeit selectively.

The fact was, all the groups seeking to exercise power were mutually dependent. The officially decreed assault on the traditions of ritual youth violence produced a fraught situation. There was no properly constituted force in existence that could either deal with disturbances or prevent them. If there was a popular revolt, the army had to be sent in to put it down. Security in the parishes was assured by the inhabitants alone, except in the towns, where there were a handful of sergeants and an urban watch of burgesses. The police, in the modern sense of the term, existed in a centralized form in only a few countries. The *maréchaussée*, set up in the thirteenth century by the marshals of France to control the armies, subsequently took on supervision of the kingdom's highways and homeless delinquents. To deal with the growing insecurity, aggravated by the rural exodus and the laying-off of soldiers from the Italian wars, Francis I decided in 1520 to create thirty companies, each directed by a provost, assisted by a lieutenant, a clerk and ten men. It was only in the reign of Louis XIV, with the reform of 1720, that this force was reorganized. A single company, divided into brigades, usually of four or five men, was allocated to every rural zone. The total number enlisted – 4,144 in 1789 – reveals the limits of their activity, though foreign travellers regarded the country as the safest in Western Europe. An identical structure, introduced by the duke of Burgundy in the fifteenth century, existed in the Low Countries. In Spain, the Santa Hermandad fulfilled a similar role before it became the Guardia Civil in 1835. Of the great European cities, only Paris, from 1667, had a specific organization, the lieutenancy of police, whose commissioners, inspectors and 3,000 officers watched over some 600,000 inhabitants by the end of the eighteenth century. London still awaited the creation of the 'bobbies'.[21]

The growth of torture and the spectacle of public executions make sense from this perspective. The initial objective was certainly to terrorize those who were tempted to disobey the divine precepts of which the prince was the guardian. By demonstrating that the eagle eye of the king was everywhere, preventive dissuasion was also one of the principal missions assigned to the Parisian lieutenant of police. He was responsible, in particular, for maintaining grain stocks to prevent riots, and for keeping all suspects under surveillance, employing a large number of spies, or *mouches*. The nascent modern state was all the more eager to instil fear in that it lacked real means to punish the majority of delinquents, who escaped it. The excesses of this symbolic terrorization were slowly abandoned, from the second half of the seventeenth century, because the power of the central authority grew and its message was increasingly effectively transmitted by the principal heads of families in each parish.

Contrary to the descriptions of Foucault, based on the eighteenth century, the spectacle of legal tortures essentially lasted only for a short period, that of the imposition in Europe of a judicial revolution which transformed the accusatorial medieval system into a formidable inquisitorial procedure. England alone retained the old practice of citizen juries, presided over by a judge, and rejected the use of torture except when authorized by the king or the Privy Council, largely confined to the period 1540 to 1640. Everywhere else at this period, a new penal code was instituted, which drew both on the heritage of Roman law and on that of the ecclesiastical Inquisition.[22] It was written, secret and required proof before reaching a judgement: there had to be two eyewitnesses to the offence or a confession by the accused. The decision was taken by a college of judges and not by juries from the people. The power of the magistrates was greatly increased, in particular that of the members of the French *parlements*. From the second half of the sixteenth century and until the apogee of the system in the middle of the next century, they had a free choice of penalties giving them the discretionary right to reach a decision on the basis of simple presumption.[23] If the proofs were insufficient but serious evidence existed, counted as fractions of proof, torture was considered necessary so as to obtain a confession. It thus became a crucial stage in the criminal process by the end of the fifteenth century. Practice was codified in the major states at almost the same time, during the course of the second third of the sixteenth century. The Holy Roman Empire obeyed the *Constitutio Criminalis Carolina* passed in 1532, France the edict of Villers-Cotterêts of 1539, Spain the *Nueva Recopilación* of 1567 and the Low Countries the criminal ordinance of Philip II in 1570.

Far from being an aberration, or evidence of bestial savagery, as has been claimed by many historians shocked by its use, in the footsteps of the *philosophes* of the Enlightenment, putting someone to the 'question' was perfectly normal in the eyes of contemporaries. It was even regarded as indispensable in certain circumstances. It was tightly codified, closely supervised and inflicted without emotion or morbid pleasure. Its aim was to make a hidden truth emerge, revealed not by the suffering itself but by the bodily signs induced by the pain, such as the pallor regarded as an indication of guilt, and, even more, by confession.[24] It could not, on principle, be administered to the weak, the old, pregnant women or children. It was inflicted in a variety of ways, according to place. In the *parlement* of Paris it was 'by water', that is, by forcing the patient to ingest large quantities of liquid. It was used only on a minority of persons, who were under a high degree of suspicion. Even then, it was sometimes felt to be enough, in France and also in Germany, in the context of the torture *mit Güte* ('without pain'), to terrify the suspect by presenting them with the instruments of torture, without necessarily using them. Those who refused to confess, in either case, saved their life because they could not be sentenced to a corporal punishment and had to be set free. In which case the magistrates, reluctant to recognize their total innocence, usually decreed an *hors de cour* or *plus ample informé*, which left the suspect under threat of a reopening of proceedings if new facts came to light. The *parlement* of Paris after 1535, and that of Bordeaux around 1550–65, sometimes ordered the question 'with reserves of proof', which automatically involved a punishment, even in the absence of a confession, but stopping short of the supreme penalty.[25] In France and some other countries *question préparatoire* ('preparatory torture') was distinguished from *question préalable* ('preliminary torture'); the latter was inflicted without restrictions or precautions on some of those condemned to death, just before their execution, to force them to denounce their accomplices.

The golden age of judicial torture was generally confined to the sixteenth and early seventeenth centuries. The *parlement* of Paris applied it to 20 per cent of the criminals from its vast area of competence in 1533–42, compared with 5 per cent in 1620. Murderers always provided more than two-fifths of the total, even more than half in the first decade of the seventeenth century, whereas thieves, the only other significant category, were increasingly less often subjected to torture, a maximum of 7 per cent around 1610.[26] It is clear that the judges were using this method in an attempt to distinguish self-defence, often pleaded by suspects, from premeditated murder. The *parlement* of Brittany subjected 5 per cent to *question préparatoire* in the first half of the seventeenth century, but less than 1 per cent in the second half of the century; the use of *question préalable* fell from 27 per cent to 13 per cent in the same period. The *parlement* of Toulouse was accused of exceptional cruelty and fanaticism by the *philosophes* of the Enlightenment, who were revolted by the punishment inflicted on Calas in 1762, but it tortured only 68 persons between 1600 and 1788. Further, there was a marked reduction in the use of torture in the first half of the seventeenth century, by as much as 50 per cent between 1640 and 1660. An identical phenomenon happened a little later in the courts of Germany. In Frankfurt, the rate fell from 59 per cent in 1562–94 to 15 per cent in 1661–96, and from 44 per cent in 1650 to 16 per cent in 1690 in the case of the council of Bavaria. French judicial centralization explains the precocity and the scale of the decline, because the *parlement*s, following that of Paris, which set the tone for the whole kingdom, gradually imposed automatic appeals for any sentence of torture decreed in a lower court. Not only does this makes the percentages calculated for the sovereign courts more reliable, but the effectiveness of the principle emerges in the case of the *sénéchaussée* of Libourne between 1696 and 1789, where only one example of the use of torture is recorded for the 1,529 persons accused.[27]

The decline of the practice was accompanied, particularly in Toulouse, by an increasingly strong discourse of validation, which insisted on the importance and gravity of torture, claiming that pain made it possible to accede to the truth, necessarily revealed by the suffering body. This reasoning was based on a theological reading of the world by lawyers. Muyart de Vouglans was still defending it in 1780, attaching an eminent value to corporal punishment because it was an aid, he claimed, to the salvation of the soul. It is from this perspective that we must seek to understand the spectacle of corporal punishments and public executions. In both cases, great changes had begun to appear by the middle of the seventeenth century, even though the punitive rituals appeared to remain set in stone until the French Revolution.[28]

In pursuit of the ungrateful son: the spread of the blood taboo

The judicial revolution of the sixteenth century was accompanied by a massive increase in the number of public punishments, executions in particular. Unlike the medieval towns, which had fined or expelled criminals, and the monarchs, who, through lack of resources, had concentrated their efforts on the 'atrocious' or 'royal' cases they saw as the most serious, the new justice aspired to educate subjects through a salutary terror.[29] In the Germanic countries, the phenomenon grew from 1500, then rapidly declined in the first half of the seventeenth century. The chronology in England is virtually identical in the case of homicide, but the death penalty, which was used in particular for thieves, remained very common in the eighteenth century. Huge crowds, some estimated at nearly 100,000 people, flocked to Tyburn to watch the hangings ordered by the London judges. Almost all the murderers brought before the courts in Amsterdam were executed, but they numbered scarcely more than one a year for a town of 200,000 inhabitants, and this type of spectacle also became less common during the seventeenth century. In Finland, death sentences for homicide and infanticide greatly increased around 1620–30, after a change of procedure reflecting a greater determination to prove the guilt of the accused.[30]

All over Europe, capital punishment was a veritable sacred theatre, which conveyed many messages. First and foremost, it validated the power of the prince and that of his judges. However, it also demonstrated the power and prestige of the great cities: the gibbet at Tyburn, the scaffold erected in the Place de Grève in Paris and the Columns of Justice in Venice were symbols which made even the most hardened criminals blench, while at the same time reassuring honest folk. And it provided some sort of release for those who came with avid curiosity to watch the legal suffering of a tortured person, and tried to carry off some relic that had belonged to them for protective or magical purposes. The contemplation of a body humiliated, mutilated, martyred, tortured, hanged, decapitated, burnt or broken on the wheel both satisfied a well-documented popular taste for violence and blood and established a distance, as this gradually became a taboo. The public execution was a way of educating the sensibilities; it produced an effect of the sacred, by means of a gripping ceremonial that was the same all over the continent. It accustomed those present to withdraw from murderous practices in favour of representations of them, which were alone validated by the law. The constant repetition of this event in the towns attracted crowds from the surrounding countryside and it played a fundamental role in helping them to purge their emotions, as did the theatre of Shakespeare, Marlowe and Corneille at the same time. Thus a sort of pact of an economy of blood was established between the king as dispenser of justice and his people. The latter began gradually to perceive in a more concrete fashion the importance of the Christian message of peace and the limitation of violence propagated by the sovereign, who claimed to have a monopoly on the killing of human beings. Paradoxically, life assumed greater importance in everyone's eyes by being taken away publicly, solemnly and seriously, without hatred or emotion, in the name of the justice delegated to the prince by God.

The same ethic was conveyed by other means, through an emphasis on the disastrous consequences of the passions, which led to a spiral of criminality and ultimately damnation. In 1609, in *Le procès civil et criminel*, Claude Le Brun de la Rochette described the inexorable descent into hell that was associated with idleness, mother of all evils. He placed the latter in four categories, in ascending order of gravity: lechery – which included the various sexual offences; larceny; public or private force – in other words, violence against persons; divine or human lese-majesty. For Le Brun de la Rochette they fed off each other – larceny was 'eldest son of poverty, engendered by lechery'.[31] Homicide thus topped the list of the most serious crimes. It was implicitly linked to regicide through the intermediary of parricide. Considered the most infamous of murders, parricide was then interpreted as including any act or attempt against the life of a close relative, even that of a master by an apprentice; it was doubly punished, by death preceded by the severing of a hand. There is no need to resort to Freud to understand that the lawyers of the Baroque age constructed the prohibition on blood as a series of stages, starting with the ultimate model of the assassination of the sovereign or a great prince, like Henri III and Henri IV in France and William the Silent in the Low Countries. The theory was designed first to strengthen the sacredness of the royal person, in order to counter the tyrannicidal ideas circulating in troubled and unsettled times. Next, it led to an increase in the value put on the life of men of power and judges, whose assassination was punished in exemplary fashion, then on that of fathers of families, and after that, little by little, on that of all subjects. Even though life had a different price according to social position, an attempt on it acquired something of the diabolic aura projected by the concept of lese-majesty, which made it possible to demand unwavering severity towards those guilty of that. The legists revived and adapted to their own age the old Christian commandment: 'Thou shalt not kill', which had been something of a dead letter in the preceding centuries.

The exceptionally cruel punishment reserved for the regicide made it the essential axis of the divine vengeance exercised by its representatives on earth. The imperative necessity of punishing all murderers followed from this. If they lacked the excuse of self-defence or accident, they must ineluctably suffer a law of revenge that was legalized, moralized and developed as an edifying spectacle for the masses. The change was fundamental, when we remember that this had not previously been the case. In the past, young men had injured each other in play and killed each other without deep remorse, almost sure of receiving a royal pardon. The religious culture of the jurists meant that they drew on the Bible to bring out the extreme horror of this act. Damhouder regarded it as a direct consequence of original sin and spoke of the 'second crime', which had appeared immediately after that of Adam and Eve. His contemporaries knew that he was referring to the odious act of Cain, son of Adam, who killed his brother Abel from jealousy. The Christian connotation merged with the implicit definition of man as a creature profoundly sinful by nature, disobedient to the most sacred laws. After Adam, his son had broken God's commandment and all their descendants risked doing the same, unless, that is, they were dissuaded by the fear of a pitiless punishment. The much stricter repression of murder thus developed ad infinitum the theme of the paternal bond. He who killed his companion from a festive kingdom of youth, or a rival of similar age from a neighbouring parish, now seemed as much of a danger to social peace as he who killed his brother or his father. The image of Cain was implicit in the sentences passed and in the proliferating decrees punishing homicidal violence. This was all the more obvious in that it matched the youthful characteristics of the majority of those accused, and there were few women in this category, except in the very specific case of infanticide. To use the terminology of our own age, the accusation of murder was now subliminally associated with the male adolescent.

Moralists and preachers disseminated everywhere the same definitions of the murderous violence caused by the weakness and sins of the descendants of Adam begotten by Cain. These definitions were transmitted by new media to the mass of the people as well as to the upper ranks of society. The *canards*, little illustrated pamphlets sold cheaply in the streets of Paris, especially between 1575 and 1631, and aimed at the former, told stories with a strong moral slant, especially accounts of crimes.[32] The tragic tales of François de Rosset, published in 1619, and those of the prolific bishop of Belley, Jean-Pierre Camus, a decade later, both huge bestsellers in their day, shaped the taste of the bourgeoisie and the nobility. They told of violence, love and ambition. They were moralizing in intent, and they taught their readers how to conduct themselves before the law, divine and human, by describing examples of transgression followed by an inevitable punishment. Camus wrote nearly a thousand such stories after 1630, the year of publication of his two most famous collections, *L'Ampitéâtre sanglant* and *Les Spectacles d'horreur*. So as to edify through terror, each one culminated in a notably bloodthirsty final catastrophe, which led the suffering man, penitent or martyr, towards redemption. The fashion for them was short-lived, however, over by the 1640s.[33] These various literary forms, adapted to very different publics, were complemented by large numbers of engravings on similar themes aimed at the illiterate, and together they propagated to saturation point examples of bloody brutality, murder and misery. They were associated with the powerful upsurge of Catholicism and the Baroque at the beginning of the reign of Louis XIII in France, and they warned their readers, especially in the towns, against the extremes of the human passions, in particular if they were linked to homicide or sexuality. Their exact chronological coincidence with the age of torture was not by chance. They were all part of a multiform pedagogy aiming to distance sinners as far as possible from worldly temptations and the demands of the body, so that they could achieve eternal salvation. There were similar developments in other countries, most notably the Germanic *Teufelsbücher*, written between 1545 and 1604 by Lutheran pastors in order to teach people about the snares of the devil.

Public executions conveyed in powerful images the sensations and sentiments experienced by the consumers of these works. Like them, and like the Baroque theatre, the executions assuaged, in the distanced form of a spectacle, an ancient taste for cruelty and the brutal expression of the desires, which continued to motivate very real acts of violence. The executions also slowly helped to strengthen a rejection – ethical in origin, vigorously promoted by religious morality and insistently repeated by the legists – of blood shed too freely and of lustfulness, in particular that attributed to women. With terrible regularity, the death penalty demonstrated to one and all that these two mortal sins were an obstacle to the attainment of eternal happiness. Thus the punitive theatre became the site of a sacred communion between the established powers and the people. The latter were not nearly as shocked as the *philosophes* of the Enlightenment, who saw judicial atrocities as proof of the tyranny of absolute monarchs. Recent research has shown that ordinary people welcomed these practices, which they believed were necessary to the restoration of order in a world disrupted by the criminal who mounted the scaffold.[34]

Perceptions varied, nevertheless, according to social group, because everyone found an echo of their own culture in these practices. The cruellest forms of execution have been linked by some scholars to ancient beliefs destined to ward off the vengeance of the dead. This was the case in the Germanic world with decapitation, dismembering and the custom of leaving the corpses of the hanged on the gibbet. The breaking wheel, which was imported from Germany into France by Francis I and used until the Revolution for the most fearsome bandits, including Mandrin and Cartouche in the eighteenth century, suggested the magical symbol of the circle, and perhaps also an ancient conception locating the soul and life in the skeleton. To break the bones was to remove any possibility of a return of the ghost. The same was true of burning at the stake.[35] It was also an ultimate Christian punishment, accompanied by the scattering of the ashes, to prevent a resurrection at the time of the Last Judgement. To drive a wooden stake through the heart of a dead witch, as in Switzerland and the future Romania, was more a sign of fear that she might return to do harm to the living than an act of gratuitous cruelty. The same was true of burying a woman alive or the trial of the suicide's corpse, which was then dragged through the streets before being hung on the infamous forks.

So many meanings were attached to public execution because it was a prime site of cultural and social meditation. It played a crucial symbolic role, like human sacrifice among the Aztecs at the beginning of the sixteenth century. It should be seen as a sacrificial ceremony intended to produce consensus in a world which, since 1520, had been profoundly shaken by major crises. The staging of the event, which was remarkably similar throughout Europe, is one sign of this. It adopted medieval elements but gave them a much greater sacred significance. The declared objective remained the same, because the purpose was to execute someone while also offering them the possibility of a spiritual reintegration into the Christian community. The religious element was omnipresent. The condemned person was prepared for death by men of the church and accompanied in procession to the place of his Calvary. There were minor variations according to the country. In some parts of Spain, the victim was led on a donkey, as Christ had been; elsewhere, for example in Paris, they were taken on a cart. In Catholic France and in the Spanish Low Countries, the ritual was often accompanied by an *amende honorable*: stripped to his shirt, bareheaded, a large candle in his hand, the condemned man was forced to kneel before chapels and churches and at crossroads to beg the forgiveness of God, the king and the law. He was sometimes beaten with rods at the various halts. Many petty offenders, too, were subjected to a similar ritual of reconciliation. They might be asked to kiss the gallows, as a reminder of the fate that awaited them if they committed a more serious crime.[36]

For the others, the death sentence was read publicly after they had mounted the scaffold. They were granted a few moments in which they could address the crowd, to profess their repentance and to exhort the spectators to avoid making the same fatal mistakes.[37] This was a highly codified and tightly organized genre. Any rebels were rapidly reduced to silence by the executioner. Their tongue was sometimes cut out beforehand or they were stopped from speaking if the judges feared they might set a disastrous example to the audience. Yet some still managed to proclaim their revolt or their hatred, to blaspheme or to struggle. To avoid this, the *parlement* of Paris instructed its criminal clerks to be sure in advance of the cooperation of the condemned person and to persist until the last moment in the attempt to get them to make a public repentance. Documents incorrectly called 'last dying speeches' reveal the efforts made by the authorities to ensure that each occasion was a deeply edifying spectacle.[38] This sometimes extended to forgiveness for the executioner, a short prayer, kissing the cross and religious singing, taken up by the crowd. The executioner then did his job.

Very different visions of this 'art of dying' coexisted and intermingled on these occasions. On the one hand, the classically Christian liturgy conveyed a pedagogy of the last days, solemnly staged, and in the presence of representatives of the law and the established institutions. On the other, magical ways of thinking resurfaced, and were not confined to the lower classes. In England, hanging was treated like a wedding. It summoned up different conceptions of death, in particular the belief in the therapeutic powers of the corpse and the return of the dead.[39] People rushed to the scene to get their hands on a piece of the hangman's rope or a scrap of the victim's clothing, or a drop of blood after a beheading. It was widely believed in Denmark and Germany that to drink this blood was a cure for epilepsy. At night, treasure-hunters prowled round the foot of the gibbet in search of mandrake, a plant that resembled a homunculus, and was supposed to bring wealth and to spring from the male semen discharged during the erection caused by strangulation.

The execution was the site of a constant mix of scholarly and popular culture. Each drew closer to the other, but without wholly merging. The common people mostly accepted the phenomenon and played the role that was expected of them. The complaints recorded by educated observers, angered by the disorder, the noise and the shouting of the crowd, are evidence of a different sensibility, but not of the hostility of ordinary people to these practices. On the contrary, the occasion was turned into a sort of grand gala around a scene of legal brutality, which replaced the old, bloodthirsty entertainments that were now forbidden, in particular the doing to death of live animals and the ritual armed battles between young men. The romantic vision of mute opposition on the part of most of those who attended these spectacular executions, inherited from the Enlightenment, is based only on exceptions. Though these were numerous, they were always caused by a temporary rupture of the consensus, when the crowd believed that justice had not been properly done, as the ritual had been disrupted or conducted in an abnormal way. This was the case if the victim suffered needlessly at the hands of an inexperienced executioner, if he took several blows to sever a head, for example. His own life was then at risk at the hands of an angry crowd, who claimed a sort of right of vengeance against the incompetent official.

In fact, the increase in the number of death sentences invested the office of executioner with a more pronounced shameful dimension than it had possessed in the Middle Ages.[40] In the sacrificial liturgy, his indispensable task now appeared ignominious and, even more, frightening; he now killed frequently and he was the sole commoner legally possessed of this terrible right, delegated by the monarch. He was the dark face of the latter; he was both sacred and contemptible, banned from society, so greatly was he feared, and he bore on his own shoulders the whole weight of the accumulated prohibitions, religious but also magical. His role was even greater: he deflected from the person of the sovereign the anger of those under his jurisdiction, although it was from the sovereign that he got his power. 'Long live the king without the executioner!' might well have been a cry of the age, modelled on that of the peasants rebelling against the *gabelle* ('salt tax'). He served as a useful screen when the spectators spotted an 'injustice' or an excess of zeal, or took pity on a lovely woman, resigned to her fate, or a brave and charismatic man. The executioner even suffered the consequences of unpopular decisions made by the authorities. In England, in 1752, it was decreed that the corpses of hanged criminals should be handed over to the surgeons to be dissected, for the purposes of medical research and education. Scandalized relatives and friends started numerous riots, as this practice of total elimination, which already happened sporadically, was interpreted through a double culture, both religious and magical, that attached great importance to the integrity of the corpse of a deceased person. The situation was only aggravated by the obvious desire of the judges to use these 'marks of infamy' as a way of imposing a new discipline more generally on the people.[41]

Such revolts make it possible to identify a 'popular' conception which accepted the total validity of a torment that was deserved. Yet the crowd sometimes corrected, in one direction or another, a sentence it did not accept as legitimate. In Nuremberg, in 1612, the city messenger, sentenced by the local court only to a beating and banishment for treason and moral offences, was stoned to death by the crowd. On the other hand, in Paris, on 28 September 1582, the crowd freed a young man about to be hanged for having impregnated the daughter of the president of the Chamber of Accounts. His friends, who were armed, came to the rescue, joined by 'the majority of the people' present. Two sergeants were killed and others wounded, while a woman cut the bonds of the condemned man, who fled and was never found. The chronicler Pierre de l'Estoile explains how shocked people had been at the injustice of the *parlement*'s decision, when one of its own councillors had recently got away with a small fine for acts regarded as far worse. Added to which, the seduced girl, Artémise Bailly, had consistently claimed that she had consented, and that the couple had contracted a 'true and legitimate marriage' before having sexual relations. Her father, what is more, had a bad reputation because he slept with his chambermaid. The chronicler, a cultivated bourgeois, admitted to his own sympathy for the touching lovers, while at the same time accepting that violent rebellion against the authorities was pernicious and deserved to be punished. To distract attention, on 16 October next, the *parlement* hanged an out-and-out rogue, 'who they said couldn't do anything about it', observed l'Estoile. As he deserved his fate, the people did not protest. But they continued for a long time to laugh at the earlier trick they had played on the judges, and to revel in 'all sorts of romantic verses and bawdy epigrams' sold in the streets on the subject of Artémise, though her story turned out tragically; for, while her lover was safe, the little girl born of their love died a fortnight later and the heroine was shut up for life in the monastery of Montmartre.[42]

The populace often expressed strong feelings – inexpressible tenderness for a couple doomed to a terrible fate in one case, fierce hatred in another, pity frequently. They would not allow a hanged man who survived, or whose rope broke, to be hanged a second time. They forced the officials to respect the traditions of mercy. In France and in the Holy Roman Empire, they insisted on a pardon when a young virgin offered to marry a condemned man at the foot of the gallows. A man about to be hanged in Cologne, in 1561, received two such proposals in succession, both of which he refused. The spectators still demanded that he be spared; they threw stones at the executioner and then set the man free. More often, they suffered along with the victim or even tried to cut his misery short. The method of hanging then in use risked prolonging the agony, because the victim died not of a broken neck but by slow strangulation, struggling to the end. The hangman or his assistants or his wife often pulled on the legs to hasten his end. It was not unknown for the wretched victim's relatives or friends to force their way through and do the same.[43]

An observation of Montaigne in his chapter 'On cruelty' sheds light on this sort of collective attitude. He describes how he saw a notorious thief hanged in Rome:

> The crowd showed no emotion when he was strangled, but when they proceeded to quarter him the executioner never struck a blow without the people accompanying it with a plaintive cry and exclamation, as if each person had transferred his own feelings to that carcass.

Montaigne thought differently:

> My advice would be that exemplary severity intended to keep the populace to their duty should be practised not on criminals but on their corpses; for to see their corpses deprived of burial, boiled or quartered would strike the common people virtually as much as pains inflicted on the living.[44]

The gentle scholar whose good sense and tolerance are generally lauded was familiar with judicial realities, as he had been mayor of

Bordeaux. His remarks help us to understand, without anachronism, the attitude of the spectators before the suffering body, but also the purpose served by penal repression in the eyes of the authorities and the lawyers. As long as the punishment seemed normal and proportionate to the offence, the fascinated crowd watched without visible emotion. Not only did it accept the appropriateness of the punishment, but it put the condemned man at a distance from the community whose norms he had seriously transgressed. Yet the subsequent fate of the dismembered corpse caused an outpouring of emotion, because it involved a collective identification, made up of individual shudders, with this martyred carnal shell, unrelated to his crimes. Montaigne, who was deeply contemptuous of the 'common people', was in favour of exploiting this feeling. To strengthen the control of governments over populations, he recommended terrorizing them. The crucial element was probably not the violence or the morbidity of the spectacle itself but the shared anguish of the spectators, who understood the message without its having to be spelt out. Beyond the execution there loomed an even more intolerable fate: once dismembered or boiled, the corpse no longer possessed its integrity and was denied a tomb. The same applied in the case of the witches and heretics who were burned at the stake. The Christian dimension of such a punishment cannot alone explain its importance. It touched on an obsessive theme in popular culture, rural and urban, which explains the virulence of the London riots of 1752, when the hanged bodies were handed over to the surgeons. In the Spanish Low Countries Montaigne's proposals were already applied in the second third of the sixteenth century. The towns were surrounded by rings of corpses and human remains, bodies hanging from the gibbet, exposed half burned or on a wheel, heads stuck on pikes, severed hands, to discourage bandits from passing through the gates and to reassure the inhabitants in troubled times.[45]

This liturgy of fear, about which not enough is known, was designed to provoke fear in the living more than to punish the condemned in a notably barbarous fashion. Whether or not it turned people away from crime, it seems to have been successful in educating the population. The principal lesson they learned concerned the meaning of death. The theatre of execution linked it closely to religion, salvation and the actions of the king, through his judges, his officials and the executioner who represented him. Different perceptions also emerged. Linked to traditions and to magical beliefs, they related to the integrity of the body, the return of the dead and the ways in which this could be prevented. We may even ask if the huge increase in the number of corporal punishments and dismemberments of corpses, over a fairly short period, the second half

140

of the sixteenth and first decades of the seventeenth centuries, may have been more of a response to a need on the part of the masses than to the wishes of the elites. It may be that a long transitional period, and a constant reiteration of the visible 'proofs' provided by the ritual of executions, was necessary before the crowds could accept the Christian perception of the body and the non-return of the dead, except when the devil animated a corpse. At the very least these different conceptions were all present on such occasions.

The 'disciplining' of the social body could not have been achieved without the consent of the adult males who dominated parish and community life. Observing the increasing number of executions for homicide, a sign in their eyes of a great upsurge of insecurity, these men accepted the desire of the state to control it, as this enabled them to strengthen their own position locally, which seemed to be threatened on all sides. It is unlikely that they saw murder as a taboo, like Muyart de Vouglans, at the end of the *ancien régime*, when he spoke of 'this maxim of our public law which does not permit any person to take justice into their own hands and which wills that whoever kills is deserving of death'.[46] More pragmatically, it was in their own interests to prefer judicial mediation to a violence that had become extremely risky, which differentiated them from the young men who were still attached to the customs of manly brutality. Cultural migration does not happen without pain. In France, it took more than a century in the areas most closely controlled by the central government, much longer in remote or isolated regions such as the Auvergne. The *parlement* of Paris held its last Grand Jours ('extraordinary sessions') there in 1665–6, in an attempt to pacify a mountainous area still steeped in violence, where it was the gentlemen who were the principal agents of insecurity. Murders, acts of brutality, duals and the carrying of arms accounted for more than a half of the 692 identifiable crimes punished on that occasion. A total of 347 death sentences passed in absentia and 23 actual executions testify to the royal determination to take the situation in hand. Subsequently, a more routine treatment of criminality was enough to attach the region more firmly to the kingdom.[47] Other parts of France resisted these changes for longer, like Quercy, where violence was a distinguishing feature of the many popular revolts of the seventeenth century, and remained an insistent daily reality up to the nineteenth century.[48] The Mediterranean states worried less about this issue or were less able to impose their mediation, and here progress was slower and more hesitant. In Castile, prosecutions for homicide reached a peak in the seventeenth century. The curve then fell, though with another upsurge in the second half of the eighteenth century.[49] Each new wave of violence can be linked to weaknesses in the state and to generational effects. The traditional juvenile culture revived at regular intervals, before once again losing ground, until the last third of the twentieth century.

The principal process was that of a power struggle between the masculine age groups. The attitude of the established adults towards homicide was never the same as that of the authorities and magistrates, but it grew closer to it of necessity. In the attempt to avoid greater unrest and fiercer challenges on the part of the frustrated young men, they used the courts as a weapon of last resort when the customary forms of regulation proved inadequate. The formal complaint became a way of adding to the pressure to reach a settlement, including among rivals of similar social standing. Though it was often later abandoned, when a private agreement had been reached, so as to limit the costs of proceedings, it made it possible openly to demonstrate the superiority of he who had inflicted on his opponent the shame attaching to an appearance before the judges. The triumph was even more resounding if the trial ended in humiliating fashion for the defeated party, if he was forced to offer an apology or make honourable amends, or even delivered into the shaming hands of the executioner. The transition from a closed system of honour to a new form built around new norms, under the influence of criminal or civil justice, completely changed the game by introducing an external mediation that enhanced the prestige of the winner, but diminished that of the loser. Thus a new grade was inserted into the scale of self-esteem. Legal arbitration prepared the ground for a shift in social relations by binding the interested parties more closely to royal sovereignty. As Scandinavian research has shown, the mechanism of court appearances was an agent for change among the population as a whole.[50] It spun an invisible golden thread which firmly attached to the monarchy 'the better part of society', that is, the married and propertied men who wanted to defend their honour against any threat. The Europeans of the seventeenth century were not delivered body and soul to a many-tentacled state, to which they submitted through fear of torture; rather, they learned how to use the law courts to repair the communal fabric damaged by the great crises of the age. Those who wielded power locally did this without rejecting the traditions. On the contrary, they breathed new life into them in a context of general anxiety. They accepted the new official definition of homicide because it gave them, personally, better protection against dangers and challenges, without the need to resort to force or arms to defend their rights.

In France, royal declarations stipulated that private persons should be disarmed, notably in 1660 and 1666. In Paris, in 1673, the recently established lieutenant of police prohibited the valets and lackeys of noblemen, who had been responsible for numerous riots, from carrying sticks or canes.[51] Though they had little practical effect, such measures are emblematic of a desire to police the kingdom so as to reduce insecurity. What is important here is not the principle, clearly, which was already old, but the fact that it now met a need on the part of the people. All over Europe, in the mid seventeenth century, a deep, widespread longing for peace was apparent, after a century and a half of incessant turmoil. The rejection of violence, with the exception of that of the state, which punished legally and waged just wars, was accepted because it was the outcome of a new social pact forged between the rulers and the representatives of those they ruled. It was based on a rejection of murderous excess, and it delineated a sort of negative image of an ideal young man who shunned all festive brutality and an ideal young girl who refused all sexual temptation so as to avoid being driven to infanticide.

In the eyes of the spectators, most of those condemned to death or to corporal punishment richly deserved their fate.[52] The fact that the spectators did not identify with the victims, a phenomenon that has been too little studied, was a further validation of the punitive action because it often prevented a transfer mechanism from operating. The crowd was a true cross-section of society, made up of persons of both sexes and of all ages and social conditions, including many peasants who had travelled from a distance to watch the spectacle in town. The victims, most of whom had committed acts of homicide, violence or larceny, were predominantly young unmarried men.[53] In 1536, the judge-magistrates of Arras recognized the importance of this phenomenon, in the case of attacks on property and against a backdrop of war, an influx of refugees and rising unemployment, because their sentences now bore the marginal note '*josnes garchons*' ('young men'). Between then and 1549, the thirty-seven individuals so described accounted for 39 per cent of the male thieves. Like the others accused of the same offence, they were typically rootless. Often from some distance away, from Lyon or Paris or Picardy, they had usually been born in other towns in the Low Countries, in particular Lille, from which they had later been banished. Like the others, they mostly stole cash to survive. Though they rarely risked death at this stage, they were systematically exiled, in some cases after being whipped through the streets. They were also sometimes branded or had their ears clipped to alert other justices to their incorrigible behaviour, as was the practice of the magistrates of Amiens, Antwerp, Bruges and Ypres among others. In 1536, a young lad from Antwerp, aged fifteen, his ears already cropped on both sides, had the image of a rat, a reference to the town's emblem, a play on words – 'a-rat' – branded on his back with a hot iron. That same year, a young man from Brussels, with two previous convictions, who had already had the top of both his ears cut off, had them further mutilated 'at the bottom' to signal his third offence. An only too obvious vicious criminal circle led young bachelors who were too disruptive towards a disastrous fate. One such was Jacquet Corroier, a native of Arras, who got mixed up in a brawl which ended in murder at a dance, one Sunday in December 1547. Though he was found innocent, he was still banished on account of his bad reputation and because he went out armed at night, a juvenile custom once considered normal but now condemned. In despair, he several times broke his ban. He even returned to the town on one occasion, knife in hand, threatening to kill anyone who approached him and shouting that he could only die once. All he could do was try his luck elsewhere, like Jehennet Ruyelle, called May Pottier, who was only about ten years old when he was chased out of Arras in 1538. He was expelled a second time in 1542 as a vagrant and thief, because he refused to practise his alleged trade of shoemaker, by which date he had an impressive delinquent past, having already been banished in turn from Lille, Béthune, Tournai and Cambrai. Frédéric Mouton, a young man born in Tournai, both of whose ears had been clipped, had a similar career. He crisscrossed the country with other cutpurses from 1537 to 1540. Colin Noizetier, called Malespargne, born at Corbie, ears clipped on both sides, a vagrant and a thief, who travelled with a small band of accomplices, was expelled from Arras in 1533, having already been driven out of Ypres, Saint-Pol, Tournai and Lille. On the road, many of these exiles encountered the terrible provost-marshal, reputed to hang before he judged, who brought their criminal careers to an abrupt end.[54]

From unruliness to banishment to theft to survive, and finally to armed robbery, the road to ruin was short for these young exiles without any hope. The association of youth and larceny was to last for a very long time. Between 1650 and 1750, 45 per cent of the thieves punished in Amsterdam were between twenty and thirty years of age,[55] as were three-quarters of those hanged in eighteenth-century England.[56] The bands of armed robbers also consisted largely of young men. That of Hees, in the United Provinces, recruited boys of twelve or thirteen in the middle of the seventeenth century. The late seventeenth-century Valencian band of Berenguer, in Spain, had 113 members, whose ages ranged from twelve to forty-six, most of them being in their twenties. The French Orgères bandits had an average age of thirty-three, and that of the accomplices of Salembier, executed in Bruges the same year, was thirty-four.[57] Cartouche, broken on the wheel in the place de Grève in 1721, was twenty-eight; Mandrin was thirty-one when he suffered the same fate in Valence in 1755.

As for the women who were executed, we should not be misled by the stereotype of the old witch. It applied on a large scale only in the Holy Roman Empire. The persecution largely spared England and the Mediterranean countries and it was small-scale in France, where the female crime par excellence was infanticide, broadly defined as 'concealment of pregnancy'. In the area under the jurisdiction of the *parlement* of Paris, which included nearly half the population of the kingdom, 58 per cent of the 1,505 men sent to the scaffold in the years 1575–1604 had committed murder. Of the women, 68 per cent of the 441 executed over the same period were guilty of infanticide, 15 per cent of murder and 9 per cent were accused of witchcraft. The majority of the first group were unmarried, vulnerable women who had concealed their pregnancy and then killed their child to avoid dishonour and destitution. Similar severity was typical all over Western Europe.[58]

In the reigns of Henri III and Henri IV, the crowds of Parisians who watched the executions in the place de Grève or elsewhere must have noticed the predominance of young people among the 1,946 men and women sent to their deaths by the *parlement* in three decades. The constant repetition of the punitive ceremony, some sixty-five times a year, that is, more than once a week, cannot but have linked youth to the potential danger it represented for contemporaries. As elsewhere on the continent, judicial action continued the new pedagogic efforts of the churches, both Catholic and Protestant, aimed at supervising children more closely as they reached the worrying age of puberty. Was it not the age of all the temptations that could lead to eternal damnation if these fragile creatures were not firmly guided onto the right path? The powerful educational vocation of the Jesuits, in particular, really took off at the end of the sixteenth century, so as to counter the Protestant academies and to form the elites by teaching them to avoid the snares of the devil. For girls, daughters of Eve, believed to be particularly vulnerable to the seductions of the devil and excluded from secondary and higher education, this role was played first by the little parish schools and the Catholic catechism, but most of all by the strict supervision of men, father and then husband. The gallows loomed as the last resort to punish those young men and women who failed to conform.

The penal revolution of the sixteenth century was intended to supervise more than to punish. By directing its thunder at masculine and feminine adolescence, it helped to foster a deeply distrustful conception of this stage of life. It was part of a major trend in the West to redefine sexual norms and make them mandatory, by showing that to transgress them could prove fatal. If they valued their lives, boys and girls were told, in no uncertain terms, not to imitate Cain, for the former, or Medea, for the latter. Families and those who watched executions had to be convinced, too, so that they would supervise more closely the children whose potential excesses threatened the validity of the social pact. The age of terrifying speeches delivered by the condemned at the foot of the gallows lasted for a century, the time that was needed for it to be accepted gradually in the core communities. In two or three generations, the task was complete. This is the reason for the marked and rapid decline in bodily mutilations, death sentences and the use of torture by the second half of the seventeenth century, well before the emergence of the philosophic Enlightenment. Though there were significant variations according to country and jurisdiction, the decline is apparent everywhere. In France it was the *parlement* of Paris that led the way. By 1545, it had already abandoned bodily mutilation in favour of branding with a hot iron, except in the case of the parricide, who still had a hand severed, and it made only moderate use of 'preparatory torture'. Between 1575 and 1604, it ratified only one in four of the death sentences passed by the lower courts in its immense area of jurisdiction.[59] Despite the lack of a similar central regulatory body, the same trend can be seen in the Low Countries, the United Provinces, the Holy Roman Empire and Italy. The number of executions fell everywhere by the seventeenth century, more rapidly and more markedly in some places than others. The great cities like Brussels, Amsterdam, Frankfurt and Florence led the way. In England the decline dated from the 1630s. It subsequently became more marked, although the number of executions rose once again in the eighteenth century. By then, however, it was primarily attacks on property that were defined with great severity by new laws. With the exception of Amsterdam, where there was a temporary rise in the half-century 1700–50, before a new decline, England seems to have been alone in Europe in increasing the use of capital punishment in the Age of Enlightenment.

Forms of execution also became more humane everywhere. The *parlement* of Paris no longer boiled counterfeiters alive in oil after the mid sixteenth century. The *parlement* of Bordeaux still issued such sentences in 1532 and 1545, but ordered a lighter punishment in two other cases.[60] The practice also disappeared in Germany. The quartering of Damiens in 1757 was a spectacular exception, driven by an accusation of regicide, now as rare as it was extraordinary. The most common form of execution on the continent was hanging, though, in France, beheading, which had become much less common since the sixteenth century, remained a noble privilege until it was democratized by the Revolution. The sentence of breaking alive on the wheel was reserved for the very worst bandits and their leaders, such as Cartouche and Mandrin. Its use, rare and terrible, contributed to the legend of these youthful bandits, giving them an aura of infinite transgressive power. In other cases, secret orders, known as the *retentum* in the *parlement* of Paris, often caused the executioner to cut short the sufferings of someone condemned to the wheel or to the stake by discreetly strangling them at the beginning of the ceremony. A similar alleviation of sentences has been noted in Prussia after 1779, in the Austrian empire after 1776 and in England in the case of women sentenced to be burned alive.[61] Contrary to the thesis of Michel Foucault, the softening of punishments was not an eighteenth-century phenomenon, but dated back at least to the middle of the previous century. From this period, the rapid reduction in the number of death penalties went together with the spectacular decrease in the number of homicides. The two phenomena are closely linked. The Western 'factory' applied the *lex talionis* strictly only for a century, from 1550 to 1650. It was legalized so that it would deter young lads from murdering each other and pregnant but unmarried girls from getting rid of their babies.

Medea, the guilty mother

In the sixteenth and seventeenth centuries, the perception of violence on the European continent varied greatly depending on the sex of the perpetrator. On the part of a man, it did not become uniformly negative under the influence of the process of the criminalization of homicide. Masculine brutality remained deep-rooted in parish traditions, especially in the festive form of manly fights between young males. Further, it was acceptable, even admirable, for a man to kill in the defence of his life, his family, his rights, his community or his country, even when he beat his wife, his children or his servants in order to impose his discipline on them. As a result, manliness was fundamentally ambiguous, because, while the law demanded obedience and self-control, society lauded an aggressive potential necessary to the common good. It was now left to the judges to separate the wheat from the chaff. In England juries also applied these stereotypes. In a domestic context, the fathers and masters whose brutality caused the death of a child or servant were treated more leniently than the wives or mistresses accused of the same offence. In the case of the former, the charge was usually reduced to manslaughter or accidental death. According to the medicine of the age, masculine violence was linked to the hot, dry temperament of the male, which made him brutal and eruptive. It was often regarded as natural, honourable and even necessary. On the part of a woman, however, violence was universally perceived as abnormal and deeply wicked. It revealed the dark, dangerous and frightening side of femininity as it was imagined by the men of that period. A wife who killed her husband or a maidservant who killed her master fitted a negative model that caused deep anxiety to the judges. The image of the female poisoner, feared by the English husbands who were Shakespeare's contemporaries, though rare in the judicial archives, was one of its principal expressions.[62]

147

It was a matter of masculine fantasy rather than criminal reality. With the exception of infanticide, murder committed by a woman very rarely came before the courts and it was less likely to result in a death sentence than in the case of a man. Between 1575 and 1604, the *parlement* of Paris dealt with appeals from 269 female murderers, that is, 9 per cent of the total number accused of this crime. It condemned sixty-eight of them, or one in four, to death. By contrast, 869 men were executed for the same offence, that is, a third of the total.[63] In England, 75 per cent of the women who appeared escaped any punishment, compared with 50 per cent of the men. In the German towns, few death sentences – usually taking the form of beheading – were passed on women, if we except cases of witchcraft: eleven at Hall and eleven at Esslingen between 1500 and 1700, and eleven at Memmingen, compared with sixty-one men, between 1551 and 1689. The women were mainly, and increasingly, executed for infanticide, the men mostly for homicide or theft.[64]

By the Renaissance, the difference between the sexes was spectacularly emphasized by all the European criminal courts. Men were essentially prosecuted for attacks on persons or property, women for witchcraft or infanticide. In the *parlement* of Paris, between 1575 and 1604, women provided only 20 per cent of the 4,281 persons accused of violence or murder and 15 per cent of the 4,523 imprisoned for theft. The proportion rose to 48 per cent in the case of the 487 persons suspected of satanic magic and to 93 per cent in that of the 529 persons imprisoned for infanticide.[65]

While the alleged members of a demonic sect were vigorously prosecuted only in certain countries, which included the Holy Roman Empire, the shameful mothers who did away with their child were punished with great severity almost everywhere. Here, there was a universal precocious judicial standardization. Yet the act had not been seen as particularly criminal in the Middle Ages. Not only had it been difficult to prove, but it was largely tolerated by communities and served as a form of birth control in the absence of effective contraception. In France, in the second half of the fifteenth century, it had even been possible to obtain a royal pardon in case of prosecution for this offence. The new legislation suddenly put it in a radically different perspective. Women pregnant outside marriage were instructed to declare their condition to the civil authorities. The aim was both to prevent infanticide and to publicize the name of the father so as to ensure he made adequate provision for the child. Crucially, the judges were no longer required to prove its death. The onus was now on the woman to prove her innocence, even in cases of natural death or accident. In fact, the judges applied a presumption of guilt with regard to every woman who had concealed her condition and given birth without witnesses. The first law of this type seems to have been passed in Bamberg, in 1507. Identical provisions appear in the *Constitutio Criminalis Carolina*, granted to the Holy Roman Empire by Charles V in 1532. The majority of the German territorial princes and European states introduced the same principles during the course of the sixteenth or seventeenth centuries. In addition to France, where a royal edict of 1557 forbade 'concealment of pregnancy', and England after 1624, Denmark, the United Provinces, Lithuania, Russia, Scotland and Sweden passed laws to this effect.[66]

This remarkable, systematically applied new policy, which ignored state and confessional differences, was marked everywhere by phases of harsh repression. Infanticide, very broadly defined, became the unpardonable female crime par excellence. The edict of 1557 unleashed a wave of fierce persecution in France. The *parlement* of Paris saw a steady increase in the number of appeals for this offence, from a dozen or so a year to about thirty by 1640. The annual average of death sentences at this period stabilized at around ten. It then declined until 1670, but the number of accusations then returned almost to its previous level until 1700, although the number of executions started to fall in the 1690s, continuing in steady decline after that. In all, nearly 1,500 women were hanged for concealment of pregnancy between 1557 and 1789 on the orders of the *parlement* of Paris. The figure for the kingdom as a whole may have been twice as high.[67] The Parisian magistrates were especially merciless between 1575 and 1604, when they sent 299 of the 494 appellants to the gallows, that is, 60 per cent of the total. Their extreme horror at this crime stands out even more clearly when this figure is compared to the 33 per cent of murderers of both sexes and 17 per cent of alleged witches (40 out of 234) for whom these magistrates signed death warrants at the same period.[68] The *parlement* of Dijon was equally harsh. Between 1582 and 1730 it confirmed more than 80 per cent of the death sentences passed by judges in the lower courts and sent fifty women convicted of infanticide to the gibbet, but not a single one of their twenty-three male accomplices. It began to soften its attitude after 1668.[69] In England, the law of 1624 also resulted in some extremely harsh decisions. In Essex, between 1620 and 1689, thirty-one of the eighty-four women accused were pronounced guilty by juries and executed, a third of them during the decade beginning 1630.[70]

The profile of the accused women was very specific. It was remarkably similar right across the continent and it continued unchanged up to the nineteenth century, in spite of developments in the judicial systems. From 1575 to 1604, more than three-quarters of the 494 women who appeared before the *parlement* of Paris were single: 271 young women and 117 widows. Mostly from rural backgrounds, they appear to have been highly vulnerable in the face of the advances of a seducer. No doubt horrified to find themselves pregnant, they were often without the material means to cope with their situation. On average, they spent twenty-six days in prison. The magistrates were much more expeditious in their case than when investigating a homicide, especially in the case of males, who were usually allowed a delay of twice as long. This only confirms the extreme gravity with which they viewed the act of infanticide and their tendency to feel little doubt or hesitation in such cases. The consequence was that, exceptionally, they enforced the royal edict almost as rigorously as the judges in the lower courts, notorious for their cruelty and bloodlust.

In Burgundy, the seventy-six women accused between 1582 and 1730 included sixty unmarried women and eight widows. Of these, nineteen had lost their father. Many seem to have come from modest backgrounds, frequently rural, and to be finding life hard. The stereotype was slow to die. It was still there in Brittany between 1825 and 1865, when 636 women were sentenced for infanticide at the assize court of Rennes. In this case, their ages were recorded, which is rare for previous periods: half were aged between twenty and thirty. A total of 355 were from the rural world, 86 per cent were unmarried and almost 7 per cent were widows. Their crime was essentially that of women excluded from marriage and whose social position was precarious. Yet the assize juries were much less harsh than in the past. Most of these women were sentenced to hard labour or imprisonment. Only twelve were condemned to death, one in her absence for having buried her child alive.[71]

The typical woman found guilty of infanticide by the courts from the sixteenth century on was young, unmarried, of rural origins and humble background, often a servant, who had killed her baby at birth.[72] The law would not have made such an impact without the cooperation of the communities. The English example, which is better documented, reveals the extent to which the judicial pressure responded to a demand from the communities, relayed by the dominant males who sat on juries. The number of prosecutions increased well before the statute of 1624. After the Poor Laws of 1576, promulgated at a time of rapid population growth, repressive activity against those who had committed crimes against property and against infanticidal mothers significantly increased, more so than that against homicide. In the case of infanticide, attention was primarily focused, that is, in 70 per cent of cases, on the murder of illegitimate children, at birth, by women who had in most cases concealed their pregnancy. The law proved inadequate, because the authorities had to prove that it had indeed been murder, not a natural death, as many women claimed. For this to happen, there had to be cooperation from the neighbours, even the family. Perhaps this, too, was pressure from below to stigmatize the extreme abnormality of the potential suspects? Guilt, which was difficult to establish by irrefutable proofs, was increasingly constructed by a case-by-case negotiation between the judges and the inhabitants, represented by the jury and the witnesses. The law of 1624 only theorized these new practices, so the innocent could more easily be distinguished from the guilty. The number of accusations greatly increased, eventually accounting for nearly a fifth of all indictments for homicide. Acquittal was more common than in the case of male murderers, but those who were found guilty were hanged in 72 per cent of cases.[73]

The victims of this process, who received no pity, were selected by tacit accord between the magistrates and the dominant males of their community. They constituted only a minority, though its size is extremely difficult to establish. At Terling, in Essex, in the seventeenth century, the number of actual infanticides identified by demographers is two and a half times higher than the number reported. The order of magnitude was very much the same in France between 1831 and 1880, according to the official statistics: 8,568 sentences were handed down in the country as a whole, while 19,959 cases were brought to the attention of the courts but not followed up.[74] The 494 women who appealed to the *parlement* of Paris in the years 1575–1604 represented scarcely one in 10,000 of the women of all ages who had lived within its area of jurisdiction during an entire generation, even fewer if we consider only those who were hanged. It seems clear that in all these cases, including in the nineteenth century, the real number of infanticides was significantly higher than that suggested by the judicial statistics. Nevertheless, the crime concerned only a tiny proportion of unmarried mothers, 95 per cent of whom, according to one estimate for seventeenth-century England, did not kill their baby.[75]

The remarkable dramatization of the problem throughout Europe was exactly contemporaneous with the great witch hunt. The aim, in both cases, cannot have been systematic elimination. It was more a matter of intimidating those who fitted the developing stereotypes, by defining the boundaries they could not cross on pain of losing their life. Men of influence, judges, witnesses and the 'better sort' in the parishes were alike in stigmatizing the aspects of femininity that were now found unacceptable, by constructing two repulsive models which stood one on either side of the only path that was morally acceptable: that of the legitimate wife and mother. The prosecutions for witchcraft and infanticide encouraged a similar deep shame regarding the killing of newborn babies and little children. In various places, especially the Spanish Low Countries, the disciples of Satan were reputed to kill their own babies or those of others women, and give their unbaptized corpses to their master, so that baleful unguents and powders could be extracted from them. They were even accused of cooking them in a horrible fashion to be eaten during the Sabbath. In England, a quarter of them were charged with bewitching children and 62 per cent with, amongst other things, casting at least one spell on a child. Even before the repressive law of 1624 against infanticide, the correlation was obvious to contemporaries. It is revealed to the historian by the parallel evolution of the two curves of indictments for Essex from 1563 to 1623 and for Middlesex from 1613 to 1618.[76]

The fear of women, young or old, who killed children reveals a deeper masculine fantasy, a fear of the destruction of the community through the sins of women who escaped the control of men and gave free expression to their sexuality. The stereotype of the witch applied primarily to old women, in particular widows, who gave themselves, body and soul, to the devil. It was a metaphor for a sexual appetite that was unnatural, in the cultural terms of the age, because it was not expressed in the context of marriage and could not be fruitful after the menopause. Infanticidal young women similarly transgressed against the prohibition by slaking their lust outside marriage, seeking pleasure, not procreation, as demonstrated by their reaction to the birth of the unwanted child. In reality, their condition was usually precarious. Many of them were servants and some were fatherless, which made them vulnerable at the hands of a master who abused his position to make sexual demands. But, in the eyes of respectable people, they were primarily seen as temptresses with dissolute morals.

Both witches and infanticidal women were regarded as disruptive elements who were likely to cause scandal. They became a focus for fears of disorder and social collapse, exacerbated by the tensions of a period of conflict and change. The growth of a stricter religious morality in sexual matters, irrespective of the dominant confession, drew them to the attention of their fellow citizens. In England, the Anglican bishops assured the supervision of their parishioners' behaviour through the churchwardens, who were chosen locally and required to produce reports with a view to the correction of the immoral acts they described. In 1630, the bishop of Bath and Wells, in Somerset, demanded a detailed report on all forms of immorality: simple fornication, conduct likely to offend against female chastity, lustfulness on the part of persons of either sex, pregnant young women, the possible fathers, young men who married these dissolute women to conceal the father's sin, not forgetting the names of any who gave material assistance to the sinners. The aim was to force the suspects to defend themselves before the religious courts, even if they were simply the victims of malicious rumour.

The reports describe a very liberated peasant sexual life, even for women, married or not. The only exceptions were the daughters and wives of the prosperous yeomen farmers and representatives of the country gentry, who had been more affected than the rest by the moral-izing turn. The influence of these two dominant minorities helped to consolidate a more ancient social control based on the need of unmarried girls to avoid the public scandal of pregnancy. Attempted abortions are often mentioned, country girls being familiar with a variety of methods, which seem often to have been effective. Yet many rejected such action, more from fear of physical damage than from that of eternal damna-tion. Few bastards are noted in the documents, 3 per cent on average, with a sharp decline over the century. Prenuptial conceptions, revealing the number of women pregnant at marriage, varied between 16 and 25 per cent of baptisms, depending on the region.[77]

If sexual norms changed, in England as elsewhere, it was not only under pressure from strict morals coming from outside. The example of Somerset shows that the local worthies adopted the prohibitions more readily than the mass of the people, from conviction, but also as a way of strengthening their hold over the community. They had the support of the government in dealing with the ancient problem of bastardy. According to the old Tudor legislation, the seducer had, in principle, to marry the woman he had impregnated or, if already married, to take responsibility for the fate of the child and contribute financially to their upbringing. Yet the problem was a difficult one to resolve, given that the only thing that limited the sexual freedom of boys was fear of venereal disease.[78] The new emphasis on the responsibility of the girls who suc-cumbed to temptation makes sense from the perspective of the hanging which awaited infanticidal mothers. Yet it is doubtful if they constituted a real danger in the eyes of their fellow citizens, unlike the witches, whose spells they might genuinely fear. More prosaically, the local worthies took advantage of the legal and religious prompting in the case of illegitimate pregnancies to try to control more effectively the threat they posed to the stability of the community. The worthies accepted, therefore, an implicit redefinition of the sexual roles, which lessened the responsibility of the male by shifting most of it onto the partner he had seduced. The execution of those who did away with an illegitimate child was not aimed only at curbing such wicked ways through terror. It reinforced a previ-ously little-observed prohibition on sexual relations outside marriage, by issuing a solemn warning, to the female partner alone, of the fatal con-sequences of a transgression.

In order to limit the supposed lustfulness of the daughters of Eve, censorious males invoked both the fear of hell and the fear of the pitiless justice of men. All over Europe, they constructed two feminine figures of inhumanity, the infanticidal young mother of an illegitimate child and the aged witch who devoured the corpses of babies, in an attempt to bring out even more clearly that of the docile wife whose mission on

153

earth was to produce beautiful babies. This was an increasingly important theme from the sixteenth century, linked in Catholic countries to
that of the Virgin suckling Jesus, maternal love for a tiny sacred being
evoking precisely what was lacking in the two negative models. The
message the latter insistently conveyed was of the necessity of male
supervision to help them avoid the traps of the devil. To varying degrees,
according to country, the prohibition was materialized in the stake and
the gibbet.

In France, mothers accused of infanticide were indeed seen as the most
dangerous of women. A veritable obsession with them permeated the
culture of the age. One sign of this is the popularity of the literary theme
of Medea. The tragic story of the woman who seduced the ancient hero
Jason with the aid of her spells, and then cut the throats of the children
he had fathered, out of jealousy, was taken up by many authors in the
late sixteenth and early seventeenth centuries. After the example of
Corneille, Belleforest, Rosset and bishop Camus, whose books 'were then
in every library and every memory', retold the savage myth. They depicted
all the brutality of their 'barbarous century' through an infinitely dangerous female figure. Heroine of Evil, lustful, unbelievably violent, a monster
capable of committing a founding act against nature, that is, against
God, she was the very 'opposite of maternity'.[79]

The first of these three writers, François de Belleforest, developed the
bloodthirsty metaphor in his *Histoires Tragiques*, published in 1559, in
the story entitled 'On the lustfulness of Pandora and on her cruelty
against the fruit of her own belly, for finding herself deserted by the one
by whom she was pregnant'. In 1619, François de Rosset, author of the
Histoires mémorables et tragiques de notre temps, destined for huge
success, described 'the strange and unheard-of barbarity of an unnatural
mother' in a tale set in Rouen. Gabrine, old and ugly, lives alone with
her daughter. She conceives a great passion for a married friend of her
son's. She persuades him to help her to kill both her son and then his
own wife so that he can marry her daughter and inherit everything she
has. All she asks in return is that he sleep with her for the eight days
preceding the projected marriage.

The story constructs the murderous violence as the worst possible sin
by explicitly linking the 'parricide' perpetrated with unequalled fury by
the shrew, who despatches her wretched son with a hundred dagger
blows, to 'he who sullied with the blood of the first good man the bosom
of our ancient mother', that is, Cain. The assassin of Abel had said to
God, when asked where Abel was: 'Am I my brother's keeper?' The
phrase is echoed by the virago – 'I am not his keeper!' – in her reply to
the valet who comes looking for his dead master. True exterminator of
her male offspring, she thus concentrates in her person all the fantasies

154

of the destruction of the human race: 'Have you ever heard of such an inhuman act? Is the fable of Medea not comparable to this story, as full of truth as of horror?' For the narrator, the diabolical Gabrine merges into the figure of the witch who is an accomplice of Satan, whom she evokes, what is more, when she faces without remorse the ultimate penalty: 'Her hair was like intertwined snakes; her two red eyes like fire cast glances capable of killing those she looked at.' Her accomplice, by contrast, publicly confessed his crimes on the scaffold, before asking his Creator to forgive him. Thus the author distinguishes the guilt of the man, punished by the law but capable of a contrition that might earn him divine mercy, from that of the old woman, inexcusable and inhuman, portrayed as a pit of lust and a Gorgon thirsting for blood.

Jean-Pierre Camus, bishop of Belley, explored the same theme, in 1630, in *La mère Médée*. A jealous, deceived wife kills her children with blows from an axe, including a six-month-old baby in its cradle, before killing herself. The author takes this as 'a lesson to husbands to treat their wives humanely and faithfully', because they are 'weak vessels'. The cruel and evil nature of the daughters of Eve is also emphasized in other works aimed at a wider audience. The *canards sanglants* sold in the streets of Paris spread fear of the savagery of women. One *canard* published in 1608 had the title *The Prodigious Story of a Young Lady who Caused a Young Gentleman to Eat the Liver of his Child*; another, which appeared in 1625, told *The True Story of a Wife who Killed her Husband, who afterwards Inflicted the most Unbelievable Cruelties on his Body*. This husband-killer was so obstinate that she even refused to repent at the moment of execution; if she had the choice, she said, she would do it again. 'Finally, this wicked woman, this horrible monster, died in her obstinacy, not wishing by true contrition patiently to accept this temporal punishment, minor in proportion to her crime, to avoid eternal torments.'[80] The same masculine vision of the second sex permeates the painting and engravings of the Baroque age, leaving women with only these alternatives: conform to the maternal model which leads to salvation, or become a fallen woman devoted to the devil.[81] However, some representations of feminine virtues carried an ambiguous message, like the Biblical image of Judith, who seduced Holofernes so she could kill him to save her besieged town. Frequently idealized by the advocates of tyrannicide under Henri III, and often lovingly painted, Judith had put at the service of the community the natural violence attributed to the whole of her sex. But the bloody head of her victim on a plate must surely have inspired in its male observers a certain unease.

In France, prosecutions of women who had concealed their pregnancy were at their height in the first third of the seventeenth century; the curve of death sentences peaked around 1620. The subsequent decline was probably partly due to a new case law of the *parlement* of Paris, which decided in 1619 to apply lesser penalties than hanging if the corpse of the baby bore no traces of criminal violence.[82] Even more important, however, was a shift in cultural attitudes. At the end of the 1630s, the educated public suddenly lost its taste for 'tragic literature'. The bloodthirsty and moralizing stories of Rosset and Camus went out of fashion, to be replaced by a more classical aesthetic, a more refined language and new norms of civility. They were described in 1630 in Faret's *L'honnête homme* (*The Gentleman*), and subsequently taken up by many authors, who now favoured good manners, moderation and urbanity.[83] The sensibilities of the upper classes moved away from the fascination with violence which had previously permeated literature and art, at just the time that executions became less frequent and the golden age of the duel came to an end.[84]

These same phenomena can be observed in other countries at the same period. The persecution of witches and infanticidal women also died down after the first decades of the seventeenth century. This has been attributed to advances in medicine, such as those questioning the validity of the search for the mark of the devil on the bodies of his alleged accomplices. A new test also appeared, brought into general use as the century progressed, in which a piece of the lung of a dead newborn baby was placed in water to see if it floated; if it did, the judges concluded that the baby had drawn breath and suspected the mother of murder.[85] In fact, what this really shows is that the courts were demanding stronger proofs than in the past before deciding on the guilt of an accused woman.

After two or three generations of severity, the relaxation of judicial pressure was due both to changes in repressive practice and to a lesser demand on the part of communities. The authorities seem to have decided that they had achieved their objective by stigmatizing the deviant behaviour of women believed to present a serious threat to the divine order and to society. The trials for infanticide had made it possible to define an intangible taboo by demonstrating the inhumanity of the perpetrators. They had also helped to impose, by contrast, the absolute principle of 'natural' mother love, whatever the circumstances, linked to the only acceptable normative model, that of the fruitful and docile wife. The judicial theatre constantly reproduced this feminine ideal. Women defendants who wanted to move the magistrates to pity, so as to increase their chances of survival, presented their 'true' nature by drawing on a well-defined repertoire of emotive behaviour and expressions: they raised their arms, they threw themselves on their knees and, above all, they wept.

The judges were not duped by women who shed false tears or who thrashed about in an exaggerated manner. In their eyes, the body spoke clear. They interpreted the pallor, the trembling, the sighs and the signs of agitation as indications of guilt. By contrast, those who grieved from the bottom of their hearts, deeply and in silence, before proclaiming their innocence, were believed. One German woman defendant was described in 1670 as obstinate, wicked and incapable of showing any trace of emotion. Another, Anna Martha Laistler, accused of infanticide in 1665, was tested and subjected to close scrutiny. The tiny body was placed in her arms before it was buried. She kissed it several times, moaning and repeating, 'Oh, my dear treasure, be calm, I will soon be with you. Oh my holy child', before saying that she was indeed a great sinner but that she had not killed her child. However, those watching remarked that, though her gestures and her eyes suggested distress, she was incapable of shedding a single tear. The bailiff concluded that her attitudes revealed terror, not grief. She was sentenced to death by beheading.[86] The female face, in particular, was scrutinized in the attempt to discover the truth. It was believed that it could be read like an open book, and that it was possible to decide with certainty if a woman belonged to the good or the bad part of her sex. Even though they were not always successful, the desperate efforts of these women, in the second half of the seventeenth century, to conform to the positive feminine model make it plain that they were well aware of it. The fact that it had spread throughout the population made the systematic attempt to eradicate the crime of concealment of pregnancy less necessary.

For the male population, a persecuting phase had come to an end. The reasons for their acceptance of this trend have as yet been little studied and remain obscure. They probably had less to do with the strict morality imposed from above, which was primarily accepted by the local notables, than with an internal need for a rebalancing of the relations between the sexes and the generations. Infanticidal young women and elderly witches were scapegoats, sacrificed to assuage the extreme anxieties of an age of great disruption and tension. They both represented forms of sexual and social liberty, in relation to the adult males, and they both had a privileged relationship with young men. The latter assiduously wooed the young women and were educated by the old women in the use of an ancient magical culture, while the wives of intermediate age reigned over childhood. The principal changes imposed on the communities, especially the rural communities, weighed most heavily on the unmarried men. Under pressure from the religious and moral diktats that reinforced the effects of the traditional codes of honour, unmarried men were expected to abandon their manly ritual violence, on pain of death if they killed someone, and to keep away from the marriageable girls. Could it be that the proliferation of convictions of young mothers for infanticide provided those who ruled the communities with an indirect means of strengthening their control over the increasing aggression of young men?

In other words, the chief problem may have lain in the relationships between the masculine age groups.

It was primarily the established men who actively collaborated, on juries and as witnesses, in the punishment of witches and women who concealed their pregnancy. The fact that they saw these women as a greater and more pressing danger than their predecessors had done, who had shown little interest in such matters, was probably due to a clearer perception of where their own interests lay. While strengthening their tutelage over the least docile sectors of feminine society, they further separated them from the masculine juvenile world. Added to this, they did not appear to be the ones most directly responsible for the persecution. They were simply enforcing the law, which had made serious crimes of what had once been the perfectly acceptable attitudes of violent bachelors, seduced girls and old medicine women. We are given a glimpse of the world of the rural *veillée*, the evening gathering at which the young lads courted the girls under the eagle eye of the old ladies, while the adult men congregated separately, a little apart. This world had been destabilized by the new religious and moral ideas introduced from outside and it needed to change to adapt. The village worthies took advantage of this to strengthen their hold over everyone else, including the women who were too independent, but even more the aggressive young men, while also managing to avoid becoming the focus of the latter's deepening discontents.

In the eighteenth century, infanticide was prosecuted less frequently in the courts and the conviction rate fell. In England, the attitude of the juries changed. Whereas in the past, in doubtful cases, they had tended to severity, they now tended to acquit, in much higher proportions than for the murder of an adult.[87] This return to leniency on the part of the representatives of the community shows that they now saw these women, who were often very young, as victims rather than as culprits. In 1803, this led to the abrogation of the statute of 1624, in the context of a law that was extremely harsh in the case of many capital crimes, including abortion by drugs. Finally, an act of 1938 decreed that infanticide would no longer be regarded as murder if the mother had not recovered from the birth, or was still breast-feeding or had killed her own baby aged less than twelve months. Similar changes were made in other countries. In France, the edict of 1557 was no longer strictly applied after 1700, when an alternative practice began to emerge. The abandonment of babies made it possible for desperate girls and impoverished married mothers to get rid of them discreetly, without judicial consequences. In Paris, the average annual entry to foundling hospitals rose from 825 in 1700 to 6,000 a little before the Revolution. Louis-Sébastien Mercier sang the praises of this moral advance, claiming it had 'prevented a

158

thousand secret crimes: infanticide is now as rare as it was formerly common'. In fact, it simply assumed a different form, taken over by the community. In Rouen, for example, of the newborn babies received in the hospital, 58 per cent died before the age of one in the decade 1710–19, and more than 94 per cent in the years 1770–9.[88]

The attitude to infanticidal mothers changed radically because their fellow citizens generally felt more pity than detestation for their act of desperation. The law might still be harsh, but it could no longer be imposed on a public that had once again become tolerant in this regard. Article 302 of the French penal code of 1810 still provided for the ultimate punishment, but the reluctance of juries and of public opinion to apply it forced a major change in 1824. The government denounced 'scandalous dismissals, or at the very most derisory sentences to feeble correctional punishments', but accused women could claim extenuating circumstances, which precluded a harsher penalty than hard labour for life. New provisions limited the punishment to fixed periods of hard labour in 1832, and in 1863 to a maximum of five years' imprisonment in the absence of proof that the child had taken breath.[89]

Recent research has invalidated the thesis of Michel Foucault, who attributed the changes in the Western penal system to Enlightenment ideas, which led to the move away from the spectacle of the physical tortures decreed by the prince towards the confinement of deviants in prisons, for the greater good of the triumphant bourgeoisie. Repressive methods based on social exclusion and hard labour had emerged by the sixteenth century. In 1545, the *parlement* of Paris already spared the lives of 19 per cent of the appellants, who were sent instead to man the royal galleys. The same was true of the Mediterranean countries, Spain in particular. In the seventeenth century, England, soon imitated by the United Provinces and Sweden, began to transport prisoners to its colonies. Another way of expiating for misdeeds appeared in 1555, near London, in the form of an institution of confinement, Bridewell Palace. Here, vagrants were forced to work and subjected to a rigorous religious and moral discipline destined to turn them into obedient and productive subjects. The same principles were applied in the Rasphuis and the Spinhuis of Amsterdam, founded in 1596. By the late sixteenth or early seventeenth century, the English model of houses of correction had spread to Leiden, Bremen, Antwerp, Stockholm, Lyon and Brussels. Then, early in the reign of Louis XIV, France in her turn produced a place of confinement for the poor and beggars, the *hôpital général*. Some of these institutions soon started to receive criminals. The fact that they provided an alternative to the death sentence or corporal punishment is suggested by the timing of their spread, which corresponds precisely to the beginning of the steady decline of these penalties and of judicial torture.

The modern state of the mid seventeenth century, consolidated by the great crises, was no longer in need of extreme demonstrations of power and cruelty to establish its hold; all the more so, as the elites were losing their taste for blood and the spectacle of death. The 'books of the devil' went out of fashion in Germany in the early seventeenth century, just as the macabre and bloodcurdling tales ceased to amuse the cultivated French public by about 1640. Classicism is simply a convenient category for describing a profound shift of sensibilities in the land of Molière. Equally visible in many other states, it corresponded to a rejection of the extremes of passion and torment that had characterized the mannerism of the late Renaissance and the Baroque age. It is reasonable to conclude, therefore, that the marked reduction in the number of public executions was one of the consequences of the strengthening of the state, because it gave its peoples a feeling of greater security.[90]

The social contract forged between citizens and authorities was consolidated all over Europe after the peace of Westphalia in 1648, which brought to an end a century of general unrest. After that, the cruel excesses of the public scaffold seemed increasingly less necessary as a way of reassuring the people about the ability of their rulers to stem the tide of evil and criminality. In the eighteenth century, the chief worries of both rulers and people moved away from fear of the savage brutality of young unmarried men and the infanticidal fury of unworthy young mothers and took new directions. The greatest fears were now concentrated round robbery, while the need to save one's threatened life grew less urgent in a society that was increasingly pacified and where fewer civilians carried weapons and homicide was increasingly rare.

— 6 —

THE NOBLE DUEL AND POPULAR REVOLT:
THE METAMORPHOSES OF VIOLENCE

The duel, incarnated in the collective memory by the heroes of swash-buckler films, is in no way timeless. It was invented in the sixteenth century and it reached its apogee in France under the first two Bourbon kings, just when the great peasant revolts were at their height. The coincidence was not fortuitous. It has been neglected by historians, because the two phenomena appear to belong to completely different social spheres, but it is surely worth searching for a common denominator. The whole of Europe was affected and blood flowed copiously on its soil from the 1520s to the mid seventeenth century. The period was marked by constant insurrections, beginning with the massive armed uprising of 300,000 German peasants in 1525. There were countless religious riots, especially in England and the Low Countries. These two states both experimented with a 'revolution', which led in the latter to the rejection of Spanish royal tutelage and the creation of the Calvinist republic of the United Provinces, in 1579, and in the former to the beheading of the Stuart monarch and the installation of the protectorate of Cromwell, in 1649. Confessional confrontations raged: French Wars of Religion from 1562 to 1598, the Thirty Years War in the Holy Roman Empire between 1618 and 1648. Thrones tottered. Kings were assassinated, like Henri III and Henri IV in France, or died in battle, like Gustavus Adolphus of Sweden. Pretenders were eliminated, including the duc de Guise in France and William of Orange, leader of the revolt in the Low Countries. Others, who displayed too much ambition, conveniently died, like Don John of Austria, half-brother of Philip II of Spain, and the latter's son – at the instigation of his father, some said.

Yet this era of bloody fury and violence was also one of great structural and political change. The detailed study of the religious conflicts has too often obscured a major positive phenomenon; the extreme disorganization of the continent caused by the incessant rivalry between competing

Churches and ambitious princes has masked the steady advance of unifying processes in Western civilization. Of these, the most obvious is the gestation of the modern state, which needed to control the aggression of its subjects in order to channel that of its armies towards the fundamental sphere of lawful clashes with its enemies. The state took two antagonistic forms, whose mechanisms constantly evolved and improved in confrontation. The centralized model, as in France, was based on the upward aspirations of its most dynamic elements. According to the classic analyses, it harnessed some of the extreme violence of the aristocrats and placed it at the service of the sovereign on the battlefield.[1] The other archetype is that of the city-state, whose power was based on a flourishing economy: Venice at the end of the Middle Ages, Antwerp in the mid sixteenth century, Genoa a few decades later, Amsterdam in the seventeenth century. However, the city-states had to adapt to the growing threats coming from the most powerful monarchies, tempted by their wealth. They sometimes accepted princely tutelage: that of the 'Grand Duke of the West', Charles the Rash, in the Low Countries, then the 'imperial' but more flexible tutelage of Charles V in the same region, especially at Antwerp but also over the Free Cities of the Holy Roman Empire and the prestigious Italian metropolises. Later, the increasing religious rigidity of the ageing emperor, and even more the iron fist of his successors, encouraged proud cities to organize extensive networks of resistance to preserve their founding principles, like the United Provinces rebelling against Philip II, or the German Protestant urban leagues preferring the leadership of local lords, while also seeking the support of foreign kings, even Catholic ones.

England, protected by its isolation, was an exception. It moved slowly from the first to the second model, rejecting the absolutism of the Stuarts after tolerating that of the Tudors, to become a sort of vast economic suburb of London. Dominated by a capital expanding rapidly after the industrial revolution of the eighteenth century, it kept up the semblance of a monarchy. After the Glorious Revolution of 1688, it was ruled by an elite with urban values which distrusted excessive centralization and favoured the separation of powers. This is shown by a deep crisis of the aristocracy, whose essential values came increasingly to be based on money and the entrepreneurial spirit rather than on birth.[2] English justice reflected these particularisms. From 1550 to 1630, it was the only country in Europe to punish without mercy those who committed crimes against property. The number of hangings reached nearly 75,000 in the century from 1530 to 1630, in a country with fewer than five million inhabitants. Between 1580 and 1619, 87 per cent of those executed were guilty of theft, armed robbery or burglary, as against 13 per cent guilty of crimes of violence. It was not until the decade 1660–9 that the proportions were more evenly balanced, at respectively 55 per cent and 45 per cent. The increasing criminalization of homicide was later here than elsewhere.[3]

The backdrop to all these changes was war. In Europe, it was waged almost non-stop between rival monarchs; it was also endured at the hands of the Turks, who were advancing in the south-east, and exported to the rest of the world in the age of the conquistadors, Cortès and Pizarro. The status of military conflict changed radically, partly as a result of the spread of the concept of the just war, but also because soldiers, who were now much more numerous, were clearly differentiated from other subjects. The only legitimate culture of violence became that of the soldiers and officers acting on the orders of the state. Civilians had to accept the loss of their weapons and had to entrust their safety wholly to the law and those charged by the sovereign with the maintenance of order. It took generations, even centuries in some cases, for such principles to be accepted universally. The process was easier and more rapid in the towns, which already had long experience of effective methods of internal pacification.[4] In contrast, a military culture of extreme brutality developed. It was increasingly oriented towards the desire to kill and it often led to appalling horrors being inflicted on the defeated, including ordinary people, women and children not excepted, as shown with realism by the engravings of Jacques Callot. Between these two extremes, forms of mass resistance to the abandonment of traditional violence emerged, which were actually ways of adapting to the prohibitions imposed by the law and morality. It is hardly surprising that the two social groups principally concerned were the two for which bloody violence was part of the common currency of social relations, encoded in ancient collective rituals necessary to the manly definition of individuals, especially that of young men: the aristocracy and the peasantry.

The noble duel and the rural revolt were collective or individual adaptations to the new codes that were being imposed. In each case, the participants claimed an eminent right to a straight fight, even if it resulted in the death of the adversary. They came up against repressive legislation prohibiting this, and they tried to find ways of getting round it in negotiation with the authorities. The aristocrats invented a new way of expressing their superiority over the commoners. This ascendancy, which was linked to the use of the sword, a privilege they now claimed as exclusively theirs, was supposed to confer the tacit privilege of killing, on condition the strict rules of the honourable conflict were respected. The monarchs were embarrassed by the increasingly strong opposition to an ethic of such barbarity coming from the Christian morality of which they were the representatives, and so introduced extremely repressive legislation against it. But they made little effort to enforce it, as they themselves often shared these aristocratic ideals, like Louis XIV, even though he had sworn to abolish duels at the beginning of his reign. In fact, the systematic prosecution of victorious duellists would have deprived warlike kings of the cream of their officers. This type of murderous confrontation demanded a long technical apprenticeship and the assimilation of values based on courage, which made it indispensable to the growth of the militarized state. This is why it flourished above all in the triumphant France of the Bourbons.

The rebellious peasants also demanded the right to continue to indulge freely in an age-old youthful festive violence. They, however, were much less sympathetically treated. Their demands were of no value to the advance of monarchical power. On the contrary, even if they did not challenge this power openly, they risked undermining it by their rejection of the pacification the monarchs were seeking to impose, in the hope of making the country an impregnable fortress, without dangerous internal enemies. In an obscure way, however, the rejection of the peasants joined that of the nobles, for very different reasons. This strange conjunction was often visible on the ground, because the peasants forced many small country gentlemen to take up arms and lead a rising, whether they liked it or not, as the rebellious German peasantry had tried to do in 1525. However, the villagers showed no interest in anything remotely resembling class war. Indeed, they rejected the new distinction, previously virtually unknown, between those privileged by birth and themselves, that is, between warriors specializing in mortal combat and tillers of the soil, enjoined to abandon their weapons and their brutal practices. The society they wanted to preserve was based on a clear distinction between the three orders, clergy, nobility and third estate, certainly, but they refused to accept the introduction of impenetrable barriers in daily life. Backward-looking, when they were being urged to look to the future, they tried to make time stand still. They wanted to preserve the mythical image, celebrated by the story-teller Noël du Fail, of an age when lords and peasants had played, fought and drunk together, sharing the same manly ethic; an age when the sword, far from being a noble monopoly, had been simply a sign of a lusty youth which thought it normal, even necessary, to shed blood, to wound and to be wounded in the quest for personal pride and social respect.[5]

The duel, a French exception

After 1500, the Western 'military revolution' turned the European continent into a machine for war and conquest, which tested the innovation on its own soil before exporting it all over the world.[6] The least visible – but probably most far-reaching – consequence of this general trend was that it drove all states to try, more or less rapidly depending on circumstances, to disarm and pacify those of their citizens who were neither soldiers nor keepers of the peace. The accumulating horrors and the new religious demands, both Catholic and Protestant, played a role in this process, but the real explanation lies elsewhere. With the passage of time, it became an imperative need for the absolute monarchs to exclude extreme violence from their own state 'citadel' so that they could direct all their fire against their enemies. In France, Louis XIV succeeded in doing this. The country was transformed into a fortress by Vauban; any internal resistance was demolished, like the walls of Marseille. Instructed to lay down their arms, the population had to fall back on the security assured by the royal *maréchaussé* and the law, while a professional army, quartered in barracks and commanded by a nobility skilled in the game of death, emerged. The other political model, that of the city-state, was also forced to adapt, and to become skilled in war, both to protect its territorial sanctity – when Louis XIV invaded the United Provinces – and to conquer colonial and European markets. Born of the pacificatory urban system, the city-state was well prepared by tradition to enforce the internal peace necessary to its economic expansion, but it now needed to develop a particular bellicose culture indispensable to its survival; it was no longer enough for it simply to hire adventurers or foreign *condottieri* to wage war on its behalf.

Paradoxically, the proliferation of conflicts ultimately had the effect of disconnecting the culture of the professionals in violence from that of the ordinary people. Only soldiers were now considered to have the right to kill another human being, in the course of a 'just' war. Which, increasingly, they did. Medieval chivalric practices, and the economy of blood practised by mercenaries seeking high ransoms for prisoners, were replaced by clashes that were increasingly often fatal, using very destructive weapons, cannons, rifles and pistols, before the arrival of the formidable sabres of the Napoleonic age. The one-to-one confrontation, governed by strict rules and not necessarily resulting in death, had become less common even in the eighteenth century, during the Lace Wars; it was now a myth. It claimed to be incarnated in the duel, which was fought not so much on the battlefield as in ordinary life or between resting troops. This form of combat became increasingly important as a way of marking the specificity of those who engaged in it, by contrast with the prohibition imposed on the rest of the population and the increasingly harsh punishment of homicide.[7]

Bastard child of the new murderous efficiency of the military nobility and of the disarmament of civilians, all the more prestigious in that it was both cruel and rare, the duel should not be viewed through rose-tinted spectacles. It was premeditated murder, rarely prosecuted at a time when an increasing number of ordinary people were being executed for this very crime. Its supporters, like the duellists themselves, demanded the outrageous privilege of a continuation of the right to kill a human being without paying the price. As the death toll rose, they put themselves above divine law and that of the king, in the name of the 'point of honour', elevated into a sign of the superiority of their caste. Whereas, in the past, all subjects, of whatever origin, had had a good chance of obtaining a royal pardon after committing such an act, the duellists claimed this privilege exclusively. The duel was an aristocratic appropriation of the regalian right of life and death, and it depended on a huge propaganda effort designed to conceal its common origins and to force the prince to show a particular leniency.

Historians have often been misled by the discourse of writers who were devotees of 'blue blood', and anxious also to proclaim a different racial origin. As a way of establishing an impassable barrier between nobles and commoners, this ideology emerged in France by the sixteenth century. The tall, fair, conquering Franks, the argument ran, had imposed their yoke on the small, brown, degenerate Gallo-Romans.[8] In actual fact, the codification of the duel served both to promote a 'natural' specificity of the nobles and to mask the extreme violence of the confrontations between them. Destructive cruelty and folly were the order of the day more often than the magnanimity that features in the theoretical descriptions. A confrontation between the lords of La Garde and Lignerac, for example, began with smiles and embraces before turning into a furious battle in which the latter stabbed the former fourteen times. Jacques de Séran, chevalier d'Andrieux, was one of the few persons of his rank to be executed for duelling, at the age of thirty, on 14 July 1638. He was a man of exceptional savagery. He had neither faith nor law. He had been accused of three rapes as well as many murders before his twenty-third birthday, and also of having killed seventy-two adversaries in duels. If we are to believe Tallement de Réaux, when some of them had begged for mercy, he had agreed, on condition they renounced God; he had then cut their throats for fun, so as to destroy their souls as well as their bodies.[9] The romantic vision bequeathed by the nineteenth century obscures the dark side of the phenomenon. The specialization of the French aristocracy in all things warlike produced a true art of ruthless killing which distinguished them from the ordinary violent practices of the other young males, who were more likely to demonstrate their valour by wounding someone than by killing them.[10] Aristocratic aggression, glorified by the ethical code of the duel, strained nature to produce a culture of death suited to the appetite for conquest of the princes of their century. It was a departure both from the rituals of the ordinary manly confrontations, intended simply to prove the superiority of one fighter over another, and from the practices of many animal species, where the emission of signs of submission by the loser stops the fatal escalation. It put its stamp on the age of unfettered French expansion, from the Italian wars to the conquests of Louis XIV.

The duel was truly 'a French phenomenon'.[11] Nowhere else in Europe did it assume the importance it acquired in the Most Christian Kingdom. It is true that the schools of fencing emerged in Italy, which also produced the most celebrated masters and the best manuals. Yet the honourable challenge enjoyed only a brief golden age in the peninsula, in the first half of the sixteenth century, before going rapidly into decline. The standard explanation cites the Council of Trent, which prohibited the practice in 1563. But there was also a deeper loss of vitality, expressed in literature and laughter, in a society where the nobles were more cultivated than in France, and where there was no legal pressure to criminalize the phenomenon.[12] Given the extreme touchiness of the Italians in affairs of honour, and also the murderous practices of the Renaissance, in the towns as well as the princely courts, such a sudden decline may seem surprising. In reality, the bellicose culture that underpinned the duel never became established in an Italy that was dominated by foreigners and hardly expansionist. As in many Mediterranean countries, the traditional model of the ritualized violence of the young continued to flourish until a later period. The persistence of the knife fight aimed at inflicting a wound, in the name of a concept of honour found at all social levels, and not requiring the elimination of the opponent, prevented the duel from putting down deep roots.

The situation was similar in Spain under Philip II, where only a small number of people broke the laws which, at an early stage, prohibited the duel.[13] In the Low Countries under Spanish tutelage, 'placards', or princely edicts, forbade the duel in 1589. A placard of 1610 provided for the loss of nobility or office and confiscation of half the property of anyone who issued or accepted a challenge, and for death and total confiscation for those who fought and their seconds. It was repeated in 1626. In 1636, proceedings against 'the body and memory of the deceased' were added. The author of a collection of case law which records these details for the decade beginning in 1630 quotes not a single concrete example of what he calls a 'bestial thing', while observing that the king of France had failed to eradicate it despite all his best efforts. This author noted, however, that a general could authorize a duel against enemies in war, which was common practice in the Spanish armies.[14] Although the cohesion of the territorial empire of Philip II was maintained by military force, the duel was not common there, in the Iberian peninsula or elsewhere. The main reason is clearly the survival in force of the practice of the ritual combat between young men. Artois provides proof, because the number of pardons for homicides in this context was at its height in the first third of the seventeenth century. The killers and their victims came from all sectors of society. There was, however, a greater propensity than in the past to kill in these confrontations. Is this perhaps evidence of the influence of the ethic of the mortal challenge which had developed in the powerful neighbouring kingdom? This was surely the true secret weapon of the Bourbon kings. While the old Hapsburg rival continued to tolerate the traditional forms of violence in its vast territories, France developed a new and formidable technique of extermination. Admittedly, the Iberian armies amply demonstrated such an attitude in the sixteenth century. The Aztecs of Mexico, accustomed to 'flower wars', which involved conquering without killing in order to maximize the number of prisoners with a view to later sacrifices, were powerless before the ruthless tactics of Cortès in 1519. Like Pizarro in Peru in 1532, he had the benefit not only of better weapons but also of a mental superiority in the art of conquering without allowing the enemy to recoup their forces. The slow weakening of the Spanish monarchy in the seventeenth century may be related to an erosion of this all-conquering aggression. Contemporaries deplored the fact that the aristocratic elites seemed to be losing the taste for battle and drifting away from the bellicose style incarnated by the duke of Alba under Philip II. Things were very different on the other side of the Pyrenees, where the art of slaughter was perfected during innumerable duels.

The duel was never particularly fashionable in the Holy Roman Empire, either. In spite of early prohibitions, in Saxony in 1572 and everywhere in 1623, convictions were rare, even in the army. They were slightly more frequent after the terrible Thirty Years War, in the second half of the seventeenth century. Soldiers and students, both susceptible to an exotic phenomenon of French origin, were the two groups most involved.[15] Before 1650 the political and religious fragmentation of the country made it the sick man of Europe; it was threatened, not aggressive and it was looked at hungrily by the great military powers, including Sweden and France. For the duelling ethic, this was not fertile ground. That ethic became a highly prized virtue, however, in the nineteenth century. A bourgeois elite rehabilitated these values, especially in the Prussian army, which also had many noble officers, some of them of French and Huguenot origin. University students were equally steeped in these values.[16] This new mind-set was crucial to an increase in military power, demonstrated against France in 1870, and later further accentuated. It would be interesting to know if ordinary juvenile homicide was criminalized at the same time. The concentration of warlike values in those who could provide the army with its officer class was probably more effective when the rest of the population lost the right to shed blood. This was the case in the Nordic kingdom of Sweden-Finland, where the much more frequent use of the death penalty for murder after 1620 coincided with the beginning of a century of military conquests and the creation of a vast empire, inaugurated by the spectacular interventions of Gustavus Adolphus in the Thirty Years War.[17] The precise status of the duel in Swedish society at this period is as yet unknown.

England imitated France from 1570 to 1640, when the nobility often sent their sons to academies across the Channel to learn the use of arms. Duels were at their height between 1610 and 1620 in both countries, but the English soon lost their taste for them. Except under the Stuarts, who modelled their monarchic style on that of the Bourbons, duelling seems to have been to some degree alien to the local cast of mind, which 'saw blood as money'.[18] Threatened by the invasion of the 'Invincible' Spanish Armada, the country was no longer the great military power of the age of the Hundred Years War. It had already gone some way to eradicating violence by orienting it towards the spectacle of animal fights and codified bare-knuckle fighting, ancestor of boxing. The Elizabethan theatre also played a role in the formation of a more peaceable sensibility, at least for those who watched the plays in London. The theme of vengeance, which was rarely dealt with in France at this period, was a veritable obsession of English writers. The avenger, heroic before 1607, became antipathetic between 1607 and 1620, after which moral debate prevailed until 1630.[19] The same period in Paris saw the growth of the literature of the 'tragic tales', which accustomed the dominant sensibility, that of the noble and bourgeois readers, to bloodshed of the most horrifyingly cruel kind. Before it lost popularity in the 1640s, this literature constituted a sort of subliminal apprenticeship that made it easier to accept the new law of the mortal duel, whose golden age in France was at precisely this period, that is, between 1600 and 1640. Oceans of literary blood and the casuistry of the point of honour prepared the sons of good families to commit murder without qualms, in spite of the law and religious morality. This was also the age of the *canards sanglants*, ancestors of the *faits divers*. The horrific stories they told encouraged the shift in norms by making the cruelty of the duel seem ordinary in most people's eyes. Gradually, a highly flattering image developed of the manly noble hero. Protector of widows and orphans, like the knights of old, he killed with good reason, to defend his honour, ignoring the tortuous machinations of a coldly repressive state, though deep down a secret supporter of its core values. Alexandre Dumas had only to elaborate on this theme, already suggested under Louis XIII, to immortalize a pure aristocratic myth by skilfully inviting everyone to see something of himself in it. The appropriation of the violent heritage by the nobility and the military made it even more difficult for the other young males to persist in the traditional expression of their competitive manliness, which was now stigmatized as an unpardonable crime if it ended in a death.

Noble youths sharpen their swords

The duel was a French passion. It acquired unrivalled prestige after the middle of the sixteenth century because it epitomized all the masculine virtues necessary to the conquest of Europe and the world. To fulfil the monarchical mission of bringing peace and Christianity to the people, it was necessary to have access to men of war who knew how to kill in order to conquer and to be killed in order to safeguard their honour. The stated rules were simply a facade, a means of educating in murder. They made it possible to bypass the powerful moral, legal and perhaps also biological prohibitions, which often prevented a victor from remorselessly administering the death blow, or from fighting with what the Italian contemporaries of Machiavelli already called 'French fury'. The realities were more brutal. The demons let loose by this tacit death pact between the prince and his finest warriors encouraged frenzies of bloodletting revealed by innumerable sources. 'A heroic and/or villainous episode involving a clever sword stroke',[20] le coup de Jarnac of 1547 was a famous duel in which the victor unexpectedly dealt a crippling thrust to the back of his opponent's knee; it exposes the desire to kill without mercy concealed beneath the normative code. The seismic shock caused by this singular duel, authorized by the king of France, sent ripples through the whole of the nobility. From then on, the frenzied pursuit of an outstanding technical skill, crowned by a botte secrète, a 'secret thrust' impossible to parry, made the basic contradiction crystal clear: to kill a fellow human being whatever the cost, but while maintaining the forms – or appearing to – so as to be sure of the indulgence of the sovereign.

Homicide took on a new meaning. It was still criticized and it was increasingly seen as a crime if it was committed by a commoner, but it was still often pardoned by the monarch, until the Revolution. The figures given by contemporary observers are difficult to verify, but they suggest that between 6,000 and 10,000 gentlemen were slain in duels in the reign of Henri IV, that is, between 1589 and 1610. Pierre de l'Estoile says 7,000 pardons were granted to victors.[21] Admittedly these figures are for all lettres de rémission for murder, only a fraction of which went to the nobility, though far exceeding their demographic weight, estimated

170

at 2 per cent of the population. One scholar has calculated that 772 gentlemen were killed in duels between 1550 and 1659, that is, an average of about six a year.[22] The exaggerations testify at least to an awareness of the problem among alarmed contemporaries. They helped to stop the duel from being seen as banal. In hammering home the idea that it risked leading to the extinction of the nobility, these writers reinforced the efforts of Henri IV to ban the duel, shown by the edicts of 1599, 1602 and 1609. At the same, time, however, the first Bourbon's many acts of mercy validated the aristocratic discourse on the legitimacy of the point of honour. The net result of these insoluble contradictions was to define the duel as an exceptional right which ought to be rare, no one but a warrior of blue blood being allowed to cut short a life without a properly constituted judicial decision.

The question of the age of the duellists has attracted little interest from historians, no doubt in part because the sources are so unhelpful on this point. Yet it is fundamental. Although there were some elderly, even old, duellists, the sources consistently associate the phenomenon with youth. Desportes is quite specific:

> The strict point of honour which with hot flames
> Pursues young hearts and the fairest of souls.

Added to which, the periods when these encounters were at their most numerous were not those of war, but those of peace.[23] A generational effect can be detected. The arrival at the adult state of teenagers whose ranks had not been decimated by conflicts, but, on the contrary, swollen by decades of relative calm and prosperity, explains both the proliferation of confrontations in the villages of Artois in the period 1600–30 and that of duels in England and France around 1620. A closer study of such considerations might make it possible to identify surges at intervals of roughly thirty years, corresponding to the rise in frustrations and internal conflicts among the young unmarried men whose numbers had become inflated, especially the younger sons of the nobility, often forced to leave their paternal home to seek fame and fortune at the point of a sword. Some contemporary authors saw this very clearly, to the point of wishing to send these superfluous gallants off to fight in the army.[24]

The decade from 1620, just before France embarked on war, after more than twenty years of peace, was crucial. The same was true elsewhere in Europe, where the beginning of the Thirty Years War, in 1618, had brought general instability. The emblematic Bouteville affair, in 1627, happened in precisely this context of surplus juvenile energy and phoney war.[25] The decision to pass a death sentence on the comte de Montmorency-Bouteville, together with his second and cousin, the comte

Des Chapelles, after a duel was exceptional, and it reveals profound social and cultural shifts. Although it had been a crime of lese-majesty since 1602, little effort had been made to repress the duel under Henri IV. In 1626, a new royal edict threatened offenders who fought in the company of a second with capital punishment and loss of nobility, extended to the whole family, because such confrontations often involved two pairs of gentlemen. Bouteville was twenty-eight when, in 1627, he broke the law. He had fought twenty-two duels since reaching the age of fifteen. Having fled after an encounter in 1624, like the others involved, he had already been sentenced in his absence to be hanged in effigy in the place de Grève. One night, some persons unknown had sawed through the gallows bearing the degrading images, to demonstrate their disapproval. Bouteville, a friend of Chalais and a familiar of Gaston d'Orléans, the king's brother, had believed he was well protected, even untouchable. Public opinion favoured a less harsh punishment, in contrast to Richelieu, his friends, the Parisian petite bourgeoisie and the judges. Even some of the latter, moved by the eloquence of Des Chapelles, a charismatic figure in all the ardour of his twenty-seven years, exhibited some ambivalence.

Reasons of state demanded a spectacular example in the face of such a flagrant denial of royal authority. Yet the affair resembled hundreds of others, for which the supreme penalty was not used. The two defendants did not yet belong to the world of established adults. Having embarked on careers of violence at the age of fifteen, like the bachelors of the kingdoms of youth, they had fought in a few military campaigns, then become veterans in brutality, without ever emerging from adolescence. Des Chapelles cleverly proclaimed his own youth before the judges, knowing it to be an extenuating circumstance. Another of Bouteville's cousins defended him by saying that he had 'the sickness of his age'. The twenty-two men this expert duellist had fought had been of a similar age, the average being twenty-four. The fights had had a traditional ritual character, specific to young bachelors as a whole. In 1624, for example, Bouteville faced Pontgibault. As they were without daggers, they decided to use knives, then tossed to decide who would have the bigger and sharper one. Pontgibault's second sharpened the weapon on a stone while waiting for Bouteville's second to arrive. 'During this time they amused themselves playing leapfrog.' These immature individuals attached little value to life, even their own. All that differentiated them from the commoners who sought royal pardons was the extreme murderous fury of the codified duel. Yet Bouteville sometimes chose to spare the life of those he vanquished. Under cover of noble honour, he was reverting to the practice among commoners of wounding and defeating rather than killing. Further, the fights always took place on a Sunday or holiday.

Bouteville's enemies took advantage of this to accuse him of impiety, although these were the normal days for battles between members of the kingdoms of youth, as we have seen in Artois. It was on Easter Day 1624 that Bouteville challenged Pontgibault, in church, during a service. The fact that they were not carrying daggers and had to draw lots for weapons to fight with suggests at the very least an absence of premeditation. It is all reminiscent of the clashes between peasants that happened in the locations and at times of great sociability. The practice of choosing seconds who also fought each other similarly points to the survival of old traditions of solidarity between pubescent boys. The initial characteristics of the confrontations had not changed. Only the code of the duel fought exclusively between nobles was really new, and the use of the rapier, when it is attested, was more likely to prove fatal. The fight remained an initiatory act, a rite of passage to adulthood for the new generations, even if fathers of families and mature men sometimes risked their lives in this way.[26]

The ritual was feared by rulers and established people, all the more so in that it overtly evoked the need for the older generation to give way, one day, to the next. There is no need to evoke the shades of Freud to understand it; or to interpret the disobedience of Bouteville as a challenge to the king himself, whose place was claimed by the noble rebels, until the crisis of the Fronde.[27] The pressure from the young, observed by contemporaries, is explanation enough. It warns us not to exaggerate aristocratic resistance in the face of the innovations of the modern state.[28] This very visible opposition hid a deeper reality. Blue-blooded adolescents were not challenging the principles underlying the authority of their fathers, any more than the young peasants were. They simply wanted to step into their shoes, without changing the order of things, and were feeling the pain of having to wait too long for their turn to launch their careers. Fighting was in any case also a way of passing the time, because they had failed to find a place in the world, as Bouteville proclaimed. For adults of their caste, the duel had at least the virtue of occupying idle young warriors and preventing them from thinking about turning their swords on their elders. This was a real possibility, especially when hopes of a rapid accession to titles and wealth receded. But in the Baroque age, that of the plays of Shakespeare and the tragedies of Corneille, at a more general level, the duel was an instruction in the main rules governing the world of those privileged by birth. The duellists tried to prove that they could fit into this world perfectly. The avowed causes of the challenges related to women, quarrels about money, lawsuits and rivalries aggravated by questions of precedence or membership of hostile factions. Most of them reveal difficulties of insertion or hierarchical conflicts, and involved the young who were in waiting far more often than respected greybeards. The romantic vision of the act of hopelessness and desperate resistance to the relentless advance of the modern state is pure aristocratic propaganda. It may even have acted as a brake on the ambitions of the most turbulent, by asserting that the hoped-for gain was tiny or non-existent. It suited a feeling of decline and impotence among some discontented nobles, but it carefully concealed the fact that the second estate was lining up for battle behind the absolute Bourbon prince, to help him to conquer the world.

The battle against the duel was never either real or effective in France. The execution of Bouteville and Des Chapelles changed nothing. Richelieu in person prevented the prosecution of an offender in 1628. Bouteville's opponent, Beuvron, having fled to Mantua, obtained his pardon in 1629. In spite of new edicts, including that of 1679, which strengthened the apparent severity of the punishments, laxity prevailed and the fashion for the duel persisted into the eighteenth century.[29] Indeed it played a fundamental role in the construction of a new relationship between the king and those who died for him in the face of the enemy. The young noble officers became the spearheads, literally and metaphorically, of the formidable French army of conquest.

The duel was an elite military academy. It operated a ruthless system of selection, allowing only the most gifted in the art of killing to survive, which augured well for their ability to conquer in battle. Further, it gave the nobles a monopoly of carrying and wielding the sword, because the prohibitions emanating from the sovereigns were not applied to them. In the sixteenth century, every man could still announce his pride by wearing a sword in his belt. In 1555, the chronicler Claude Haton exclaimed that no son of a good mother was without a sword and a dagger. The priests themselves, he added, were often as quick as the rest to draw their sword and among the first to get mixed up in a quarrel, at the inn, at dances or in games of skittles or fencing. In 1610, in his *Traicté de l'espée francoise*, Jean Savaron, four years later a deputy in the third estate, wanted the privilege of carrying a sword to be extended to all good Frenchman, as had 'everywhere and at all times' been the case.[30] Later, the morality of the point of honour culminated in a monopolization of the rapier by the aristocracy, who wanted to demonstrate their peerless virility in an exclusive fashion. Everyone else had to make do with a knife, concealed beneath their clothing, even with its point blunted on the orders of Philip II in the Low Countries, in order to reduce the number of homicides. The symbolic castration of the commoners thus achieved by legislation did nothing to stop the survival of the traditions of armed juvenile confrontations. While the sword was ennobled by means of the codified duel, the knife fight, which featured in a majority of the pardons issued in Artois in the seventeenth century, was now

174

synonymous with baseness, treachery and crime. It was increasingly devalued, successively characterizing the poor, who were firmly instructed to stop spilling blood, the cruellest bandits in remote regions and, finally, the Apaches of Paris at the beginning of the twentieth century.

In France, the myth of the sword dates from the seventeenth century. In the space of a few generations, it brought about a total transformation in the social significance of this weapon. In the words of an enraptured master-of-arms, in 1818, 'it is the sign of command, the weapon of the officer'.[31] Given noble status in the age of territorial expansion, under Louis XIII, it served to reorient the extreme internecine violence found all over the kingdom in the direction of a specialized body of elite warriors, which the sovereign was desperately in need of to accomplish his sacred mission. Its technical function and objective changed at the same time. It became a machine for killing, once the subtle rules of a purely aristocratic swordsmanship were mastered, and no longer bore any relation to the practices of the sixteenth and seventeenth centuries. In war and in the villages of Artois, estocs, or 'verduns', called after the town supposed to manufacture them, came into frequent use. The finest of them were capable of piercing armour, due to their long blade, with a square or triangular cross-section. They were used to cut more than to thrust, as is shown by the engravings of infantry encounters. The records of the injuries of the veterans of the companies of Montluc and Brissac, drawn up in 1576, reveal that four out of five of their scars resulted from sword blows to the head, the face or the limbs, with those on the trunk or belly accounting for less than 6 per cent. Ambroise Paré says that it was the last of these that were most often fatal.[32] Military swordsmanship targeted the head in every sense of the word. It was not necessarily intended to kill, given the helmet. Further, a defeated prisoner might fetch a high ransom, especially if of high rank. The army was the main source of the technical education of the entire population. In Artois, the predominance of head wounds in the persons killed by those seeking *lettres de rémission*, often young peasant lads, suggests a show of force without deliberate murderous intent.[33] The same was generally true of Picardy, on the other side of the frontier, under Francis I. A sword had been used in more than half the murders pardoned. The cranium and the face were most often hit, in 37 per cent of cases, followed by the limbs, the shoulders, the back and the sides (32 per cent), and then the chest and the belly (both 15 per cent).[34]

The rapier of the musketeers immortalized by Alexandre Dumas, longer, thinner and more fragile, could only be used to thrust, so as to pierce a body. War changed its nature after the abandonment of the heavy armour that was easily penetrated by a bullet. Plume fluttering in the wind, the noble cavalryman swooped down on the common pikemen, firing and killing, then valiantly used his sword against one of his peers. He needed a new kind of bravery, skill more than strength, all instilled into him by three indispensable masters: those of dancing, riding and fencing. They all called for the same qualities of finesse, skill, endurance and valour to form a new type of conquering aristocrat. Under a veneer of politeness, provided first by the manuals of civility and then by the etiquette of the court of Versailles, the nobleman had never been so highly motivated to behave with animal savagery in a duel or in war. A physician of the Sun King, Martin Cureau de la Chambre, put this baldly in *Les Charactères des passions*, published in 1658, in which he speaks of the courage 'which birth has placed in the heart and which is proper to the sensitive appetite because it is common to all the animals'. To which he adds strength, to characterize the second estate by the use of those two 'qualities which nature has rendered so noble, having destined them to be the foundations of power and superiority'.[35]

The duel was a frenzied and savage hymn to death, sung by thousands of ambitious young men inspired by a 'race' prejudice which encouraged them to believe they were superior beings. It is hardly surprising that the church and the king, appalled by the inhuman ferocity of the combatants, tried to limit its effects, even though they assured the glory of the sovereign in war. One musketeer made this point lucidly in a work published in London in 1768, and intended to refute the arguments of the critics: 'But they do not realise that it is the duel that nurtures this French valour, fatal to the enemies of the state.'[36] And it did indeed take exceptional courage to risk one's life with no other protection than the thin blade of a rapier. One survivor described such an encounter. He pierced the stomach and then the throat of his adversary, but his sword remained stuck in the second wound. He was himself then hit in the side, fell back, then prepared to throw himself on the man, who had just picked up his weapon, which had fallen to the ground. Against all expectations, his adversary handed it to him: 'You have done for me, but I am a gentleman', he said, before falling dead on the spot.[37] This story can be read admiringly, certainly, as a eulogy to the principle of the point of honour taken to a peak of elegance, panache and respect for the other. A reading less susceptible to noble propaganda detects a furious and deadly ballet on both sides, an absolute determination to eliminate a human being, including in the duellist with the perforated stomach and a sword stuck fast in his throat, who continued his frenzied attack. Indomitable courage, certainly, but what a deep disregard for life!

A history purged of the passion for the duel leads to a disturbing conclusion. The 'civilizing process' described by Norbert Elias was no more than a facade. Cruelty was more deeply hidden under imperative rules of civility, but it also became more extreme and more drastic in the specialists in the art of killing. Unlike the young peasant lads, who used violence to demonstrate their manliness without seeking deliberately to kill their opponent, and were sometimes imitated by Bouteville, the French nobles of the seventeenth century were encouraged to kill intentionally and coldly, cloaking themselves in the point of honour to defend the indefensible. In this way they offered the state a violence taken to extremes, which made them the prototypes of Rambo, the military superhero of the cinema, capable of exterminating enemies by the hundred. Subsequently, the steady increase in weapons of mass destruction is more easily explicable if we accept that Europe perfected, on the basis of the French model under Louis XIV, methods of warlike elimination, up to the terrible world wars. By forcing nature and by producing a culture of death, the duel inaugurated a formidable shift towards barbarity assumed in the name of allegedly transcendent values. It is as if the aggression inhibited by the civilizing codes was largely concentrated into a destructive sense of superiority which gave the right to kill to a tiny chosen fraction of society, before it later led armed populations into military confrontations on a larger scale. From this perspective, man increasingly became a wolf to man on the continent of Europe, from the seventeenth century to the middle of the twentieth century...

The 'brutalization' of French society after 1700 makes sense viewed from this perspective.[38] 'The nobility alone are permitted to bear arms', stated the police dictionaries of the Age of Enlightenment. Honour where honour is due! Although there were many offenders among the commoners, it was the aristocracy, therefore, who were chiefly responsible for a volume of bloody violence that was on a much larger scale than tends to be believed. The age of the *philosophes* was marked by great eruptions of cruelty. Far from declining, the duel was common in the streets of Paris. Duels accounted, by the lowest estimate, for a tenth of fatal acts of violence in the first quarter of the eighteenth century and for 333 court cases recorded between 1692 and 1792. The curve of judgements on appeal before the *parlement* has two peaks, from 1722 to 1731 and from 1742 to 1751, each followed by a decline, before a final rise during the last decade of the period in question. Among the victims deposited in the morgue of the Grand Châtelet, those who seem to have died in a duel had been hit in the chest in 70 per cent of cases, in the stomach in nearly 10 per cent of cases. Most of the thrusts had been to the area around the nipples, with a slight preference for the right. The desire to pierce the trunk and the heart is clear. It testifies to a cold desire to kill. Nearly 300 corpses were the result of confrontations of this sort, according to these documents, for which thirty years are missing.[39]

The fights mainly involved the military, including a large number of ordinary soldiers as well as nobles, if we are to believe the professional descriptions, which are provided for only one in three victims. A quarter of those who can be identified were common citizens, from a very wide range of occupations. This does not mean that the duel had been democratized, but rather that these men were continuing to practise the old bloodthirsty brutality which was now, according to the ideology of the honourable challenge, reserved to the aristocracy and soldiers. When age is recorded, which is in less than half the cases, it reveals the youth of the victims: almost half were under thirty, and only a negligible number over forty. The peak was between twenty-six and thirty, which has been the principal age group, in the case of both the accused and their victims, for homicides in the West from the thirteenth century to our own day. Some of these men may have been married and established. This is unlikely to have been the case for the majority of them, however, at a time when men married a little before thirty, in the context of increasingly late marriage as the century progressed. This probably only accentuated their anger, like those retarded adolescents Bouteville and Des Chapelles in 1627. The next largest group was of men between twenty and twenty-five, followed by an almost equal number aged between thirty and thirty-five. A generational effect also appears in the curve of the 810 duels recorded between 1700 and 1790. There were rises at the beginning of the century, from 1732 to 1751, after 1762 and again in 1782.[40] Every twenty or thirty years, there was a collective eruption of deadly violence which involved mainly young men. The cause seems to have been a surplus of energy and an intense rivalry between the unmarried, to whom we may add some of those who had just taken a wife but remained attached, for a while, to this earlier world. The postponement of the age of marriage is classically interpreted by demographers as a way of regulating the number of births in an overpopulated world. It also helped to delay the date at which sons succeeded their fathers, at the cost of serious sexual and social frustrations. The increase in the number of unofficial couples and illegitimate births in the towns was one way of relaxing this iron law. The duel was another.

A new procedure aimed at the pacification of noble behaviour had been introduced in France in 1566 by the royal ordinance of Moulins. The court of honour, instituted under the aegis of the marshals of France, was designed to limit the violence of potential duellists by offering them a form of judicial redress likely to reduce the chances of armed conflict. The abandonment, two years later, of the practice of enrolling *lettres de rémission* in the registers of the Trésor de Chartes was another sign of a desire to change practice in the case of homicide. The legislation failed, however, to prevent the traditions from persisting or the duel from reaching new peaks up to the middle of the seventeenth century. The ambiguity of the reactions of the state apparatus, and even more the hesitancy of

178

the sovereign in the face of this forbidden but deeply entrenched phenomenon, which proved a formidable aid to the militarization of the nobility in the service of the aggrandizing ambitions of the monarchy, are explanation enough. In the event, the marshals dealt with only a small number of cases. Their help was sought only by the more cautious, who had no desire to risk their life in a duel, and who were relieved that they could avoid losing face by resorting to a court which might be equally effective in restoring their honour. The punishments stipulated for the aggressors were: *l'éclaircissement* (a sort of excuse), the obligation to seek forgiveness, sometimes on bended knee, loss of arms and personal nobility, banishment and a fine or, lastly, imprisonment, for a maximum of twenty years, for he who 'who struck from behind, although alone', took unfair advantage or had a second. The archives, which survive only for the years 1720–89, contain 643 case files. Their chronological distribution echoes that of duels: few before 1730, a marked increase from then until 1759 (382 complaints, of which 161 were for the years 1730–9), a sharp drop to 116 cases during the next two decades, and then a sharp rise to 106 cases between 1780 and 1789.

Of those accused in the 160 cases recorded between 1774 and 1789, 99 per cent were men. Only 10 per cent of the victims were women. Half the protagonists were nobles, closely followed by soldiers, of whom only 4 per cent were officers. Members of the bourgeoisie and craftsmen making complaints in connection with *billets d'honneur*, that is, for the unpaid debts of aristocrats or officers, accounted for 7 per cent. Nearly two-thirds of the cases came from the towns, mostly from Paris itself, or in Normandy. Guyenne and Gascony provided most of the rural disputes. Few cases originated in the centre or east of the kingdom. The issues underlying the conflicts were predominantly financial in nature: 70 per cent of the 100 cases where the cause is known concerned debts unpaid in spite of a *billet d'honneur*, 22 per cent concerned a patrimony, 3 per cent gambling and 5 per cent women. There had been insults, followed by an action for redress before the courts rather than a duel, even though both the plaintiffs and the accused were almost all from the second estate or the army. It was rare for blows to have been exchanged. When this had happened, the feet or fists or a stick or a cane had been used three times as often as a sword, the latter involved in only six cases. The last information of interest concerns age. Though it is rarely recorded, for only twenty-three of the accused and twenty-six of their victims, it confirms the youth of the former: fifteen were under twenty-five and three between twenty-five and twenty-nine. Only four of the plaintiffs belonged to these age groups; fourteen were between forty and forty-nine and the others even older. In other words, the cases for which we have information tended to be between generations separated by twenty years or more.[41] This seems to imply difficulties of insertion on the part of the defendants and an aggression turned against the adult plaintiffs as a consequence of problems that were much more often financial than sexual. Symbolically, we may see this as 'sons' blaming 'fathers', who stubbornly insisted on debts of honour, for not allowing them the means with which to live honourably. This is perhaps why the court was preferred to the duel in these cases. The phenomenon throws light on the difficult situation of sons of good families in a period of late marriage and inheritance. It seems to suggest that they felt they had the right to demand an advance on their inheritance from society as a whole as the price of their patience. The spendthrift mentality and refusal to honour their debts imputed to the aristocracy by their bourgeois creditors is also made a little easier to understand. The unpaid *billet d'honneur* was sometimes an insidious form of juvenile aggression. If things turned nasty, the dispute might lead to a real duel, often unequal, where the younger man, carried away by his desire for revenge, and by the lust to kill instilled by his lessons in swordsmanship and his superior physical strength, was likely to outclass his older adversary.

This French passion gave no sign of dying out with the abolition of privileges by the Revolution. The murderous rage persisted into the nineteenth century, adapting to new techniques and becoming bourgeoisified.[42] After 1815, there were once again dozens of mortal challenges every year. Any man who refused to fight was deemed a coward. The greatest names – Victor Hugo, Lamartine, Alexandre Dumas, Proudhon, Gambetta – all fought duels. Clemenceau confronted Déroulède, and then Drumont. The mathematician Evariste Galois gave his life for the honour of a woman in 1832, like Pushkin, killed by a pistol shot from a French officer in 1837. So great was the courage demanded by the duel that the armies of the Revolution appointed a provost of arms to test the new recruits in each regiment. Every new arrival had to pit himself against an opponent during a violent initiation rite inspired by the old practices of the kingdoms of youth. In a nice example of 'what goes around comes around', the Revolution appropriated the duel and returned it, unknowingly, to its 'popular' origins. 'With us, a slap in the face is a murder', said Camille Desmoulins.[43] The model warrior who sustained the phenomenon was as necessary to the France of mass conscription and to the 'left colonizers' of the nineteenth century as it had been to the sovereigns of the *ancien régime*. It was not by chance that the unified Germany of Bismarck similarly constructed, in the universities and within the bourgeoisie, military heroes who would assure the national triumphs of the nineteenth century and lead the charge in two world wars.

It was not until after 1945 that the age of the medieval towns eager to halt the cycle of violence by fining the most trivial blow, before things got out of control, returned. The duel then went into very rapid decline in France, with a last dying flicker in the confrontation between Gaston Defferre and René Ribière in 1967. Like the rest of Western Europe, France longed for peace and rejected the practices that had too enthusiastically promoted the aggression of youth to make it a weapon of conquest, such as compulsory military service. To kill became a crime, without exception, whatever the circumstances. The taboo is today virtually absolute. The most violent male adolescents constitute only a tiny minority. The ritual initiatory violence of the gangs is directed primarily against objects, as in the torching of cars, and only rarely with ferocity against persons, even in the case of rivals from different districts.

The swashbuckler novels of the nineteenth century, which have recently had new life breathed into them by numerous films and television series, made a major contribution to this pacification. They gradually helped to vaccinate their young readers against the temptation of real violence by offering them oneiric release. The exploits of d'Artagnan, Lagardère and Pardaillon are totally inaccessible to ordinary mortals, given their lack of skill in fencing, never mind swordsmanship. Substitutes of wood or plastic are hardly likely to inflict serious injuries, though they reassure the boys who brandish them as to their manliness and enable them to claim their place in the world. The genius of the authors was to fuse different violent traditions and make all of them contribute to the calming of youthful passions. The heroes of page and screen are always younger sons, poor and simple gentlemen from the provinces who, with panache and generosity, turn the duellist's cold art of killing into a mission to defend widows, orphans and the persecuted. These heroes remain committed to the common good, for ever coming out with familiar claims that ought to alert the sovereign to the wicked schemes of his evil ministers. Thus is reaffirmed the old habit on which monarchy is based, which was echoed by rebellious peasants right up to the gallows: long live the king without the *gabelle*! The king is good! Everything that has gone wrong must be the fault of those around him.

It is the Republic that has so far made best use of this precious heritage. Further, Cyrano and the Three Musketeers obscurely incarnated the inalienable right of youth to excess, gaiety and the fights with their peers that serve to strengthen group solidarity. Youth must have its fling! Like the prince who granted pardons, adults were expected to be indulgent towards those who were impatiently awaiting their turn for a share of the social cake, even if they engaged in a certain amount of violence in order to let off steam or out of boredom or anger. Deep down in our imaginations, d'Artagnan and his friends are the very archetype of the band of youths, always ready for a fight, whose members may kill but remain, nevertheless, full of charm. It was originally a challenge that led d'Artagnan and Athos into a duel, in which Porthos and Aramis were the seconds. Two against two, as in the encounter which led to the execution of Bouteville, but, like the young peasant lads who fought on holidays in front of a crowd, they ended up by falling into each other's arms. As mature men, twenty years later, the indestructible friendship survived, a metaphor for everything that a fight between boys should be: ludic, rough but fair, strengthening bonds and contributing to the common good. It was along these very lines that the sovereign was thinking when he pardoned large numbers of young unmarried men who had become Sunday assassins, enabling them to resume their place in the community without too much difficulty.

In essence, the romanticized swashbuckling tales produced in the nineteenth century mingled the popular and aristocratic heritages in order to teach how to become a young Frenchman. Just when the nation was launching itself into the great colonial adventure, they linked the ancient rituals of manliness, necessary for each individual so he could carve out a place for himself, to the more specific mechanisms that had transformed the nobles of the seventeenth century into machines for war and conquest. Later, in the age of decolonization, these pen-and-ink heroes struggle to offer the generations of doubt an ideal which is gradually going out of fashion. The peace which has reigned since 1945 and the ongoing construction of Europe have devalued the symbol of the conquering sword in favour of the serene expansion of universal noble ideas. The swashbuckling films are losing their appeal, or are produced in a very different spirit in Hollywood. It is as if we are seeing the end of an imperial chapter which opened with fire and the sword at the beginning of the sixteenth century, when aggression first started to be directed away from the heart of the communities and the kingdoms of youth to be redirected against external enemies.

Popular violence and the frustrations of youth

The questions posed by historians are always determined by those of the age they live in. The popular revolts which shook Europe between the end of the Middle Ages and 1789 illustrate this to perfection. They gave rise to passionate debates during the Cold War period, in the 1960s and 1970s. A Russian specialist, Boris Porchnev, started the ball rolling by analysing in classic Marxist fashion the French insurrections of the years 1623–48, in a 'context of a still dominant economic feudalism within which a capitalist system was developing'.[44] This book, which was translated into French in 1963, provoked a vigorous debate, led by Roland Mousnier. For Mousnier, the class war could not explain any of these

182

movements. In a strongly hierarchized 'society of orders', the insurgents never showed any sign of a 'revolutionary' ideology, even during the Russian uprisings of the same period, with the sole exception of that of Stenka Razin, in 1667–71.[45] The revolt was usually sparked by the imposition of new taxes or some bureaucratic abuse, because the state was consolidating its centralization and stepping up its demands. The castles and the nobles were rarely the targets of the revolts. On the contrary, they often provided themselves with aristocratic war leaders to increase their military effectiveness, if only by pressuring the local lords to train the troops. Nor was the monarch himself ever challenged. The frequent cry, 'Long live the king without the *gabelle*!' reveals the refusal to blame him for anything. Their anger was directed primarily against the local officials, especially the tax-collectors. Many pupils of Mousnier were set to work searching the archives all over France to produce regional theses. They repeatedly proved that the class war never happened in the Most Christian Kingdom, while a few rare mavericks risked challenging the accepted view.

One of these was Robert Mandrou, who drew attention to certain features obscured by the fierce ideological dispute. He noted the extreme localization of these revolts in the west and south-west of France, the great emotionalism of the common people, the seditious role of women, the importance of violence as 'collectively life-affirming' and the savage but not entirely random nature of the insurrections. For the peasantry, he added, the main problem was not so much the ownership of land as the small size of their holdings and the inadequacy of their equipment. The higher taxes helped to unbalance even further an already fragile system. The fiscal uprising was simply a 'wildly fluctuating thermometer of a crisis situation', including in the towns, even though the situation of their inhabitants was frequently less precarious. The rebels did not form class fronts and had no political consciousness, apart from the monarchic loyalism expressed by most of them during the rebellions, which did not prevent them from being cruelly repressed on the orders of the prince. They were usually hostile to the rest of society, moving from anti-fiscal demands to an anti-seigneurial movement in the Dauphiné in 1649, or ending up burning châteaux as in Périgord in 1637. The country-dwellers thus usually alienated the townspeople, who were in any case by nature inclined to mistrust, even despise, them.[46]

At the beginning of the twenty-first century, the historiographical quarrel has died down, and the subject is no longer in fashion. The proliferation of works devoted to different European countries has probably helped to bring this about, by giving the impression that everything, or almost, has been said on a subject which no longer stirs doctrinal passions.[47] And, although violence was central to these manifestations and to their brutal suppression, the overall view of them today is still strictly limited to the issues classically debated in the aftermath of the confrontation between Porchnev and Mousnier. It is as if there were watertight barriers preventing any discussion from straying beyond a now well-established consensus.[48] From this perspective, the long cycle of popular revolts started with the great peasant Jacquerie which ravaged the Ile-de-France in 1358. The fifteenth century was principally an age of reconstruction after terrible ordeals, but the major religious, political and social changes of the early sixteenth century coincided with social explosions on a large scale, beginning with the German Peasants' War of 1525, which later spread to the towns and mining districts. Some revolts were the direct result of confessional protests, like the conquest of the town of Münster by the Anabaptists in 1534–5, the Pilgrimage of Grace in England in 1549 and the Protestant iconoclasm in the Low Countries in 1566. Others escalated and caused revolutions, like the splitting of the rebellious Low Countries into two distinct entities in 1579, resulting, in one case, in a return to the Spanish fold and, in the other, to the creation of the Calvinist republic of the United Provinces. In many towns in both France and Germany, the systems for keeping the internal peace broke down as the inhabitants became more turbulent, especially in the seventeenth century.

In an iron century, marked by the growing fiscal demands of states seeking to wage endless wars, which devastated many regions, life became increasingly hard. The 'little ice age' brought colder and wetter summers, fluctuations in the price of bread and more frequent and more serious famines. Weakened populations with empty bellies had to face both numerous epidemics and the havoc wreaked by the armies. Their anger led to constant food riots in both town and country, further aggravated by a range of problems, such as the enclosure movement in England, the problem of aristocratic hunting rights and intensely local quarrels almost everywhere.

The peasantry, which accounted for more than three-quarters of the population in most countries, resorted to violence over a very long period. Small 'emotions', as they were called, lasting no more than a few hours or a few days, occurred in their thousands in the cities and in the countryside until well into the nineteenth century. The great rural wars that involved thousands of people and went on for months were more localized, and mostly confined to the period 1550–1650. That in Guyenne, in 1548, directed against the introduction of the *gabelle*, the new tax on salt, marked the beginning in France of a movement which culminated in the riots led by the Breton Bonnet Rouges in 1675. As in the Holy Roman Empire in 1525, the authorities could not tolerate such a radical challenge. These serious explosions of anger, which were cruelly punished, testify to a huge increase in the spirit of violence, on the part of rebels and governments alike. The origins of such a massive and widespread phenomenon on the continent pose a major problem. It can only be resolved by the introduction into the closed world of the study of popular protest of a paradigm that is very rarely evoked by historians: the transformation of the juvenile sensibilities of the ordinary people under the influence of the growing number of prohibitions designed to strip them of their age-old rights to ritual violence.

The immediate causes of the risings were essentially related to a deterioration in living conditions, following a great increase in fiscal pressure or terrible famines. The phenomenon was endemic throughout Europe, including in the eighteenth and nineteenth centuries. However, the great peasant revolts are evidence of a much deeper malaise. In France, veritable armies of rebels, trained by nobles, confronted royal troops under Louis XIII and early in the reign of Louis XIV. From May to July 1637, the Croquants of the Périgord assembled many tens of thousands of rebels and left hundreds of dead on the battlefield after their defeat at the hands of the soldiers on 1 June. From 16 July to 30 November 1636, the 'Army of Suffering' of the Nu-pieds of Normandy had as many as 4,000 men. Defeated under the walls of Avranches, it left 300 dead. The pursuit of the scattered rebels that followed was spectacular and bloody. From May to July 1662, 3,000 insurgents, nicknamed the 'Lustucru', roamed the countryside around Boulogne-sur-Mer. Nearly 600 were captured, most of whom were sent to the galleys. In April 1670, the Vivarais was in a state of unrest until 25 July, date of a rout which left 100 victims. In Brittany, the peasants of Cornouaille took up arms in the spring of 1675 against the imposition of indirect taxes on stamped paper, the marking of pewter and the sale of tobacco. In July, they turned against many châteaux and demanded that their lords renounce the *corvées* (forced labour) and certain seigneurial dues. When the troops arrived, in September, the peasants dispersed without a fight.[49] The Bonnet Rouges were brutally suppressed, nevertheless. Madame de Sévigny complained she could no longer walk in the woods of Brittany because of the number of men hanging from the branches of trees.

These rebellions, which were doomed in the face of seasoned soldiers and ruthless authorities, were actually an expression of a strong attachment to traditions. The rebels objected to the fiscal 'novelties' and, more generally, to any sort of challenge to age-old customs. They were respectful of the social equilibriums, of the king and usually also of the aristocrats, whose help they sought to obtain justice. Their prime targets were the excesses to which they were subjected and they frequently chose tax officials as scapegoats. Conservative and backward-looking, they rejected the advance of the modern state, but without theorizing their rejection.

185

Their collective protest defined a culture of humiliation and opposition which is the distant ancestor of the workers' strikes of the industrial age. It was rooted in poverty, made all the harder to bear by the fact that living conditions were deteriorating for the lower classes in the seventeenth-century countryside. Without contesting the established order, the actors in these innumerable dramas turned to the prince to ask for bread, as still happened in the hunger riots of April 1789, because this was the protective and nurturing role of the sovereign. However, the sociology of the rebellious crowds merits further study. They often included women, who were particularly active during the innumerable food riots but also present on many other occasions.[50] No one has paid any real attention to the age of the men concerned, often for lack of information in the sources, but also for lack of interest in the subject.

Yet the great peasant revolts display specific features which ought to make us consider this aspect. They happened mostly in the season of warm weather, from spring onwards, culminating in the summer months. This was precisely the calendar of juvenile festive violence.[51] The month of May was traditionally devoted to amorous pursuits, after the long winter and interminable Lent. The curves of pardoned criminality show a steady increase until the middle of summer in the manly confrontations that resulted in homicides. To this we should add the opportunities provided by Carnival, when the usual excess could result in a proliferation of bloody disputes.[52] This was a phenomenon found all over Europe. In Lisbon, when a Jew cast doubt on the miracle of a shining crucifix, the Easter festivities of 1506 turned into bloody riots that lasted for three days, in which 2,000 people were allegedly killed. The serious disturbances in Pamiers, at Pentecost 1566, were directed against the Protestants who had prohibited the Catholic festivals at which popes, emperors and abbots of youth were elected. Those who proceeded to march through the streets behind a statue of St Anthony and danced, to the accompaniment of musicians, crying 'Kill! Kill!' were clearly unmarried men reclaiming the rights that had been taken away from them. The fighting went on for three days before the Catholics were finally defeated. In England, a riot in the Forest of Dean, in Gloucestershire, on 25 March 1631, involved 500 men, who marched through the forest accompanied by fifes and drums and carrying banners. Their declared objective was restoration of free access to areas that were now enclosed and forbidden to them. However, the form taken by the uprising was that of the Skimmington, the English charivari, which ended in the destruction of an effigy of the encloser. On the following Saturday, 5 April, the eve of Palm Sunday in the Catholic liturgy, a larger crowd of some 3,000 returned with drums and banners, destroying other enclosures and burning several houses.[53]

186

One of the essential but neglected aspects of the popular rebellions was their expression, through acts of violence conveying a symbolism of opposition, of a refusal to accept the disappearance of the customary privileges of the masculine kingdoms of youth. The important role played by women and pre-pubescent boys in the riots, particularly those with a religious dimension, has received more attention.[54] The festive dimension of many insurrections has also been emphasized, and sometimes even related to the frustrations of unmarried men, but without this being seen as of much general significance. Yet many bans were issued in the 1530s to address such issues. The Protestant authorities were deeply hostile to any manifestations considered to be pagan and licentious. The Carnival games were forbidden in the Reformed German and Swiss towns, such as Berne and Nuremberg, where the last *Schembart* was held in 1539. The Catholic countries adopted similar policies. At Lille, the Feast of the King of Fools was suppressed by an edict of Charles V in 1540. In France, an ordinance of François I of 1538 tried to abolish the abbeys of youth in certain provinces on the pretext that they were helping to propagate the Reformation. There was stronger resistance in the countryside. It retained its traditions in spite of the pressure, for example in Geneva, in the Jura and the pays de Vaud, and in the Low Countries, the United Provinces and the German Holy Roman Empire. The participants were sometimes able to adapt them to new times so as to ensure their continuance. In sixteenth-century England, the custom of burning an effigy representing Carnival on the night of Shrove Tuesday was transformed into a bonfire for a straw pope, which made it more acceptable to the strongly anti-Catholic authorities. The Puritans successfully replaced Hallowe'en and its ghosts and goblins (1 and 2 November) with the celebration of Guy Fawkes Night (5 November), in memory of the discovery of the papist Gunpowder Plot in 1605. They were unable, however, to put a stop to the old festivities and drinking sessions on this occasion. They were similarly unsuccessful in their attempts to prevent the acts of violence and sexual licence associated with Shrove Tuesday and Easter, or the erection of Maypoles inaugurating the season of love on May Day, with their obvious symbolism.[55]

The censorship of youth customs was only partially successful, which explains the tenacity of the religious and lay authorities. The efforts of the former on this front were stepped up in the seventeenth century. The Catholic priests, now much better trained, spearheaded this assault and wielded the formidable weapon of confession to dissuade sinners from vices stigmatized as mortal sins. Dancing was particularly frowned on. In some dioceses, the number of feast days – some sixty on top of Sundays – was reduced to thirty to cut down on occasions for disorder. In most cases, these festivities 'boiled down to the youthful high spirits of the summer months', with two high points: the dance in the village square and the communal drinking session in the inn. It was inevitable that an attempt to deny all pleasure to people whose everyday life was hard and dull would come up against fierce resistance, especially in the presence of a particularly strict bishop. In fact, the successive prohibitions issued by the various authorities never wholly succeeded in eradicating the ludic rural customs before the departure of the young en masse for the army or the factory in the industrial age. Among the forms of refusal, the propensity to dress up as a woman during a revolt was not only due to the need for anonymity; it was very clearly a carnivalesque protest. The transgression of a clothing taboo, punishable by law under the *ancien régime*, added an additional anti-establishment dimension. It was present in the enclosure riots in the West of England, led by a peasant known as Lady Skimmington. It was also found in Wales in 1820, and again in 1840 in the Rebecca riots. In Ariège, during the war of the Demoiselles against the forest code in 1829–30, the rioters roamed the countryside at night in bands some twenty strong, disguised as women and with blackened faces, especially during Carnival or on Sundays or feast days.[56]

The great peasant revolts of the sixteenth and first half of the seventeenth centuries were very different from the short, spontaneous 'emotions' when a small number of people from a rural parish or urban district came together to protest about a famine or for some other reason. The great revolts constituted a sort of mass protest movement on a regional scale, lasting for many months. The anger driving these thousands of peasants had deeper causes than the immediate events described by social historians since the 1960s. It led them to break through not only the barriers of disobedience but also those of the deep xenophobia existing between neighbouring communities. These heterogeneous assemblies suffered moreover from a basic weakness, in that each group followed its own leaders and colours to go into battle. This made it much easier for the much more disciplined and better-armed regular soldiers to put these rebellions down.

Nevertheless, the rebels went to war as if to a festival, even jauntily. They were convinced they would be victorious because they were sure they had right on their side: 'If the king only knew!' They marched cheerfully off as if to some entertainment, with fifes and musettes to the fore in attacks, for example in Quercy in May 1707. If they were victorious, they got drunk, toasting 'the king's health' without irony; they lit great fires like those for Carnival or St John's Night, rang bells and paraded to music. During Carnival in Bordeaux in 1651, an effigy of the execrated Mazarin was beheaded on the night of Shrove Tuesday, after being trailed through the streets on a mule, escorted by 300 armed men. On the fol-

188

lowing Sunday, the effigy was burned a first time in the palace square, scene of executions, then again, a week later, in the ditches of the Hôtel de Ville, during a great firework display, while bonfires were lit by the hundred in the surrounding villages. Monster drinking sessions and improvised dances accompanied what was effectively a variant – expanded and many times repeated to add to the general enjoyment – of the traditional battles of Carnival and Lent, which had been concluded by festivities round the bonfire on which the effigy of Carnival was burned.[57]

As regular participants in festive occasions, the members of both the rural and the urban bands of youth would certainly have been present in large numbers in the ranks of the insurgents; it was, after all, their custom to parade, armed, through the streets. Further, they had the energy needed for long weeks of marching followed by rough mêlées; and they had much less to lose than their elders, given that they were neither married nor established. It was probably their vitality that gave the rebellion its ludic dimension and a certain insouciance with regard to the dangers faced or even the heavy penalties they would incur. The absence of deliberate massacres and the selection of a small number of deeply detested targets was also characteristic of the customary rites of violence, based, as they had been, on brutality but without the systematic desire to kill. Only the hated tax-collectors were at risk of being done to death and then dragged through the streets like a trophy. Sometimes the victors tied their prize to a tree before throwing axes or knives at him, to test his courage and to make him bleed amidst general rejoicing, on the model of animal baiting or the rough games of *soule*. The cultural code operating here, which lauded the inversion of ordinary values for a festive period, was precisely what the authorities were all trying to destroy. The rebels acted in the same way as the young at the Feast of Fools or in Carnival or on the many occasions for festivities in the summer months. For a brief moment, they lived the dream of the hungry, of reaching the shores of a mythical land of Cockaigne, where wine flowed like water, food was plentiful and everything was for the best in the best of all possible worlds.[58]

The great peasant wars were a massive collective protest against new Puritan moral norms which were not fully enforced, but nevertheless seriously disruptive of everyday life; they were about more than the articulated demands, but, rather, symptoms of a profound malaise. They reveal a stubborn refusal to abandon the ancestral cultural traditions which extolled manly violence as a way of carving out a place for oneself in an unchanging world. Since the end of the Middle Ages, however, Western Europe had chosen to criminalize homicide and condemn the roughness of relationships among the people. Both the law of God and the law of a prince now stronger than before were invoked by the authorities to promote this major change. Only the aristocracy surreptitiously won the right to continue to kill without restraint, in the name of the point of honour. The morality of the new times, based on triumphant religions, demanded that all other subjects abandon their violent practices.

The long-drawn-out upsurge of peasant revolts, over several generations, shows that the confrontation with governments was focused on this issue. The forbidden violence was displayed in spectacular fashion by those who resisted. Meanwhile, under the influence of both repressive and educative processes on the part of the authorities, a new model of masculine behaviour slowly emerged, which banished brutality and excess. In the attempt to make as many young bachelors as possible abandon the ritual confrontations, they added the power of persuasion and shame to coercion. They put great stress on the cruelty of their games, the animal sacrifices in particular. This marked the beginning of a gradual transition which culminated in the transformation of the carnivalesque entertainments into sport, such as boxing in eighteenth-century England or football today. Once they became spectators, the participants, including the unmarried young men, were more in control of the pleasure they continued to get from watching men and beasts suffer, and they could identify with the players while indulging in an exuberance that was now frowned on in ordinary life.[59] The increase in the number of executions and their impressive judicial liturgy place the distant foundations of this phenomenon in the sixteenth century. The new spectacle of the executions did not so much demonstrate the power of the king as create a new attitude to death and blood among the observers. Admittedly, the crowds still sometimes broke the rules, rushing to the rescue of a condemned person or lynching an incompetent executioner, just as football supporters today sometimes invade the pitch. Most of the time, however, they had to be content with watching from afar. One of the principal functions of the endlessly repeated executions was to force those present to distance themselves from the scene and to instil into them the notion that the prince alone had the eminent right to end the life of a human being who had been lawfully condemned.

To be accepted one day as a true adult, the young country lad or town boy of the fifteenth and sixteenth centuries had to prove his manliness in the theatre of the street. This meant he had to take part in fights with his peers and in dangerous rituals, such as the English and French ball games, the Spanish bull hunts, the horse races of the Sienese *palio* or the battles on the bridges of Venice. One identical code of violence underlay both the cruel festivities that punctuated the year and the obligation of vengeance symbolized by the story of *Romeo and Juliet*. The progression from one to the other was only made easier. It needed only a spark to transform a merry Carnival into a veritable slaughterhouse, as at Romans in 1580 or Udine in 1511. On the latter occasion, the Zambarlani faction defeated the Stumieri faction, after two hundred years of inexpiable battles, then dismembered the corpses, leaving the remains exposed to the pigs and the dogs for days on end.[60] After the Renaissance, monarchic justice tried all over Europe to appropriate the symbolic language which made the body a metaphor for society as a whole, and violence an act productive of links between individuals. However, it was careful to sacralize to an extreme degree the ceremonies of execution and torture. To strengthen the authority of the state, it was important to demonstrate that these were not simply public reprisals but a punishment justified in the eyes of God, and that its cool enforcement transcended the passions of this world. The contemptible executioner bore alone the burden of direct responsibility, sparing the king, merciful by nature, from the appearance of a cruel tyrant. And the event was conducted with great solemnity: the procession leading the condemned person to the scaffold, the exhortations of the confessor, the public repentance. The process served to calm the passions and satisfy the morbid curiosity of the spectators, while also teaching them both to master their emotions at the sight of the spilling of blood and to control them in ordinary life, so as to avoid an equally terrible fate. The distancing of the crowds achieved by the erection of elevated scaffolds on permanent sites, such as the place de Grève in Paris and Tyburn in London, had the same effect. True, some of the crowd still rushed to the front so they could dip a piece of cloth in the victim's blood or carry off some relic, but the tendency to keep at a distance from the martyred body gradually strengthened from one generation to the next, in line with the slow rise of a taboo. The execution was watched from afar, without contact and without smell. It was probably the steady advance of this threshold of tolerance, more than fear of the supreme penalty, that explains the reduction in the number of homicides and assaults on persons from the second half of the seventeenth century.

The great popular revolts, which followed a similar chronology, made abundant use of the old gestural and symbolic repertoire. They reveal a mass refusal to accept the disappearance of the ritual right to the violence that permeated the whole of life, and taught boys how to become men. In a context of multi-factor crises, they invented a culture of protest in the face of the pressure from rulers and churchmen. The apogee of the revolts, in the first half of the seventeenth century, amounted to an assertion of identity, at precisely the time that this pressure was at its peak in a Baroque Europe disturbed by the Hundred Years War. The insurrections expressed in acts the refusal of the rebels to abandon festive

191

violence and become simply spectators of the tragedies of life, docile subjects and faithful Christians. The end of the great peasant wars was not, however, the end of the contested customs. Rather, it revealed that an equilibrium had been reached. The authorities moderated their demands, though continuing to launch sporadic offensives. Country people were sometimes ready to opt for less dangerous games or to differentiate themselves from those who inflicted suffering on people or animals and justified it as sport.[61] Thus they gave an appearance of adapting by making changes that were more apparent than real. Murderous violence remained a basic fact of life in regions that were isolated or remote from political centres, which preserved their traditions with greater success. The vendetta continued to operate at the heart of human relations, indeed still sometimes does so today, for example in Corsica, Liguria and Friule, but also in Iceland, the Highlands of Scotland, and Gévaudan and Quercy in France.[62] The proletariat of the industrial age also exhibited a certain brutality of manners inherited from the past. When this was sublimated, it eventually produced a workers' culture of protest which still today inspires many strikes, especially in France.

The role of young males in the revolts of the past would repay further study. It appears indirectly, in particular, in the great French peasant risings of the seventeenth century. The fact that they were mostly confined to the west, and even more to the south-west, of the kingdom suggests that the classic explanations of fiscal discontent, distance from monarchical power and local traditions of independence are inadequate. The deterioration in living conditions was aggravated by tax rises, but it was also the result of a neglected structural phenomenon, that is, the rules of inheritance among the peasantry. French customs were put into writing from the sixteenth century on. Though they varied greatly in detail, those governing the division of peasant property between successors essentially contrasted regions where the constraints made the fragmentation of holdings difficult and regions where the principle of equality prevailed.[63] The latter included the Orléans–Paris region, which was little affected by the great insurrectionary movements after the Jacquerie of 1348 due to its exceptional prosperity, the huge influence of the capital and the fact that the monarchy kept a close watch on this crucial area.[64] By contrast, egalitarian areas that were much less closely supervised from the political centre, largely located in the west, demonstrated a high level of agrarian individualism. The family was privileged at the expense of the household. It was in precisely these areas that rural protest movements were most common after 1620. After some twenty years of peace, reconstruction and demographic increase, the situation deteriorated, here as everywhere, for the young men who were reaching adulthood. The consequences were more severe in these communities, however, because

192

if a father left several sons, they had to share lands already reduced in size by the automatic consequences of previous successions. Their frustrations were also heightened by the postponement of the age of marriage, which further delayed their entry into the group of established adults. Added to this, the juridical and cultural importance of lineage made for a greater attachment to the customs linked to festive violence and familial vengeance. The great revolts probably acted as safety valves for a whole raft of accumulated discontents, made explosive by the authorities' offensive against dancing and youthful rites of confrontation. A similar sensibility was present in Flanders, another area of egalitarian succession, where the habit of rebellion, both rural and urban, was well established.

A further indication of the importance of the youth factor can be found in an analysis of the popular 'emotions' in France from 1661 to 1789.[65] The end of the peasant wars did not mean that the countryside had been pacified; far from it. Jean Nicolas has counted nearly 8,500 movements of lesser or greater importance, of which 39 per cent were directed against taxation, 18 per cent were food riots and 20 per cent the result of conflicts with the authorities, in particular the machinery of state. A total of 60 per cent were rural, though the over-representation of towns, 40 per cent for 15 per cent of the population, is indicative of significant urban tensions. A first peak came around 1705, another in the years 1740–60 and a last, which was particularly marked, in the period 1765–89. These were waves of generational discontent, which were probably stronger in the cities, then experiencing rapid economic and demographic growth, than in the countryside. The 634 disturbances clearly identified as predominantly youthful in character confirm this: 131 took place in the years 1741–60 and 308 in 1770–9. They included many nocturnal or carnivalesque eruptions, mostly concentrated between June and September and on Sundays or one of the major festivals of St John, St Peter and 15 August. The old ludic and manly calendar was still in operation. The forces of law and order and those holding local power were challenged on 365 occasions; there were 61 confrontations between gangs, 59 charivaris and donkey-rides and 40 riots involving schoolchildren or students – including some from Toulouse, famous for their excess. In other words, the many and harsh edicts to control them were frequently flouted. The great waves of legislative intolerance of the middle of the century and the years 1778–86 were followed, in direct response, by peaks of transgression, which cast doubt on the efficacy of the prohibitions that were supposedly being strengthened. Popular culture put up a strong resistance to the offensives mounted against it and even demonstrated considerable vitality. The young males had abandoned neither their nocturnal traditions nor their brutality. Some of the latter was turned against the servants of the state, soldiers and the members of the *maréchaussée*.

Yet this is only the tip of the iceberg. At just over 7 per cent of the total, youth disturbances seem relatively rare. But only those who were prosecuted appear in the figures, and they had mostly taken their revenge on those who had prevented them from dancing in a circle or otherwise behaving as they had done in the past. Many other ritual happenings went unpunished, like fights between gangs, which are rarely mentioned in the documents. Such activities were conducted discreetly, away from the prying eyes of the keepers of the peace, who were probably not actively looking for trouble as long as there was no wave of repressive fervour to spur them on. Further, we may be confident that many of those who participated in other 'emotions', ranked under other headings, were adolescents. They would certainly have turned out with the rest of the community on the occasion of fiscal or food protests, or protests against the authorities. These provided an outlet for their long-established animosity towards their elders and the *maréchaussée*, as well as an opportunity to demonstrate their manliness by employing, against hated targets, a customary violence which generally had the approval of the rebellious adults they accompanied.

As everywhere in Europe, the seventeenth century was particularly violent in France.[66] The worsening living conditions and the increased fiscal demands of the state were major factors in this, but the main cause was the revolution in sensibilities brought about by the 'civilizing process'. This radically altered the behaviour of the prosperous townspeople, among whom the ground had already been prepared by the urban peace of the fifteenth century. It then spread to the courtiers at Versailles.[67] The other population groups were similarly urged to abandon ritual violence, which had cemented their group cohesion but also resulted in a high degree of indifference towards injuries and homicide. It was not easy for them to accept theories that were so far removed from their own realities. At the two extremes of the social spectrum, the nobles, on the one hand, and the urban and above all rural poor, on the other, refused to abandon their traditions. The twofold rise in violence which resulted, visible in the proliferation of duels and of great popular uprisings, reveals a stubborn refusal to accept the imposition by rulers of a law of the economy of blood and of the passions. Around 1620, just when the principle that human life was protected by God and by the sword of justice of the prince was beginning to prevail in the West, the explosion of mortal challenges between aristocrats and of peasant revolts issued a strong warning that this principle was not universally accepted. The brutality displayed was in itself the principal claim. The aristocrats came off best,

194

because they were too necessary to the monarch and his armies for him not to tolerate the murderous folly of the duel; though they were threatened with harsh punishment, this was only a facade. They were able to invent a privileged culture of violence, a warlike model based on the ruthless elimination of the opponent, traces of which survived for a very long time. The peasantry did not get off so lightly. Nevertheless, the constant reiteration of the prohibitions testifies to the survival of the traditions they were meant to make disappear. The rural world proved able to adapt to external threats while preserving its internal equilibrium. As with the young noblemen who fought ever more duels, it was based on the need of the new masculine generations to demonstrate their manliness. It was only much later, with the conjunction of population decline in the countryside, the exodus to the factories and universal conscription, that real and profound change became possible. And some regions still cling today to the habits of youth violence and familial vengeance, as we see from the Mediterranean vendetta and the mafias which have appropriated their chief features.

The blood taboo was accepted first among the continent's urban elites, after the terrible devastation and traumas of the Thirty Years War. It then spread, but very gradually. At Romans, in 1768, a riot broke out because of a rumour that children aged under fourteen had been abducted by well-dressed men who wanted to 'draw some of their blood' to use in anatomical demonstrations.[68] The allegation recalls the Parisian riots of May 1750, during which one policeman died, which had been sparked by rumours that the ageing Louis XV had ordered children to be abducted so that he could revitalize himself with their blood.[69] The sacralized vital substance, a social metaphor, had to be used sparingly. The exuberant body of the people was urged to show restraint, to avoid excess, to be disciplined.[70] These two riots show that the common people of the cities did not always heed this advice, but that they were beginning, in the age of the *philosophes*, to take it more seriously. It is an irony of history that the crowds turned their aggression against the king and the grandees who were accused of seeking to monopolize the body, the flesh and the blood of the subjects, especially the youngest. They were conscious of the symbolism, at a time when boys who were approaching adulthood were much more closely controlled than in the past. The European 'factory' tried to persuade young males of the absolute necessity of curbing their violence. It was now denigrated by the dominant moral discourse and stigmatized by the representatives of law and order and the schoolmasters, and increasingly deflected towards spectacles that were believed to defuse it, such as public executions or, in England, boxing. The young men who were particularly stubborn, and committed homicide, inflicted injuries or stole, had to expect to be harshly punished.

195

It was still necessary, however, for the accepted moral authorities, represented by the sovereign and gentlemen of quality, not to break the tacit pact by making unlawful use of the precious blood of youth, which they were in general so insistent should not be wasted.

A cultural and social dividing line emerges with great clarity. The more civilized, those who were strongly in favour of the pacification of behaviour, now saw everyone else as gross and brutal barbarians. The racial prejudice of the nobles, clearly visible by the sixteenth century in France, and the deep contempt of the upper classes of the industrial age for drunken workers and their violent habits and lax sexual customs, for example in Victorian England, resulted from this division of the world. Did it perhaps initially help to sublimate the old xenophobic reflexes that had been crucial to the cohesiveness of local communities, so as to forge the modern states and then the nations of the nineteenth century? It is now accentuated by the way we educate our young, as we persist in separating off an elite in spite of the contemporary egalitarian discourse, and it continues to produce before our very eyes, in France and elsewhere in Europe, a two-speed society.

— 7 —

VIOLENCE TAMED (1650–1960)

In 1648, the peace of Westphalia ended the Thirty Years War and over a century of confrontations between Protestants and Catholics for the domination of Europe. Conflicts continued to be numerous after that, and increasingly bloody up to the climax of the two world wars of the twentieth century, but they had very different meanings. The emphasis ceased, for the most part, to be on religious causes, in favour of notions of a just war between states or nations, while a significant part of the continent's lifeblood was invested in colonial conquest and exploitation.

The Western 'factory', which was engaged from 1650 to 1960 in a massive effort both to dominate the rest of the world and to respond on its own soil to the constant clashes between expansionist countries, came to draw an increasingly clear distinction between two forms of violence, legitimate and illegitimate. The former was essential to sustain the bellicose spirit necessary to the defence of the homeland and the domination of vast territories overseas; the latter came to be regarded by the authorities and by established people as disturbing, dangerous and disruptive of social harmony. Yet both these forms were closely connected to identical phenomena of manly aggression. How, then, was the violence that was legitimate to be encouraged without validating the use of the other sort in the general opinion?

The process of making this distinction was long and complex. It was slower in some countries and regions than others, and ground gained was often lost, especially during major crises. The result, nevertheless, was the acceptance, all over the continent, of a dual model of masculine behaviour: on the one hand, the 'imperial' man, capable of brutality when it was necessary or legitimate; on the other, the peaceable citizen, the good husband and father, happily fulfilled in a serene household.

197

The ideal of what has been called the 'Peaceable Kingdom' of England, capable of producing the military energy necessary to rule a vast world empire, was found throughout Western Europe, especially in France, the Low Countries and Germany.

The pacification of everyday behaviour was based not only on the power of ideas, but also on methods of collective control adapted to such needs. Norbert Elias and Michel Foucault clearly identified these, each confining his discussion to one of the two principal aspects of a phenomenon whose full significance can only be understood globally. The civilizing process described by Elias makes it possible to understand how the authoritarian state claimed a monopoly of violence, and how it 'fashioned' the subject by urging him to internalize self-control and in this way limit displays of aggression in public space. Politeness, a code unifying the members of the upper social ranks, configured appearances so as to pacify normal relations, without sapping the energy indispensable to vital and legitimate battles. However, the mass of the population was only partially and slowly affected. They were the subject of other techniques for the management of brutality, in the form of the 'disciplinary' practices described by Foucault. For him, the purpose of prison or, to be more precise, 'the carceral system', was not solely to punish or render docile those who might break the law. Confinement was part of a 'general tactic of subjection', which led, in succession, from the police gaze to incarceration and then to delinquency, because the surveillance of pre-defined targets regularly despatched some of them to the cells.[1]

It would be mistaken, however, to oppose too literally these two models for an education in conduct only in relation to social criteria. Many people from all backgrounds were shaped by the contradictory messages, within families, in educational institutions and even more during military service. The norm that consisted of strictly limiting the right to kill to one's sacred duty to the homeland and one's loved ones and to self-defence was difficult for most people to accept. It was infringed, in particular, by the aristocrats, who demanded respect for the point of honour, and by adolescents from the lower classes, whose survival was dependent on their ability to defend themselves in a hostile environment. It spread, nevertheless, closely controlled by numerous agents of socialization. Criminal justice was one of the most important of these. For the three centuries in question, it played a fundamental role in auditing the efficacy of the dissemination of the principles and prohibitions concerning ordinary violence. Those who ignored them, and then appeared before the magistrates, were predominantly unmarried young men of modest origins; the proportion of women involved steadily declined. The same characteristics apply in the case of property crime, which became the principal preoccupation of the industrial societies.

Over and above their repressive action and the restoration of internal peace, the courts shaped the new masculine generations according to the prevailing criteria. An analysis of their role makes it possible to insert a missing link between the theories of Elias and Foucault, because the courts addressed a normative message to all citizens, accompanied by penalties if the codes were broken. Those who failed, or refused, to adapt to the demands of the civilizing process, of whom there were many, were potential targets for the courts. Their activities were judged not only according to the law, but also to the degree of danger they posed to the community. They had to demonstrate that they could at the very least keep their aggression in check if they wanted to escape prosecution. This mechanism of self-control, linked to a clearly perceived self-interest in the face of a specific threat of punishment, reinforced that of the civility which cemented relations between honest folk. It resulted, not in an absolute reduction in the destructive potential of the human being, but in an effective form of its cultural control by Western civilization. The adult world succeeded in significantly limiting youth violence by deflecting it into external conquest or legitimate war and by ruthlessly criminalizing the remainder. Combined with the disappearance of great military conflicts from European soil after 1945, the end of the colonial era has destroyed this balance, leaving the field clear for some decades now to a new increase in murder and physical violence.

Between 1650 and 1960, violence was truly tamed in Europe. Not only were homicide rates in long-term decline, before reaching the absolute minima of the mid twentieth century, but the more ordinary use of force evolved towards less dangerous practices, both within the home and in public space. This, in the latter, bare-knuckle fighting, conducted according to precise rules, gradually replaced fighting with knives. The urban metropolis was the principal motor of change. Contrary to a widely held belief, the European town has done much to damp down violence. To pacify its streets, it never stopped moulding its young and it kept a close watch on the immigrants who arrived in large numbers in the age of industrialization. The countryside, which lost its demographic preponderance at this same period, also changed radically, but at a slower pace. The decline of rural violence owed much less to the offensive of the civilizing process than to a readiness to adapt to the criminalization of murder, even, on the part of the village worthies and established adult males, a strong desire to adapt. This radical change in relations between the masculine age groups took the form of a gradual abandonment of the defence of manly honour by means of weapons or the use of physical strength, in favour of a new perception of the value, symbolic but also monetary, of human life.

Murder is forbidden

The spectacular downward trend in homicide in Europe is well known. It began in the seventeenth century and it developed primarily in the towns until the industrial age, when it gradually spread to the country-side. In France and Germany alike, there was a slow reduction in the rate in the nineteenth century, in spite of occasional upturns. In France these occurred around 1830, 1850, 1870, 1880–90 and, even more markedly, around 1910. Contrary to a common belief, urbanization and industrialization did not have the effect of aggravating violence, but rather of lessening it over the long term. In both countries, however, the curve of non-fatal assaults rose, in precise inverse correlation with that for murder. In other words, conflicts were more frequent but their con-sequences were less dramatic. One historian, having noted that the highest rate in France – nearly 21 homicides per 100,000 inhabitants – was in Corsica, has pointed to the tradition of violence as one of the most important determinants, and seen its decline as 'a victory for urban values and social organisation'.[2]

To this we need to add the youth dimension, which alone makes it possible to understand the sharp rises in the murder rate observed at roughly twenty-year intervals in France, and also identifiable in Germany around 1850 and in the 1880s. These statistical peaks seem to be primarily related not to economic, social or political crises, or the unsettled atmosphere of the pre-war periods, which merely accentuated the phenomenon, but rather to generational effects. The prohibitions on the shedding of blood were now imposed on an ever-larger majority of young males. Nevertheless, these prohibitions were still openly rejected by a minority, who continued to fight in the streets, but now less often killed each other. The more dramatic upsurges, which happened with some regularity in France every twenty years, were probably linked to the emergence from adolescence of a new age group. It was a sort of fit of youthful rage against the imposed norms. It reveals a sharper perception of their situation among the offenders, who were usually of humble origin, in the face of the domination of adults, which was felt particularly strongly in the economic sphere. By obliging the police and the judicial authorities to tighten a control that had gradually been relaxed, from habit, during the preceding period, it sporadically helped to swell the figures for crimes against persons.

In Sweden, the homicide rate fell slowly from the 1840s, and the crime gradually came to be specifically associated with the working classes.[3] In England, the number of cases known to the police – just under 400 a year – fell by half in the period 1860–1914. Convictions declined even further, to settle at 0.6 per 100,000 inhabitants at the end of the period. Assaults and woundings initially moved in the opposite direction, then began to decline sharply, from the mid nineteenth century in the case of the former, around 1870 for the latter.[4] A regional study of the great mining district of the Black Country, north of Birmingham, although it deals with age criteria only in passing, and does not provide raw figures, shows that young men in the 16–25 age group were over-represented. Although they formed 23 per cent of the population in 1850, they provided 45 per cent of those accused, all offences included, even 50 per cent in the 1830s. No other category had a delinquency rate higher than its demographic weight, with the exception, in each case less pronounced, of the 14–15 and 26–29 age groups. Overall, two-thirds of those prosecuted were aged between fourteen and twenty-nine, although this age group represented only a third of the total number of inhabitants. They were significantly less well educated than the majority, and belonged to a rough proletarian world where brawling was frequent but rarely resulted in murder.

Between 1835 and 1860, in this region with a population of over 300,000, 258 persons were prosecuted for manslaughter and 56 for murder. Not a single death sentence was passed. Transportation or penal servitude were ordered in only a dozen cases, and most sentences were of six months or less in prison. The proceedings against 499 persons accused of non-fatal assaults confirm the conclusions as to the overwhelmingly masculine and juvenile nature of ordinary violence: 92 per cent of the offences were committed by men, of whom over half were aged between eighteen and thirty. In the case of attempted murder, the proportion was as high as 80 per cent. Infanticide, lastly, was little prosecuted. The thirty-nine women accused of it were mostly young, often domestic servants, and they were treated leniently. Half were found innocent, the others imprisoned for at most a year, in two cases for less than a month. Everything suggests that violence, even when it was fatal, was not the prime concern of the authorities, or of the local working classes. In spite of the heavy costs incurred, charges were laid much more often in the case of property crimes, which emphasizes both the high degree of acceptance of the legitimacy of the law and the lukewarmness of the desire to take the pacification of human relations any further.[5]

For France, the *Compte général de l'administration de la justice criminelle* for the years 1871–1940 reveals that 49 per cent of the felonies had been committed by young men or women aged thirty or less. The rate was above 71 per cent for infanticide, the most frequent female crime, before theft and abortion. For men, who constituted 83 per cent of the contingent, the figure was 71 per cent for manslaughter, 66 per cent for premeditated murder, 77 per cent for aggravated assault and also over three-quarters for aggravated robbery. The number of very young persons accused was low, less than 1 per cent of the total – the life of crime really only began at the age of sixteen. Up to the age of forty, robbery was by far the main offence, after which it was consistently child molestation or statutory rape, the two arbitrarily lumped together in the same judicial category. Between the ages of twenty-two and thirty, manslaughter came second, well ahead of robbery, followed by child molestation or statutory rape, premeditated murder, then infanticide. An additional correlation appears with the unmarried state. Recorded on average in 57 per cent of cases, it was particularly characteristic of aggravated violence.[6]

From these figures, which are never a perfect reflection of reality and which need always to be used with care, two clear trends emerge. In Western Europe in the nineteenth century, it was primarily a sector of the young of both sexes who seem to have been unable either to assimilate the norms or to integrate socially that lapsed into delinquency. For both sexes, the process usually began with theft. In the case of young men, this was followed by the molestation of little girls and acts of violence, fights either with peers or to get food, whereas vulnerable young women resorted to infanticide to get out of a difficult situation. The young men who went on to marry and settle down moved on to offences more typically based on fraud, abuse of confidence, illegal schemes or the sexual abuse of young girls. A total of 29,369 cases of girl molestation were denounced in the years 1871–1940, that is, 14 per cent of the total, which puts it in second place after grand larceny. It seems unlikely that this was a practice confined to members of the upper and middle classes, frustrated by 'bourgeois marriage', shamelessly pursuing young, unprotected, working-class girls.[7]

One of the questions this phenomenon raises is that of incest among the lower classes, as it was included by the penal code in the category in question. More generally, we are made to think about the displacement of violence from public space to the intimacy of the family. This novelty was of little interest to the authorities, as happy to see a reduction in visible conflictuality as they were reluctant to intervene in private life. The fact is, men of all ages preyed on little girls. It was the second most common crime among bachelors in the 16–21 age group, and the third most common among their elders up to the age of thirty; it was second among married young adults, and consistently the most common among men over forty. These figures cast a disquieting light on relations between the sexes in the lower social ranks, from which the majority of the individuals prosecuted came.

The emergence of a large number of complaints probably reveals a need among women to seek external help against a very widespread masculine tyranny, which often led to the abuse of young girls. It is equally probable that the law of silence and fear of reprisals prevented other denunciations, in particular by mothers of abusive fathers. It is also possible that the greater tolerance of infanticide on the part of the magistrates and the jurors was motivated at least in part by a clearer perception of the disastrous situation experienced from childhood by many girls, especially the poor servant girls who provided many of those accused.[8] As in England, not only were masters ready to believe they had a right to the sexual favours of these girls, but the girls were also exposed to rape at the hands of male servants or lodgers.[9]

In France, female criminality declined during the course of the nineteenth century, eventually settling, in the last three decades, at 14 per cent of the total, infanticide and abortion included. Women played an increasingly small role in violence: 6 per cent for homicide or theft with violence, 9 per cent for assault and battery, 13 per cent for premeditated murder. Further, juries displayed a growing tendency to treat women leniently, and they were acquitted more often than men.[10] Only certain specific types of woman attracted attention, such as *La Servante criminelle*, to whom Raymond de Ryckére devoted a book in 1908; it had the suggestive subtitle *A Study in Professional Criminology*.

We should beware, however, of too readily concluding that the condition of women improved. In fact, the second sex provided an increasing number of victims. Sexual abuse of minors, predominantly girls, increased, in France and in many other countries, including the Vienna of the age of Freud. In England, there was a significant increase between 1860 and 1890, in direct contrast to criminality in general, which fell rapidly after 1850 and continued to decline until the end of the century. Of those accused, 99 per cent were men, and in 93 per cent of cases they had molested little girls. The 'discovery' of the problem was linked to a burgeoning of the movement for the protection of children and a romantic conception that dated from the Enlightenment and emphasized the innocence of the child. Little attention was paid to young boys, due to a different perception of the genders, which still linked the feminine creature to her sexual reputation. Only little girls who had been abused posed a real social threat. They received more attention, therefore, which explains the increase in complaints, but they also suffered rejection. Many institutions refused to accept them, for fear they would corrupt the other girls. At the age of twelve, or even younger, they were frequently placed in refuges or prisons which accepted adult prostitutes.

At a time when both femininity and childhood were being re-conceptualized by the British, so as to promote throughout the nation a masculine model of the 'vigorous colonist' and a feminine model wholly devoted to 'the sacredness of motherhood', the little female rape-victims, who did not fit into this schema, were a source of as much fear as pity. Further, contemporaries refused openly to confront the problem of incest, although it was quite often the reason for these children's 'fall'. Though a sin in the eyes of the church, incest was not made illegal in the United Kingdom until 1908. Before that, the sexual abuse of children was dealt with only under the legislation governing the age of consent. Until 1885, the excessive affection of a father for a daughter of between thirteen and sixteen did not seem illegitimate. Indeed, some fathers seem to have believed that their marital rights extended to their children, all the more so as the rape of a spouse could not be prosecuted until 1991.[11]

Despite major social, religious and cultural differences, the two principal colonial powers of the nineteenth century, France and England, evolved in a similar fashion as regards offences against persons. Homicide and physical violence continued to decline in public space, to reach an absolute low: at the beginning of the twentieth century, the courts prosecuted fewer than one alleged murderer per 100,000 inhabitants. Violence was not so much eradicated, however, as deflected, by the efforts of the political and moral authorities who taught the necessity of restraining it in public. The first English laws against the ill-treatment of cattle, in 1822, were part of this trend. Cock-fighting and cruelty to domestic pets were banned in 1835. With the support of a public opinion increasingly hostile to acts of cruelty, the criminalization of brutality entered a new phase in seeking the complete pacification of collective space. The main target remained young males, from the working classes in particular. Since the Middle Ages they had been successively urged, on pain of death, to stop carrying weapons, to abandon their ritual fighting, to avoid aggressive challenges to the authorities and not to steal in an effort to ameliorate a hard life. Finally, the acquisition of a vast empire overseas contributed to this pacification by despatching some of the most turbulent young men to make a military career or become settlers in the colonies.[12]

In the nineteenth century, Western Europe redefined the notion of violence once again, to adapt to major shifts in social relations and, even more, in relations between age groups and sexes in an industrial era characterized by massive change. In both France and England, the courts became increasingly severe towards male defendants while, in contrast, treating women with greater leniency. This apparent paradox reveals a desire on the part of governments and of adult men of standing from the upper and middling social ranks to control men more closely, especially if they were young and from the working classes. In their eyes, the right to punish, including a legitimate recourse to force, belonged exclusively to masters, superiors and fathers, who might use it in moderation to protect their home and their property.

Women, many fewer of whom came before the courts, were also punished increasingly less harshly in England in the second half of the nineteenth century. They were usually given short prison sentences, and almost never condemned to death. Further, more of those found guilty of violence were acquitted on grounds of insanity. The fact that such verdicts rose to 17 per cent in the 1890s is telling with regard to the perception of feminine 'weakness' that lay behind these decisions. In France, the juries of the late nineteenth century were remarkably tolerant of abortion, which was now practised by an increasing number of wives, who used it as a form of birth control, in spite of the pro-birth policy of the government and the exhortations of the church. The act was decriminalized by a law of 1923. The acquittal rate for infanticide, mostly committed by poor, tyrannized and unmarried girls, rose even more rapidly, reaching 58 per cent on the eve of the First World War, three times higher than in 1860.[13]

Such leniency seems suspect to some feminists, inclined to see this 'non-recognition of women's potential for violence' as a mechanism designed to soften manners by highlighting the old figure of the 'civilizing woman', linked to an assertion of woman's inferiority.[14] However, it might equally well derive from a perception on the part of the judges and juries that there had been a decisive shift of physical brutality from outside the home to inside it, and a desire to limit the impact of this without interfering directly in private or intimate matters. The large increase in the number of accusations of molesting or raping little girls is one of many signs of the growth of judicial sanctions designed to soften the roughness of relations and extremes of behaviour within marriage. Regarded as the inviolable sanctuary of masculinity by the triumphant bourgeoisie, it was in practice the only place where aggression was legitimate, on the part of the master against the rest of the household. It must not, of course, pass the thresholds of tolerance laid down by the law, but had to remain hidden, unknown to the authorities; otherwise it could be severely punished. This was the case with the murder of a spouse. Between 1841 and 1900, there were seventy-eight trials for husband murder in England and Wales, and 701 for wife murder. The disproportion greatly increased during the period, the number of wives accused falling by half, that of husbands rising by three-quarters; it was the only type of homicide to increase during this period.

It is unlikely that this was due only to an intensification of conflicts within the home. Such things had been invisible or rare in previous ages.

No accusation of this type figured among the 579 cases of assault prosecuted in Essex between 1620 and 1680. As elsewhere in Europe, domestic disputes were then punished by the community, without recourse to the courts. Complacent or weak husbands were told in no uncertain terms to assert themselves under pain of a humiliating public punishment such as the *chevauchée* on a donkey, inflicted on cuckolded husbands alone. If the husband went too far, and the wife did not survive, the act was classed as manslaughter and treated with great leniency by the courts – if, that is, it ever reached them. More non-fatal cases came before the courts in England in the eighteenth century, but they were usually dealt with by mediation rather than punishment. This practice continued in the nineteenth century, but there was at the same time a growing trend to criminalize the act, probably only partially effective.[15] This is difficult to interpret. It is by no means certain that it sprang purely from a desire to protect the weaker members of the household. The magistrates and jurors seemed to define real boundaries only in the sphere of the lethal excesses of a husband. At the same time, they refused to take effective action against paternal incest. And if they tried to give little girls greater protection against sexual abuse, especially by adults, it was primarily to prevent their fall from leading to a wider corruption of the feminine world on which the demographic future of the nation depended. As in France and other countries experiencing industrialization, the repressive effort was primarily directed against the lower classes, who were regarded as dangerous and singularly violent.

England was something of an exception in Europe. It was the only country to have oriented its courts at an early stage towards the repression of attacks on property, under pressure from the principal inhabitants of the parishes, the 'middling sort', who were alarmed by the rapid rise in vagrancy between 1570 and 1630. The problem arose as a consequence of the extreme difficulty experienced by young people in getting established and marrying, because 67 per cent of those apprehended for vagrancy were under twenty-one years of age and 43 per cent under sixteen.[16] In the eighteenth century, the Bloody Code continued to send more young thieves than murderers to the gallows. It was abandoned in the 1830s, as the principal anxieties of both the authorities and the population shifted increasingly towards assaults on persons. They were dealt with, belatedly, by a general disarming of citizens and by police forces, reinforced by a great strengthening of forms of social surveillance and of the regulation of public order. Seen as an English peculiarity by anglophone authors, this evolution seems rather to be a case of England catching up with other states, which had been engaged since the beginning of the seventeenth century in the 'civilizing process' and the curtailment of murderous violence. From this perspective, the strong condemnation of the murderer was more of a move to correct a backwardness that is amply demonstrated by the figures and to bring the country into line with others than an expression of a specificity, as Victorian newspapers were wont to claim at the end of the nineteenth century.[17] In particular, they called the murder of an unfaithful wife essentially un-English, as a way of lauding self-control, restraints on violence and the attention paid to the weaker sex. Such traits were deemed to characterize the British subject, by contrast with everyone else – Frenchmen, Italians, Spaniards and Greeks, in particular, all presumed incapable of controlling their impulses or their rage. The immorality of the French, vilified for the extreme leniency of their national juries towards crimes of love and passion, attracted especial criticism. It is true that women were the chief beneficiaries of the changes in England in the nineteenth century. Alcohol fuelled brutality, in particular among the lower classes. The evidence comes in the very restrictive legislation and the fact that fines or imprisonment for such excesses more than tripled between 1860 and 1870, reaching 185,000 in the last year. Cases of wife murder by a drunken husband echo this trend, rising from 63 in 1841–70 to 152 in the next thirty years.[18] The reality of this growing social scourge explains the severity of the courts. The ode to the 'ordinary reasonable man' intoned by contemporaries helped to conceal the extreme difficulty of eradicating violence, which was now excluded from public space but concentrated in the home, where it was probably more extreme and more widespread than the crime statistics suggest.

In France, the situation appears to have caused less concern. The longstanding battle against all forms of aggression seems to have prevented an excessive concentration of them in the home, if we are to go by the leniency of juries in this matter. Between 1903 and 1913, they were harsh only in cases of murder or aggravated murder, especially during a robbery. They acquitted 40 per cent of the other defendants. They were particularly understanding towards those who killed from love, jealousy or distress, but also when the victims were of bad reputation, belonging to turbulent milieus where fights were common, or in cases of brawls in a bar or between lovers from the working-class world.[19] The essential difference between the two great rival countries probably lay in a different collective perception of the value of human life. Around 1830–4, France occupied a middle position in Europe as regards the use of the death penalty, with an annual rate of 1 per 1,000,000 inhabitants. In Prussia the supreme penalty had practically disappeared in the preceding fifteen years and was rarely used except for murder. In England, by contrast, the annual average of death sentences rose from 1,000 in 1810 to 1,350 in 1830, a rate, in relation to size of population, ten times higher than in Prussia and three times higher than in France. The majority of these sentences were for crimes against property. Although the number of hangings steadily declined in the first third of the century, settling at 1 in 29 death sentences between 1831–3 (the others were transported to the colonies), it was primarily simple theft without violence that was so harshly punished.[20] The symbolism attaching to execution was not primarily intended, therefore, to dissuade potential killers. As a result, homicide had a much more banal dimension than on the continent. The proliferation of wife murders probably reflected the difficulty for the collective sensibilities in adapting to the criminalization of an act which had not previously seriously concerned the authorities.

The fall in fatal violence and the reduced use of the death penalty were closely connected. They were the two faces of a same process, that is, the increase in the value attached to human life, an original feature of Europe and of the universal values it has exported since the nineteenth century. In this age of conflicts, internecine strife and class war, the general trend towards the pacification of ordinary relations happened everywhere on its soil, though at very different rates. In Italy, for example, there was a radical transformation in the second half of the nineteenth century. The national homicide rate fell from 13 to 2 per 100,000 inhabitants. In the province of Naples, with a population of some seven million in 1861, this crime was twice as frequent as in Germany, France and England put together. The courts tried it seven times less often in 1880, although the population had increased by 20 per cent. In Sicily at the same date, the rate remained very high, at around 17 per 100,000 inhabitants, but this was already half, perhaps even a third, of what it had been at the beginning of the century. The gradual decline of the death penalty, at different rates in different states, forms the backdrop to the steady pacification of manners. In France, the use of the guillotine fell to a very low level in 1901–5, then fluctuated, before this form of punishment was abolished in 1981. The evolution in England was even more dramatic, with death sentences falling from a maximum in 1830 to a rate lower than that in France at the beginning of the twentieth century. Meanwhile, Norway, Denmark and Sweden abolished the death penalty. These changes are a sign of a new attitude to young people of humble origins, who had accounted for most of those condemned to death. In England before 1800, young men of under twenty-one had been the most heavily represented in this doomed cohort.[21]

On the eve of the First World War, which was marked by great outbreaks of collective ferocity, many Europeans, paradoxically, were disinclined to engage in violent confrontations in everyday life. The bourgeoisie could pride themselves in having tamed homicidal violence by drastically reducing the number of non-criminal murders. It had channelled or

208

diverted the brutality of the working classes to render it less disquieting. The increase in the number of assaults and woundings and in domestic violence reflected this shift towards acts with less tragic consequences, which would subsequently decline in their turn, less rapidly and to a lesser extent in the southern than the northern countries.[22] This was the result of a multiform surveillance of adolescents, in particular those of working-class origin, whose 'natural' unruliness caused great unease to governments, men of property and lovers of order and civic peace. The Western 'factory' developed many ways of curbing their disruptive potential. The ultimate filter was criminal justice. It was aimed less at punishing the recalcitrant and those beyond redemption, or at rehabili-tating them through confinement, in accord with certain normative dis-courses of the age, than at isolating them from the community and forcing them to undergo the training they had refused.[23] Prison, as described by Michel Foucault, was both a link in the chain and a scaled-down model of Western society. It largely housed anomic young males. It continued the massive effort expended on making their age group conform through a variety of institutions, such as the school and the army, and many less official procedures. The training in behaviour under-taken by all the socializing bodies endlessly reiterated the need for self-control and good manners when sharing public space; youthful aggression, meanwhile, was deflected in countless ways, in particular into sport, which was believed to produce healthy minds in healthy bodies, colonial enterprises and, even more, the defence of the endangered fatherland.

Nevertheless, in spite of a real reduction in the danger, clearly visible in the extremely low figures for homicide at the turn of the century, Europeans believed they were witnessing an increase in the ferocity of young men. The unease was probably caused by the arrival at adulthood of a large generation, whose rising numbers could alarm established people, also shaken by demands for workers' rights and tensions between states. French intellectuals were fascinated by these problems. They defined criminal stereotypes from a highly moralistic standpoint. On the masculine side, they were organized according to age: violence was char-acteristic of youth, theft and fraud developed with maturity, the sexual abuse of little girls typified old age. It may be that the whiff of archaism given off by these typologies has helped to devalue them in the eyes of modern scholars. Yet if we consider this flourishing literature as a symptom, it reveals a deep anxiety in the face of the threat represented by the new generations and their disastrous consequences for the col-lectivity. Paul Drillon presented a dissertation in 1905 on *Criminal Youth. Science and Religion. Studies for the Present Day*. In 1907, J. Grosmolard discussed *The Struggle against Juvenile Criminality in the Nineteenth Century*, while Raoul Leroy offered a *Medico-Legal*

Examination of a Young Criminal Aged 20 Prosecuted for Rape and Murder. In 1908, Albert Giuliani entitled his law thesis *Criminal Adolescence. Contribution to the study of the Causes of the Constantly Growing Criminality of Adolescence and of the Remedies to be Applied*. The year after G.-L. Duprat held forth on *Criminality in Adolescence. Causes of and Remedies for a Contemporary Evil*.[24]

The carnage of 1914–18, which decimated the young above all, defused these fears and made it possible for the pacification of manners to continue. By 1930, murderous violence had reached its lowest point on the continent. Only a residue of homicide remained in Western Europe, from Scandinavia to Spain, by way of France, where recorded murders varied between 0.5 and 0.9 per 100,000 inhabitants; the exception was Finland, where the rate was 10.1 per 100,000. In a second group of countries – Germany, Belgium, Portugal, Italy, Czechoslovakia and Austria – the rate was on average between 2 and 3 per 100,000. Further west and south, lastly, in Hungary, Poland, Romania and Greece, the rates were between 4 and 6 per 100,000 inhabitants, compared with 8.8 in the United States and 51.8 in Mexico at the same period. Nearly fifty years later, in 1976–8, the situation revealed by the world health statistics had evened out. The rate generally fluctuated around 1 per 100,000, that is, nine times lower than in the United States, and the gaps had grown smaller, including for Finland, although the rate there remained three times higher than elsewhere. Europe was the only continent on the planet to present these features in the third quarter of the twentieth century. Lethal violence was a residual phenomenon, mostly associated with organized crime. Prosecutions were now principally focused on forms of private brutality. The very marked increase in cases of rape in Sweden and Germany, and their slower rise in France, England and Italy, were an indication less of a real worsening of the phenomenon than of its increasing criminalization. Driven off the streets and more often denounced by the victims, aggression became an absolute taboo. The family unit was under greater surveillance, which led to more prosecutions of acts that had previously been widely concealed. These included incest and paedophilia, which were to become a main concern of the repressive authorities at the beginning of the twenty-first century. Other shifts or transfers of violence may be observed. The conclusions of Durkheim regarding suicide, more common among the prosperous French classes than among the poor, are still applicable, and Europe in the 1970s had the highest mortality on the roads anywhere in the world, though it varied considerably between countries. In contrast to the United States, crime was a lesser threat to life than road accidents or suicide.[25]

The way in which the Old Continent was transformed into an oasis of security for its inhabitants was linked both to the assumption of responsibility for this problem by every state and to the widespread individual acceptance of the new more peaceable values. This did not result in the complete disappearance of lethal violence, which reached a pitch of intensity during the rebellions, revolutions and wars which deeply scarred the continent until 1945. However, it accelerated its retreat from public space and ordinary social relations. We may wonder whether the two are not closely connected. Might the collective price paid for the increasingly effective control of manly aggression have been the military carnage and the protest movements leading to violent confrontations? In the current state of knowledge it is impossible to say. We may at least believe that the proliferation of constraints around the blood taboo profoundly altered the psychic equilibrium of young males, at a time when other prohibitions, of a sexual order, bore heavily down on them. The sons of privileged or wealthy bourgeois families were sometimes driven to suicidal despair, and more often, by a mechanism of sublimation, to types of legitimate competition put at the service of the community: the army, colonial conquest, missionary work among remote peoples, commercial enterprises and extreme sports.[26] How did the others, in particular the less well-off, urged to discipline their passions, to stop fighting each other and to wait until marriage before enjoying the pleasures of the flesh, endure this subjection without much hope? There is no simple answer to such a vast question, which has been too little studied. At the very least it requires that we distinguish between the urban and the rural worlds.

The civilizing town

Western societies have made the policing of the urban streets a priority. The Paris lieutenant of police, a post created by Louis XIV, saw that the streets were lit, kept them under surveillance to avert any potential popular uprisings, assured the provisioning of the city in cereals and kept his ear cocked for any rumblings.[27] In the eighteenth century, with the growth of commercial capitalism, colonial wealth flooded into the continent and especially the cities. They attracted, therefore, large numbers of vagrants and rootless individuals, many of whom could not be re-educated in the houses of correction or general hospitals. The vast majority of delinquents still came from the juvenile world, masculine and feminine. Although they may often have internalized the imperative message of the authorities and guardians of morality concerning the blood taboo, they nevertheless suffered deep frustrations within a strongly hierarchical system in which the adult males had all the rights. For many of them, theft was a vital necessity as well as an outlet. The West increasingly made a fetish of property. At the symbolic level, it gradually became the mark of a success. Meanwhile the French Revolution loomed, with its emphasis on the values of merit so as to counteract those of birth. It is hardly surprising, therefore, that the social dialogue united decision-makers from the top and the bottom of society, from the king or head of state to ordinary fathers of families, in a desire to marginalize, in new ways but as firmly as ever, young people who were in a hurry to enjoy what their civilization regarded as essential. It was the task of criminal justice to demonstrate the supreme importance of the new prohibitions.

The principal change, which was slow to be effected, was the gradual expulsion from public space of the young, especially the young bachelors who had once fought in the streets at night and on holidays, to be put in schools and workshops, then factories and the army, through compulsory military service. The concern and the familial affection for these stages of life which developed after the Age of Enlightenment reveal not just a transformation of sentiments but an increase in the control by adults of generations who were potentially disruptive to the peace of the community. The parental home, which had the task of providing an initial socialization, preventing children from straying into vice and then entrusting them to institutions able to limit adolescent contact with the disquieting street, thus gained greatly in importance. It was a place of protection, but also a focus for heightened tensions as it took over the formative functions previously performed by the youth bands. Domestic violence seems to have increased steadily during the period, to the point where, around 1970, almost one in four homicides committed in Europe was a family affair.[28]

Although the cities still represented only a minority in the eighteenth century, scarcely more than a fifth of the population in France, they became the laboratories for change. With the end of the age of a terror decreed by a state anxious to demonstrate its power, they rediscovered the old ways of pacifying behaviour that had characterized the golden age of the *bonnes villes* at the end of the Middle Ages.[29] The contrast between the legal terror still used by central governments and the more flexible procedures for ensuring control employed in the modern metropolises was often very marked. The targets might be the same, property crime being the most prosecuted everywhere, but the system of punishments was very different. In Lorraine, a sovereign principality, the Code Léopold of 1710 aimed judicial severity primarily at thieves. Of the 139 judgements on appeal made between 1708 and 1710, thieves provided 59 of the 70 criminals who were condemned to death. Half of them had stolen food products, livestock or clothing, without the use of violence. The few murders punished by death were all considered to be exceptionally serious: two parricides, six homicides and one infanticide.[30] The depression and poverty in this region in the hard winter of 1709 cannot alone explain the harsher repression of theft, as the same phenomenon was apparent elsewhere in Europe, in particular, as we have seen, in the England of the Bloody Code. In the Age of Enlightenment, this shift of direction in the criminalizing process indicates that homicide was no longer the authorities' principal concern. Their campaign of intimidation had borne fruit, leaving only a small number of hard cases, who were still ruthlessly eliminated. The full weight of the law now bore down on those who committed larceny, and were thus guilty both of disobedience and of a challenge to the fundamental inequalities of society.

The suppression of property crime was the principal preoccupation of the urban authorities, too, but the response of the police and the local courts was less brutal. The records of the court of the Jurats of Bordeaux for the decade 1768–77 show that 2,100 persons were punished for petty crime by this lower court in ten years.[31] This was a prosperous city, enriched by the Atlantic trade, embellished by the *intendant* Tourny and rapidly expanding, with a population that increased from 45,000 to 110,000 during the eighteenth century, making it one of the largest in France, after Paris. It faced a subsistence crisis of exceptional gravity in 1771–2. Women, according to these sources, played only a marginal role in crime. Inter-personal disputes accounted for almost 36 per cent of the total, followed by theft, at 25 per cent. The most common criminal profile was that of a young man from the crafts or one of the lesser trades, a recent immigrant in 41 per cent of cases, and more often from the country than from some other city. Those in the 20–34 age group accounted for nearly four-fifths of the contingent, with a predominance of young men aged between twenty and twenty-four. Craftsmen, above all those working in the wood, clothing and building trades, very few of them masters, provided two-fifths of the accused, followed closely by those from lesser occupations, such as sailors, porters, domestic servants and wine-growers. The age of the plaintiffs is rarely recorded. Almost half came from the ranks of the more prosperous; they were mostly natives of Bordeaux and a higher proportion of them than of the defendants were able to sign their names. In 80 per cent of cases, they knew each other, through work, neighbourhood or cohabitation, or even simply through meetings in the street or at one of the March and October fairs, both crime hot spots according to these records.

Insults and blows causing injuries are the mark of a brutal sociability inherited from the past, and which was primarily a summer phenomenon. Half the quarrels were between persons of equivalent social rank, often neighbours or workmates. They concerned money – loans, unpaid rent, debts – or followed altercations, usually in a bar, or, in a few cases, sprang from a desire for revenge. Verbal aggression, insults, threats and blows that left no wound accounted for almost two-thirds of the total. They were mostly aimed at persons of higher rank and also accounted for much of the female delinquency. For the rest, wounds requiring the attention of a surgeon were inflicted in 36 per cent of cases by young men aged between twenty and twenty-four, three-fifths of whom were journeymen craftsmen, who had usually clashed with one of their peers. A hangover from the intense and frequent homicidal violence of the past, this testifies to a significant lowering of the threshold of tolerance in this matter, but also to the survival, with less tragic consequences, of the manly confrontations between unmarried men that were particularly characteristic of manual labourers.

Robbery was a very different matter. It closely followed the curve of fluctuations in the price of bread and it reached its maximum intensity during the crisis of 1771–2. It was less common in summer but flourished during the March and October fairs. Though simple theft in one in every two cases, it rarely involved food. It was mostly money, linen, silverware and jewels that were stolen. Most of the thieves were members of the lesser crafts or recent immigrants still unemployed, and they stole from the better-off. The scourge was much greater than the figures suggest, because the victims had to find the thief themselves to bring him to justice, with little help from the police. Heavy penalties, even hanging or penal servitude for life, show that the judicial authorities identified a grave and endemic social threat without having real means to stamp it out. The penalties also reveal a tense stand-off between, on the one hand, the most unstable sector of the poverty-stricken juvenile world of recent immigrants and, on the other, prosperous established society. The residual homicidal violence, which had a very different calendar, and which seems to have caused less disquiet because it was confined to disputes between equals, may have been typical of a different, slightly more settled sector of this age group. This is probably the case with insults and derisive or defiant language on the part of inferiors, especially women, directed at superiors or the better-off. The simple police misdemeanours recorded only confirm this impression, because they prove the 'existence of a rowdy, rebellious, gambling and cheating spirit' among the youth of Bordeaux, who liked to resist the watch and attack or incite the populace against them. Lastly, affairs of morals suggest a high level of local tolerance of prostitution and a marked masculine propensity for 'kidnapping by seduction', so as to enjoy the favours of a girl and then abandon her when she got pregnant. We see here the extreme vulnerability of female servants, inevitably sent away by the masters and then tempted by infanticide; this was hardly a new phenomenon, of course, as it is recorded elsewhere, for example in England in previous centuries.[32]

The changes observed in the other great European towns were broadly similar. Theft became the main concern everywhere, notably in Paris.[33] In Amsterdam, the judges issued a very large number of death sentences for this crime around 1720, although it had previously been treated with great leniency. This change was directly linked to that in the status of lethal violence. The lists of inspections of corpses make it possible to observe a dramatic decline in this crime up to the 1690s, followed by a short-lived sharp rise: the homicide rate per 100,000 inhabitants fell from 47 in the fifteenth century to 25 in the sixteenth century, then to 3 around 1670, before rising to 9 in the years 1693–1726; it then settled at between 2 and 3 in the second half of the eighteenth century. The rise recorded during three decades corresponded to a specific period of frequent knife fights in the streets, which ended during the 1720s. Lethal aggression then moved from outside to inside the home, where more murderous disputes developed. Those who engaged in one-to-one knife fights were essentially young males from the lower, but not the lowest, strata. They tended to come from a median position, at the lowest levels of the 'respectable' categories. Further, half of them were occasional petty thieves, even sometimes men who lived off their spoils.[34] It seems that the pacification of behaviour was advancing at this period, leading to resistance on the part of the bachelors deprived of their traditional rights to manly violence. Instructed to stay away from public space at night, they defied the authorities on two fronts, by the popular duel using knives and by theft.

The urban masculine youth culture moved away from murder, which society was increasingly less ready to condone, to theft. This, which had previously been only half-heartedly repressed, indeed often seen as a private affair by the police, in Bordeaux as elsewhere, was more than simply a means by which the least well-off managed to survive. In a world where the gulf between rich and poor was increasing, and where temptations were more numerous, it was also a form of protest by adolescents against the authorities and those who were comfortably established. It was the act not of the poorest or the vagrants without hope, but rather of the children of the people, who felt they were getting a raw deal and who were feeling the pressure of the stronger moral and social constraints imposed on them. The law made no mistake. Faced with these new challenges, which shifted onto property the focus of the symbolic conflict between the rising generations and adults, it responded by increasing the use of the death penalty. Simple theft, or, for domestic servants, pinching anything at all from their masters, even just a handkerchief, could lead to the gallows. The new lesson taught to every son was not to oppose the law of the fathers, and not to try to subvert the natural order of things by taking what did not belong to him; he must stay in his proper place, work and obey, so that, one day, he would accede to the position he longed for. *Industry and Idleness*, Hogarth's famous series of engravings of 1747, carried the same cruel warning: the vicious and idle apprentice ends up on the gibbet at Tyburn, while his industrious friend, who respected the norms, becomes mayor of London.[35]

London was on the way to becoming the largest city in Europe. Its population more than doubled during the century, to reach nearly 900,000 by 1800, and its per capita income fell sharply. Nevertheless, there was a big reduction in the number of murders committed in its streets. Men accounted for 87 per cent of those accused of this crime. The number of women fell, as they very rarely responded violently to the many provoking insults to which they were subjected in public space. Allowing for the increased population, the total number of fatal clashes, which were in any case mostly entered into without any intention of killing, was six times less in 1791 than in 1690. In the last decades of the eighteenth century, the rate settled at 1 per 100,000 inhabitants, which is the same as that for the United Kingdom as a whole in 1930. The two types of homicide which declined most were those resulting from resistance to the police – which implies a greater acceptance of the law – and those resulting from disputes over honour. In the latter case, the tendency to walk away, already noted in the case of women, increased among men, too, as, from the middle of the century, an increasing number of them no longer responded to provocation by resorting to a weapon. Further, bystanders of every social class intervened in 39 per cent of recorded disputes in the second half of the century. The pacification of manners affected young gentlemen in particular, many of whom stopped carrying a sword in the 1720s and 1730s. The intolerance of any form of brutality is revealed even more strikingly around 1760 in the frequency of complaints lodged by Londoners who had been pushed, taken hold of, knocked down or kicked when walking in the streets. Open external space was becoming much more policed. By the end of the eighteenth century, more than half the homicides denounced had been committed inside houses or in enclosed public spaces such as taverns, coffee houses and shops.[36]

The decline in stages of relational violence in London corresponded to a growing acceptance of the need for greater self-control among the generations concerned. The point of departure for the sensitizing of public opinion to the problem was probably the Mohocks affair. For many months, in 1712, the capital was in the grip of a veritable moral panic. Mysterious groups of debauched young aristocrats were accused of terrorizing the city by night and of assaulting respectable folk. The queen called for vigilance and even offered a generous reward to informants. In fact, the whole affair was an invention of a Grub Street scribbler, and there were always many sceptics. The result, nevertheless, was to make both citizens and authorities considerably less tolerant of libertines of quality, or rakes, who were in future more often and more enthusiastically prosecuted by the courts. Though it had its origins in a troubled fantasy, the long crisis revealed a reality, by drawing attention to the dangers resulting from youthful aggression – and to the need to do something about it.[37]

The subsequent statistics for homicide record a residue that continued to decline, in spite of the ever more acute social and cultural problems posed by the cohabitation of disparate populations that were constantly increasing in size. Violence did not disappear, of course, but it became more trivial from generation to generation. Surveillance by the police and fear of capital punishment are not enough to explain this. The principal motor for change is to be found in the everyday control of the gestures of each individual by the community. The civilizing process was taking effect, here as in all the large towns of Europe. It was not being imposed only by rules of politeness and civility. They effectively created ideal types of sensitive, charitable men and women, capable of mastering their impulses and purging their vocabulary so as to avoid insults and confrontations in public.[38] However, their effect was primarily visible among the upper and middle classes. Though these rules also spread among the common people, and could be learned by frequenting coffee houses, pleasure gardens and other public places, and though they even increasingly influenced the master–servant relationship, they were far from determining the behaviour of the working classes as a whole. The use of words belonging to this verbal code is very rare in the thousands of trial testimonies of the period, which largely involved ordinary men and women.

Yet there was clearly a major shift in the attitude of the masses and the poor to brutality. It seems to have resulted principally from changes in urban space, which had become overcrowded. In the last third of the century, in particular, many foreign observers commented with astonishment on the way Londoners behaved in the streets: they avoided eye contact and they kept physical contact to a minimum by using their elbows rather than their hands to clear a passage; they did not look back if they bumped into someone, which might make it seem intentional. Reputation was not established in the street as it had been in the past, which defused some of what would otherwise have been inevitable clashes over a public challenge to someone's honour. The sites of sociability in which ordinary people congregated, the pub and the workplace, were probably regulated by even more imperative rules for the avoidance of conflicts, because they provided indispensable havens, set aside from the external tumult. To affect affable manners became a necessity so as not to appear a troublemaker. Respectability was not now associated with a fiercely proclaimed manliness so much as with a peaceable demeanour that posed no threat to the order prevailing in these places.[39]

Londoners of every background distanced themselves, in a sense, from the dangers and overcrowding of the street, to construct a more intensely 'private' personality, less sensitive to the gaze of others, which made them less ready to engage in invective or thump someone as a way of winning respect. This new attitude seems to have come as much from below, from the crowds in the process of turning into collections of individuals in an overpopulated world, as from above or from the civilizing process. It led to a profound change in the implicit definitions of masculinity and femininity, hence also in relations between the genders. For, while men behaved less aggressively towards each other, they seem to have assaulted women more often, more spontaneously and more brutally. The violence of women, meanwhile, declined, to the point of becoming almost negligible in the judicial archives. When they did resort to violence, however, women behaved towards each other and towards men with a particularly intense, passionate brutality, ready to pounce on a policeman, for example.[40] The apparent contradiction suggests that the masks women wore in most circumstances conformed to stereotypes deliberately adopted so as to exhibit the required norms. In the general opinion, the suffering of insults without responding and the patient endurance of masculine blows, especially those of the husband in the home, was what characterized the second sex.

Male violence, once it had been tamed in public space, seems to have been given freer rein within the conjugal unit, and even more against women who were not protected by their good reputation or a husband. The large number of complaints of sexual assaults is one sign of this. The steep rise shows both that the authorities were beginning to criminalize this phenomenon, and that the victims were developing defensive strategies against masculine abuse. While 80 per cent of those charged with rape were acquitted by the English courts, to the distress of their victims, women who denounced a simple attempted assault or ill-treatment were given a sympathetic hearing and easily obtained satisfaction. Pregnant women and battered or betrayed wives appearing before the Westminster justices of the peace in the years 1680–1720 produced accounts that tended to wander from the facts. They insisted on their dependent state and their weakness in order to move a magistrate who, in a sense, occupied the place of patriarch and was ready to accept their truth, even if the allegations it was based on were vague. Taking advantage both of public sympathy and of legal proceedings favourable to the ill-treated feminine type they represented, they used the very stereotypes

218

of weakness associated with it to win their cases.[41] Though cleverly circumvented on such occasions, the domination of men, so quick to violence within the home, remained a fundamental fact of life. It is because it recognized this that the law tried to restore a little balance to the benefit of these women, probably without being entirely taken in by their discourse or apparent docility.

It is true that London was very different from the rest of England, especially the rural areas where disputes were much more often settled informally. All over Europe, the big town radically altered behaviour, in a variety of ways. It forced individuals to limit their demonstrative excesses, gestural and verbal, so as not to alarm the dense crowds in which they had to move. The codes of politeness invented in the Renaissance in the courts of northern Italy, and proposed as models by Erasmus in his *On Good Manners for Boys* of 1530, spread widely among the members of the upper urban strata, for example, in Paris in the reign of Louis XIII, because they met a vital need for a more peaceable management of the public space in which they developed.[42] Such norms were only one visible aspect of the relational urbanity that became increasingly necessary in the huge and potentially highly conflictual metropolises of the eighteenth century. The town both policed and polished attitudes. Like the women who exaggerated their pose of subjection before the courts, the common people, too, were forced to adopt a profile to suit their needs, in dealing with a customer, for example, or an employer or even just a passer-by. As they constantly rubbed shoulders with others, they learned to avoid the problems associated with exuberant forms of conduct. Vagrants and beggars were well aware that aggression did not pay, even if they were sometimes driven to it by drink or frustration. The most restive were probably the young, anxious to demonstrate their worth in public. Nevertheless, they were still generally caught up in the web of prohibitions, which were all the more difficult to escape in that they were constantly conveyed not only by the authorities, morality, religion and the handbooks of civility, but by the reproving and anonymous gaze of the crowd. Every citizen who negotiated the urban jungle had of necessity to find protection from others by keeping himself to himself more than in the past, sheltering within a sort of invisible personal cocoon.

This 'hidden dimension' defines the way the human being sees himself and behaves in relation to his peers. It is larger or smaller according to the rules laid down by societies and to the place the individual wishes or claims to occupy.[43] In the villages, where living space was less crowded and where the sense of honour required public demonstrations of manliness, by contrast with ladylike modesty, this dimension remained wide for all men, but varied as a way of demonstrating hierarchies between them. It was most important for the swaggering aristocrat, who proudly wore a rapier at his side, who would tolerate no contact and who might seize on the pretext of a mere raised eyebrow to challenge the impudent offender. The fact that noblemen stopped carrying swords in London after 1730 is symptomatic of a general contraction of this cocoon. This was also true of the disarming of the ordinary citizens of Europe. To appear respectable, a gentleman must now restrict the number and intensity of his clashes with others. As for women of quality, they had to demonstrate even more submissiveness in towns than in the countryside, fleeing before an insult and taking refuge in the home. The bourgeois norms that spread in the nineteenth century, of a voluntary confinement of wives and of masculine courtesy in public space, were simply a theorized version of the new necessities of urban life. Protected from external tumult by a sort of invisible armour, the urban masculine 'me' became less sensitive to the tyrannies of the local milieu, which urged him to avenge in blood a flouted honour that belonged more to the family or clan than to the individual concerned.

The same probably happened in other large cities. No close study of it has as yet been made for Paris, principal rival to London. In the case of the French capital we know more about street violence, which has long attracted the attention of historians.[44] They have revealed the resistances and the continuities which are the other aspect of this phenomenon. On the one hand, the authorities and respectable people wanted to pacify the urban streets, with the assent of many adults from the working classes. On the other, young men tried frequently to recover their lost rights to ritual violence, in particular in the city centre and in the nocturnal world, now increasingly well lit and orderly. The discourses on hygiene, health and work joined those devoted to security and peace in order to control a rapidly growing and explosive capital. After 1850, rent increases and property speculation further accentuated social segregation and drove the so-called 'dangerous' working classes eastwards, then out into ever more distant peripheries and suburbs.

In the face of this bitterly resented exile, the return to Paris became an obsessive popular theme. It marked the great revolutionary eruptions of 1848 and 1871. Proletarian youths, symbolically illustrated by the figure of Gavroche, also more routinely expressed their resentment at an increasing marginalization, which was worse for them than for their elders. They made use of a very wide range of derisive, insolent and sometimes defiant gestures and acts, epitomized by the type of the *titi parisien*, the street-urchin of Paris. When they could, they took over public space, as at festivals. They also returned to violent practices which recalled the manly traditions of the past, through the Apache phenomenon at the beginning of the twentieth century or in the context of youth gangs.[45] But their room for manoeuvre was gradually being reduced. They now had to go out into the streets to express themselves, whereas before the industrial age the street was where they spent most of their time. A deep longing for a repossession helps to explain the importance of strikes, often held in spring or autumn, and some of their ludic features, inherited from the old youth customs – even though the mixing of sexes and ages today has transformed the meaning of such actions. Male adolescents, already literally disarmed, since carrying a knife had become a sign of potential criminality, were now symbolically disarmed by the culture in which they had to find a place, under pressure from normative codes originating elsewhere but also among the adults of their own world.

Masculinity had totally changed its meaning since the sixteenth century. It had become detached from the local gaze, primarily preoccupied with the honour of the group, and become much more personal and 'urbane'. The blood taboo had stripped the duel of its prestige, much more quickly in England, where it had almost disappeared by 1850, than in France, where it survived for another century.[46] The status of the popular knife fight had slowly been eroded by the official discourse that labelled it bestial and despicable as a way of destroying the peasant traditions of fighting with a bladed weapon, which had once been how adolescents demonstrated their manliness. In nineteenth-century Finland, the province of South Ostrobothnia was terrorized by bands of knife fighters who attacked people and property. The inhabitants demanded the assistance of the police and even regarded as heroes officers who used methods that were effective, but on the margins of legality, to rid them of this scourge.[47] In Paris, the only period during which homicide rates increased, before the purges of 1944–5, was between 1890 and 1913, when the rate rose to 3.4 per 100,000 inhabitants. It then fell once again, to reach a minimum of 1.2 between 1939 and 1943. In spite of the constant complaints and the anxieties of the comfortably off in the face of the so-called dangerous classes, the capital was hardly a nest of assassins at this period. It is true that criminality was greater in the towns than in the countryside at the beginning of the twentieth century, but this was primarily because the countryside had lost its numerical predominance during the Second Empire. The great cities, including Lyon, Marseille and Bordeaux, were the scene of more frenzied outbursts than elsewhere, and in Prussia the urban homicide rates were significantly higher than those in the countryside at this period.[48]

The classic explanations, which cite the atmosphere of the Roaring Twenties, when people played and killed more than in the past, in a frenzy paving the way for the Second World War, are inadequate. The crucial factor was the silent escalation of the demands of the adolescents, in France as much as Germany, in a world shaken by modernity which did not allow them enough space, even though their numbers were con-stantly increasing, and further swollen by rootless lads of the same age from the country, come to try their chances in the city. The return in force of the culture of the knife fight, symbolized by the Parisian Apaches at the beginning of the twentieth century, points to an imbalance in the system for transmitting property and rights from the adults to the young, which is probably an indirect form of protest which would repay further study. Fear of the dangerous classes obscured a deeper fear, that of being assaulted and killed by young men from the proletariat who were finding it increasingly hard to get a place in the sun. As in Finland, this fear grew among adults of proletarian origins, too.

All through the nineteenth century, successive generations of estab-lished workers adopted, and adapted to their own milieu, the rules for the pacification of behaviour instituted by the law; until, that is, a time when their example no longer satisfied the young men queuing up in a world that left them without enough hope. The mechanisms for settling ordinary urban disputes appear clearly in England, best studied from this point of view. Brawling had not disappeared, obviously, and was prob-ably no less frequent, but its consequences had become far less tragic. The manly code of honour had been reoriented towards the definition of 'the fair fight' or 'up-and-down fight', as in boxing, which had been the fashion in town and village alike since the eighteenth century. This was an encounter which was agreed on by both parties, in which no weapons were used and which involved only the two combatants. In 1896, a quarrel between two married women, which would once have led to a general mêlée in which the husbands fought with knives, was stopped by the police. The two husbands met later in a pub, where they quarrelled. They asked a neighbour to let them adjourn to his stables, where they proceeded to fight in front of witnesses; they then left sepa-rately. Once back home, one of them complained of a pain in his abdomen; he had ruptured his bowel during the fight. His opponent was eventually arrested on a charge of manslaughter, but the spectators declared that the fight had been a 'fair one' and he was discharged. It was by no means uncommon for juries to reach such decisions, as long as no weapon had been used. Bare-knuckle fighting was regarded as honourable and 'English', whereas the use of a knife was considered proof of cowardice, a specific mark of foreigners, especially the Irish. One lawyer defended an Argentinean sailor by pointing out that 'foreign-ers...did not look on life as seriously as Englishmen did'.

The realities were often rather different, especially as there was no law forbidding the carrying of knives or firearms until 1920. Some towns were deeply marked by the insecurity associated with their use, for example Liverpool and Manchester. The latter was also the scene of much juvenile violence. Between 1870 and 1900, 250 cases involving gangs of 'scuttlers' have been identified. Of the 717 young people accused, 94 per cent were working-class boys, mostly from the 14–19 age group; they were imitated by a minority of girls of similar age, typically single and factory workers. Their behaviour has echoes of a rite of passage, as they waited for adulthood. Unlike the kingdoms of youth of the sixteenth century, however, the threshold of the violence practised was much lower. It was confined to assault and woundings, as only five homicides were recorded. They kept to the rules of the fair fight as laid down by adults. They were often themselves victims of adult brutality, and learned the importance of force in establishing a reputation and asserting social status, in particular on Sundays and holidays, during codified public fights in which it was important not deliberately to endanger the life of the adversary. The tradition of great brutality had not disappeared. It had simply been adapted to the supreme need to show respect for human life which was hammered home by the law. Excessive savagery was also stigmatized, sometimes bringing opprobrium on whole regions. Thus Lancashire had a bad reputation thanks to a local form of fighting called 'purring', in which men fought with their clogged feet; seventeen people were accused of this before the county courts in the single month of August 1874.[49]

The European town had a calming effect on violence. It had played this fundamental role for some five hundred years and it provided the rest of the population with a model for the pacification of manners. The urban melting-pot was not exempt from brutality, of course, but it was constantly trying to lessen its destructive effects by promoting the urbanity necessary to a life of more intense relationships. One of its principal objectives was to integrate the young, whose arrival at the adult state constantly risked upsetting the balance. However, it also sought to drive the most unruly of them out towards remote peripheries, together with all those who rejected the established codes. More than the distant state, which was always tempted to use coercion or terror to impose its own order, the city tirelessly mended a social fabric constantly being torn by new developments. It therefore urged its most vigorous elements, including adults from the lower classes, to keep a watch on each other and to keep the young closely controlled, so as to maintain, in its preferred manner, a security which could not be achieved solely by the carrying of weapons and the death penalty. This is why political, moral, religious or economic explanations are not enough to explain the long Western march towards the goal of making homicide and physical or verbal violence a rarity.

The pace of change varied from country to country, which gives some significance, at a secondary level, to the study of cultural variations

223

between the south and the north and the west and the east of the continent. In the 1960s, for example, intentional assaults and woundings remained numerous, but fell below the level of road crimes. England and France, though singularly different in so many ways, were alike in having the lowest conviction rate for this crime, calculated as a function of demographic size; the rate in Germany was 50 per cent higher, while in Italy it was twice as high.[50] There is some value in looking for reasons in the 'Latin' or 'Nordic' temperament, levels of religious commitment, the importance of alcoholism or other criteria, for comparative purposes. What is of most significance, however, is that Western Europe had collectively achieved the lowest level of inter-personal violence that any civilization has known, under the direct influence of its principal metropolises. London, Paris and Amsterdam had led the way. The relative tardiness of Italy was due to the lateness of the move to pacify its big cities. Rome still had homicide rates of between 8 and 15 per 100,000 inhabitants in the years 1850–90, whereas the rate was only 0.5 in London, 2 in Liverpool and 1.3 in Paris in the decade 1860–70. The knife duel remained an important tradition in the streets of the Eternal City. At the turn of the century, however, the curve fell sharply, settling at just under 5 on the eve of the First World War.[51] The process of repressing the murderous knife fight began to make an impact among the new generations at precisely the time that the population doubled, between 1879 and 1914, bringing it close to 600,000 people. As in London a century earlier, the rapid increase in population density made a reduction in open aggression a necessity.

And yet, in a recurrent fantasy, the big city is still seen as a dangerous and horribly violent place. Could it be that the more or less regular resurgence of this collective terror is the deliberately veiled symptom of the arrival at adulthood of a large number of adolescents, in particular of lads from the lower classes? The fear of the London Mohocks in 1712, and that of the Parisian Apaches of the *belle époque*, focused attention, respectively, on debauched aristocrats and the lowest criminal depths, but in both cases expressed an obscure collective anxiety about the young men who were believed to be thirsting for blood and champing at the bit on the margins of the established world. They gradually assumed the position of the potential worst enemies of respectable people, as violent rebellions and riots grew fewer. There can be no doubt that their claim culture made it easy for them to be confused with strikers, whose numbers rapidly increased in France from the 1880s, and even more with the murderous bandits who incarnated absolute evil in the industrial age.

Contemporary scholars were desperate to find the secret of these noxious creatures, this 'evil muck', this 'violent machine', by scrutinizing their physiognomy, or their brains, or their corpses deposited in the morgue. As Camille Granier, inspector general at the Ministry of the Interior, wrote in 1906 in *The Criminal Woman*, those responsible for the maintenance of order 'are scared by the idea of a powerful and imaginary coalition, and have invented, by turns, the dregs of society, the dangerous classes and, lastly, the army of crime'.[52] Perhaps this was, each time, a way of avoiding a direct confrontation with the most frightening of their fantasies, that of being engulfed by a bloody tide of proletarian youths thirsting for revenge? The emergence in 1910 of the Oedipus complex in the thinking of Freud can usefully be read in symbolic terms as the irruption into European culture of a very real youth problem, an increasing obsession up to the First World War. Was it not the case that the fathers, in other words the established adults, feared brutal dispossession at the hands of the sons, the adolescents kept so firmly under tutelage, who had become too numerous and impatient to take their place?

Violence and changing concepts of honour in the countryside

The systematic study of violence in the countryside largely remains to be done. This is especially the case for the industrial centuries, where research has primarily focused on the towns and the workers. The European rural population was reduced to minority status in the nineteenth century, whereas it had accounted for over three-quarters of the total in 1789, and it shrank even more rapidly in the last quarter of the twentieth century, under the impact of modernization. Around 1970, a strong wave of nostalgia for this world we have lost led to a brief flowering of research, but few of the historians concerned were interested in criminality. Old, deep-rooted stereotypes regarding the crudity of village manners and morals probably helped to divert attention from these matters, on the quite erroneous assumption that everything was known.

In fact, the violence of the peasant changed radically, in a way that was much more disruptive of established traditions than the changes in the towns. In the space of two or three centuries, this civilization, cradle of our own, changed more drastically than during the preceding two millennia. It accepted, more or less willingly, a relative pacification of individual and collective behaviour. The French example, which is slightly better known, makes it possible to observe the coincidence, which was in no way fortuitous, between the sharp fall in homicides and the end of a great cycle of rural revolts, by the middle of the nineteenth century. The blood taboo, which was now associated with the cruellest armed robbery, or with some abnormal behaviour, only came to apply in the countryside about a century after the towns. The tardiness of this development reveals a reluctance to accept the new norms sacralizing human life and condemning an excess of aggression. However, this was not due to a barbarity that had scarcely been affected by the new religious, moral and ethical developments, as external observers claimed. Rather, it was a consequence of the resistance of a social and cultural model which had proved its worth.

The people of the countryside tried to preserve its essentials, while doing enough to satisfy the external powers that increasingly weighed down on them. They managed to choose what was useful to them from among the material and cultural tools that they were offered or had imposed on them. The law was the subject of a subtle appropriation, which made it easier to resolve disputes. The population was disarmed and manners were pacified, as demanded by the civil and religious authorities, but without destroying the old value system based on the ritualized expression of manly confrontations. Reduced to bare-knuckle fighting, like the English 'fair fight', violence was largely the preserve of young men in the eighteenth- and nineteenth-century countryside, because it continued to enable them symbolically to proclaim their value and assert their rights within the group.

Neither the civilizing process, which had little impact in the villages, nor fear of the police, nor the power of the unfamiliar discourses is enough to explain these changes. They were equally caused by a realization that the only way of safeguarding the essentials was abandoning or concealing the most strongly condemned traditions. Gradually, however, the internal balance of the communities shifted, because the towns cast an ever longer shadow over lands abandoned by waves of migrants. Murderous criminality then developed primarily within the family, in particular as a way of resolving the problems of transmission to the next generation, or it was transmuted into banditry in the remote areas that largely escaped the control of the police. The rural world simultaneously wilted and weakened from within, paving the way for the rapid disappearance of the habits of physical confrontations, as young people left the islands, mountains and hamlets, where only the old remained.

Gonesse was a big village of about 3,000 inhabitants, a few miles to the north-east of Paris, which had many bakers, who went several times a week to the capital to sell a white bread that was highly regarded by Parisians. Thus modernity arrived early in Gonesse, in the seventeenth century, under the influence of the nearby metropolis. Violence was still common, but it was much less brutal than in previous centuries.[53] In its small royal court, the provost heard 522 cases between 1620 and 1700: 86 per cent involved assault and woundings, 4 per cent insults, simple or aggravated by blasphemy, 4 per cent theft, 4 per cent affairs of morals

226

and 1.5 per cent homicides. In total, 1,326 individuals are named in the sources, that is, 522 defendants, 208 accomplices and 596 plaintiffs. Men provided 85 per cent of the defendants and 82 per cent of all those mentioned in any capacity. Not all of them were peasants. Apart from a small number of nobles and ecclesiastics, they came from a wide range of occupations: bailiffs, prosecutors, gaolers, shepherds, carters, prosperous farmers, labourers, wine-growers, shoemakers, masons, carpenters, millers, merchants, barkeepers and servants. The inevitable bakers accounted for 19 per cent of the male defendants. The majority lived in Gonesse itself. Only 13 per cent were 'strangers', mostly from neighbouring villages. Age is only recorded, sadly, for fewer than one in ten male defendants and for one in twenty women and plaintiffs of both genders. Of this small and unreliable sample, two in five defendants were in the 20–25 age group and half the male plaintiffs were in the 20–30 age group.

The sources record only eight homicides for the whole eighty-year period. Such a low number is plausible; however, it is also possible that the gravity of the crime justified its direct referral to a higher court. Four of the cases were described by surgeons on the basis of inspections of corpses; the other four resulted from complaints. Two of the accused were sentenced to be hanged. The first, a native of a neighbouring parish, had wounded his opponent with a knife in the marketplace, one August evening in 1638; the second had struck his victim, also with a knife, in a tavern in August 1681. The other two were sentenced, respectively, to perpetual exile and the galleys, as, in both cases, there were mitigating circumstances: one pleaded provocation in his own home, where he had done the deed with blows from a sword, one evening in August 1653; the other had been drunk, in the tavern, on a November evening in 1679, but had used only his feet and his fists. The last case, exceptional in its dire consequences, already hints at the consequences of the prohibition on carrying a weapon. Only gentlemen, royal officials and accredited persons had this right. Surveillance was stepped up during fairs, holidays, market days, Sundays and at night. Offenders risked heavy fines and a greater severity on the part of the court, as was learned to their cost by the two men who had used knives in the marketplace and an inn, and been sentenced to death.

Their bad example was rare. A total of 837 injuries, some described in great detail in 213 surgeons' reports, were declared by 529 victims of physical violence, consisting of 395 men and 134 women. Only 8 per cent had been caused by blades or firearms. Of the latter, in all barely 2 per cent, half had been inflicted by royal sergeants, who were also legally entitled to carry a sword. They were professional in their use of this weapon, inflicting wounds that bled, whereas the bakers who used a sword had more often struck their opponent on the head with the flat part. A few soldiers carried a knife, which they drew in a brawl. Most men used their feet or their fists: the former are mentioned in 22 per cent of cases, the latter in 33 per cent. Various types of stick, including a club-headed cart strut, a whip handle, brooms and wooden utensils, especially rakes and hammers, accounted for 22 per cent. Stones were used in 8 per cent of cases, and metal objects – pots, bottles, candlesticks, iron-tipped staffs, a shepherd's crook and a spade – in 6 per cent. There are only five references to bites. One woman had used her teeth against a royal sergeant who was attempting to confiscate her belongings in 1626. She had hurled herself at him, hit him on the head with a stone, torn off his shirt, then bitten him in the leg. Neither head-butting nor the use of elbows and nails is mentioned, and there is only a single reference to someone being kneed in the stomach, in 1623.

We are given a picture of firm social control. It went further than required by the legal prohibitions designed to stop the use of weapons and restrict the majority of confrontations to fights with fists and feet, reminiscent of the fair fight or boxing matches of eighteenth-century Britain. However rough, these hundreds of encounters seem to have been relatively codified, so there was none of the murderous rage or ruthless cruelty which might have resulted in the participants smashing each other's heads in with a stone or club, disfiguring each other with the fingernails, biting off a nose or an ear or attacking the most sensitive parts. An analysis of the injuries confirms this impression, as 55 per cent of them had not bled. It is true that the average conceals differences according to the sex of the victim: only 39 per cent of the women had open wounds, compared with 51 per cent of the men. The women mostly had contusions or ecchymoses, occasionally fractures, which suggests a degree of restraint on the part both of male aggressors and of other women. For both sexes, the parts least often hit were the shoulders, the back, the chest and the belly, which together received only 14 per cent of the injuries. Arms, legs and hands were struck in 29 per cent of cases, the head in 26 per cent and the face slightly more often, at 30 per cent.

There were significant differences between the sexes. Women were more often struck on their limbs or in the face, in 40 per cent and 34 per cent of cases respectively, as against 25 per cent and 29 per cent for men, and they were much less often hit on the head than men (10 per cent as opposed to 31 per cent). Wounds and bruising on the hands, arms and legs were sometimes bad enough for the victims to take to their beds, but without preventing them from working for an extended period. To damage the face by causing ecchymoses, lividity or scars was a way of ensuring that the victim lost prestige in the eyes of others, as well as demonstrating the superiority of the victor, because the marks would remain visible for a long time. For women, we may suspect that the humiliation was all the greater in that the face, the only part of the body to be uncovered at the period, with the hands and the arms, was the very symbol of femininity. Worse, they were unable to conceal a scar under a beard or a moustache, or, for that matter, under makeup, which would have been highly incongruous in a village. The injuries inflicted on men's heads demonstrate a greater desire to cause damage, to win without killing and to trounce an opponent, stigmatizing him in the eyes of all. The most common injuries were to the top of the head, the parietal bone and its continuation to the front, the coronal bone in the vocabulary of the surgeons. A hat or a cap could muffle the shock but did not prevent bleeding, especially if a stone, a stick or a tin vessel was used. There were also lesions to the temples and, though less often, to the forehead or the occiput, these last signifying a treacherous attack, as in the case of a corpse found lying in the road in 1683.

The population revealed its great sensitivity to the problem by concentrating its complaints on the everyday violence, intense but small-scale, committed by 474 individuals, 21 of whom were guilty of abuse or blasphemy without physical aggression. Women accounted for fewer than 10 per cent of the offenders. Only eighteen cases of theft were denounced. They consisted of larceny aggravated by assault (six cases), acts committed by strangers to the village or highway robbery. Crimes of morality were only slightly more numerous: two rapes, one with violence, eighteen pregnant girls seeking to force the father to marry them and pay them an allowance, and two cases of prostitution. To avoid the heavy expenses entailed in legal action, the community probably itself dealt with the cases that lent themselves to a private settlement. The fact that people were so quick to resort to the law in cases of ordinary non-lethal violence suggests it was proving difficult to deal with this problem by the traditional methods.

The sentences are recorded in only a fifth of cases, probably because in most others proceedings were abandoned after an agreement had been reached between the parties, which was less costly than formal justice.[54] They allow us to see the importance attached by this local court to the various types of offence, and also to understand what the victims were hoping for when they brought an action. Three death sentences were passed, two for homicide and one for the theft of money from a house in the village by a stranger. In cases of allegations of serious injury, the defendant was given preventive imprisonment in the local gaols to make provision for the necessary medical costs. The penalties, strictly speaking, were usually fines. Blasphemy was officially taxed at 60 *sous* in 1642, and at 10 *livres parisis* in 1697. A merchant from Picardy who had repeatedly blasphemed in a hostelry in 1662, when in his cups ('God's death! God's head! I deny God!'), was fined 60 *sous*. When insults were added, without assault, the judges adapted the punishment, bearing in mind the social position of the person insulted. The man who, in 1679, laid into a lieutenant in the French artillery, a former colonel *du ban et de l'arrière ban*, was sentenced to a fine of 60 *livres*, banished for five years and obliged to pay the costs of the proceedings, which came to more than 256 *livres*.

Just how heavy these fines were emerges from a comparison with the fairly average wealth of a gardener from Montreuil under Louis XIV, estimated on the basis of the inventories after his death: 200 *livres*. Similarly, injuries were generally punished by fines, which ranged from 24 *sous* to 300 *livres*, according to the same criteria and taking account of any aggravating circumstances, such as insults or blasphemy. The heaviest fine, in 1665, which was accompanied by perpetual banishment, was for an attack in the street on sergeants engaged in the transfer of a prisoner. The additional penalties of exclusion were rare, except in the case of thieves, who were banished or sent to the galleys. Of those guilty of violence, some were sentenced to punitive imprisonment, whipping or exposure in the *carcan*, or iron collar. Others were required to make a public apology to their victim. Sometimes, candle in hand, they were made solemnly to ask for the forgiveness of God, the law and the victim for having offended them. For example, a 26-year-old carter was sentenced to pay a fine of 6 *livres*, to purchase an expiatory candle and to a two-hour exposure in the iron collar of the prison of Gonesse. His offence was to have resisted an official sent to arrest him following a denunciation for blasphemy. On 23 December 1670, when the prosecutor had arrived at the Hostelry of the Golden Lion to perform this task, the man had rushed at him, bitten him in the hand and growled, 'Who are you to speak to me? I don't give a damn about you! You must be very proud of yourself!' before blaspheming: 'I deny God! God's death! God's head! God's blood, I won't follow you!'

Those who made the accusations wanted most of all to obtain substantial damages, together with a sop to their pride and even, in some cases, a very public restoration of their wounded honour. The guilty party, destabilized by the fine and the costs of the lawsuit, humiliated in the eyes of others, imprisoned if believed still to represent a threat, was unable to take revenge without risking even worse trouble. The law thus succeeded in making its calming role appreciated. It is difficult, however, to discern the true objectives of the plaintiffs, only half of whom offered a motive. This deliberate silence seems not to have worried the magistrates unduly. It suggests, nevertheless, a need for caution with regard to the motives that were articulated. Among them, matters of material interest take first place, followed by denunciation of a desire for vengeance on the part of the enemy or of a slur on their honour, followed by acts of solidarity, for example assisting a wife being beaten by her husband, and, finally, quarrels after drinking in the tavern.

Unlike in the sixteenth century, however, bars were no longer the scene of most of the violence. They came second, mentioned in 20 per cent of cases, evidence that the police surveillance was having some effect and that the prohibitions on opening during divine worship or on Sundays and holidays were being observed, at least to some degree. Nevertheless, taverns with names like the Golden Lion, the Shepherd, the Greyhound, the Cage, the White Horse, the Sheep, the Three Ways and the Stag remained important sites of local sociability and of its occasional break-downs. The *manse*, that is, the house, its outbuildings and yard, was the scene of 30 per cent of conflicts. Here, women clashed with other women in 44 per cent of cases and with men in 29 per cent of cases. The plaintiff was more often the occupier than a visitor, come, in some cases, to settle a dispute, a touch aggressively, especially in the evenings. Among other enclosed spaces, 6 per cent of cases took place at mills, 2 per cent each in churches and shops. Only a minority of cases overall had taken place out of doors, in the street (15 per cent) or in the square, on the highway or in the fields (7 per cent each). Violence was now better controlled than before in public places, in particular the inn. By contrast, it was much greater in the home. This trend only accentuated over time. On the one hand, the excesses committed within the conjugal home became more visible, because everyone was more watchful; on the other, the home became the main site for relational problems that could no longer be as easily settled out of doors, in full view.

Conflictuality died down in winter and was at its lowest level around Easter; it then increased from May on, reaching a peak in August, with a renewed surge in December. Sunday and Monday were the favoured days, each accounting for 20 per cent of offences, followed by Thursday, with 16 per cent. The time of day of the crime is known in a fifth of cases, from which it emerges that aggression developed mostly in the afternoon, culminating in the early evening, after which it diminished slightly, more rapidly after midnight. The house played a minor role in winter, the time of the communal evening gatherings, or *veillées*, and until April, when it was the scene of only 8 per cent of offences; the number rose slightly in May, June, August and October, reaching a peak of 33 per cent in November. The bar was over-represented from September to February, and the scene of as many as a third of cases in November and December.

Insults, the subject of half the complaints, were the most common starting point for altercations. The time was usually between mid-afternoon and early evening. Half of the insults cast aspersions on morals. Men were regularly called *bougre* ('bugger'), *janin*, a term of contempt

231

suggesting cuckoldry, or *foutre-jean* ('effing useless'), women were usually called *bougresse* or *putain* ('whore'), *garce* ('slut') or *cul chaud* ('hot-arse'). More than a quarter of the other terms of abuse related to a bad reputation: 'thief', 'crook', 'good-for-nothing', 'troublemaker' etc.; the rest implied stupidity or are not recorded. References to witchcraft were very rare. Women quarrelling with each other used mostly 'whore' and 'slut', sometimes in a veritable crescendo: 'whore, doubly a whore, her house is a brothel, slut, bitch' or 'whore, doubly a whore, she rents out her arse'. Men called each other mostly 'bugger', 'thief', 'scoundrel' or 'crook', which reveals their hostility to offences against property, even if they rarely resorted to the courts in such matters. When abusing women, they had a preference for 'whore', followed by *bougresse*, a term women rarely used of each other.

Insults and abuse were stereotyped but also variable according to the social position of the protagonists. They reveal the importance of a very touchy sense of honour, because anyone who felt they had been discredited, personally or by slurs on the reputation of a relative, resorted to blows so as not to lose face. What was new in relation to earlier centuries was that the losers often continued the battle through a formal complaint, even if it was they who had started the altercation. The provost's court, as we have seen, had little interest in motive, which made it possible for many plaintiffs to leave this vague. The aim was not so much to punish the aggressor as to compel him to pay the costs of the victim's care, compensate him and restore his honour, tarnished by the injuries he had sustained, especially if they were clearly visible. The inhabitants became accustomed to using the court to obtain the financial and symbolic compensation which had previously almost always been negotiated between the parties through the intermediary of unofficial arbitrators.

In the seventeenth century, in Gonesse, a large, active and prosperous village dependent on Paris, violence was very rarely murderous, which distinguished it from the Artois of a century before. Yet the calendar of the confrontations was basically unchanged. The increased surveillance of places of friction, like the tavern, and of behaviour was a major factor in this. In fact, there had been a decrease in external sociability in favour of a new concentration on the home, together with an almost universal disarmament, which limited the carnage between young men. The crucial factor, however, was probably the appropriation of the law by the inhabitants. This was not simply from fear of punishment, but rather in the hope of financial gain and greater protection. In this eighty-year period, nearly 600 plaintiffs sought the aid of the law, primarily in connection with insults or assaults they had suffered. Given a population of 3,000 persons, the annual rate of conflictuality recorded in these sources was around 250 per 100,000. In other periods, this might have led to dozens of homicides, which were now defused at an early stage.

The transformation was not the result of any real pacification of manners, which remained very violent. It was primarily caused by a reduction in the ferocity of the blows exchanged during physical encounters, which themselves remained as frequent as before. The many sworn surgeons appointed by the provost and mentioned in the documents were kept busy. More than a quarter of the 275 treatments recorded recommended bleeding as a cure for injuries, which were mostly open wounds, in the case of men, or, in that of women, contusions. Thus one patient with a cut upper lip was bled in one arm in 1662, while another, who had received a bullet from a pistol in his right eye, was bled in both arms ten years later. Rest, diet, dressings, the lancing of purulent wounds followed by suture, plasters, ointments, potions, tisanes and enemas were all part of the surgeons' armoury. The death of a client is recorded only eighteen times, that is, in 6 per cent of cases. In 1681, the two surgeons summoned to visit a man with a knife wound in the lower belly, whose intestines had spilled out, could do no more than offer a diagnosis of 'imminent, almost inevitable death', which duly came to pass a few days later.

These observations make it difficult to attribute the reduction in the frequency of homicides to significant advances in medicine. The rarity of fatal consequences is much more likely to have been due to a new restraint in the physical encounters, which remained very numerous. The codes had changed radically in the space of a few generations. Fights between men with the aim of spilling blood with a bladed weapon had become extremely rare, which points to greater social control of male adolescents, and greater self-control by them, even though the sources almost never reveal the age of the combatants. The language of the blows still suggests the defence of honour and desire to humiliate an opponent, especially in a man-to-man bare-knuckle fight. However, there was nothing indiscriminate or bestial about it. On the one hand, it was probably more inhibited than in the past by the fear of having to pay ruinous medical costs to a victim who had been too seriously injured and too long confined to his bed, and who would not hesitate to lodge a complaint before the courts. On the other, brutality was restrained, except in cases of madness or destructive rage, by a growing obligation to show respect for human life. This message had been dinned in for decades by the civil and religious authorities, but it also had the support of the community, who demonstrated their hostility to those who failed to observe it. The plaintiffs were well aware of this. They presented themselves before the court as honourable men who had never done any harm to anyone, or said anything nasty about anyone, and who, if the accusation seemed credible, denounced outsiders or fellow villagers who were violent, odious or drunks.

These documents also make it possible to see that the brutality of the deeds varied according to sex, age and position on the social scale. Just as ties of family, work and friendship required the defence of a victim of aggression, or even support for an aggressor, a subtle code of deference meant nuancing or reining in the force of the blows struck and the seriousness of the injuries inflicted. Fear of judicial or economic reprisals toned down the attitude of inferiors faced with important or formidable persons. Their hard reputations and their weapons meant that the honour of the royal sergeants was rarely questioned – unlike their honesty – and they were usually struck on the hands or legs. Millers, powerful in a society where bread was king, and envied, were also badmouthed for their dishonesty and mostly hit in the face, rarely on the head. *Laboureurs*, that is, prosperous peasant farmers, who employed a large number of people permanently or seasonally, were usually struck on the arms or the face. Merchants, who were often outsiders and generally less respected, were more often subjected to slurs on the purity of their wives, and hit on the head or in the face, as were labourers and bakers. The latter, of whom there were many, had a longstanding reputation for brutality, linked to their hard life and frequent, long and sometimes dangerous journeys to Paris to sell their bread in its markets. Labourers were generally assumed to be thieves, easily despised, called drunkards and fools and condemned for their low morals, especially as many of them were not natives of Gonesse.

Women were generally defined by their weakness, which meant that most men restrained the blows intended to punish them or force them to obey, and they tended to aim at the face or the arms so as to humiliate them by leaving the signs of masculine superiority to be clearly visible when the women next walked through the village streets. A socially superior situation on the part of the husband guaranteed them more respect, whereas an additional element of contempt was attached to unmarried servant girls, over whom all the men of the household assumed they had rights.

The peasants of the seventeenth century, confronted with a justice intruding ever further into their universe, and imposing respect for increasingly strict religious and moral norms, bowed to the inevitable, but managed to make the system work to their own ends. They learned to become wily litigants and to lay more charges in the hope of procuring substantial gains. The inhabitants of the wine-growing villages of Vanves, Issy and Vaugirard, not far from Paris, proved themselves experts in chicanery in the years 1760–7. They were extremely litigious and played the law like a favourite instrument in order to settle their incessant disputes and assert their position. They still made use of arbitrators and negotiated compensation agreements with their adversaries, but the courts offered them an additional means for putting pressure on the recalcitrant. They were not concerned only with restoring their tarnished honour, as they usually demanded a large financial recompense for the harm suffered, as at Gonesse under Louis XIV. The most trivial affairs, an insult or simply a punch, could result in the payment, on average, of the exorbitant sum of 200 *livres*, and the demands increased in line with the seriousness of the injuries. This greed went with a determination to obtain compensation. Even more formidable was a clever strategy of provoking an adversary, luring him into abuse or physical assault, to make a victory even more resounding, especially if the culprit had refused to accept the sentence, resisted a seizure or laid hands on the representatives of the law. Plaintiffs could procure large sums this way, more than they could ever have acquired in a lifetime of labour.

The thirst for profit encouraged litigants to personalize cases as far as possible and bring out the private dimension of the confrontation, because, if the culprit was punished for having disturbed the public peace, the victim risked receiving only symbolic satisfaction. This explains the vagueness of many of the depositions and the silence as to the real causes of the aggression. An apparent ignorance regarding the legal subtleties often concealed a remarkable aptitude for navigating the procedural jungle of the period in such a way as to achieve the best possible result. Of course, the defendants responded in kind. They argued back, they reacted skilfully and they sometimes made counter-claims, presenting a totally contradictory version of the dispute, which made a definitive decision difficult, especially when witnesses were reluctant to get too deeply involved in a complex matter. Nor were challenges to the law or its representatives unknown. These tended to come not from the poor so much as from the better-off inhabitants, and their principal targets were locals who had acquired office, for example that of sergeant, clerk, procurator fiscal or lieutenant. These children of the village elite were envied by those who were proud of their rank but lacked the prestige attached to office.[55]

The pressing demand for justice in the rural communities seems to be linked in part to the possibilities it offered for getting rich without having to work for it, by making someone pay – literally – generously for an insult or a blow. This also helps to explain the fall in the number of prosecutions for violence in the eighteenth century and the growth of property crime, because notions of value and wealth acquired a new importance in the countryside. The progress of the pacification of manners was then due more to a clearly perceived self-interest and dread of ruin than to fear of the law strictly speaking. At Fâches-Thumesnil, a small cereal-growing village north of Lille, as few as ten cases of delinquency are recorded in the archives of the seigneurial court for the period 1677–1789. This was a village of thirty-four households in 1553, that is, just over 150 inhabitants, with 14 horses and about 100 sheep. A census of domestic servants in the parish made in 1701 lists ten males and twelve females. The population increased rapidly in the eighteenth century, a total of 202 men, single, married or widowers, between the ages of twenty and sixty being recorded under the First Empire. Half the offences dealt with dated to the years between 1677 and 1697. All related to woundings, four of which had been inflicted between 1689 and 1697 by an awkward customer and repeat offender, Laurent Petit, a farmer born around 1652, who had attacked four different men, including the local sergeant. He was sentenced only to fines with costs.

The other five offences, all committed between 1701 and 1789, included one that was unspecified, two nocturnal thefts with breaking and entering – one of cheese among other items, the other of money – and two offences against persons. In one of the latter, on 14 July 1724, Vincent Defretin, son of Jean, had thrown stones at the door of a house at night, hurling 'atrocious insults' at the daughter of the house and her father. This was clearly pique on the part of a rejected bachelor. In the second, on 28 January 1742, a man had entered a bar with his firearm and felled with a blow the servant of the blacksmith, uttering abusive threats, before being overpowered. These stories appear in the periodic reports on criminality drawn up on a six-monthly basis. Even if they contain gaps, they often fail to record a single offence. For the years 1738–46, they note only one theft and disturbances in the tavern; between 1762 and 1772 not a single incident is recorded.[56]

The situation in the rest of Europe was probably more varied than is suggested by these few French examples, which show just how far violence had been tamed in parts of the countryside close to large towns. Young men were still disorderly. Between 1696 and 1789, in the *sénéchaussées* of Libourne and Bazas, which came under the *parlement* of Bordeaux, more than a third of those accused of physical violence came from the 20–29 age group, and a fifth from the 30–39 age group. Verbal violence was more often committed by older men aged between 40 and 49, who were responsible for a quarter of cases, as against a fifth for those aged between 20 and 29. The traditional youthful behaviour at festivals still led to acts of violence and verbal or symbolic insults. The latter reveal the existence of a deeply contentious spirit, directed against the authorities. In 1741, for example, two troublemakers chanted offensive songs about the mayor of Libourne, then, when he pressed criminal charges against them, came one night with a gang of supporters and tried to force his door to get their revenge. Another gang, in 1787, covered a later mayor's door with excrement. The charges laid by older men against well-established adults who had insulted them probably sprang from the hope of receiving substantial damages, which would have been beyond the abilities of the impecunious unmarried to pay. The great precariousness of the latter's life in a period of late marriage is shown by the fact that 51 per cent of the thieves of both sexes whose age is known were twenty-nine or under. Women accounted for only 15 per cent of this total; men aged between twenty and twenty-nine made up the largest group, responsible for a third of the offences.[57]

In spite of the negative stereotypes so frequently peddled with regard to rural violence, it declined significantly from the seventeenth century on, as the few studies devoted to this question show. In the nineteenth century, the rural world suffered even greater disruption. Opened up by the roads and the railways, its population became much more mixed, while its local young people were sucked into the factories. In resisting change, it came up against the hostility of the disciples of modernity. They denounced its filth, brutality and backwardness, all convenient ways of describing its difference. Its social and cultural traditions survived by adapting to new factors.

Hostility to 'strangers', particularly from a neighbouring parish, remained strong, as it still cemented the community and made it possible to defend its territory and its women against external threats. Those who risked entering this hostile territory responded by closing ranks, with the result that blows were often exchanged on the occasion of a festival. It was by no means uncommon for a dance to culminate in a fight between the champions of two adjoining villages. More often, collective mockery, primarily directed at sexual failings, kept alive a rivalry that was regarded as a necessity. In Vexin, for example, they had a song which said, of the girls of Longuesse, 'they uncover their backsides to cover up their heads'.[58]

It was not only the regions that were difficult of access, where life remained hard due to the material conditions, that experienced waves of resistance to modernity when it proved too disruptive of the local communities. The forests of Hurepoix and Yveline, close to Paris, were the scene of fierce clashes between natives and gamekeepers after the introduction of the hunting permit in 1844. Resistance to the police was an ingrained mind-set widespread in the countryside. It led to support for 'bandits of honour' who had taken refuge in the woods or wastes after some police or judicial pressure that was locally seen as excessive. These men bore no resemblance to the faithless, lawless bandits who had burned the soles of the feet of rich peasants to force them to reveal where they had hidden their gold. They were valued because they were seen as suffering doubles of those who still had their own homes, and their adventures sustained the spirit of protest against injustice.

Among many such places of refuge, mountainous regions like the Pyrenees, the Mediterranean islands and southern Italy were constantly marked by these phenomena, which prepared the ground for the advent of the organized mafias. This was strikingly illustrated in Ariège during the War of the Demoiselles. Peasants disguised as women revived disquieting memories of the old carnivalesque festivals, when young men won fame by their violent and murderous acts. Now subdued but restive, they never missed an opportunity to let off steam and they sustained an atmosphere of endemic challenge at a time when, in the mid nineteenth century, the great revolts that were the heirs of the medieval Jacqueries died out in France.

Nevertheless, in spite of some resurgences, the countryside abandoned collective armed protest. An era drew to an end. Overtly injurious violence had long been in decline, due to the temptation to resort to the law, which made it possible to dispense with private vengeance while obtaining substantial financial damages. Violence now gradually disappeared from the countryside. Those who resisted this most strongly were denounced for their archaism. It was they who were most likely to hang on to their weapons, for example on the pretext of hunting, and who remained most deeply attached to a sense of honour associated with the purity of women and the theatrical demonstration of the manliness of young men. Around 1882, Corsica was the area with the largest number of homicides and attempted homicides, followed in descending order by the Pyrénées-Orientales, Lozère, Ardèche and Bouches-du-Rhone.[59]

If violence was no longer the preferred method of resolving disputes and tensions in the nineteenth-century village, it was because villages were increasingly integrating into the surrounding world. The principal motor of this dramatic change was the transformation in relations between young and adult males. The language of traditional honour and obligatory vengeance gradually became a dead letter, which no longer bound them together. It was replaced by new idioms drawn from the outside world and adapted to local needs, and it no longer constructed the norms of inter-generational exchange, though this was slower to happen in some regions than others. This revolution was greatly accelerated by the massive intermixing of young men caused by two world wars, and it was constantly kept going by major integration mechanisms, both formal, like the school and the army, and informal, like the cult of novelty celebrated by the mass media and the growth of leisure. It reduced the importance of the collective in favour of that of the individual, and it devalued the destructive impulses in favour of universal ideals inherited from 1789, which came to be enshrined in a model of personal success that exalted wily finesse at the expense of brute force.

The people of the countryside had always been capable of benefiting from innovations which brought them significant concrete and symbolic advantages. However, by accepting the disciplining of violence in public space, the near-total abandonment of the use of weapons in fights, especially the knife, and the transfer of codes of honour from the group to the person, they helped to shift the principal site of disputes to the home. In the past, the major excesses of the young unmarried men had been enacted out of doors, between peers from the kingdoms of youth. Now, though homicides were less common in the nineteenth-century countryside, they were more often committed within the family. In Quercy, confrontations within the home were among the most brutal, together with those between neighbours. The most frequent causes related to the choice of heir and the transmission of the patrimony, because this was a region where one child was favoured at the expense of his brothers and sisters, who were generously rewarded with a small compensation. Next came internal contention over the exercise of power within the household. Disputes between spouses, which were often very bitter, resulted primarily from accusations of alcoholism or idleness, which also reveal a fear of seeing the prospects of survival and development of the successors jeapordized.[60] Parricide was a rare and steadily declining crime, in spite of one peak in mid century and another in the 1880s; committed only a dozen times a year in France, it confirms the importance of generational conflicts, linked, in two-thirds of cases, to economic factors. In the south, the tragedy was often set in motion by the eldest son, anxious to get his hands on the family property. In the north, an egalitarian region where the children paid an annual pension to the parents, those who committed this crime were seeking to lighten their financial burden.[61]

With all due reservations, we may assume that the French example holds good for the rest of Western Europe: driven out of the streets and the squares, closely controlled in the taverns, rural violence got back in through the window of domestic exploitation. Whereas it had once been seen in a positive light in the village, because it made it possible to defend the honour of a group and demonstrate the manly power of the new generation, while also urging sons to wait their turn to replace their fathers, it was now seen simply as abnormal, and deeply disturbing in that it was increasingly inflicted on a member of the family. The tensions for which the family became the focus also made visible other types of violence, previously hidden behind house walls. From the 1880s, with the emergence of new sensibilities resulting from the 'rise of the individual', which had deeply marked the century, there was an increase in the number of accusations of the rape of little girls, incest and cruelty to children.[62] It is true that the authorities were still more preoccupied with the repression of youth crime, which was likened to a veritable plague at the beginning of the twentieth century, but this nascent movement was a sign of a growing unease in the population at large with regard to the abuse of children; it was the first step in the direction of the later definition of paedophilia as the most despicable monstrosity imaginable.

Crime statistics, which were increasingly well kept from the eighteenth century, reveal a major transformation of the repressive gaze rather than a change in the criminal realities. It was 'the judicial ritual which constructed this social object that we call the accused'. It designated him as an 'other', as an inverted double of the 'gentleman', during the course of a legal process which enabled the state symbolically to assert its authority and to offer the citizens an ideal of equality before the law.[63] Yet the main target had remained the same since the judicial revolution of the sixteenth century: the rebellious young likely to pose too serious a challenge to the rights of established persons, of fathers and of rulers. As society changed, however, along with its basic values, the emotive formulations of this fear of dispossession among adults and the comfortably off changed, too, adapting to the new circumstances. The trial of strength between the sexes and, above all, age groups shifted along potential fracture lines, which then became more important. With the general acceptance by young men of the blood taboo, at the cost of many minor clashes and frequent outbursts of violence, the authorities gradually turned their attention away from a problem that had been largely solved; all the more so, as the definition of a legitimate violence in just wars made it possible to mobilize this powerful repressed collective aggression and channel it to make it serve aggressive and patriotic objectives.

The growth of a capitalist commercial economy in the eighteenth century produced new challenges by causing hordes of rootless young people to leave the countryside for the thriving towns, such as Bordeaux, Amsterdam, London and Paris. The living conditions of these workers, who were often ill-adapted to the new needs, were so difficult that they led to major outbreaks of robbery, which were the only way the workers could survive; they were joined in this by many domestic servants of both sexes, reduced to poverty after displeasing their employers or succumbing to temptation. The weakest and the youngest, and those least protected by family or other solidarities, formed a worrying underclass.

In the nineteenth century, their famished armies were known by established prosperous citizens as the dangerous classes. The demand for

240

protection hugely increased, encouraging the urban authorities to press on with the criminalization of theft and idleness. England was one of the first countries to experience the commercial and industrial revolutions, and it was not by chance that it produced, by the second half of the sixteenth century, a cruel Bloody Code whose main purpose was to punish without mercy those guilty of crimes against property, to reassure the well-to-do. This legislation was softened only when the threat seemed to be growing less urgent, after 1830. In spite of its much-vaunted insular originality, England then embarked on the pacification of private space, like the other European countries, turning its attention to the family.

In a striking paradox, the beginning of the twentieth century saw violence become totally unacceptable among those who regarded themselves as civilized just when the terrible human butcheries of 1914–18 were in preparation. Did this amount to a massive return of the repressed? Everyday brutality in all its forms was fiercely criticized in Western civilization. The aversion to the sight of blood went so far as a new repugnance at the spectacle of the slaughter of animals and a growing pity for them, which heralded the later development of their protection and the defence of their rights.[64] Healthy, moral persons turned away not only from the spectacle of death, which was increasingly hidden, before its modern concealment deep inside hospitals, but from the spectacle of suffering.

In 1847, in France, the aversion to pain led to the use of the anaesthetics ether and chloroform. The artificial paradises of drugs, including the opium so much appreciated in the age of Baudelaire, perhaps went some way to compensate for the repression of the emotions, especially among the young, as they were subjected to a relentless education in the blood taboo and the ban on violence. It was no longer simply the rural brute, inverted image of the man of quality, who continued to behave with unacceptable savagery, unable to control or divert his morbid impulses, because the countryside, too, opted for modernity and repudiated violent excesses. With the active assistance of much media hype, these were now incarnated in the absolute monster capable of killing for pleasure and revelling in his revolting cruelty, like Jack the Ripper in London and Jacques Vacher in France. The latter, born to a farming family in Isère, in 1869, called himself 'God's anarchist', and was charged with killing four boys, six little girls and an old woman. Released from an asylum, he committed his last crime on 31 August 1895 at Bénonces, in Ain, where, according to his own confession, he cut the throat of a sixteen-year-old shepherd boy before tearing off his sexual parts with his teeth.[65]

The figure of the murderous monster, which fascinates a wide public avid for horror, speaks of the final human boundary that is crossed only by rare individuals who must surely be insane or deeply unbalanced. At the beginning of the twentieth century, innumerable works of fiction took up this theme. As the First World War loomed, the insatiable appetite of the Western imaginary for these bloody fantasies showed that there had been no resolution of a fundamental contradiction between the relational mildness demanded of every civilized being in their daily exchanges and the warlike exaltation of nationalistic virtues.

— 8 —

MORTAL THRILLS AND CRIME FICTION
(SIXTEENTH TO TWENTIETH CENTURIES)

The sharp fall in the number of homicides from the end of the sixteenth century was accompanied in France by the emergence of a literature and an imagery intended to edify the reader or observer by recreating the emotions so spectacularly staged by the ritual of torture. The dramatized accounts of the latter and the *canards sanglants* sold in the streets of Paris, and the *histoires tragiques* ('tragic stories') destined for a more cultivated public, seem to have had as their sole aim to prove that crime doesn't pay. The gallows literature of eighteenth-century England delivered the same moral lesson. Something changed, however, in both countries around 1720, with the appearance of a much more ambiguous type of literature, which elevated certain bandits, such as Cartouche, to the rank of mythical popular hero. Then, in the nineteenth century, these bandit tales spread to the great industrial towns, where they became both strangely popular with and a source of deep unease to the good bourgeois citizens. Murderers and thieves then formed an army of savage shadows, led by Fantômas, hunted down by Sherlock Holmes, whose violent exploits defied the established decencies and morality. Shortly before the First World War, the Apaches were suddenly everywhere, both in the streets of Paris and in the columns of the mass circulation newspapers. Can the aficionados of these sensational tales have been confined to the lower classes, who had escaped the 'general softening' of manners and who had not had the 'rough edges of their individuality' rubbed off?[1]

The colonization of the Western imaginary by cruel fantasies is surely more likely to have been a sign that the taboo on murderous brutality had been accepted, leaving space only for evocations of what had been forbidden. Transgression had become impossible, without being taken for a brute beast or insane. It was available only in distanced and oneiric forms to boys reaching adolescence. Increasingly driven out of public space and closely supervised, it was only in their dreams that they could rediscover the manly youth culture of earlier centuries. Mandrin, Cartouche, Jack the Ripper and their innumerable fictional imitators, first propagated by the book and the image, and then, throughout the twentieth century, by the strip cartoon, the cinema, song and music, are surely ways of conjuring up nostalgic memories of a violence that had once been ordinary and largely tolerated by adults. To varying degrees, the crime story, in all its many forms, questioned the morality of appearances and the order imposed by established society. It painted, and constantly updated, the picture of he who dared to resist, whether evil genius, youthful honourable bandit or disillusioned private eye with unorthodox methods. The success of this chameleon genre was based on a powerful internal contradiction present in our culture since the process of eradicating homicide had begun. The relational softness demanded of 'civilized' males in daily life went together, at the express demand of the state, with an exaltation of their warlike qualities, which were indispensable to the successful retention of colonial empires and the defence of the endangered fatherland. Fictional violence, omnipresent in magazines, detective stories and many other media, served two opposing ends: it pacified the manners of pubescent boys, by offering them the outlet of mortal thrills without getting involved in action, but it also prepared them for this eventuality, as the terrible slaughter of two world wars testifies. The symbolic education in these two contradictory roles is what gives the crime novel its significance. This literature also defined the function of the weaker sex in a world dominated by manly values. Women were effectively offered a choice only between the sweet, maternal, tender victim of masculine passions, often a blonde, and the deadly femme fatale, hard and usually brunette, who drives men to crime and ultimately disgrace.

The devil, assuredly: the birth of crime fiction

In 1558, Pierre Boaistuau published *Le Théâtre du monde*, the first French manifesto of an anguished humanism which broke away from the optimistic vision of the preceding generations: 'But, Good God! How the devil has taken hold of the bodies and souls of men today and made them so terribly industrious and ingenious in doing evil.'[2] Boaistuau was also the creator, in 1559, of a new type of literature in the land of Rabelais, the *Tragic Stories Extracted from the Italian Works of Bandel, and Put into our French Tongue by P. Boaistuau, Surnamed Launay, a Native of Brittany*.[3] His source was Italian, Matteo Bandello, who died in 1561, and had himself been inspired by Boccaccio. Many new editions, translations into English and Flemish, adaptations and plagiarized versions testify to the immediate success of this work. It was added to by François de Belleforest in 1570, and a new and much longer version, running to seven volumes, came out in 1582.[4] The world it presents is a nightmare world, overrun by violence and the monstrous, totally opposite to the prevailing codes. The individual is as subject to the 'prodigies of Satan' as to the terrible vengeance of God. Weak, carried away by the fury of his passions, he strays from his divine nature.

In the last decades of the sixteenth century, the trickle of 'tragic stories' swelled, with Vérité Habanc (1585) and Bénigne Poissenot (1586) among others, and, by the beginning of the reign of Louis XIII, it had become a flood, with François de Rosset and Bishop Jean-Pierre Camus.[5] Their writings appealed to a baroque taste among the cultivated public, which also enjoyed very different works, such as the chivalric romances, the gallant tales and *L'Astrée* (1607–28), a long pastoral novel by Honoré d'Urfé. Rosset and Camus offered 'stories of our times', based on violence, love and ambition. They were often sandwiched between a moralizing introduction and conclusion and they taught their readers how to behave before the Law, divine and human, by providing them with examples of transgression followed by an ineluctable punishment.

Rosset, born in 1570, probably to a noble family, settled in Paris in 1603, where he seems to have become a lawyer in the *parlement*. He was the author of various volumes of letters and love poetry and, in 1614, produced a French translation of the first six *Novelas exemplares* of Cervantes as well as his own *Histoires tragiques de notre temps: où sont contenues les morts funestes et lamentables de plusieurs personnes (Tragic Stories of Our Times: Containing the Baneful and Lamentable Deaths of Many Persons)*. The latter, which consisted of fifteen stories, to which eight others were added in 1619, presumed date of the author's death, proved one of the greatest publishing successes of the seventeenth century. It was republished at least forty times between 1614 and 1757, augmented by many other stories by anonymous authors, long after the death of Rosset himself. A contemporary of the Counter-Reformation, he presented the unhappy history of mankind with an emphasis on the vanity of all things.[6] Famous events provided him with plenty of material, including the murders of Concini and Bussy d'Amboise, whose exploits were also described by Alexandre Dumas in 1846 in *La Dame de Montsoreau*. Rosset wrote of sinister fates and tragic and frequently violent deaths – there are no fewer than fifty-three in the collection – and he liked to describe the gory scene in meticulous detail: Fleurie, a woman raging against the man she hates, 'drew out a little knife with which she stabbed him in both eyes, then she wrenched them out of his head. She cut off his nose and his ears and then, with the help of the servant, pulled out his teeth and his nails and cut off his fingers, one by one.' Rosset, a moralist, denounced his century as 'the sewer of all the villainies of the others', glutted with abominations.[7] He laid the blame on depraved humans, and even more on the devil, one of the principal characters he portrays.

This is a literature that insists on the terrifying divine vengeance which awaits transgressors. It seeks to persuade its readers to accept a pitiless punitive morality, after luring them into exploring an imaginary prohibited world. Rosset appeals to the sort of morbid curiosity displayed by the crowds who attended public executions to take his readers on an oneiric journey that produces thrills of horror at the spectacle of forbidden things, followed by feelings of mingled confusion and relief at the inevitable punishment of the guilty, before a return, soothed, to the universe of the God-fearing. By providing a taste of forbidden fruit without the danger of losing one's soul, these stories helped to distance the atrocities they described. They opened a new window in Western culture by transforming blood into the ink of collections of stories and engravings, concrete reality into macabre fantasy. The age of the repression of the destructive impulses had begun. Even committed to paper, these stories were highly ambiguous, which they remain to this day, in spite of their constant reformulation and the use of an increasing variety of media. Their role is ultimately a dual one: to impose the taboo on murder, but not totally to extinguish man's deep fascination with this mystery, which has enabled him, as predatory hunter, to acquire his dominant position on earth.

Not forgetting his damned side... For Rosset and his emulators, the devil was assuredly man's most faithful companion. And women were his principal allies. Rosset demonstrates this in the story of a lieutenant of the watch in Lyon who was abused by a devil who had seduced him in the guise of a beautiful young lady. The sinner died as a result and was damned, as he should be, because 'libertinage attracts adultery, adultery incest, incest the sin against nature, and then God lets you sleep with the Devil'. To which Rosset adds: 'I, for my part, am firmly of the opinion that it was the dead body of a beautiful woman, which Satan had taken from some grave and that he had made move', changing its odour of corruption and its colour. The edification through horror that is offered here paved the way for the murky crime thriller. The readers had to enjoy themselves while being educated through fear; they had to take pleasure in teetering on the edge of the abyss to which they had been led by their guide.

In the reign of Louis XIII, France experimented with the pathetic, the tragic and the baroque. Life seemed ever more sombre and more disquieting, so many were the traps laid by an omnipresent devil.[8] Jean-Pierre

Camus conveyed and disseminated this sensibility. Born in 1582, dead in 1652 or 1653, bishop of Belley from 1608 to 1628, he was one of the most prolific writers of his age, author of 265 works, 21 of which were collections of tragic stories, containing a total of 950 tales.[9] Their brevity and their variety were ideally suited to his moralizing purpose. A Christian humanist and fierce supporter of the Counter-Reformation, Camus' aim was to spread devotion at every social level. His first collection of tragic stories, *Les Evénements singuliers*, published in Lyon in 1628, consisted of seventy tales and quickly became hugely popular. That same year, he resigned his bishopric and produced a second volume in the same vein, *Les Occurrences remarquables*, followed, in 1630, by *L'Ampitéâtre sanglant* and *Les Spectacles d'horreur*, two of his most famous collections, and *Les Succez différens*. In 1631 came *Le Pentagone historique*, *Les Relations morales* and *La Tour des miroirs*, in 1632 *Les Leçons exemplaires* and *Les Observations historiques* and in 1633 *Les Décades historiques*. Eight new titles appeared between 1639 and 1644, including *Les Rencontres funestes*, to which were added many posthumous collections published between 1660 and 1670.[10]

That Camus had a great influence on potential readers, although they were few in number, is clear. He reached both the specialists in knowledge, of whom there were between 2,000 and 3,000 in the classical period, and even more a 'society' public which, in 1660, consisted of between 8,000 and 10,000, 3,000 of them in Paris. They included nobles, prosperous bourgeois and ladies of all ages, keen readers of poetry, novels and epistolary literature and setters of fashion. The same readers also consumed treatises on civility and good manners, modelled on Faret's *Honnête homme*, published in 1630.[11] The twelve tragic titles produced by Camus between 1628 and 1633, together with the new editions that rapidly followed, amounted to tens of thousands of copies, which suggests that few cultivated readers can have been unaware of their existence. It is likely, furthermore, that it was by identifying their needs, and after several failures in more mawkish genres, that, in 1628, Camus turned to churning out dark stories with the intention of instilling piety by the example of its opposite. Master of the morbid and the cruel in an age deeply marked by an obsession with the devil and sin, he was a very self-conscious moralist, but one who did not deny himself the pleasure of writing or seek to skimp on the details of the terrible scenes he describes.

Few writers after Camus and his contemporary Claude Malingre continued to write in this vein, with the exception of F. de Grenaille, author, in 1642, of *Les Amours historiques des princes*, and Jean-Nicolas de Parival, whose *Histoires tragiques de nostre temps arrivées en Hollande* were published in Leiden in 1656. The end of the reign of Louis XIII coincided with the end of the fashion for tragic stories, which were soon replaced by the more entertaining works of Sorel, Segrais, Scarron and Donneau de Visé.[12] The quality public had probably eventually grown weary of them. These people were losing their taste for blood, as they increasingly turned towards classicism in literature and embarked on the 'civilizing process'.[13] The period of these works' greatest influence, from 1559 to the 1640s, was precisely that of the first great retreat of homicidal violence in France, under pressure from a judicial criminalization at its most effective in the 1620s.

Camus presented a human comedy peopled with a wide range of characters. His preference was for the nobility, who embodied his own aristocratic ideal, even if he often adopted a satirical tone towards them. He had little liking for the rich bourgeoisie and was fiercely critical of financiers, the world of money, lawyers, the police and hypocritical monks. Nor was he much interested in craftsmen or tradesmen and, though he described peasants with some sympathy, he also revealed a certain repulsion for them: they 'lived as a rule among animals, and resemble them in many ways'. He paid more attention to the passions of the soul than to the individuals who experienced them. He also took great pleasure in the picturesque and the anecdotal. Marriage, women and adultery, subjects to which he constantly returned, were always located in an atmosphere of incredible violence and cruelty, close to the realities of the moment. From a pessimistic Augustinian perspective, his implacable Biblical God was very sparing with his mercy. Like the justice of his own day, which aimed to deflect people from crime by the spectacle of corporal punishment, Camus used brutal examples in order to provoke a horror of vice in his readers.[14]

Murderers, traitors and perjurers fill his pages. There are 126 deaths in *Les Spectacles d'horreur*, one of his masterpieces. The devil is omnipresent and pulls the strings of the tragedy of existence. Readily falling into his traps, humans are drawn into a bloody frenzy which destroys all their hopes of salvation. Camus mines the seam of murderous atrocity by presenting a gallery of monsters who are archetypes of he who is deaf to divine entreaties. When the cruel betrayed wife of *La Jalousie précipitée* murders her sleeping husband, she 'repeatedly plunged a large knife that she had prepared for this horrible execution *into* his throat, *into* his abdomen and *into* his stomach and, with frenzied blows, chased the soul from the body of the deplorable and too loyal Paulin'. To avenge herself on an unfaithful husband, *La Mère Médée* kills her children with an axe. The deceived husband of *Le Coeur mangé* serves up, as a delicacy to his other half, the heart of her lover.[15] There is always a brief conclusion evoking a terrible God who punishes the sins of men without pity. Simple words like 'punishment', 'unhappiness', 'deception', 'brutality', 'tragic', 'lamentable', 'execrable' and 'infamous' epitomize an exhortation to his readers to mend their ways to escape damnation. The impact of Bishop Camus' conventional sermons must have been heightened by the way they came close on the heels of a colourful description of the dangerous byways of vice, illustrated with an abundance of titillating details.

A friend of St Francis de Sales, Camus can hardly be suspected of any lack of apostolic zeal, but he broke new ground because he loved to pile one terrifying anecdote on another. His scenes of horror were meant to edify while describing with realism instances of destructive fury. He combined a lofty perception of divine ideals with a remarkably clear vision of the extreme baseness to which mortals can sink. This was probably the only way he could attract a wide readership, bored with all the usual ecclesiastical perorations. With a good grasp of the psychology of his contemporaries, the former bishop of Belley gave them the dose of unfathomable mystery they needed by making the devil the fundamental explanatory principal of human perversity. The device was perhaps oversimple, but his skill as a writer enabled him to get away with it, over and over again. In this way he helped to entrench this idea, which persists to our own day, deep in any explanation of the too frequent but unacceptable breaking of the blood taboo.

The devil was, in a way, the inventor of the *fait divers*. A new genre of printed material, destined for a rather less cultivated public than that of Camus, bore his mark. The vogue for the *canards* followed a chronology very close to that of the *histoires tragiques*. Like them, these short printed pieces catered for a very pronounced 'popular' taste for the macabre and the sensational, though it was also a taste shared by some cultivated bourgeois, such as the chronicler Pierre de l'Estoile. Poorly preserved and difficult to study, the *canards* seem to have flourished primarily between 1600 and 1631. Nearly three-fifths of those known were printed in Paris, and more than a quarter in Lyon.[16]

Stories of marvels accounted for over a third of the total, tales of calamities, celestial phenomena and dreadful crimes each for a fifth. The latter were recounted with a wealth of morbid detail and dwelt at length on the fury of the participants. There was no shortage of horrifying scenes, as, for example, when a deceived young woman makes her lover eat the heart or the liver of their child. Miracles and sacrilege were frequent occurrences. The devil was rarely absent and indeed the leading character in the stories of spells, bewitchments, baleful apparitions and executions of witches. Frequently reworked and re-used, like the engravings adorning their covers, these stories taught a very simple moral lesson, linking human misfortunes to the wrath of God, unleashed by the proliferation of sins and forbidden passions such as lust.[17]

A direct correlation exists with the works of Rosset and Camus, who took many of their anecdotes from this hotchpotch of real events, gory *fait divers*, also picked up by newspapers such as the *Mercure françois*, and imaginative literature. But the strictly literary treatment differed, because it was aimed at a quality readership, which meant it was necessary to include 'these violent spices suited to the taste of the most refined of palates'.[18] Both genres offered supposedly different readerships a simplified explanation of the trials and miseries encountered in this world. The more ambitious, illustrated by Rosset and Camus, prepared the thinking man for a morality of controlled passions, which was also being proposed in parallel, between 1620 and 1640, by the model of the urbane and polished gentleman of the manuals of good manners.[19] They shaped the collective imaginaries of right-thinking people by interposing between their gaze and reality an interpretative key dominated by the idea that any violation of divine or earthly law would inevitably be punished.[20]

The *histoires tragiques* drove home a message of obedience, but they also provided the pleasure of a relatively risk-free transgression. They familiarized their readers with a paper devil, captured by the words of the author and a prisoner of the mind of the reader, which probably lessened the anxiety regarding him. The cultural break of the 1640s was perhaps in part due to a reaction against the excessive familiarity with the pathetic and the diabolic during the preceding hundred years. Encouraged by the challenge to the primacy of theology resulting from the new ideas, in particular Cartesianism, it also revealed a growing repugnance among the upper urban ranks for gore, the base and the trivial, which paved the way for the triumph of the harmonious principles of classicism. The tragic stories had dealt primarily with violence, sex and lese-majesty.[21] They taught that the least false step could lead to the abyss, within a notably cumulative morality. The simplest acts risked ending in total disaster, because Evil was always on the lookout for an opportunity to use them to bring a man down. The eighteenth tale in the first book of Camus' *Les Spectacles d'horreur* tells the story of two small boys who, having seen their father cut the throat of a calf, imitate him by killing their little brother and hiding his body in the stove. Camus simply wanted to show that you must avoid doing wrong in front of children, virgin wax on which everything made its mark. The third tale of the second book of the same collection, 'Les Morts entassées', describes a fatal series of events which shows how the devil stubbornly stalks his prey. An angry farmer kills his son without good cause, then commits suicide in despair; his wife, horror-struck at this terrible scene, lets her last-born child fall into the fire. Evil is everywhere. There is no remedy and it accompanies everyone from the cradle to the grave.[22] Yet nothing happened without God's permission, not even the sin which tested, in order to punish, a wretched, depraved and execrable humanity.[23] The mental state generated by the fear of transgression spared no one, not even the saints. It was a *mise en abîme* of a parable on necessarily destructive desire, against which everyone must protect himself by overcoming his animal part, that is, his violent and sexual impulses.

The guilt described by Rosset and Camus had not yet, however, been fully internalized by thoughtful people. The omnipresent devil played the role of a double. Capable of entering the bodies of his victims, he was not fully consistent with the soul of those he tyrannized. Further, his figure lost its impact among a cultivated public as the horror linked to the notion of sin was threatened by the taste for behaving well and for speaking properly in an uncluttered language, in other words by social politeness, more agreeable to bear than fear of the devil. He became increasingly less necessary as a marker for sin for the members of high society in pursuit of the more enjoyable style of life of the Age of Enlightenment.

From bloodthirsty murderer to well-loved bandit

Canards and *histoires tragiques* were two avatars, each destined for a different audience, of gallows literature. The latter, which flourished from the sixteenth century, recounted, in a few pages, the disastrous career of a person condemned to death, and was on sale to the crowds at or soon after the dismal ceremony. The archetypes described could be quickly re-used and the accompanying illustrations were interchangeable. The emotion felt by honest folk was thus prolonged. The genre gave them more to shudder at, with its descriptions of the terrible exploits of the criminals, recounted with a profusion of detail, if often scant regard for the facts. The end of the story was necessarily fixed in advance. All the anonymous authors could do was add a few curious or surprising details to a strictly codified theme. Very few prisoners were rescued at the last minute by a posse led by their friends, a royal decree or the discovery of circumstances necessitating a stay of execution, such as a woman's pregnancy. Contrary to what was dreamed up by popular novelists in the nineteenth century, seeking to introduce an element of suspense into their descriptions of such scenes, death was almost always the end of the story. Further, the ritualization of the spectacle meant that only slight variations were possible. The crowd watched out for them, all the more keenly in that they were familiar with the fixed sequence of events in this implacable tragedy. They kept a close eye on the gestures and physiognomy of the person who had taken on a role prepared for them, in which they were expected to demonstrate both courage and repentance to serve as an edifying example to all. All they could hope for was divine mercy, which depended on the sincerity of the contrition they displayed.

The gallows was not there solely to punish. It was also a powerful educational tool for the use of all who watched a human life end tragically. For the officials responsible for organizing this solemn moment, the most difficult part was getting the principal character to cooperate, so that they did not disrupt the desired consensus between justice and the watching crowd. The confessors worked hard to achieve this, and to good effect. The magistrates of the *parlement* of Paris did their bit by ensuring that the victims' last hours were closely supervised. They were questioned as to their intentions by the clerks of the court who came to read out the death sentence. If they detected a desire to disturb the harmony of the ceremony, to proclaim their innocence, insult their tormentors, or make some embarrassing public revelations, the clerks did everything in their power to make them change their minds. Recorded in the documents incorrectly known as 'last dying speeches', their persistent efforts until the last minutes on the scaffold testify to the importance attached to the collaboration, at least apparent, of the condemned. This was just as strongly desired in England.[24] They were expected finally to sublimate their evil passions so as to validate in the eyes of all present the notion that crime never paid.

The dualist logic of the judicial documents permeated the whole of the literary and artistic production devoted to the description of these crimes. There could be no such thing as a positive hero, because the murderer or the bandit had to be perceived as an offender against divine law, an accomplice of the devil and an agent of Evil. Yet it is by no means certain that this approach was universally accepted. The gallows literature was so insistent and it expanded so rapidly in the great age of executions, from the late sixteenth to the early eighteenth centuries, that the question of its social function is posed with some force. Its 'popular' success may suggest that it formed public opinion by inculcating basic notions concerning the prohibitions which, if they were transgressed, led to the ultimate punishment. But the scale of this success also suggests that the desire to educate is not enough on its own to explain the golden age of this literature. There needed also to be readers fascinated by the blood-curdling tales it told. Producers and consumers were not necessarily looking for the same thing in the works whose success they together guaranteed.

In England, the phenomenon was at its height between 1680 and 1740. It took three contrasting forms, produced, respectively, by the authorities, a chaplain and journalists. As in France, the first of these, the official *Proceedings*, were very quickly put on sale to the public.

252

Their format was always the same, first a description of the composition of the court, then a summary of the case and the verdict. To please lovers of concrete detail, they became increasingly full and lively, expanding from a couple of pages in the late seventeenth century to forty-eight on average by 1730. The second type was the work of the chaplain of Newgate, who provided his own version of events the day after the execution. He gave the criminal star billing, but only so as to relate his spiritual biography according to a standard model: first his fall and then his repentance, which had to be based on the love of God and not only on fear, if he was to achieve his salvation. The press, lastly, highlighted the sensational and the bloody, illustrating the text with stereotyped engravings in which the characters spoke in balloons. The journalist usually took the side of the victim, proclaiming his horror at the culprit who mounted the scaffold and offering a moral judgement. However, a new element, still rare, was that a journalist occasionally expressed admiration for some of the most famous bandits, such as John Sheppard or Mary Carleton.[25]

This limited novelty apart, the three types of text were alike in producing a routinely disturbing image of the criminal as a villain, a second-rater, a sinner, inexorably got rid of by society. Yet the discourse as a whole gave the criminal an important symbolic role. By publicly proclaiming the justice of his punishment, he allowed the community to reaffirm its unity and, each time, revalidate its rules. The individuality of the criminal was lost sight of, together with the real reasons for his acts, in favour of the edifying lesson offered to one and all. This meant that the reader or observer need have no compunction in revelling in the detailed account of the criminal's cruel deeds or the spectacle of his well-deserved agony. The emergence of some journalistic admiration for a few exceptional bandits is a sign that this process was losing some of its power. It suggests that some among the public had gone beyond the normative vision to appreciate the seduction of the transgressor, or simply dared to feel deeply in a way that ran counter to the dominant ethic.

This was slower to happen in France than in England. A positive mythic image of Cartouche developed only after his execution in 1721, whereas the phenomenon was visible in England a decade earlier. The exploits of Jack Sheppard, Blueskin Blake and Jonathan Wild attracted attention to the subject and filled the columns of the newspapers, especially the *Original Weekly Journal* of John Applebee, to which Daniel Defoe (1660–1731) was a contributor between 1720 and 1724. The vogue for the theme also gave rise to many books, including several anonymous anthologies of trials, such as *A Compleat Collection of Remarkable Tryals* (1718) and *A Compleat Collection of State Tryals*

(1719). Based on official records, these works shared the same basic structure. They presented in succession the origins and childhood of the scoundrel, the juiciest episodes from his or her deplorable life, the arrest, the trial and, lastly, the execution. The moralizing binary structure, from crime to punishment, was traditional all over Europe at this period. Other more elaborate and signed works opted for a different approach. Their authors still drew on the official records for their facts, but then went on to compose stories that were partly fictional. The models were either much-loved popular heroes, such as Robin Hood, Long Meg of Westminster and Moll Cutpurse, or idealized criminals whose values were remote from those of the aristocracy or bourgeoisie. These subversive figures battled against the authorities and attacked characters feared by ordinary people, such as usurers, the privileged or the tyrannical rich.

One such work was *The Lives and Histories of the Most Noted Highwaymen, Footpads, Shoplifts and Cheats*, published in 1714 by 'Captain' Alexander Smith, and followed, in 1726, by his *Memoirs of the Life and Times of the Famous Jonathan Wild*. In 1734 'Captain' Charles Johnson assembled the stories of nearly 200 bandits for his *A General History of the Lives and Adventures of the Most Famous Highwaymen, Murderers, Street Robbers, etc.*, to which he added, two years later, a gallery of the most illustrious pirates, which was actually the work of Daniel Defoe. In the preface to his earlier book, Smith justified his project by the desire to instruct and convert the corrupt and profane individuals of his licentious age, which did not stop him from cramming his collection with ingredients supposed to please a mass public, a little violence, pornography and humour and a lot of action. Ridiculous, even grotesque, episodes, sometimes repeated unchanged in other lives of other wrongdoers, were supposed to institute a healthy distance between them and the readers, so that the latter were not tempted to follow their example. Morality was safe, because no criminal ever escaped the gallows; the wicked were invariably punished. Further, the highly theatrical illustrations to Smith's book shunned any pleasing dimension, unlike the text, in an ostentatious demonstration of its instructional intent.[26]

It is difficult to know exactly what were the real objectives of Alexander Smith and Charles Johnson, and in particular to believe the latter completely when he claims that his sole aim was to amuse. All we can be sure of is that their works were successful, which suggests that the expectations of a readership that is hard to define were changing. One approach to these readers, probably Londoners, citizens, well-off and of the middling sort rather than working-class, may be through the content of the books. From this it is clear that these readers were tired of having criminals endlessly held up as an example to them, and that they preferred flamboyant heroes capable of challenging the abuses of the established powers, whom they seem to have feared rather less than disturbing stereotypical shadows. The latter, present in large numbers in the streets of the metropolis, were incarnated by the apprentice who went to the dogs and the fallen woman who fell into prostitution and theft.

The same fears were abundantly peddled by the conduct manuals, moralizing works and great literature. They seem not to have been characteristic of the poorest citizens, but rather to reveal the worries, real or imagined, of worthy citizens, of masters prosperous enough to employ servants and of craftsmen, who were deeply dependent on workers of both sexes if their businesses were to survive and grow. The grave danger of disorder represented by delinquent adolescents and by women living outside the sacred bonds of marriage was a commonplace of the age. It is found in literature and engravings, in Lillo's *Barnwell*, for example, or Hogarth's *Industry and Idleness*, and it masks a silent fear of the seething mass of the young, chained to their precarious state by the iron laws of economics. These had been decreed, of course, by the solidly established adult males of earlier generations. Rebellious, depraved or lazy apprentices and dissolute serving maids existed, but they were also metaphors for the rise of an uncontrollable youthful danger. Was there not a risk that they might one day band together, form a common front and dispossess those who kept them in such strict tutelage and delayed their access to a full life?

By about 1720, the practice of torture and capital punishment seems no longer to have been enough to reassure honest folk. In London, as in all the great European cities, there emerged a deep fear of subversion which was focused chiefly on the unskilled, unmarried young men of working-class origin, local or immigrant, who had become too numerous and too unruly. It also applied, though less urgently, to the young country girls who arrived in large numbers to become domestic servants, but who were often forced into prostitution to survive. In the face of these fears, the reformulation of the image of the murderous bandit seems to have been both the crystallization of a fear of dispossession and a way of assuaging it. Helped by the individualization of feelings and by the decline of the demonic explanation of crime, it made it possible to use laughter to exorcize fearsome bandits, made to look ridiculous. It also eased deep frustrations by offering hope of revenge to those who identified with the new fictional model of the murderer with a big heart, capable of sparing children or the innocent and reserving his cruelty for the wealthy and the worst exploiters. The various heirs of the gallows literature gradually paved the way for the crime novel, by preparing an urban readership that was neither very rich nor very poor, neither

255

powerful nor powerless, mostly adult and male, and anxious to forget its fears by drowning them in the reassuring ink of a teller of thrilling tales. The intrepid cutthroat thirsting for social vengeance offered the next generation in particular an oneiric escape, far from the burdensome obligations and the repression of adolescent behaviour forced on them by the prevailing morality.

Paradoxically, the eighteenth century saw more gangs of murderers than ever, even though the police and the law were in reality more effective than in the past, and though homicides and assaults continued to decline; this was true even of the parts of the countryside most resistant to the law. Indeed, it is precisely this increased efficiency that explains the emergence of these gangs in the archives of repression. In France, the eradication of organized banditry dates from the 1750s in the case of smuggling, and from the end of the century or First Empire for the armed bands. With the notable exception of the Mediterranean regions, they soon after ceased to represent a serious threat in the continent. Yet in the eyes of contemporaries, bombarded with stories that circulated more widely and more rapidly than in the past, the situation had never seemed so bad. They developed a keen interest in the bloodcurdling adventures of bandit gangs, who became the subject of veritable legends.

These gangs were led by young men, such as Philippe Nivet, dead aged thirty-three in 1729, Cartouche, executed in 1721 in his twenty-ninth year, and Mandrin, tortured to death at the age of thirty-one, in Valence, in 1755; similarly, they also largely consisted of young men.[27] They were unremittingly violent, in spite of frequent claims to the contrary, but rarely operated in large numbers, except in the Mediterranean countries, because the state and the forces of law and order made this impracticable. Their favoured spheres of activity were frontier regions, marginal zones and areas difficult of access. They were especially active during wars or in their aftermath, when demobilization meant the return to civilian life of many recruits who found it impossible to reintegrate and who retained their taste for blood. The reputation of the gang depended on that of its leader, incarnation of a 'popular' hero, feared by the strong, loved by the weak.

The band led by Cartouche was dismantled between 1721 and 1728, during a long trial involving a total of 742 men. Yet it survived his death by becoming for centuries a myth based on the deeds of a youthful demi-god, righter of wrongs and social rebel forced to operate outside the law after suffering various abuses at the hands of the regime and the powerful. The stereotype, destined to take many forms, bore little relation to reality and it was not based on an organized criminal subculture, as imagined by romantic novelists and certain historians.[28] It sprang from a collective urban imaginary that was conscious of a major gulf between those who dominated and those who were subjected. It was not an attack by the poor on the values and principles of the ruling classes, but rather a sign of dissatisfaction among the middling urban ranks. Wishing to differentiate themselves from the aristocracy and from the rich bourgeoisie who despised them and dominated urban life, they concocted these indomitable rebels as a way of dealing with their frustrations. They were also seeking, by endowing their mythical leader with a generosity that was often belied by the facts, to exorcize the fear of subversion associated with the unruly and dangerous rising generations.

The affair of the London Mohocks, in 1712, started the ball rolling. Though the fabrication of a writer, it nevertheless started a veritable moral panic in the capital, which went on for months, and in which mysterious groups of debauched young aristocrats were supposedly terrorizing and assaulting respectable citizens by night.[29] The prolonged crisis revealed both the fierce disapproval of wild upper-class behaviour among ordinary citizens and their deep unease with regard to the aggression of pubescent boys, inclined to every excess if not kept under close control.

Cartouche incarnated the new archetype of the honourable bandit, a man of humble origins, but behaving more nobly than the aristocrats themselves. Within a week of his execution, in 1721, he appeared on the stage of the Comédie Française in a play by Marc-Antoine Legrand with the title *Cartouche, ou l'Homme imprenable*. For the authorities, and in some of the 'laments' sold at the time of his execution, which harked back to the traditional gallows literature, he had a negative aura, but for many Parisians it was wholly positive. His legend elaborated on the theme of someone not fundamentally wicked, but forced to steal in order to survive, doing so with panache, constantly making the forces of law and order look ridiculous. Some contemporary authors made him a 'king' of the bandits, more just than the real sovereign, master of a society turned upside down, which allowed them to criticize the inadequacies and failings of the monarchy. Active in the countryside round the capital, where he attacked farms, inns and mail coaches, Cartouche was all the more sympathetically regarded by the Parisian lower classes in that he was always victorious and openly mocked the police, who were far from popular; the inhabitants of the faubourg Saint-Antoine, for example, had several bruising encounters with the latter in the early 1720s.[30]

Another famous criminal, Schinderhannes, had very similar characteristics. From 1798 to 1802, his band had roamed the Rhineland, the western part of which then belonged to France, the east to various Germanic states. A joint action led to the arrest of seventy men, who were tried before a special French court, in Mainz, with the result that the leader and nineteen of his accomplices were executed, on 21 November 1803. With his arrest, the legend of Schinderhannes began. A popular hero and a social bandit, he was reputed to steal from the rich to give to the poor, to detest violence, to personify rebellion and the spirit of freedom against the French enemy and to attack, in particular, the detested Jewish moneylenders. A vigorous counter-propaganda, which emphasized his brutality, including towards his companions, failed to overturn the stereotype. It triumphed in the nineteenth century and continued into the next, by way of novels, short stories and two films inspired by a play performed in 1922. In the first film, made in 1927, Schinderhannes was turned into a romantic fighter, a rebel who hated the French and the Jews. The second, in 1958, adapted to the new values by glossing over these aspects, neither of them now acceptable; it transformed its hero, played by Curt Jurgens, into a champion in the battle against all forms of oppression.[31]

The idealization of the bandit in the eighteenth century was not automatic. Why, we may ask, did many others not achieve this status, or even remain bloodthirsty monsters in the general view? Let us take, for example, the case of Lodewijk Bakelandt, who, after rampaging through the Flemish countryside from 1798 to 1802, was finally executed in November 1803, along with several companions. His career closely resembled that of Schinderhannes, and was similarly played out in a context of opposition to French power. He, however, was seen in an entirely negative light at the time, accused of cruelty, debauchery and being inspired by the devil. Some later writers tried to invest him with a social aura, but the hostile judgements continued to dominate the reformulations of his character. Another Flemish gang leader, Jan de Lichte, active in 1747–8, was broken alive on the wheel in 1748 with four of his accomplices; eighteen others were hanged and a further fifty-five whipped and banished. Jan de Lichte seemed doomed to oblivion. Then, in 1873, a short story was published in which he was portrayed as a bestial brute, without scruples, a man even more dangerous than Bakelandt. It was only at a much later date that he became a champion of the poor and the exploited, in a novel written in 1953.

Yet the difference between the actions of the 'good' and the 'bad' bandits was often very slight. Everything depended on the favourableness, or not, of the opinion of them and of the counter-society over which they ruled that was adopted, from the beginning, by the established citizens who found them so endlessly fascinating. They wanted a hero who represented a break with the order to which they belonged. The prototype brigand had to be amiable and merry, an enemy to violence, disinterested and 'noble' by nature, when so many aristocrats behaved like tyrants. He must be not only brave but able to rule, with a firm hand but without excessive harshness, a well-structured and harmonious community, liberated from the ordinary constraints, especially of a sexual nature; in fact the ideal was for women to be entirely absent or highly ethereal. Cartouche and Schinderhannes were immediately recast in this model, whereas Bakelandt and Jan de Lichte were just as rapidly despised, because their conduct, though structurally identical to that of Cartouche and Schinderhannes, was regarded with revulsion. In their case, the absence of rules turned into sexual debauchery and hard drinking, the perfect counter-society into a terrible tyranny, the crime made necessary by the pressure of the authorities into simple egoism and the desire to help the poor into indiscriminate cruelty.[32]

The crucial factor was how the violence was perceived by those who composed and consumed these myths. The bands of *chauffeurs* got their name from the way they terrorized the countryside by attacking isolated farms and burning the feet of the inhabitants to make them reveal where they had hidden their wealth. They were hardly a new phenomenon in the Age of Enlightenment, and their activities continued, though in smaller groups, after that. But once better protected by their walls and police forces, townspeople could afford to construct an image of this terrible problem that relieved some of their anxiety. The heroes also had to be accessible, similar to them, in short civilized, hence sparing in their use of physical force. Real or cleverly presented, the rebel had to abhor bloodshed and violence if he was to become the subject of a rosy legend. It was necessary, in short, for the disquieting elements to be forgotten if he was to be admired by the masses. In 1798, Vulpius offered a famous literary synthesis when he created his romantic bandit *Rinaldo Rinaldini*. Now firmly embedded in Western culture, the model has continued to be updated and adapted to changing times. Its principal characteristic is the bandit's ability to control his aggression; without this, he is quickly cast into outer darkness.

The prototype of the social bandit, the *betyár*, flourished in nineteenth-century Hungary. He was typically a young, unmarried country boy, who had committed some minor offence and been forced to flee justice, like Jóska Sobri, born Jószef Pap in a little village in West Hungary, who died in 1837, in combat or possibly by taking his own life. His legend developed in three quite different forms: in one he was the son of a poor man, in another of aristocratic birth, in a third had turned to crime as a result of a love affair. He stole from the rich, to give to the poor, obviously. A Hungarian national hero until 1867, he later converted to Marxism. Between 1993 and 1999 he seemed to have been reincarnated in the person of Attila Ambrus, who, born in 1967 and known as the 'Whisky Robber', became more famous than the president of the Republic after attacking twenty-seven banks and making the forces of law and order, who were unable to catch him, look ridiculous. Later, however, having escaped from prison, his glory rapidly faded after another attack on a bank, because the public did not forgive him for having, for the first time, injured someone. His fame, linked to the low esteem for the police and the banks in post-Communist Hungary, was irrevocably sullied when he broke the fundamental taboo regarding non-violence.[33]

In the eighteenth century, the idealization of the 'noble' bandit was a sort of collective exorcism of the youthful violence that was both destructive and disruptive of the established order. The last great bands of robbers and assassins had disappeared from Western Europe by about 1815, and the death penalty was less often used for murder, but prosperous people felt the need to reassure themselves by imagining a sort of acceptable marginality, a controlled deviance, on the model of the revised version of the exploits of Cartouche. Youth must have its day, but not at too great a cost to adults. The authorities continued to punish harshly the crimes committed by representatives of the new generations, but the established adults, rich and poor alike, viewed the problem from a less repressive perspective. They were no longer totally convinced by the normative discourse of the gallows literature, but began to recognize their closeness to those among the criminals who did not display either egoism or brutal savagery. Perhaps they felt their own alienation more strongly at the time of the new ideas of the Enlightenment? At any rate, they turned a more indulgent eye on the adolescents who rebelled against injustices, while still trying to control their brutality.

The traditional generational conflict seems to have eased, because social and political oppositions intensified, the law and the police being increasingly seen as the instruments of a tyrannical domination. The figure of the well-beloved bandit, young and a bringer of hope, acquired a vaguely anti-establishment dimension, especially in France, where the Revolution was largely led, we may add, by young men in their twenties and thirties. The proliferation of the criminal gangs throughout the eighteenth century is further evidence of the importance of this theme. The rising generations now began to invite themselves in a variety of ways to the collective banquet at which they had previously been left very little space. This dimension, which has largely been ignored, may help us to interpret the phenomenon more accurately. The structured bands of outlaws settled on the geographical and cultural margins of the communities. Between 1730 and 1774, in Limbourg, the 'Goatriders', or *Bokkerijders*, formed secret societies whose members led a double life. The same was true in Ariège, a century later, of the rebels of the war of the Demoiselles, who wore masks and dressed as women for their sorties.[34] Were they not both resurgences of the kingdoms of youth of the sixteenth century, sites for the expression of adolescent identity and a ritualized physical violence, adapted to an age that had become hostile to such behaviour?

Yet the conformist morality of the old gallows literature was not wholly superseded. In England, it still inspired great writers to produce plays, such as Gay's *The Beggar's Opera* (1728) and Lillo's *The London Merchant* (1731), and novels, like Fielding's account of the life of a famous criminal in *Jonathan Wild* (1743). Contemporary urban readers also developed an interest in more complex tales of transgression. Daniel Defoe was fascinated by the subject, to which he repeatedly returned, in a highly original fashion.[35] Contrary to the accepted conventions, his heroes and heroines – Moll Flanders, Jack, Roxana and Singleton – went unpunished. A Protestant individualist, Defoe tells their story at considerable length. He makes no pretence of offering an intangible truth, the motives of his criminals remaining mysterious or remote from the norms supposed to determine them. He invites his readers to exercise their freedom of judgement by offering them a work of fiction. In the preface to *The Fortunes and Misfortunes of the Famous Moll Flanders* (1722), he describes his aim as 'to make us more present to Ourselves'.[36] *Colonel Jack* (1722) includes what amounts to a definition of the very new concept of the individual by means of the character's use of the personal pronoun. Jack, overcome with remorse, returns the money he had stolen from a poor widow a year earlier. In a clever narrative device, he addresses his conscience mentally using 'I' – which evokes the register of moral failure – but speaks to the widow using the third person to refer to the robber, that is himself, in order to emphasize his repentance and his hope of being pardoned by God. In a similar vein, Roxana, the heroine of another of Defoe's books (1724), explains that 'Sin and Shame follow one-another...like Cause and Consequence'.[37]

Defoe's *Robinson Crusoe*, published in 1719, contains a vigorous critique of established society. In 1726, in his *The Political History of the Devil, As Well Ancient and Modern*, while accepting the existence of Satan, he treats the belief in the infernal punishments which await sinners as ridiculous; the devil, he claims, acts only on the minds of his victims. His approach to criminals was thus no longer dependent on the simplistic demonic principle previously used to explain their crimes. This allowed him to present a more nuanced picture of the criminal's conduct and invite his readers to meditate on the human condition through his case.

The golden age of the tale of the highway robber came to an end in England around 1740. This was probably less because the market had reached saturation point, as is usually argued, than because tastes were changing. The decline of the genre is linked to a decline in its symbolic usefulness as a producer of a consensus between the authorities and the audience for executions. The myth of the repentant scoundrel, of the sinner become saint at the moment of his death, was no longer as effective as it had once been in strengthening social cohesion by its demonstration of the defeat of the devil who had inspired the wrongdoers. And the crowds, gradually influenced by the spirit of the Enlightenment, came increasingly to suspect that the whole pious production was a fraud. They were less ready to believe in the sincerity of the condemned man who claimed that his execution was the happiest day of his life, and they doubted the sanity of those who came 'happy' and 'smiling' to the scaffold.[38] In London, people were frequently able to watch hangings at Tyburn that were a good deal less edifying, which was difficult to conceal despite the best efforts of the officials and the chaplain. It was the same in Paris, too, and the other great European cities.

Created at the same time as the idealized *geste* of Cartouche, the heroes of Defoe opened a new chapter in the perception of offences against persons. With them, the era of romanticized fiction began. Ancestor of the crime novel, it transcribed complex human phenomena, stories of love and hate between population groups, generations and sexes. A source of terror to some, healing balm for old moral wounds for others, it invented murders by the score and spilt much ink in compensation for the oceans of blood saved by the increasingly effective control of homicide and violence in Western Europe.

Blood and ink

The principal role of the fiction based on the figure of the criminal was to lessen collective anguish and calm the fear of murder by explaining it, not rationally but according to the prevailing beliefs of the age. The bandit with a heart of gold provided an eminently plastic and always reassuring type. He drew his emotional charge from old ideas, articulated, in particular, in the simple discourse of rebellious peasants since the Middle Ages: when Adam delved and Eve span, life was much more harmonious than it is today! Incarnated by the myth of Robin Hood, the just revolt against an unjust order also influenced the archetype of the noble bandit chief who fought all forms of tyranny in order to restore some balance between the poor and the profiteers who exploited them without scruple. In the 1720s, this was joined by a growing demand for the right not to be subject to constant supervision. The writers who created the legends of Cartouche and Schinderhannes were proclaiming a new sacredness attaching to the individual, as opposed to the heavy law of community. Addressing a public open to such new ideas, but often still stuck in the old ways of explaining the world, they invented models which were apparently very singular, yet which still bore the generic characteristics of their readers.

These stories gradually assured the transition from the age of dogmas imposed on everyone to that of personal reflection on the self, of which Rousseau was one of the first avowed exponents, in his *Confessions*. They constantly addressed the question of the genesis of someone who rejected the prescribed constraints. They were initiatory texts, frequently dealing with youth and adolescence, without focusing attention on the question, so unremarkable was it in its constant reiteration. The primordial theme was that of the perennially difficult process of adapting to the adult world. The proliferation of robber bands in the eighteenth century illustrates the difficulty of such an integration. They had their origins in the soaring problem of pauperism, which governments were powerless to reduce. Between 1768 and 1772, the French *maréchaussée*, reputedly the most efficient in Europe, arrested no fewer than 71,760 beggars and vagrants.[39] They included many young lads from the country, displaced and hopeless. Those who refused to be confined in the general hospitals or workhouses joined the criminal bands.

The eradication of these bands by around 1815 drove juvenile violence into more individual forms or into small groups. Youths who lived dispersed throughout the town assembled at night when the time seemed ripe for 'doing a job'. In the industrial age the proliferation of institutions of confinement, such as the army, the factory, boarding schools and day schools, helped to reduce the importance of the problem, but without ever making it disappear entirely. The illusion developed of a murderous brutality that was exceptional and characteristic of marginal or deranged individuals. However, there are always, as it were, running sores within the social fabric, consisting of poorly integrated youths who band together to survive and whose collective violence emerges in particular circumstances, as shown, at the beginning of the twenty-first century, by the nights of rioting in the French banlieues.

The nineteenth century was fascinated by crime. Accounts of terrible atrocities dominated the *faits divers* in newspapers like *Le Petit Parisien* or *Le Petit Journal*. The latter, founded in 1863, and with a circulation of a million by 1890, also printed the hugely popular and extremely violent stories of Ponson du Terrail, Gaboriau and Paul Féval. Blood and gore sold ink and paper. Though it had become unobtrusive in everyday life, lethal violence still fascinated the masses. People packed the court benches for sensational cases and thrilled with pleasurable horror as they watched public executions. Some even tried to collect the blood-soaked sand left behind after a beheading. The *Gazette des tribunaux* was hugely successful thanks to this craze. The more murderers the merrier! Their exploits filled many pages of print, in the novels based on

263

judicial proceedings of Zola, Coppée and Belot, in songs and laments and in serialized novels whose heroes incarnated Evil and Death, like Tenebras, Zigomar and Fantômas.[40]

Murder was the central theme of the detective story, itself directly inspired by judicial records. Its invention has been attributed to the American Edgar Allan Poe. An admirer of the *Mémoires* of Vidocq, he wrote 'The Murders in the Rue Morgue' for the April 1841 issue of *Graham's Lady's and Gentleman's Magazine*. In it, he presents an eccentric French detective, prototype of innumerable later sleuths. The Chevalier C. Auguste Dupin solved a 'locked room mystery' after the terrifying night-time murder, in their Parisian home, of an old lady and her daughter.[41] Like Victor Hugo and Balzac when they tried their hand at this genre, Poe wrote for people of quality, aiming to make them tremble at his scenes of horror, but also to provide them with the reassuring assistance of a skilled investigator to elucidate the deadly secret.

Like London, where an original school of this literature flourished in parallel, the French capital was at this period fertile ground for a literature of the controlled frisson, forerunner of the flood of violent American crime thrillers of the next century. The large European cities of the nineteenth century were tormented by fear of the 'dangerous classes', a consequence of industrialization. The main purpose of the genre was to invent a hero who operated outside the system of established authority, and who was revealed as alone capable of solving the most incomprehensible mysteries, when they proved beyond the police. It was as if an idealized Cartouche had become the bastion of respectable people by hunting down the gangsters who roamed the city at night, armed to the teeth!

This, at any rate, was the myth skilfully maintained by Vidocq, many times escaped convict, informer, policeman and then creator of the Sûreté Nationale. The huge success of his *Mémoires*, published in 1828, was owed to this journey of redemption, which finally made their author an indispensable bulwark of society. Not enough attention has been paid, however, to the fact that the very favourable reception received by his book was due to its structure as an initiatory story: the youthful fall, result of the temptation to shed blood, was followed by a redemption in middle age and dedication to the service of the community in the battle against crime. Victor Hugo was similarly inspired, in his creation of Valjean. In fact, the anxiety of the settled generations in the face of young urban killers embittered by poverty is the essential underlying theme of the emerging detective story.

The invention of the popular press transformed this phenomenon into a mass literature. It was now aimed at the ordinary people of the big towns, and it disseminated among the adults of the working classes a normative morality based on the notion that crime doesn't pay. Young boys of proletarian origin could also find in it an oneiric release, while learning the same lesson, and being encouraged to identify with the shrewd dispenser of justice, rather than with those he relentlessly pursued. Nevertheless, the youthful fascination with violence, traditionally the basis of the manly personality, led some authors to invent evil geniuses who appealed to adolescents while also increasing their sales. The best-sellers of the years preceding the First World War were often notable, as a result, for highly ambiguous themes, even anarchistic declamations against the values of established society.

The serialized novel packed with murders and vengeance came vividly to life in the work of Alexandre Dumas, of Eugène Sue in *Les Mystères de Paris* (1842–3), of Paul Féval (1817–87), who wrote over a hundred of them, and of vicomte Ponson du Terrail (1829–71). Rocambole, one of the latter's creations, is a truly fiendish hero, a ruthless killer and fearsome bandit. He dies, disfigured by vitriol, in 1859, in *Les Exploits de Rocambole*, but by 1862, in *La Résurrection de Rocambole*, he has become a detective, devoted to good deeds. It is not difficult to recognize here the theme of initial human cruelty, converted by trials and maturity into a quest for happiness for all.

Emile Gaboriau (1832–73), an admirer of Poe, and a man whose own youth was not without incident, was the author of *L'Affaire Lerouge*, a book which had only a tepid reception when first published in instalments in *Le Pays* in 1863, but was hugely successful two years later when it appeared in *Le Soleil*. Modelled on 'The Murders in the Rue Morgue', the puzzle was solved by three emblematic characters: the chief of police, an ambitious young inspector called Lecoq, a name clearly derived from Vidocq, and an elderly dilettante, Père Tabaret. It is the last of these who is successful, whereas the representatives of the law arrest an innocent man. However, it is Lecoq who is the main hero of Gaboriau's later novels, *Le Crime d'Orcival* (1867), *Monsieur Lecoq* (1869) and *La Corde au cou* (1873). For this to be possible, he had to mature and overcome his 'criminal mentality'. At least this enabled him to solve perfect crimes instead of committing them. A former petty offender who had made his peace with the law, he clearly incarnates the dangerous adolescent who has settled down and put himself at the service of society after being initiated by a shrewd old man.

With the approach of the First World War, detective fiction continued to explore the theme of the conflict of the generations, one of the main keys to understanding this period, which historians have not sufficiently taken into account. The golden age of the genre saw the creation of three celebrated great cycles which have left their mark even today: Arsène Lupin (1905), Rouletabille (1907) and Fantômas (1911). Together they provide a mythic and harrowing portrait of dangerous sons faced with outmoded fathers. Rouletabille also unambiguously incarnates the Oedipus myth. His creator, Gaston Leroux (1868–1927), has him solve, in 1907–8, *Le Mystère de la chambre jaune*. He is presented as a youthful journalist, aged only eighteen, born of unknown parents, and nicknamed Rouletabille because of his small round head, who is opposed to the devious chief of police. The latter piles up proofs against a false culprit but is unmasked by Rouletabille...only for him to discover that he is, in fact, his own father, a former crook and murderer hiding behind this usurped identity. Though lost at sea at the end of the book, this disturbing character returns, in 1909, in *Le Parfum de la dame en noir*. The fragrance of the lady in question conjures up in the son memories of his mysterious mother, who used occasionally to visit him at the boarding school where she had abandoned him. The father, meanwhile, carries out many more shameful and persecuting acts before he is at last exposed, and commits suicide, thus liberating Rouletabille from the frustrations of his childhood.

Anxiety about crime and those who committed it continued to grow at the beginning of the twentieth century, in a transposition of a fear of violent dispossession felt by prosperous adults in the face of the impatience of the young, poor and kept strictly on the margins. Maurice LeBlanc (1864–1941) created, at this highly symbolic juncture of the transmission of property, a character destined to an extraordinary career in the cinema, the theatre, television and the strip cartoon: Arsène Lupin, the gentleman thief. His first adventure appeared in 1905, in the magazine *Je sais tout*. A retarded adolescent who refused to settle down, supposed to have been born in 1874 of a liaison between a crook and a noblewoman, he stole not to enrich himself but to recover goods improperly acquired by dishonest, criminal or filthy-rich persons, such as the Prussian emperor, one of his victims. A protector of the weak and full of scruples, he chose not to rob a man in debt – or Pierre Loti, when he realized that he was in the house of the famous writer.

Probably inspired by the anarchist Marius Jacob, who had admitted to 156 robberies at his trial, three months before publication of Lupin's first adventures, he was even closer to the archetype of the noble bandit and righter of wrongs of the legend of Cartouche; and not least because at one point he kills a beautiful woman who was a traitor. A patriot and spy of great charm, he chose to serve France when war intervened. He was an aristocratically elegant model of the solver of puzzles, an outlaw always on the margins of the conventions, but fully capable of occupying a position of refinement in the world.

His features were consciously opposed to those of Sherlock Holmes, the frightfully British detective invented in 1887 by Arthur Conan Doyle

(1859–1930). In *A Study in Scarlet*, Holmes owes his success to his infallible method of deduction, that is, the triumphant positivist method. Suited to a different national temperament, he, too, was a retarded bachelor, aged thirty-three when he first met Dr Watson and conducted with him his first investigation. Many others followed. His battle against absolute evil, incarnated by Professor Moriarty, had a huge international success, which continues to this day. Weary of this intrusive 'son', Conan Doyle killed him off in *The Final Problem*, but had to bring him back to life due to popular demand for further adventures, which carried on until 1927. It is a curious fact that Maurice LeBlanc also found Arsène Lupin a burden, and engineered his death, only to be forced to restore him to life in the face of his admirers' protests. It even appears that, shortly before his own death, LeBlanc asked for the protection of the Etretat police 'against M. Lupin'.

A much more negative perception of human nature, against a backdrop of imminent war, transformed the aesthetic of the detective novel in the second decade of the twentieth century. In 1914, Gaston Leroux created the nefarious character of Chéri-Bibi, the savage and odious convict who went on to become a defender of the oppressed. He was probably inspired by two sagas of evil that had recently appeared. The first, published by Léon Sazie between 1909 and 1910, tells the story of the struggle between Zigomar, a king of crime, and a detective of police, Paulin Broquet. The second, written by Pierre Souvestre (1874–1914) and Marcel Allain (1885–1969), and published in 1911, featured Fantômas, the 'evil genius'. Its publisher, Arthème Fayard, orchestrated the appearance of the first novel with a poster campaign which had the menacing silhouette of the criminal looming over Paris. In 1913, in *La Fin de Fantômas*, he was lost at sea along with his two principal adversaries, the police officer Juve, his twin personifying Good, and the journalist Fandor. Thirty-two stories and some fifty serials produced up to Souvestre's death testify to his enormous success, only enhanced by a cinematic adaptation by Louis Feuillade in 1913. Allain then resuscitated all three characters and followed their adventures until *Fantômas mène le bal* in 1963. The complete series contains no fewer than 552 crimes, two-thirds of them against persons; they include assaults and woundings described in detail, kidnappings and detentions and homicides committed in the course of crimes, or in revenge or out of pride.

The collective imaginary which assures the success of a theme is not, of course, monolithic. The widespread popularity of the terrifying saga of Fantômas suggests that the public of the pre-war period had wearied of the traditional happy endings and no longer believed in the redemption of criminals. They preferred the open evocation of cruelty, realistically portrayed, with no hope that the culprit would be saved. They were unconsciously accustoming themselves to the imminent carnage when they learned to shudder with a terrible fear before the dreadful angel of evil who proclaims: 'I am Death!'

Other works of the same period also won a large audience by applying balm to this prevailing pessimism, as their young and bloodthirsty heroes loudly proclaimed that they killed only from a sense of duty, according to a strict code of honour. These very French cloak and dagger cycles acquired a huge cinema and television audience, which they retain to this day. Their characters cheerfully despatch large numbers of evil customers, dealing out blows right, left and centre. *The Three Musketeers* (1844) of Alexandre Dumas, the chevalier de Lagardère of Paul Féval's *Le Bossu* (1858) and the huge heroic epic devoted to *Les Pardaillan* by Michel Zévaco (1860–1918), a 'great original popular novel', serialized from 1902 to 1914 in *La Petite République* and then *Le Matin*, all testify to this same fascination with violence.

These skilled authors had discovered an effective formula. They legitimized the lethal prowess of their heroes by making them righters of wrongs and knightly defenders of the weak against the caricatured strong. D'Artagnan and Pardaillan, implacable young killers thanks to their fencing skills, were very different from Fantômas in that writer and readers readily granted them licence to kill the treacherous and cruel creatures with whom they crossed swords. In their generosity and their strict sense of honour, which prevented them from finishing off a defeated opponent or engaging in an unequal fight, they bore some resemblance to the idealized formulations of the honourable bandit incarnated by Cartouche. They displayed the innate panache of the French gentleman and a nobility of soul which simply reflected the nobility of their birth. Jean de Pardaillan, a sort of imaginary ancestor of Arsène Lupin, who had been created three years earlier, and may have inspired Maurice LeBlanc, performed his feats between 1572 and 1614. Endowed by his creator with an anarchistic ideology, he despised men of power and honours, preferring a modesty which brought him closer to the suffering people. These charming assassins were hybrid figures, who incarnated the juvenile murderous instinct, but toned down and closely controlled by an elevated conception of their chivalric role as defenders of the oppressed. They subsequently entered mass culture by means of the strip cartoon, cinema and television. In fact, they constitute an extraordinary symbolic success, reconciling very different social classes and providing a reassuring image of youth, because these young men killed only out of necessity, never out of hatred or self-interest. Pardaillan, the eternal adolescent, who grew old without ever settling down or abandoning his ideals, was the very archetype of the fearless, blameless hero whose exploits were reassuring to established people, by showing them that their civilization was capable of curbing the aggressive and destructive instincts of the next generation. In 1926, however, when the last adventures, written in 1918, appeared, readers knew from cruel experience the real cost of internal peace on the continent, after an unprecedented slaughter, which had exacted its heaviest toll among the ranks of European youth.

Not long before the cataclysm, the *fait divers*, the detective story and the swashbuckler novel had helped to dissipate the fear of subversion through violence. These texts, which inundated the imaginary, deflected, controlled and limited the real fears that were accumulating with the approach of the First World War.[42] By focusing attention on the army of crime supposed secretly to have invaded the slums of the big cities, they seemed to develop an obvious metaphor concerning the 'dangerous classes', representatives of a working-class world seen as nasty, brutish and avid for revenge against its exploiters. But their real importance lay elsewhere. This particular anxiety was coupled with a deep, unarticulated fear of the age groups waiting impatiently to take their elders' place. While Freud, in Vienna, invented the Oedipus complex, cleverly transferring onto sons responsibility for a general malaise in Western civilization, fathers were feeling increasingly anxious because they feared their generalized symbolic murder. Detective fiction and the cloak and dagger novel reassured the fathers while offering the sons an escape from a world too strictly controlled by the power of the old. In parallel, learned criminologists were discoursing on the causes of homicidal savagery. Lombroso invented the model of the born criminal, a category in which he included the anarchists, which was reassuring to the good bourgeois because it made them exceptions to the norm. Dallemagne even claimed to be able to predict the danger, describing the specific features of the physiognomy of the delinquent.[43] Judging by appearances is not new!

The literary or scientific frisson of horror transposed a deep anxiety in the face of the rise of a youthful peril. Admittedly, respectable people dared not broach the subject openly, which would have been out of the question in a society claiming to be at the forefront of modernity. But this unease was present everywhere in the culture. As the twentieth century dawned, and the world became too full, the affluent generations found ever more harrowing ways of expressing their fears in veiled terms, and trying to exorcize them. Thus Paris, in 1903, saw the beginning of the 'reign of the Apache'. As with the London Mohocks of 1712, it was largely a fantasy, based on a handful of facts hugely inflated to produce a massive salutary fear. A few observers described the Apaches as kind-hearted hooligans, but many more portrayed them in a far darker light. They claimed that hordes of pimps and murderers were invading the capital. Ruthless variants of the cruel, brutal and bloodthirsty knife-wielding gangster, they were accompanied by their *marmites*, the women they prostituted, off whose earnings they lived and who spread venereal disease far and wide. Up to the outbreak of war, the Apache craze ruled, generating a deepening psychosis. The most anxious claimed that there were nearly 100,000 of these terrifying and unscrupulous known criminals living in Paris. They were accused of violently assaulting respectable citizens in a multitude of ways, of speaking in secret languages, such as 'javanese', 'loucherbem' and 'verlan', and of robbing, looting and killing. Most dangerous of all, it was said, were those living in La Chapelle, Grenelle and La Villette. Though usually from the working classes, they refused honest toil in a factory, having fled any schooling. They lived in gangs of 'conscripts of crime', because they were mostly aged between sixteen and twenty-five, like the thirty members of the Neuilly gang convicted in 1899 of robbery and murder, whose average age was just under twenty. They were archetypal dangerous youths and dregs of humanity for Dr Lejeune, degenerates hobbled by foul defects for Barrès, and generally believed to form veritable anti-societies dedicated to wrongdoing.

In fact, these supposed realities were in large part a fiction. Journalists invented picturesque, exotic or savage names to characterize the gangs, like the 'Bloody Fists' of Saint-Ouen, the 'Saute-aux-pattes' of la Glacière, the 'Tattooed Ones' of Montmartre. The detective story accorded them huge importance, most notably in the great popular cycles of Zigomar and Fantômas, whose heroes were presented as leaders of this 'army of crime'. However, the literary transcriptions almost always glossed over their working-class origins, except to contrast their degeneracy with the orderly life of the virtuous and respectable proletariat. Like the anarchists, another scapegoat of the newspapers and right-minded people at the period, they incarnated a subversive power, a marginal world that was overwhelmingly young, urban and working-class.[44] Not enough emphasis has been put on this combination of features. They indicate a strong resurgence, at a time of demographic pressure, of the fear of the murderous violence of pubescent boys. The leaders of the Apache gangs, young males of humble origins who preferred to indulge their killer instincts, were the exact opposite of the idealized Cartouche of 1721. Implacable and a-social, they reverted to the old structure of the violent kingdoms of youth in order to oppose an adult world whose ideals they did not recognize. Nevertheless, it was more of an alarmist denunciation, product of a horrific imaginary, designed to justify new measures for confining intractable plebeian adolescents, than a return in force of the manly culture of the past.

The *fait divers* so beloved by contemporaries were a constant reminder that crime did not pay. According to the same principle, the anxiety provoked by the descriptions of the acts of violence of the Apaches made it possible to demand harsher punishments by denouncing the laxity of the courts. Influential persons and newspapers constantly deplored this after 1902. In Marseille, Paris and elsewhere, the question of insecurity became crucial, all the more so when a slight increase in homicides was revealed by the judicial statistics published in 1906, the year in which Clemenceau tabled a bill designed to abolish the death penalty, substituting life imprisonment. The security panic grew worse. It led, amongst other things, to a campaign against Apaches in the army in 1910 and a debate about stronger repression. It was further aggravated, in 1912, by the exploits of the vicious 'Bonnot gang'. New laws introduced harsher penalties. In 1910, a law of 'moral cleansing' attempted to separate 'healthy' young men even more firmly from the 'corrupt' by rehabilitating the *Bat' d'Af*,[45] and by creating special sections for soldiers who challenged the moral values of their corps. In 1911, the unit known as the 'anti-Apache' called for even greater harshness in cases of 'special vagrancy' with a weapon, even if it was not used.[46]

The new concept of 'dangerousness' was thus applied to thugs who challenged the institutions or disturbed the tranquillity of respectable citizens. Most of those stigmatized in this way were young men from the lower classes, who continued to meet up in the evenings and on holidays in order to relax, flirt with the girls and generally hang out together in the face of the often hostile world of adults and the agents of government. Their roughness and their difference, and their special codes, meant they were seen as criminals. Admittedly, some of them used knives to demonstrate their manliness. And, poorly integrated and hostile to the established rules, they sometimes lapsed into delinquency, theft and physical assaults. But not all of them were murderers or hardened criminals.

The shift from the ruffian with a heart of gold to the cruel henchman of Fantômas was to a considerable extent a disparaging oneiric production, designed to bolster a security offensive at a time when liberals were hoping it might be possible to abolish the death penalty. It happened because generational tensions reached an unprecedented intensity on the eve of the First World War. The crime literature that was read so widely drew attention to the urgent need to reform the morals of the nation's youth as a whole, which had been shown in a very negative light by the exploits attributed to the Apaches. This was demoralizing because it had affected even the very spearhead of the nation by introducing the seeds of decadence into the army. The principal function of detective fiction, the *fait divers* and 'popular' literature was to promote greater social integration. They were a form of education, teaching the norms and legitimizing the authorities by making the Other an object of terror. The fact that the image of the man spoiling for a fight came to be attached

271

to the young male of humble origins speaks volumes as regards the degree of internal tension existing within the European states; it makes it easier to understand the massive collective disaster which was preparing in 1914.

Everything changed with the Great War. Crime fiction continued to adapt to the times. Once overwhelmingly conservative, serving the Establishment, in particular the dominant males, it now, like Western society itself, became more complex. The monstrous *fait divers* made the reader uneasy, but the murder investigation in the hands of a competent sleuth brought reassurance. It gave a feeling of enhanced security by duplicating police protection, while at the same time making it possible to mock the inadequacies of the institution. More, the thousands of pages in the magazines and 'popular' novels saturated the imaginary with reassuring metaphors: the young male, dangerous by definition, was easily turned into a defender of the common good by the trials of life; as in the case of Vidocq, Rouletabille and Lecoq, of *The Four Just Men* of Edgar Wallace (1905), and even of Arsène Lupin, who became a patriotic thief during the War, not forgetting the heroes of the swashbucklers such as the chevalier de Pardaillon. Only a few were able definitively to reject this mould, like Fantômas, which may explain his heretical success. Even Rocambole and Chéri-Bibi eventually fell into line and became defenders of the established norms.

The model of the avenger, righter of wrongs and guarantor of collective harmony, continued to be a winning formula, even if the hero cast a disillusioned eye on life. It took very different forms, as varied as Hercule Poirot, Miss Marple, the Chinese Judge Dee, Philo Vance, Ellery Queen, Brother Cadfael and all the various world-weary American detectives, as casual as they were violent, like Lemmy Caution, or cynical, troubled but generous, like Philip Marlowe. Presented as a man both ordinary and exceptional, Marlowe incarnates the principle of redemption, of revolt against corruption but also social maladjustment and lack of maturity.[47] It is as if it was essential not to be truly part of the corrupt adult world in order to be able to defend its founding principles. These men are all defined by a strong sense of honour, close to that which had inspired the musketeers of Alexandre Dumas or the chivalric characters of Michel Zévaco. This is equally true of the gangsters of Auguste Le Breton, 'real men', true to their word and their friends, in contrast to the villainous 'jackals'. For this anarchist author, their violence, product of a society as unjust as it was hypocritical, was not blind, because they were able to control it effectively.

There was no end to the metamorphoses of Robin Hood or Cartouche in the twentieth century. They still posed the same questions of good and evil with regard to homicide and to ways of bringing children to maturity with the least possible damage to their predecessors. Yet the schools of detective fiction continue to diversify because human relations are evolving at a breathless pace before our eyes in a Western Europe that has been spared internal wars since 1945. Life expectancy is steadily increasing, which has made even more complex than before the difficult problem of the transmission of property and values to the new generations. Many volumes would be needed to analyse this fascinating enigma, crucial to our civilization, through the prism of the crime fiction found all over our modern media. Alfred Hitchcock alone would merit a whole book devoted to unravelling the troubled relationship between many of his young and innocent heroes and a cruelly stifling society.

— 9 —

THE RETURN OF THE GANGS: CONTEMPORARY ADOLESCENCE AND VIOLENCE

Since 1945, the blood taboo has been a powerful imperative in Western Europe. The memory of the slaughter of the early twentieth century has helped to strengthen a deep revulsion for homicide and violence, patiently instilled into our culture since the sixteenth century. Now, for the first time in its long history, European civilization is free from the direct pressure of war on its own soil, with the exception of some unstable margins. The result has been a silent but decisive transformation in the relationship to the ancient law of force, seen in a major shift in the balance of power between age groups and between sexes. The repeated outbreaks of armed conflict meant, in the past, that masculine power could be imposed without debate; it alone was capable of responding to danger by conducting 'just' wars in defence of the threatened fatherland or so as to expand national territory or colonize the rest of the world. The submission demanded of the so-called 'weaker' sex was a natural consequence of this. Slightly more subtle formational techniques were used to persuade young men to exercise more self-control over their aggression, while always retaining the possibility that this could be vigorously reactivated when needed, so they could become brave soldiers on the battlefield.

Since the Age of Enlightenment, this mechanism for sublimating the manly brutal impulses has been validated and strengthened by a moral economy aimed at the preservation of the vital fluids. Discourse and practice alike inveighed against any extreme experience that might result in the most precious of these fluids, blood and sperm, being squandered. Around 1710, in England, doctors invented the great fear of masturbation. As recently as the last decades of the nineteenth century, many of them were still stubbornly insisting that solitary pleasure led to a horrible death, within a few months, or at most a few years. This propaganda probably had little effect on the mass of the population, but it succeeded in filling many upper-class adolescents with guilt, as is shown by the confessions of Henri-Frédéric Amiel and William Gladstone, amongst others.[1] The underlying ethic extolled the virtues of the conscious accumulation of the vital capital of each individual, in the age of commercial, and then industrial, take-off in Europe. Sons were insistently enjoined to wait their turn to replace their fathers patiently, without violence, without sexual activity, even without recourse to the solitary vice. The established generations, who had all the power and the wealth, and who controlled access to women, dreamed of an ideal masculine adolescence. In the nineteenth century, they manufactured one, by prohibiting bloodshed, except in the 'just' defence of the national interest, and sexual pleasure outside marriage, except for the use of prostitutes, which was permitted. Never had the pubescent Western male, constrained by moral and legal pressure to avoid conflict with the Other, and to exert strict self-control in order to avoid the terrible, and lovingly described, consequences of masturbation and venereal disease, been so closely confined as in the industrial age. This extended to the working classes, though here the pressure was often met with mute resistance. This system was liable to regular crises, however, whenever young men became particularly numerous during long periods of peace and prosperity, for example in France under the Third Republic, until 1914. War, which exacted its heaviest toll on the young, devastating epidemics and a life expectancy shorter than today's acted as regulatory mechanisms, though without preventing fierce confrontations with those in authority. These sometimes developed in disguised fashion, in symbolic forms, such as the Apache phobia of the second decade of the twentieth century.

The new era which opened in 1945 was one of increasing disequilibrium in the model, as a consequence of much more rapid social change. The unmarried youths waiting their turn to be integrated were no longer decimated by war and sickness; life expectancy was steadily rising, to reach almost double what it had been a century before. The world of the baby-boomers was full of aspirants, but also of old people, who were increasingly slow to give way to the new arrivals, in a world characterized by abundance, but also by poverty, which was all the harder to bear for those excluded from the system. Never before had there been a conjuncture of such conditions. They led to a redefinition of the male and female roles, to the emergence of a third – previously forbidden – gender and to a major change in relationships between age groups.

The paradigm of murderous violence is a way of approaching this problem. Homicide and intentional woundings are now residual, responsible for only a tiny fraction of violent deaths. Road accidents, suicide and other forms of self-destruction eliminate a much larger proportion of adolescents. Few now dare to kill another human being, transgressing the supreme prohibition, but those who do are getting younger. All these signs draw attention to an increasing difficulty in integrating, which has taken the spectacular form of youth gangs, still active, constantly renewed, from the 1960s to the recent nights of rioting in inner cities all over Europe.

Death in paradise

The risk of being murdered varies greatly, at the beginning of the twenty-first century, depending on where you are in the world. In 2000, the annual rate per 100,000 inhabitants ranged from 60.8 in Colombia to 0.6 in Japan and 0.7 in France and England. The statisticians have refined their approach by also counting suicides and deaths as a result of road accidents in order to gauge more accurately the level of danger in each country. Those where all three causes together account for less than 10 per cent of deaths are those where the risk is smallest.[2] This is the case with the United Kingdom (3 per cent), Germany and Sweden (4 per cent), the United States (6 per cent) and France and Japan (8 per cent), whereas the figure is 10 per cent in Ukraine, 18 per cent in Russia and 24 per cent in Colombia.

In spite of the heterogeneousness of the figures, due to different definitions and methods of recording, they reveal islands of security, notably Japan, Western Europe and the United States, in a much more dangerous world. The relative importance of the three types of violent death varies considerably. In Colombia, homicide is nineteen times more frequent than suicide and three times more frequent than transport accidents, whereas in France, suicide claims twenty-five times more lives than murder, and the roads eighteen times more (17.5 and 12.9 compared with 0.7 per 100,000). In the United Kingdom, with a population of roughly the same size and an identical level of fatal violence, traffic causes fifteen times more deaths and suicide ten times more (0.7, 10.5 and 7.5 per 100,000). The risks are much more evenly spread in the United States, where the rates vary by a ratio of only two or three (6.2 for murder, 16.5 on the roads and 11.3 suicide).

This leads to very different collective perceptions of brutal death. Murder happens mostly to men, either young or in the prime of life. They are almost a hundred times more likely to suffer this fate in Colombia, and ten times more in the United States, than in Japan, France or the United Kingdom. Deaths from accidents are more evenly spread, varying from a maximum of 27.7 in Latvia, and almost the same figure in Russia, to a minimum of 5.5 in Sweden, a level it seems difficult to reduce. Suicide has its own characteristics. In 2000, it varied on a scale ranging from 1 to 20, between just over 40 per 100,000 in Latvia and Russia and 2 or 3 in Kuwait, Mexico and Colombia. It is no doubt a consequence of collective problems as much as of individual distress. Hungary was for a long time first in this category after 1956, as a result of the moral crisis linked to the Soviet occupation. The post-Soviet Slav and Baltic worlds now occupy first place; the rate is ten times higher in Russia than in the 1930s. France comes somewhere in the middle. Correlations exist with the long-term trend in homicide. While the latter fell sharply in the Western countries experiencing modernization and industrialization, the suicide rate tended to increase. It was rare in the traditional agrarian regions, including Russia, around 1850, but already much more common in Germany and France, where it peaked in the first half of the twentieth century. With the sole exception of China, it always affects men much more than women, and it becomes more common with age. In France, the male curve for the year 1999 starts at adolescence, reaches a first peak between thirty-five and forty, then remains at the same level for a long time, before rapidly rising again after the age of seventy. 'Suicide rates are largely linked to the economic and political history of societies.'[3]

That old age should be seen as a disaster, especially if accompanied by material difficulties or isolation, is understandable. It is more difficult to interpret the first surge in masculine self-destructiveness, at a little before forty. Might the crisis be due to a painful bout of introspection, faced with failure in life? Could it be that some of these men, having reached the prime of life, feel deeply frustrated that they have dutifully restrained their violence since puberty and conformed to the norms, when they realize that this has not brought them the hoped-for social success? By killing themselves, that is, by spectacularly transgressing against the blood taboo, they are perhaps giving free rein to the aggression they had been prohibited from expressing, so as to send a message of hatred and rejection to the community as a whole.

In this hypothesis, the relationship between homicide and suicide should be in inverse proportion, the near-disappearance of the former having as its price a marked rise in the latter at a time of stock-taking, that is, on reaching maturity or old age. The death of the self might also reveal the rejection, moved forward in time, long after puberty, of the symbolic power of the prohibition on the murder of the Other, now inescapable in our society. In France, the suicide rate reached 8.9 per 100,000 in the middle of the nineteenth century, and rose to its absolute maximum of 20.8 between 1896 and 1905, at a time when the number of crimes against persons was lower than ever before. In 1897, Emile Durkheim devoted one of his most famous works to this pressing problem.[4] The cultural context is one of an insidious malaise and a significant rise in collective anxiety. Though it is contradicted by the judicial statistics, the fear of physical aggression and murder is promoted by popular novels and the press. The first of these, in 1909 and 1911, came up with the terrible characters of Zigomar and Fantômas; the second carelessly spread fear of the violent young Apaches supposed to infest the town.[5] The suicidal surge at the turn of the century was equally visible in Germany, where it also seems to have been linked to measures for keeping violent impulses closely controlled. Conversely, contemporary Colombia has an unrivalled level of murder and one of the lowest suicide rates in the world. The interdependence of the two phenomena would surely repay further study.

In the second half of the twentieth century, in a situation that is unprecedented, the overwhelming majority of young Europeans have neither killed nor injured another person, as war has disappeared from the continent. Of the tiny minority who have caused a death, most have done so involuntarily, in a road accident, or have cut short their own life. However residual, the tiny minority who have killed nevertheless reveal an insistent truth about our civilization, and a disturbing mystery. The very notion of homicide is a social and legal construct. It adapts according to sex, age and class, and it attaches great importance to factors such as economic inequality or material privation in order to explain the deadly act. Yet it cannot predict the act. Nor can it explain why a small number of those defined by these criteria commit murder, whereas many others do not. Murder contains an irreducible element of unfathomable mystery.

In the United Kingdom, one of the countries where murder is least common, the statistics reveal a long period when the rate was virtually unchanged, between 1981 and 1999. In England and Wales together, between 500 and 600 murders a year were committed, infanticide included. The rate seems to have increased since 2000, the figure rising to 700 in 2001. But the increase was due in part to the inclusion of the figures for the victims of Harold Shipman, a serial killer active between 1978 and 1998, accused of 215 murders and suspected of 45 more.

In general, homicide in Great Britain is an overwhelmingly masculine crime, and most of its victims are of the same sex. In both cases, the age group most often represented is that between twenty-one and thirty-five. In Scotland, the majority of convicted murderers are males aged between sixteen and twenty-nine.[6] Everywhere in the United Kingdom, the risk of being killed is at its highest for young men aged between sixteen and thirty. Almost half of cases originate in a quarrel. The most common type of fatal injury is that inflicted with a bladed weapon, 28 per cent of cases in 2003–4. Those involved readily resort to firearms, too, and a third of them are slightly or even very drunk. The parties know each other in 49 per cent of cases, but are total strangers in 37 per cent. Young blacks and Asians are over-represented, given their proportion in the population. Homicide linked to another crime is rare and the role of gangs is less than 1 per cent. As the defence of manliness is the main cause, British scholars have developed the concept of 'hegemonic masculinity' to explain it. They believe that the construction of gender identity, taken to an extreme in fights between young men, lies behind 22 per cent of the deaths following a highly symbolic duel.

In contrast, women rarely murder, because their training in the feminine role prohibits murderous violence. Their motives are obscured by the frequency of explanations connected to insanity or their abnormality as 'wicked' women. Female victims are also a very distinct group, as 60 per cent are killed by their partner or ex-partner. The most common method, used in 19 per cent of cases, is strangling or suffocation. In a similar vein, the overwhelming assumption of the innocence of the child in Western civilization means that the small boy or girl who kills is regarded as demonic or possessed by evil.[7]

The English example does not tally with certain alarmist observations regarding a worrying rise in violent crime in all the industrialized countries since the 1960s. Crime rates effectively tripled in twenty years in the United States, to reach their highest point at the beginning of the 1980s, in all the main offence categories, including property crime, crimes of violence and drug offending. Among the explanations offered are major social upheavals that have led to a weakening of the informal procedures for control by means of the family, the neighbourhood, school etc. In this more relaxed context, the arrival at puberty of the baby-boomer generation, the argument runs, let loose a crime wave. The young, more mobile than in the past and less confined by parents or work, and brought up in a universalistic commercial culture, experienced a whole new set of desires and more often opted for a criminal career in the hope of instant gratification. The claim is not entirely false, but it also subtly propagates a very pejorative view of this age group, allegedly the one 'most prone to criminal behaviour'.[8] But the vast majority of its members do not break the law. Those who kill represent only a tiny fraction of their peer group, even though they are between ten and twenty times more numerous than in England, depending on period, in an environment where guns are everywhere. The discourse that attributes guilt to the whole of this age group is suspect, to say the least. In fact, it acts as a system for designating a scapegoat. The part defines the whole, so pubescent boys are suspected on principle of a particular aptitude for serious offences, in particular violent crime. Specialists and adults unite in denouncing their intrinsic dangerousness. What this really reveals is a deep distrust of this age group, at a time when their unusually large numbers are disturbing the existing equilibrium. This was the case in France around 1900–10, and it has been the case every time the advancing tide of new arrivals has disquieted the established generations.

That there has been a recent significant worsening of the problem of crime in postmodern societies is far from proved. The rises may be the result both of harsher repression and of particular circumstances, such as the discovery of the shocking activities of a serial killer in England or a temporary rise in pressure from the young. Contrary to a current belief, homicides have significantly declined in the United States since 1990. Many analysts have attributed this to the effectiveness of the punitive measures following the implementation of zero tolerance policies. These analysts have failed to give sufficient consideration to the possibility that the adolescents of the turn of the twentieth and twenty-first century may simply be less transgressive than those of the time of the Vietnam War. It is true this is at the cost of rare but extremely violent and spectacular eruptions of savagery on the part of serial killers, especially in schools and universities, and of a heavy death toll among minority groups. Further, recent decades have seen the development, as in Europe, of a growing collective fear of assaults on persons, exaggerated by a media avid for the sensational.[9] This preoccupation with security has put the problem firmly back at the heart of people's everyday concerns and provoked a fierce debate on ways of dealing with it. The results of the police and the law in this sphere, minutely scrutinized and subject to widespread criticism, have given rise to contradictory publications, which teach us not to seek for an absolute truth in the statistics, but rather to interpret them in the general context of their production.

From this perspective, it is possible to relativize the findings concerning the increasing youth of murderers in the Western world, a feature well known to criminologists. For France in 1897, Emile Durkheim put the prime age for male murder between twenty-five and thirty. In Philadelphia, in the years 1948–52, it was between twenty and twenty-four, on a line without spectacular peaks. In New York, in the years 1976–95, it was twenty, and appears in the form of a very marked bell curve on a graph which falls sharply during the third decade of life, then continues to decline, but very gently. Murderers have been getting younger since the nineteenth century.[10] The observation holds true for the whole of the United States. The number of boys aged under eighteen arrested for murder or assault and wounding doubled between 1952 and 1987, to reach, respectively, 16 and 19.5 per cent of the total. In parallel, the peak age for victims fell from 25–9 years to 20–4 years, probably in line with the reduction in the age of marriage, because the phenomenon always supposes a strong propensity to kill or wound among adolescents and unmarried men of the same generation.

The problem goes well beyond criminological analysis. Very young murderers constitute a minority, but their cases are given huge media prominence, which helps shape the public perception of juvenile delinquency by linking it directly to lethal violence.[11] Facts and fantasy reinforce each other to focus attention on the potential danger represented by the violently aggressive male teenager. Non-white ethnic origins and a disadvantaged background add extra dimensions of dangerousness to what amounts to the systematic construction of the profile of a killer.

This is clearly brought out by the work of a scholar who is a specialist in New York. His research on the nineteenth and twentieth centuries has shown that only about half of murderers are arrested. Of these, less than half are brought to trial, and just under half of them are convicted. The majority, about three in four, escape with a sentence of five years in prison, and many of these are eventually pardoned. Juries tend to sympathize with those who appear before them, another sign of a high threshold of tolerance for violence in a new country, where the use of guns is commonplace and, in the case of self-defence, constitutional.[12] The recent focus on very young killers may have its roots in a more general unease. Although they represent only a tiny proportion of their age group, they attract attention to the group as a whole. To a large extent orchestrated by the television and the press, their unacceptable offence is an invitation to strengthen the rules they endanger. The real issue here is probably not so much the homicide itself, since this has always been more easily tolerated than in Europe, as the dogma of the innocence of the child. The obsessive insistence on these very young murderers is surely a sign of an uneasy fascination with the crossing of the border of evil at the dawn of adolescence. It may also be a way of protecting the pre-pubescent from any breath of suspicion, given the dramatically increasing youth of the strange sect of murderers.

The penal is not, as is well known, an isolated phenomenon. It is closely connected to the life of societies and alters in line with the groups from which a society is composed. In the case of crimes against persons, theft, moral offences and disturbances of public order, the punishment usually consists of a prison term. In France, this affects, in particular, marginals and members of the most vulnerable sectors of the working classes, especially the young and foreigners.[13] The attempt to make the 'dangerous classes' conform has been the chief aim of the authorities since the nineteenth century. Intractable and violent adolescents have been a particular target, in an attempt to make them lose their taste for manly violence, with its often fatal consequences. Europe had practically eradicated the problem by the middle of the twentieth century, and the United States spectacularly reduced it in the 1980s.

The recent increases in homicide and physical aggression may simply be short-term fluctuations in a curve which remains very low over the long term. However, they contain new features which threaten collective cohesion, as they increasingly include boys scarcely out of infancy, with a tiny proportion of girls of the same age. The more pessimistic can see this as a consequence of a crisis in family values, the optimists of an extension of social control into private spaces and categories previously neglected in favour of more pressing concerns. The truth no doubt lies somewhere in between. The American example indicates an increasing preoccupation with the problems caused by boys as they reach puberty. This intermediate stage, that of a more or less painless transition from family and school to work or unemployment, is currently at its hardest for the most vulnerable sectors of the working classes and recent immigrants. It is the beginning of a dangerous age, susceptible to all the excesses and to delinquency, which these young people's 'big brothers' are gradually leaving behind, as they become slightly better integrated or totally disillusioned.

For youth gangs, this is fertile territory. Though distant heirs of the sixteenth-century kingdoms of youth, they have their own distinctive features, perfectly suited to the times. The principal hypothesis for explaining their growth in Europe since the mid twentieth century is that they are the modern form of expression of a deep youthful dissatisfaction in the face of the adult world and established society. However, their extreme symbolic violence, emphasized by very threatening forms of behaviour, does not prevent the majority of their members from accepting the prohibition on murder. The adolescents who kill, usually one of their peers, in a one-to-one male-on-male fight, are increasingly rare.

In Finland, in the years 1998–2000, a knife was used in almost 45 per cent of fatal encounters of this type, a firearm in 23 per cent, that is, only half as often. The national homicide rate, which has been fairly stable since 1970, at around 3 per 100,000 inhabitants, is high for Europe, but it is less than half that in the United States. One of the most interesting conclusions comes in a long-term analysis by Martti Lehti, based on statistics which exist from 1754 on. The dynamic of the development depends on two specific factors: the dangerousness of boys and young men in the 15–29 age group and that of middle-aged men from the lower classes, alcoholics and usually unemployed. The latter has remained fairly stable for 250 years, with a slight tendency to rise since 1950, whereas the former has steadily fallen, to reach its lowest ever historical level. Though short-term fluctuations are sometimes marked, they are primarily due to surges in the number of young men. According to Lehti, they then draw attention to a challenge to the legitimacy of the established social order by a sector among the new generations.[14]

In other words, while adolescents who kill have become increasingly rare over time, the peaks in the murders they commit are every time a sign of a worsening of their relations with established adult men. Even if some of the aggression is deflected, because most confrontations are between peers, the transgression of the blood taboo reveals a silent challenge to the rules imposed by the community. This is the message delivered by non-fatal assaults, too. They are much more common than homicide, so great is the value our civilization attaches to human life, but they, too, are pointers to the scale of the juvenile malaise. The gangs which are the sole refuge of the youths concerned, and which have constantly evolved since the Second World War, tell, in their own way, the story of the turbulent relationships between the generations.

Juvenile delinquency

From far back in time, the definition of the social roles in the West has been organized round a highly developed paternal power. In the sixteenth and seventeenth centuries, attitudes to 'youth', which then meant adolescence, were deeply ambivalent. It was seen both as a time of great promise and as a 'dark' and 'sinful' age, 'the worst and most dangerous time of all' according to many commentators. The English moralists constantly condemned the sins to which young lads were most prone, and, in particular, their dissolute morals. In *The Winter's Tale*, Shakespeare is only expressing the general opinion when he denounces, through the mouth of an old shepherd, the period between ten and twenty-three years, when young lads did nothing but get girls pregnant, deceive their elders, steal and fight. They were like wild colts, thoughtless, driven by their burning sensual appetites, said many others.[15] Songs, ballads and chapbooks disseminated this negative image, contrasting it with that of the brave, virtuous and pious apprentice, obedient to his master, whose qualities might raise him to the coveted office of lord mayor of London.

Such a discourse expressed an adult fear of an inability to control the fervours of youth. The positive model proposed was based on a Christian perception, according to which every man was a sinner, especially in the early stages of life, when he lacked discernment; nevertheless, he could and should resist temptation in order to achieve salvation. At a more humdrum level, the prevailing morality tried to get young bachelors to put all their strength and vitality at the service of the established order, so as to negotiate this difficult period without too many problems, with the promise of eventually acceding to a full, agreeable and prestigious adult life. The social, economic and cultural upheavals experienced by Europe in the Age of Enlightenment transformed this dualist vision. At the turn of the eighteenth and nineteenth centuries, youth crime became a major problem. However, this notion has been the subject of much debate among historians, because it seems to indicate a sudden emergence of the phenomenon, at precisely the time of the appearance of the notion of adolescence, people having previously spoken more vaguely of young men of marriageable age.[16] The debate needs to be put in a much wider context. The process of controlling the lethal violence and dissolute morals of this age group made significant progress in the seventeenth and, even more, the eighteenth centuries. Its effect was first evident in the more prosperous milieus, before it proceeded, though with more difficulty, to make an impact at the lower social levels.[17] The concept of juvenile delinquency is essentially a product of a heightened perception of these differences. It was a social marker, which made it possible to separate the wheat from the chaff, the golden youths who were simply boisterous from the hard core of the sons of the people, who continued to fight each other with knives with a fury described as vulgar and savage.

The use of a new penal vocabulary testifies to a profound shift in attitudes to childhood and the years of transition to adulthood. The docile entry into the ranks of conformists of a growing number of pubescent boys, revealed, amongst other things, by the decline in the homicide rate, slowly softened the earlier image of their whole age group as extremely brutal. A new discourse was gradually put in place in order to differentiate the mass of 'normal' youths from the few who were abnormal, because they behaved violently. It received support from the romantic perception of the innocence of the child, exalted by Rousseau, which gradually gained ground, and is now universally accepted. By the beginning of the nineteenth century, in France, the very young criminal was defined by contrast with his normal peers. Judicial practice subsequently took on marked pejorative connotations by drawing a very clear distinction between the hardened and corrupted working-class child and the innocent and pure child of the middle classes. The same applied in the case of adolescents, when it came to explaining their propensity for crime. From the middle of the nineteenth century, when states decided to address the issue, their offences began to be described officially as 'juvenile'. England was first with the Juvenile Offenders Act of 1847, followed by Norway in 1896 and Sweden in 1902. France established special courts for children and adolescents in 1912, as did Belgium, in the same year. The later shift from repression to welfare and re-education testifies to the victory of the notion of innocence attaching to these stages of life. In Germany, after the defeat of 1918, juvenile delinquency was often seen as an illness, with the growth of the idea that German youth had been physically and morally damaged by the war. In France, a law of 1935 decriminalized the offending of minors. The sharp rise in the offences attributed to them led to a renewed consideration of the question in 1941. The law of 2 February 1945 established the penal irresponsibility of minors below the age of 16 and created the post of children's judge; this was the beginning of a decisive shift from the punitive to the therapeutic.[18]

Virtually absent from this debate is the criminal girl. By the beginning of the nineteenth century, the problem was perceived as essentially one of young boys. Though sometimes described as boorish or as brutal thugs, especially when they were guilty of physical violence, boys were much more often portrayed as intelligent, cunning, brave and determined, on the literary model of the Artful Dodger in Charles Dickens' *Oliver Twist* (1838). The female stereotype, by contrast, was constructed round sexual immorality, whereas it was very rare for the young boys to be accused of prostitution or homosexuality before 1871. This twofold definition of the roles, which influenced the actions of the police and of the law, derived from a discourse which generally put boy offenders in the same category as adults, because of the strong assertion of their manliness, their sexual knowledge, their coarse language and their pastimes. What worried right-minded people and the authorities was that they were often 'thieves from the cradle', already proper little men, driven by a rejection of all rules.[19]

The concentration of social fears on working-class adolescents seems to have been universal in Europe in the second half of the nineteenth century. The fear of the Parisian Apaches around 1900 is not an isolated case.[20] Such fears were very strong in England at the end of the 1890s. 'Hooliganism' was a subject of endless fascination for journalists and the writers of popular literature. Music hall songs celebrated the exploits of members of youth gangs, and anglophone historians have carefully analysed the gendered dimension of these groupings.[21] The attention of contemporaries, however, was focused mainly on the males. It reveals a growing fear of street violence among the middle classes of big cities such as London, Manchester, Liverpool, Birmingham and Glasgow. The commentators were only interested in the girls in their carnal manifestation as molls, that is, the consenting property of violent boys. They were fiercely denounced as 'degraded' by the press and the magistrates, and generally regarded as anti-feminine.

In Manchester, nearly 94 per cent of the 717 adolescents accused of gang violence in the years 1870 to 1900 were effectively boys. Mostly aged between fourteen and nineteen, these 'scuttlers', as they were called, were manual workers and usually lived with their parents, but enjoyed considerable independence in disposing of their leisure time because they earned their own living. They differentiated themselves from other young men of a similar background by wearing a sort of uniform intended to proclaim their manliness and signal that they were up for a fight. Their outfits drew attention in particular to their shoes and their heads. They let their hair grow long at the front, plastering it down on their foreheads, and they wore their caps tilted to the left to show off the fringe. The girls tried to dress as much like the boys as they could. The fights were rarely fatal, because only five homicides are recorded for this period, but they were violent and led to many injuries. Led by 'captains' or 'kings', if we are to believe the journalists, they fought against rival gangs or attacked isolated individuals with bricks, stones, knives or belts with heavy metal buckles. Accustomed to experiencing physical violence, or seeing it from childhood at home, these offspring of the labouring classes learned to defend themselves to survive and to demonstrate their manly honour, the latter an essential attribute in the working-class culture of the time. They needed to show that they were 'hard' and that they knew how to make people respect them.

Some girls of the same age joined the scuttler gangs. They were usually unmarried and factory workers, which gave them independence. They, too, gathered informally, at street corners, and walked around together in the evenings and on holidays, or went as a group to places of entertainment that were also frequented by boys. They were as active and sometimes also as cruel as the latter in group battles. Yet the sources say little about their participation in assaults of this type or in fights with the police. They were more often implicated in the intimidation of witnesses. Called viragoes and amazons, even rippers, in a sinister echo of the reputation of Jack the Ripper after 1888, they were a source of deep unease to the authorities and good citizens, who regarded them as even more abnormal than the young lads.[22]

The condemnation of the aggressive behaviour of these young men was targeted more generally at the exaltation of a rough working-class masculinity, in which it served as an apprenticeship. The gangs of scuttlers offered their members a specific site of sociability where they could pick up the dominant values of their milieu. Their years of violence constituted a long rite of passage from adolescence to maturity and marriage, during which they acquired the brutal manly characteristics which they would display for the rest of their lives. The police and the good citizens saw them as dangerous rebels, although they were, on the contrary, extremely conservative, in that they were clinging to the norms of their class of origin. Heirs, without knowing it, to the old rural customs for the construction of identity, they created a traditional personality through the use of force as a badge of honour. If we are to judge by the small number of incidents reported over a thirty-year period for the whole of the densely populated Manchester conurbation, by no means all sons of working-class fathers joined these gangs. Their bad reputation probably dissuaded many young men from involvement. Some even preferred ostracism at the hands of their peers from the same neighbourhood to joining their punitive expeditions. One man who had experience of this related later how books had opened up a new world for him, but how he had been regarded with contempt by the others as a snob and a bookworm.[23]

In the nineteenth century, the concept of juvenile delinquency became a way of characterizing the minority of boys in the big industrial cities who stayed faithful to popular traditions of aggression. Now, however, though the kingdoms of youth of the past had consisted exclusively of males, a small number of girls joined them. They were recruited from among those who worked, and were able, as a result, to behave with great freedom as they waited for marriage. To be accepted by the gangs, however, they had to demonstrate essentially masculine attitudes and values. Flaunting a sort of feminine version of manliness, but also sexually dominated and accused of the worst debaucheries, they made the police and observers deeply uneasy, because they departed so far from the established norms in regard to the so-called weaker sex. Hannah Robin was the 'sweetheart' of William Willan, a sixteen-year-old scuttler condemned to death on 20 May 1892 for the murder of a rival in an affray. She was arrested a week later, with three friends, during a brawl in the centre of Manchester. She was drunk and wearing a formidable-looking belt with a heavy metal buckle, and, it transpired, had a tattoo on her right arm, 'in loving remembrance' of William.[24]

With the exception of the purely criminal cases, the continuities observable over the centuries in the case of violence and homicide concern the proclamation of masculine hegemony. In Sweden, for example, fights and murders retained similar characteristics from the sixteenth to the twentieth century. They were frequently a consequence of a fit of rage, coming after a dispute or a provocation relating to a question of honour or a debt, and they were often fuelled by alcohol. The protagonists mostly came from the lower social ranks. However, the number of fights and homicides fell sharply during the same period. The middle classes became more peaceable first, probably because they found other ways of asserting their manliness. The street ceased to be the principal theatre for confrontations, whereas conflicts within private space to some extent bucked the trend, automatically increasing their statistical proportion.[25]

The volume of physical violence shrank in Western Europe, to leave only a residue by the twentieth century. Despite signs of a slight increase at the beginning of the twenty-first century, and growing security fears, violence has been largely eradicated. This observation suggests that the brutal human impulses evoked by certain biological theories can at the very least be dramatically controlled by culture. Unlike the sons of the peasantry in the sixteenth century, or the noble duellists of the sixteenth and seventeenth centuries, the majority of adolescents today never kill or injure one of their peers or any other human being. They are usually able to control their aggression, or deflect it into symbolic confrontations, especially in sport or intellectual or artistic sublimation. The very rare murderers who transgress these powerful prohibitions are often from underprivileged backgrounds where honour and force remain essential values. The steady reduction in their number, including in the United States, where the trend has been for a slow decline for some decades, points to a spectacular retreat of 'macho' traditions.

Violence has been tamed and made to serve society. Some psychoanalysts see this as a way of producing in the child a generational effect unknown among the animals. The desire symbolically to kill the father, they claim, has as a consequence recognition of the position he occupies and thus of the possibility of replacing him one day.[26] More generally, could it be that the current use of violence by youth gangs derives from a similar need to claim a place in the sun, in the face of adults who are making the most of a paradise that is scarcely accessible to the young? By vigorously externalizing the manly values that are condemned by modernity, may they not be refusing to continue their acceptance of the 'auto-constraints' of the 'civilizing process', because they are not bringing them enough immediate benefit?

'Rebel without a cause', or 'eternal recurrence'

In the autumn of 2005, the gangs of rioters from the French banlieues stunned and shocked international opinion. Yet the phenomenon was hardly new. It has constantly recurred in the history of the West, like a song of youthful rebellion against excessively strict constraints. Though each time sung to a different tune, it is always a sign of the same increase in collective frustration among a sector of the age group, and of the choice of a violence both very real and deeply symbolic as a way of attracting the attention of adults blind to their sufferings.

Long periods of demographic and economic growth are more favourable to the rise of these silent generational discontents than periods of great unrest or war. After the English scuttlers and the French Apaches of the late nineteenth and early twentieth centuries, the first large-scale manifestation of youthful rebellion emerged in the 1950s, when the children of the baby boom reached adolescence in a Europe that was at peace and undergoing rapid reconstruction after the Second World War. Most of the countries in the world seems to have been affected, if to varying degrees, according to the reports of the 1960 second congress of the United Nations on the Prevention of Crime and Treatment of Offenders or the discussions at the session devoted to the same theme by the International Union for Child Welfare in 1961.[27] It is possible, however, that this is a view surreptitiously contaminated by current European preoccupations. We lack a solid comparative analysis to link, for example, the African, Japanese or Chinese examples to events in the Old Continent. Here, 'rebels without a cause', cheats, skirt-chasers and thugs proliferated in both the capitalist and the socialist states: English Teddy boys (and girls), Italian *vitelloni*, Dutch and Belgian *nozems*, Soviet *stiliagues*, Swedish *skinn knuttar*, French *blousons noirs*... With the exception of the Polish 'hooligans', who were organized in a strongly hierarchical fashion around a leader and his chief of staff, on the model of American gangs, the European gangs were relatively unstructured. Their members were not recruited exclusively from the working classes, as the sons of bourgeois families also formed homogeneous bands, *blousons dorés* in France, *vitelloni* in Italy.

It was a theme taken up by the cinema, which opted to romanticize it to make it appealing to the public. In the United States, in Laslo Benedek's *The Wild One* (1953), Marlon Brando plays the leader of a gang of bikers in studded jackets who sow panic in a small provincial town before a fight with a rival gang that leaves a man dead. In Nicholas Ray's *Rebel Without a Cause* (1955), James Dean is a spoiled boy who arrives in a new town. There he discovers the love of Natalie Wood, the hatred of the little gang to which she belongs and the friendship of the deeply troubled son of a wealthy family, who loves to play with a gun and ends up being shot by the police. The initiatory metaphor, rather on the trite side, is a call to fall into line by controlling one's adolescent violence. Nevertheless, the film created a veritable myth, helped by the fact that the actor who played the hero was obsessed with speed and killed in a road accident in 1956. Most of all, it seems that the fundamental ambiguity in the treatment of the subject, emphasized by the tragic death of the friend unable to face up to the responsibilities of adulthood, was also what assured its success among those who were fearful of the excesses of youth. In 1958, Marcel Carné's *Les tricheurs* (*The Cheaters*) described a particular type of wealthy Parisian youth who were carelessly wasting their lives away. The twenty-something 'overgrown calves' of Federico Fellini's *I vitelloni* (1953) were similarly not from the proletariat. They dragged out their aimless lives in a small Italian seaside town, refusing to grow up and leave the shelter of their families. In practice, the influence of family and of socializing institutions, especially school and university, dissuaded many more sons of the bourgeoisie from forming gangs than their fellows from the working classes. In France, the latter generally despised the former, calling them 'tricheurs' after the success of Carné's film, although they were, in fact, guilty of offences blown up out of all proportion by the press, especially stealing cars.[28]

Far from the curiosity of the media, and its fixation with the real or supposed turpitude of the sons of middle- and upper-class families, the real bands shared many features with the kingdoms of youth of the sixteenth century. The main difference is that they now existed in a pre-dominantly urban environment, after a period of unprecedented urban growth. In the middle of the twentieth century, they consisted of boys of similar background, workers or apprentices, mostly aged between four-teen and eighteen. Girls were exceptionally admitted 'as occasional hangers-on or as instruments of pleasure', very rarely in the role of leaders. Shared dress codes and symbols strengthened group cohesion. The main aim of their members was to have fun, to pass the time between the end of compulsory schooling – fourteen in France – and entry into the adult world. They wandered the streets at night, gossiped at street corners, sat in bars and cafés and went to clubs and dances. The group-ings were usually fluid, dictated by circumstances. In the 1960s, the police and the gendarmerie drew a clear distinction between them and the real gangs. Their offences were rarely planned – it was more a matter of opportunity making the thief. Thus, a party might end in casual sex or 'borrowing' a car. The unease felt by the public was only made greater by the fact that the sudden, brutal transition to a criminal act seemed not to have any identifiable reason – shades of *Rebel Without a Cause*. However, for the experts, the doctors and the historians and the journal-ists, there were reasons in plenty. They endlessly denounced, among other things, the decline of the family, school exclusions, boring jobs, the con-sumer society and its frenetic pace, overcrowded estates, the lack of affordable leisure activities, not forgetting the crisis of adolescence.[29]

The real causes lay elsewhere. The bands offered the young a socializa-tion by their peers. This took the place of an education by their fathers which had become inadequate, faltering or inept. Contemporary observ-ers emphasize the deep affective need of those who join gangs in search of security and the mutual support of their peers, so they will feel better about life. However, these observers exaggerate the part played by the increasing harshness of a competitive and lonely world. Such phenomena are hardly new. Indeed, the difficulty of integrating into the world of the established was far greater in previous periods. This was certainly the case, for example, in the seventeenth century, in the peasant communities which then accounted for some 80 per cent of the population. Famine caused thousands of deaths, and the transmission of land to the young was happening much later. In France, the average age of marriage was then over twenty-five, which meant not only that sons had to work for long years for their fathers, but that they had no other option than to accept their burdensome supervision. The warmth of relationships between equals in the kingdoms of youth provided them with a welcome release. Further, the authorities and their families tolerated their violence, even though it often ended in murder, because it deflected much of their aggression away from their parents and in the direction of their fellow bachelors, instead.[30]

More subtly, the mechanics of intergenerational relations subsequently shifted in the direction of a sort of common front of the affluent in the face of the supposedly savage hordes of adolescents, violent without a cause. This started at the beginning of the industrial age and was clearly in evidence at the time of the Apaches, in the first decade of the twentieth century. In the second half of that century, it went a stage further. It became a powerful myth enabling adults to unite against the *blousons noirs*. It was encouraged by the press and the cinema, which amalgamated the fear of gangs, visible tip of the iceberg of the fear of the 'dangerous' working classes from which they came, and fear of isolated young criminals or gangsters, whose harrowing exploits they constantly described and routinely inflated. This largely artificial fantasy constituted a 'discourse on the young'. It reveals the fear among mature men of being submerged by their rising tide. In 1963, a French sports official based an urgent appeal for funds on the fact that the number of 15–19-year-olds would rise from the 2.8 million of two years earlier to 3.8 million in 1965.[31]

Gangs of young males are neither an anomaly nor a pathology. Heirs to very ancient traditions, they have become deeply implanted in Western culture as a way of supporting their members during the difficult rite of passage from childhood to maturity. As more or less ephemeral groupings of a few individuals of similar social origin, place of residence and sympathies, these bands still, in the middle of the twentieth century, provided an apprenticeship in life. While the sons of more privileged backgrounds received the necessary education within the family and in specialized institutions, gang members explored their personality in this context. They presented it before their peers, playing a generic role, prestigious, useful or despised by those around them, as leader, lieutenant, ordinary member, fool, clown, buffoon dominated by the leader, misfit, scapegoat etc. Gangs are unobtrusive in normal times because they are of little interest to mature or older men, who are only too happy to forget the tedious or troubled hours of their own adolescence. Their sudden emergence into the glare of the media spotlight before 1914 and in the 1950s was a sign of heightened tension between the generations.

291

Usually an automatic response to a surge in the numbers of young men, it became the occasion for a symbolic confrontation, which eventually gradually died down as those involved grew older and adopted a more settled style of life. Two years before the explosion of May 1968, social workers, the police and the press announced, in all seriousness, that the phenomenon had disappeared in France!

They could not have been more wrong. It is only the media interest that dies down. Then, as soon as a new wave of young people floods the imaginary and reality, it revives. The American film director Stanley Kubrick fuelled the war between the age groups in 1971, in *A Clockwork Orange*. This tells the story of the ferocious Alex and his 'droogs', who terrorize England, committing at random a stream of violent acts, rapes and robberies. Imprisoned for murder, Alex acts as a guinea-pig for an experimental form of aversion therapy designed to make him detest violence. 'Cured' and freed, he is in his turn persecuted by his former victims, before making an unsuccessful suicide bid, then becoming again what he was, but with his aggression now put at the service of the state. The parable of the final victorious control of the individual brutal impulses by organized society is a perfect illustration of Norbert Elias' theory of the 'civilizing process'.[32] In 1973, George Lucas provided a much more 'Hollywood' vision of teenage gangs in *American Graffiti*. Set in a period of peace, around 1960, before the Vietnam War, the story presents characters who love music and freedom and who meet up in the evenings in the main street of a small Californian town. The tone is less idyllic in *Un monde sans pitié* (*Love Without Pity*), a film by the French director Eric Rochant, made in 1989. This paints a picture of a disillusioned generation, lacking models, ambition, the desire for conquest or the wish to fight. Even darker is *La haine* (*Hate*) by Mathieu Kassovitz (1995), which describes a day in the life of a small band of friends from the banlieue through the story of three lads who learn to hate after the death of a mate killed during a clash with the police that went wrong.

The age of the banlieues began in the 1970s. The *loubards* replaced the *blousons noirs*. Black or white, French or foreign, mostly drop-outs from school, often unemployed, they hang out in the streets of the estate where they live. The return of the gangs is in large part the return of the fear – now media-fuelled – of the violence of an underprivileged youth, cooped up in the ghettoes on the peripheries of the big cities. Like their predecessors, groups of friends meet, often spontaneously, in their *quartier*, at the entry to a block of flats, in the street or some place of entertainment, and, like them, they find in their peers a 'refuge against hostility, incomprehension and exclusion'. They are rough and intensely quarrelsome, but not, on the whole, hardened delinquents; rather, they live on the margins of legality and are quick to riot, especially against the police, when they sense an injustice. According to the commentators, the principal novelty in their case is the absence not only of points of reference but of a father. Even when he exists, he is totally out of his depth, lacking authority or prestige. This is a plausible explanation. It is not, however, a sufficient one, because the old kingdoms of youth similarly transgressed against paternal authority, at night and on holidays, times that encouraged the letting off of steam.

The spectacular and sometimes highly organized aggression of the *casseurs*, whether grouped according to ethnic criteria or not, is certainly a language of intimidation aimed at established adults. However, it also owes much to the fantasies of the latter, and of the media, the exaggeration of the danger serving to calm anxieties and to justify a policy of increased security. In 1990, according to the Renseignements Généraux Français, there were at most a hundred groups specializing in gang rapes, assaults on public transport, the bloody settling of scores and robbery. The hardest were black, with names like the Black Dragons, the Requins Vicieux and the Derniers Salauds. Their members adopted a culture that imitated that of young American criminals, including outfits inspired by prison uniforms and a penchant for B-movies and video clips. They patrolled the streets of Paris, congregating in Les Halles or La Défense. Their highly ostentatious and aggressive behaviour was an expression of the frustrations of those rejected by the consumer society, who wanted not only to take their revenge but to acquire all the signs of power and wealth. Far from seeking to start a revolution, they were demanding their slice of the cake of growth, and taking it by force. The fascinated curiosity of the journalists only enhanced their importance in their own eyes, leading to a spiralling overestimation of the problem: 'The press speaks of *zoulous*, so they see themselves as *zoulous*.' But when the commentators and the television lose interest, the gangs seem to merge back into the urban landscape, as happened, for example, after 1991.[33] They do not disappear, however, because they are indispensable refuges against a double hostility, that of an external world represented by the police and that of the neighbours whose already difficult lives they disrupt.

Though symptoms of the peculiar difficulties in integrating faced by young people from disadvantaged backgrounds, they are too often seen as organized gangs. But racketeering, dealing, 'stripping' (forcing people to hand over fashionable items of clothing) and rape characterize only a minority of them, who copy a 'black' American code of extreme violence and systematic contestation of the values and norms of ordinary behaviour. Their members very rarely carry guns, unlike in the United States. This was true even of the French riots of November 2005, which limited the seriousness of damage. Far more typical are the less well-known, more unobtrusive and highly informal gatherings of groups of friends seeking to pass the time in the evenings and at weekends in the banlieues. Their sociability reproduces that of the old youth traditions, adapted to the unwelcoming modern world of the urban housing estate. Lacking any revolutionary aims, or even desire to change the system, all they want is to join the ranks of those leading a more agreeable life, surrounded by all the signs of material success. By burning cars at night, they are demonstrating just how much value they attach to these objects they do not own, and taking pleasure in revenging themselves on those who do. Between these two contrasting stereotypes, a variety of mixed forms of socializing exist. They are, as it were, American transplants into the old European body of signs of protest popularized by the mass audiovisual culture, and they help to actualize the practice of spontaneous gatherings of young males in order to resist more effectively the authoritarian demands of the established generations.

Territory and sexuality are the main determinants of identity. Whatever the type of gang, the space they inhabit collectively is of extreme importance. The group makes its mark wherever it goes, by postures, by graffiti or by clashes with rivals or strangers on fiercely disputed frontiers. The young peasant lads of long ago had similarly fought the champions of another village on the margins between their two territories. The *loubards* of the French banlieues, who are much more mobile thanks to the speed of modern forms of transport, carry their territory around with them, on the soles of their carefully chosen shoes. They like to set up somewhere in the centre of Paris, such as Les Halles, or La Défense or the Gare du Nord, then fiercely block entry to rivals.

Though sometimes from different 'villages', which was rare in the past, they collaborate closely in defence of a 'hidden dimension' which they think is theirs by right: the girls growing up in their area. This had been the main purpose of the activities of the kingdoms of youth, many centuries before. In spite of the evolution of manners and the major changes that have taken place in our civilization, adolescent solidarities continue to be the main site for the expression of sexuality. This aspect is probably crucial, because each member has to provide the others with proof of his virility. The vocabulary they employ reveals deeply chauvinist attitudes, directly derived from working-class traditions, themselves rooted in immensely old peasant customs. Girls can only be sluts who agree to have sex, or virgins who refuse. To shag as many of them as possible, or at least to brag about it, is essential if one is to be admired by the others. Just as bachelor lads in the countryside had actively cheered on the amorous activities of one of their group, so the gang spurs on its members and demands an account. To boast of one's good luck, to make crude jokes and to pass swiftly from one conquest to another is good; a stable relationship is not, because it weakens group cohesion. Peers are defined as 'brothers', equals. Even if they have a different skin colour, friendship binds them together.

We need to treat with some caution, however, the conclusions of those sociologists who see this as a very modern 'self-socialization', an original and innovatory response by the young to the crisis in the authoritarian models and integration practices currently being experienced by our society.[34] The retreat by the young from the power of fathers, into specific groups providing reassurance, where they will complete their education in life among their peers, has existed for centuries in Europe. It is not, however, simply the free choice of those concerned, but rather something that is forced on them, as fathers distance themselves from unruly teenagers they see as disruptive of the existing balance, and as girls avoid them, fearing for their virtue. In the industrial age, the general distrust was greatly increased in the case of boys of working-class origin, in spite of the 'knocking into shape' they experienced during compulsory military service. Whether in the village of old or the banlieues of today, the gulf between the generations is created less by rebellious or aggressive sons than by fathers who want to make them undergo a long rite of passage before acceding to the good life. For centuries, the gang, heir to the kingdoms of youth and then to bands of conscripts, has served as an affective refuge and site of socialization for the most marginalized. It allows them to ease their frustrations during the interminable wait imposed on the whole of their age group, but which is much harder for the children of poor or excluded families to bear than for the descendants of the rich and powerful.

After the *blousons noirs* of the 1950s and the *loubards* of the 1970s, the violent gangs of 1990–1 faded, in their turn, into the background. Or rather, to be more accurate, the mass media turned its back on them, for fear of boring its readers and listeners, abandoning the 'sensitive neighbourhoods' to their everyday problems and city politics. But, similar causes producing similar effects, and the level of public interest depending on the level of anxiety gripping it, the violent urban riots of November 2005 in France were the occasion for a sudden rediscovery of the problem. In fact, nothing had fundamentally changed in the lives of the teenagers of the banlieues in the preceding fifteen years, except for the worse, due to higher unemployment and more academic failure. Bands of youths had continued to form and break up. A small but significant number of them had continued to engage in crime and violence, carving out little empires that were practically inaccessible to the police so as to conduct their lucrative 'bizness', based on racketeering and drugs. No official with contacts on the ground had imagined for a moment that the phenomenon had gone away, any more than those of today are unaware of the constant disorder and large number of cars burned, especially on holidays such as la Saint Sylvestre (New Year's Eve).

The '*racaille*' – or 'scum' – generation, to use an expression that has been hijacked by those it refers to, and used as a term of defiance, consists of youths born in the 1990s. It has replaced that of the turbulent *grand frères* ('big brothers') of those years, while they have themselves reached maturity. The bandwagon effect of an insistent security discourse was greatly magnified by this transition, in a context of deteriorating problems in the cities. As always, the picture is not as simple as it appears. To understand it fully, we need to get beyond the highly impassioned political standpoints that either prophesy the beginning of a proletarian revolution or denounce acts of truly inhuman savagery. Both are opinions that reflect a perception of the 'new dangerous classes'. In one, they are called into battle against injustice, in the other, feared like the plague. The initial lumping together is not helpful. Though often from the impoverished minorities relegated to the margins of the society of abundance and consumption, the youths of the banlieues are not all victims of social exclusion; nor are they necessarily frustrated or violent. Only a minority of them go on the rampage in the 'concrete jungle'. The others remain invisible because their life is largely led at home, in school or in the workplace. In one city carefully analysed, the former represented at most 100 of the 800 young men aged between eighteen and thirty.

It is also the case that there are major differences between the gangs, depending on the financial resources, age and ethnic origins of their members. The uniformity suggested by external observers, with reference to their language, clothing and attitudes, bears little resemblance to reality. Lastly, the behaviour flaunted by '*les chauds*', the leaders, glorifies physical force, '*tchatche*' – the language of the banlieues – and '*vice*', but also the ostentatious display of the coveted wealth, such as luxury cars, designer clothes, new mobile phones and MP3 players. Even if they acquire these emblematic products through '*bizness*', that is, trafficking, they like to present themselves as savvy consumers who draw on a sufficient 'warrior capital' to protect their friends and their *quartier*. In any case, many of them end up by going straight after starting a family, giving way to younger *chauds*.[35]

Street culture gives the appearance of changing with breath-taking speed, so readily does it adapt to technological novelties and so constantly does it invent ephemeral fashions. But its internal codes have remained the same for centuries. They are based on a glorification of manliness, which leads to an instrumentalization of girls and the resort, without any feeling of guilt, to collective rape in appalling 'gang-bangs'. However, many cases of the latter are recorded at the end of the Middle Ages in Dijon and the towns of south-east France.[36] The gulf is magnified by comparison with the values of toleration accepted by the majority of the population, in France as elsewhere in Europe, especially with regard to the rights of women and homosexuals. The young people of the cities of today are much more than is generally believed the direct heirs of the *loubards* and of the earlier youth bands. Though they are now defined by their ethnic and religious origins, they are primarily unemployed or temporary workers, whereas their predecessors were usually manual workers or apprentices, in an age of full employment. Like those, however, they are driven onto the margins by setbacks or failure at school and, like those, they are essentially trying to show themselves to advantage by developing an exultant masculinity. This has been a powerful marker of social difference since the upper classes abandoned manly violence in favour of sublimation and politeness. In seeking, in this way, to join the French model from below, given that they are unable to get in from the top, they are a source of increasing unease among respectable people. Well aware of this, they indulge in endless acts of antisocial behaviour – in other words, supposedly impolite forms of communication – both as revenge and for the sheer pleasure of giving provocation. However, their situation is far from easy, in areas of increasing multiple tensions, while they experience enormous frustration. An incident can quickly lead to disaster, when it gives rise to a deep sense of injustice.

This was the case in November 2005, when what was seen as a police over-reaction led to the deaths of two young men at Clichy-sous-Bois. The French banlieues erupted, one after the other. The massive, savage protest was not, however, a planned rebellion, or sustained by specific ideas. It was 'protopolitical', in the phrase of one commentator, and fell outside any established framework.[37] It was more like the popular 'emotions' of the seventeenth century, brutal, bloody, but lacking any programme, and always destined to be cruelly suppressed. To call it 'gratuitous' would be to ignore its dimension of revolt against daily humiliations, a powerful feeling which also motivated the peasants who rose up against fiscal excesses. The parallel may be taken further, because the peasants embarked on their fight with enthusiasm. Refusing to admit that they were certainly facing a crushing defeat, they rejoiced, drank and enjoyed themselves unrestrainedly, to the detriment of enemies they had captured. In just the same way, the young rioters of November 2005 turned the world upside down with a joyous exuberance which resembled 'a sort of carnival where the social rules were suspended'. The risks they ran in the confrontations and their judicial consequences were accepted. 'The pleasure of action was more important than victory.'[38] The protest, in other words, was its own raison d'être. However, the new power of the information networks gave it an extraordinary capacity to spread, which the rebellions of the past had lacked. Finding themselves the involuntary cause of copycat uprisings all over the country, television newsreaders discovered with trepidation just how effective they had been.

Text messaging, blogs and online videos can accentuate this even further. Added to this, the enjoyment of violence has conquered new territory by invading sport. To the great confusion of the responsible officials, sporting competitions at a high level no longer effectively channel aggression, according to the traditional model invented in the nineteenth century. They are now frequently the scene of vicious encounters between the young supporters of the great European football clubs. This return of the punch-up is as disturbing as the brutality of the urban gangs, because the violence is the work of structured groups, whose members are looking for thrills. If we are to believe the press, which now takes a close interest in the subject, the inevitable clashes are planned by tiny, highly organized groups.

The Virage Boulogne in the stands of the Parc des Princes, in Paris, is home to the most determined of the dozen dangerous small groups, known as the 'independents', who follow the matches of the club Paris Saint-Germain. They had between 150 and 200 members in the autumn of 2006, according to the Renseignements Généraux. Academically well qualified and socially well integrated, they avoided distinctive insignia so as not to be identified by the police, dressing conventionally. They were believed to go looking for trouble, which might be arranged in advance with their opponents in the form of a 'free fight', or involve a surprise invasion of an enemy stand. According to some of their statements, they fought only with their feet and their fists, not kicking a man when he was down or ganging up on isolated individuals, because the aim was not to kill but to 'dominate' the opponent.[39] We may recognize here the principle of the British 'fair fight' of the nineteenth century, which had made it possible to cool the ardour of the protagonists by forbidding the use of knives and by imposing strict rules. Its transfer to the sporting arena may be a sign that the pacification of manners in the West has reached a threshold that it will be difficult to lower, in a society where to succeed in a situation of strong economic and professional competition demands a capacity to behave aggressively. The exaltation of assertive manliness by bands of football supporters may be a consequence of a recent strong increase in the need to assert identity. Though it is sometimes linked to nationalist or racist ideologies, it seems to stem more generally from the desire to test one's physical strength against one's peers; but this is strictly forbidden to spectators at matches by the codes of good manners that have replaced the violent rites of passage to the adult state.

The return of the gangs is also the return of the repressed. The sudden irruption of the problem, at fairly regular intervals, when a large number of teenagers approach maturity and encounter too many obstacles to integration, is every time a sign of the breakdown of the tacit pact governing the transmission of property, power and values from one generation to the next. The frustrations of the new arrivals are matched by a heightened fear of dispossession on the part of their elders. Long periods of peace and prosperity are more likely to sharpen this competition than periods of crisis and war. The most vulnerable elements among the young, from the least privileged backgrounds, are hit particularly hard. In Europe, the malaise has been especially acute in the era of mass unemployment. The *blousons noirs* of the 1960s represented a fraction of boys from working-class backgrounds who refused to accept the disappearance of the old popular tradition of exultant manliness. They were mostly wage-earners, with a poor or mediocre school record, and endured a primarily cultural marginalization. Driven out to the housing estates on the peripheries of the big cities, they needed a powerful motorbike both to escape and to express their combative masculinity. The *loubards* of the 1970s came from the same population sectors, but the working-class world was by then in decline and unemployment was rising. This gave them an extra fury, which inevitably fuelled the mounting anxiety of the respectable bourgeois faced with these representatives of the 'dangerous classes'. The late twentieth and early twenty-first centuries have seen a far more profound shift in the landscape. The frequent lack of jobs, 'hate' for the institutions of confinement, especially schools, that have presided over their failure, life in the banlieue experienced as exile from a consumer paradise, ethnic and religious conflicts – these have all combined to turn the problem into a running sore; permanently festering on the social body, it now erupts at the least provocation.

Yet the number of youths who break the taboo on homicide remains very small. The overwhelming majority respect the most powerful prohibitions. And those who resort to force or intimidation to get what they want are not seeking to destroy society or to challenge its founding principles, but to denounce the blockage that has such adverse consequences for them. Even if they demonstrate their 'hate' by antisocial behaviour, provocation and vandalism, what they really want is to find a place in the sun or better their lot in a consumerist world they wholly accept. Robbery, trafficking and violence are aimed as much at acquiring inaccessible, highly valued material goods as at the symbolic expression of serious protest. The *casseurs* from the banlieues who torch cars attach huge importance to this sign of success and power. They like to proclaim their victory by stealing a prestigious model. They loot to get their hands on the most sought-after products and make a big profit by selling them on, to others like them, who want to possess them to enhance their value in the eyes of others.

Their behaviour today results from a remarkable combination of factors. Basically, it derives from the universal acceptance, irrespective of colour and family history, of macho traditions inherited from the European working-class world, first of peasants, then of factory workers. The fact that they tie in with the chauvinist values found equally strongly in the civilizations of origin of some immigrants only reinforces this. To this is added the input of American mass culture – caps, clothes, gestures and swear words. The whole fuses in the melting pot of the banlieues to produce a youth style that has the appearance of uniformity, but actually varies greatly in detail. Although the resulting violence is often exaggerated by the media, always ready to propagate disquieting fantasies, and although it has been declining for centuries, it still causes deep anxiety to adults. It is generally accepted today that it is linked to serious social difficulties and forms of exclusion. Is this enough to mean that the appropriate remedies will be put in place, so that it will finally disappear?

IS THE END OF VIOLENCE POSSIBLE?

Homicide has retained one sociological characteristic almost unchanged since the thirteenth century, that is, it is overwhelmingly the act of adolescent or recently married males, whose victims are usually their peers. Nevertheless, it has declined spectacularly all over Europe, most notably at the beginning of the seventeenth century, and then again in the nineteenth century. This trend is linked to the marked reduction in the number of fights between men using bladed weapons, which was first visible among the aristocracy, before it spread, slowly and unevenly, to the lower classes. In both cases, a small number of young men refused to accept the pacification of manners and the disarming of individuals which the monarchies, with the support of the churches, were seeking to impose all over the continent. The sword for the former and the knife for the latter remained badges of honour on the public stage. Their number steadily declined, however, to become residual by the second half of the twentieth century. In Western Europe today, where there are strict controls on the possession of firearms, there is on average one murder per 100,000 inhabitants. This is a hundred times fewer than seven centuries before; it is also six times fewer than currently in the United States, though the rate there has been falling significantly for several decades.

Non-fatal physical violence has also been considerably reduced in our world. The resort to force to settle a quarrel has been literally invalidated, both by the legally constituted state and by the growth, since the seventeenth century, of powerful 'auto-constraints' regulating relationships with others. When the norms are transgressed, it is usually in the form of collateral violence during robberies or burglary or of acts of antisocial behaviour that constitute a veritable symbolic language of challenge to the established values. This situation is due to the development, generation after generation, of a powerful system for the management of male aggression. This was initially imposed by the authorities in order to pacify human relations in busy public spaces and taverns, and then gradually became universal. The institutions of socialization, like the church, the school and the army, helped to extend it gradually to the home. The elites were quickly enmeshed in a dense network of codes of pacification and politeness, with the lower classes gradually following suit, first the townspeople, then the peasantry, and lastly the working – or 'dangerous' – classes of the industrial age. The impact of this 'civilizing process' was at its greatest for teenage boys and young men, a fact which has not been sufficiently emphasized. By 1530, they were already the prime targets for the instructions contained in the two founding texts of the new principles: the *On Good Manners for Boys* of Erasmus and Castiglione's *The Courtier*. At the Versailles of Louis XIV, the 'curialization of warriors', that is, the obligation to repress all warlike ardour in the presence of other courtiers, and reserve it for foreign battle-fields, affected them most. Unlike their elders, their impulsiveness had not yet been subdued by long experience of a ruthless world where success demanded avoiding revealing one's emotions.[1]

In medieval rural societies, by contrast, youthful brutality had been regarded as normal, even encouraged. It made it possible to form individuals capable of defending themselves in a hostile material and human environment. And it made it easier for them to tolerate an extended period of waiting, during a long rite of passage, before they acceded to the full rights of the married man. In this context, their aggression, which might have been turned against their harsh and demanding fathers, was deflected against their local peers, and even more their rivals, members of juvenile gangs from neighbouring villages. However, it gradually became the subject of a major prohibition, transmitted by religion, morality, education and criminal justice. The culture of violence gradually died out, with more difficulty in some regions and population groups than others, and masculine physical strength was eventually channelled, to be put at the exclusive service of the state. Strong traces of the earlier practices survived, nevertheless, as shown by the duel and clan vengeance, in particular.

This long Western evolution raises a major question concerning the violence of our species: why is it often crueller and more destructive than that of the animals, as has been demonstrated in two world wars? An ethologist like Konrad Lorenz and a psychoanalyst like Erich Fromm had no hesitation in designating this a phenomenon peculiar to mankind. Lorenz spoke of an innate passion linked to mankind's animal nature, Fromm of a deep-rooted destructive instinct. Freud saw man as motivated by both a life impulse and a death impulse, the latter eventually prevailing, as Thanatos finally conquered Eros. Many other interpretations try to take account of the extreme complexity of the problem.

UNESCO supports those who argue for the absence of innate destructive impulses and attribute deviant behaviour to circumstances and a poor education likely to alienate adolescents from peaceful behaviour.[2] The explanation is essentially tautological, because it takes the whole of Western experience, focused for centuries on the need to sublimate extreme feelings and desires, as the basis for a theorized truth. We may at least retain the idea of a possible cultural construction of the taboo on murder.

While historians may be in no position to decide on the relative merits of the innate or acquired origin of aggressive behaviour, they need to emphasize the extreme plasticity of civilizations. Some, like the Tarahumaras Indians of northern Mexico at the beginning of the twentieth century, may choose to control violence closely. Without any strong state organization, they were mutually supportive in their labours in the fields, generally affectionate and non-authoritarian in their relations with each other and enjoyed a relative sexual freedom, aided by alcoholic beverages, at mixed festivities. Quarrelsome individuals, prone to create opportunities for brawls, were not invited to these gatherings. However, the exclusion from social interchange of those who displayed aggressive tendencies had negative consequences because, when the Apaches attacked their villages, all the inhabitants could do was flee. The ban on aggression bound the group together, but left it very vulnerable in the face of external predators who cultivated the opposite virtues.[3]

The Europeans of the Middle Ages did not live in a society without a state. They cultivated a strong fighting spirit, which enabled them both to compete militarily with the Muslim world and to sustain innumerable conflicts at a variety of levels. The best way of keeping this spirit alive lay in the law of vengeance, to punish by the death of the culprit a serious assault on the honour of the group. This fundamental principle, which was defended by males from puberty, was directly linked to the purity of women, one of whose essential duties was to avoid bringing shame on their family. Men were under great pressure to give proof of it on a permanent basis. It was 'nothing other than mastery of the penis and the knife'.[4] If they wanted truly to exist in the eyes of their fellows, they had to prove that they had the sexual power necessary to reproduce, so as to assure the continuation of their blood and name, and also the strength and the courage necessary to defend their family or preserve the community. Everything was concentrated symbolically on their ability to make use of a pointed weapon. Cruel reprisals were an absolute imperative if an individual's honour was sullied; otherwise, the person insulted was, in a sense, unmanned, and made an object of contempt. This system has by no means wholly disappeared in our own day. It is perpetuated deep at the heart of societies. In nineteenth-century Corsica, a man had only to place his hand on the headdress or face of a woman for this figurative taking of possession to lead to a mortal vendetta. In Calabria today, a man who fails to redress such an affront is dishonoured. To avoid exclusion, he has to '*cacciarsi a ffengia*', that is, to avenge himself to compensate for the disgrace, so as to rid his blood of the venom poisoning it, a metaphor for his unmanning.[5]

The monopolization of violence by the state since the last centuries of the Middle Ages involved the replacement of the vindicatory system, so costly in human life, by the law. This imposed punishments proportionate to the offence and restored honour at a smaller cost to the community, by eliminating or intimidating those who disturbed the internal peace. The system operated increasingly effectively, with the assent of a growing number of adults, happy to observe the pacification of behaviour. The steady decline in the figures for homicide up to the mid twentieth century testifies to this. Yet our civilization has avoided ending up in the position of weakness of the Tarahumaras in the face of their enemies; instead, it has invented the concept of the just war, the only occasion on which killing is legal, even necessary. To be able to appeal, in time of need, to a large number of defenders of the endangered fatherland, states have tried not so much to extinguish the murderous instinct as to deflect it towards sublimated objectives, under their strict control.

There has been no major military conflagration on European soil since 1945. The violence of young Western males is still, nevertheless, systematically driven out of public space. It is probably considerably more inhibited than in the past within the home. The disappearance of legitimate patriotic conflict, marked by the abolition of compulsory military service in many countries, including France in 1997, has taken away the only mass outlet regarded as acceptable by our culture for a youthful belligerence it has never sought to eradicate entirely. This disequilibrium, which has recently become much more pronounced, is probably one of the principal causes, together with unemployment, of a very visible surge of anger among adolescents. The absence of a serious threat of destruction is the backdrop to a return of the repressed in the least privileged sectors of the societies of the Old Continent. The law of vengeance and the cult of manliness have never completely died out. They are now finding a wider sphere of operation to the extent that the intensifying aggression is increasingly directed inwards within the community, in the absence of opportunities to employ it against a pressing external danger. This has caused sport to lose some of the cathartic effectiveness that has characterized it since the nineteenth century. The rise of brutal confrontations between enraged supporters reveals an exultant enjoyment of their masculinity, and also a desire for revenge against the authorities and the codes which force them normally to display it with a restrained politeness.

Have we reached a turning point? Our generally pacified, rich and hedonistic civilization continued until recently to sustain the brutal youthful impulses, by reserving them for warlike confrontations. Will it be able to prevent them from swamping the disinherited margins of the great cities and stadiums, and producing a series of explosions?

NOTES

1. The figures are accepted by all the specialists, although overall expla-
    nations are still at the stage of hypotheses. See Manuel Eisner, 'Long-
    term historical trends in violent crime', *Crime and Justice: A Review
    of Research*, 30 (2003), pp. 83–142 (with full bibliography).
2. Ibid.; see also Jean-Claude Chesnais, *Histoire de la violence en
    Occident de 1800 à nos jours*, rev. and expanded edn (Paris:
    Hachette, 1982) for Europe *c.*1930 (see map on p. 57) and 1978
    (pp. 61–3); Jean-Claude Chesnais, 'Les morts violentes dans le
    monde', *Population et Sociétés*, 395 (November 2003), pp. 2–7,
    especially p. 3 (homicide rate in 2000: highest in Colombia, at 60.8,
    followed by Russia; the rate in the United States was 6.2, in Canada
    1.5, in France 0.7 and in Japan 0.6).
3. See below, ch. 1.
4. Norbert Elias, *The Civilizing Process* [1939], trans. E. Jephcott
    (Oxford: Blackwell, 1978).

1. Manuel Eisner, 'Long-term historical trends in violent crime', *Crime
    and Justice: A Review of Research*, 30 (2003), pp. 83–142, espe-
    cially pp. 122–3.
2. Laurent Mucchielli, *Violences et insécurité: fantasmes et réalités
    dans le débat français* (Paris: La Découverte, 2001; new edn 2002).
3. Sigmund Freud, *Civilization and its Discontents*, trans. Joan
    Rivière, new edn James Strachey (London: Hogarth Press and
    Institute of Psycho-analysis, 1963); Erich Fromm, *The Heart of*

Man: Its Genius for Good and Evil (New York and London: Harper and Row, 1980) (see also *The Anatomy of Human Destructiveness* [London: Cape, 1974; Harmondsworth: Penguin, 1977]); Daniel Sibony, *Violence* (Paris: Seuil, 1998); Boris Cyrulnik, *Mémoire de singe et parole d'homme* (Paris: Hachette, 1983); Boris Cyrulnik, *La Naissance du sens* (Paris: Hachette, 1995). See also Robert Muchembled, 'Anthropologie de la violence dans la France moderne (XVe–XVIIIe siècle)', *Revue de synthèse*, 108, gen. ser. (1987), pp. 31–3; Véronique Le Goaziou, *La Violence* (Paris: Le Cavalier Bleu, 2004), pp. 26–7.

4. Konrad Lorenz, *On Aggression*, trans. Marjorie Latzke (London: Methuen, 1966; rev. edn London: Routledge, 1996).

5. Author of the *Leviathan* (1651).

6. René Girard, *Violence and the Sacred*, trans. Patrick Gregory (Baltimore, MD: Johns Hopkins University Press, 1977), pp. 20, 259.

7. Henri Laborit, *L'Agressivité détourné: introduction à une biologie du comportement social* (Paris: Union Génerale d'Éditions, 1970), esp. pp. 137, 175–9. Desmond Morris, too, sees the imperative of the survival of the species as vital for 'the naked ape': Desmond Morris, *The Human Sexes: A Natural History of Man and Woman* (London: Network Books, 1997).

8. Edward Twitchell Hall, *The Hidden Dimension: Man's Use of Space in Public and Private* (NewYork: Anchor Books, Doubleday, 1969).

9. Alan D. Berkowitz, 'The social norms approach to violence prevention', article on the author's website (www.alanberkowitz.com).

10. Gustave Le Bon, *The Crowd: A Study of the Popular Mind* (London: Ernest Benn, 20th edn, 1952).

11. Alain Vernet and Franck Henry, with Cyril Boutet and Abdeenour Chalal, 'Contribution à la compréhension des comportements agressifs et violents', *Le Journal des psychologues*, 241 (Oct. 2006), pp. 60–1. Experiments on animals that live in organized societies have emphasized the development of a pathological aggression in conditions of overpopulation, even when they are well fed: Hall, *The Hidden Dimension*, pp. 39–60.

12. *Traité de Luís Fróis, s.j. (1585) sur les contradictions de moeurs entre Européens et Japonais*, trans. from Portuguese by Xavier de Castro (Paris: Editions Chandeigne, 1993), pp. 111–13, 117.

13. Yves Michaud, *La Violence* (Paris: PUF, 1986), p. 37 ('The violence of life').

14. Le Goaziou, *La Violence*, p. 81. In thirteenth-century England, 90 per cent of those who committed murder were men: James

Buchanan Given, *Society and Homicide in Thirteenth-Century England* (Stanford, CA: Stanford University Press, 1977).

15. James Lee, 'Homicide et peine capitale en Chine à la fin de l'Empire: analyse statistique préliminaire des données', *Etudes chinoises*, 10, 1–2 (1991), pp. 124–5.

16. See the works of Desmond Morris, especially *The Human Sexes*.

17. Françoise Lauwaert, *Le Meurtre en famille: parricide et infanticide en Chine (XVIIIe–XIXe siècles)* (Paris: Odile Jacob, 1999), pp. 21, 26–7, 103, 145, 158–9, 312–15.

18. Michel Foucault, *Discipline and Punish: The Birth of the Prison*, trans. Alan Sheridan (New York: Vintage, 1977).

19. See ch. 2 below; also Robert Muchembled, 'Fils de Caïn, enfants de Médée: homicide et infanticide devant le parlement de Paris (1575–1604)', *Annales Histoire, Sciences Sociales*, 72 (2007), pp. 1063–94.

20. Douglas Hay, Peter Linebaugh, John G. Rule, E. P. Thompson and Carl Winslow, *Albion's Fatal Tree: Crime and Society in Eighteenth-Century England* (London: Allen Lane, 1975; repr. Harmondsworth: Penguin, 1977), p. 116; André Abbiateci, François Billacois, Yves Castan, Porphyre Petrovinitch, Yvonne Bongert and Nicole Castan (eds), *Crimes et criminalité en France: XVIIe–XVIIIe siècles* (Paris: Armand Colin, 1971).

21. Bernadette Boutelet, 'Etude par sondage de la criminalité dans le bailliage de Pont-de-l'Arche (XVIIe–XVIIIe siècles): de la violence au vol, en marche vers l'escroquerie', *Annales de Normandie*, 12 (1962), pp. 235–62. The theory was taken up by Pierre Chaunu and his students, then supported in the case of Denmark by Jens C. V. Johansen and Henrik Stevnsborg, 'Hasard ou myopie: réflexions autour de deux théories de l'histoire du droit', *Annales ESC*, 41 (1986), pp. 601–24; it has since been abandoned by the majority of specialists.

22. Charles Petit-Dutaillis, *Documents nouveaux sur les moeurs populaires et le droit de vengeance dans les Pays-Bas au XVe siècle: lettres de rémission de Philippe le Bon* (Paris: Champion, 1908); Robert Muchembled, *La Violence au village (XVe–XVIIe siècle): comportements populaires et mentalités en Artois* (Turnhout: Brepols, 1989), esp. pp. 221–47 on young people. See also ch. 3 below.

23. Shani D'Cruze, Sandra Walklate and Samantha Pegg, *Murder: Social and Historical Approaches to Understanding Murder and Murderers* (Cullompton: Willan, 2006), pp. 14–17; Fiona Brookman, *Understanding Homicide* (London: Sage, 2005), pp. 34–5 for the ages of the accused and their victims.

24. Brookman, *Understanding Homicide*, pp. 309–10.

25. Antoine Garapon, *L'Ane portant des reliques: essai sur le rituel judiciaire* (Paris: Le Centurion, 1985), pp. 145, 159.

26. Robert Muchembled, *Orgasm and the West: A History of Pleasure from the Sixteenth Century to the Present*, trans. Jean Birrell (Cambridge: Polity, 2008).

27. Graham J. Barker-Benfield, *The Culture of Sensibility: Sex and Society in Eighteenth-Century Britain* (Chicago and London: University of Chicago Press, 1992, repr. 1996), esp. pp. 37–103.

28. Martin J. Wiener, 'The Victorian criminalization of men', in Pieter Spierenburg (ed.), *Men and Violence: Gender, Honor, and Rituals in Modern Europe and America* (Columbus: Ohio State University Press, 1998), pp. 198–203, 209; Martin J. Wiener, *Men of Blood: Violence, Manliness, and Criminal Justice in Victorian England* (Cambridge: Cambridge University Press, 2004).

29. D'Cruze et al., *Murder*, pp. 40–1, 79 for a summary of various works, and pp. 149, 157 for the concept of 'hegemonic masculinity'.

30. Marie-Elizabeth Handman, 'L'Enfer et le Paradis? Violence et tyrannie douce en Grèce contemporaine', in Cécile Dauphin and Arlette Farge (eds), *De la violence et des femmes* (Paris: Pocket, 1999), pp. 128–9.

31. See ch. 4 below.

32. Muchembled, *La Violence au village*, esp. pp. 39–42.

33. Ibid., pp. 43–5. For Mediterranean societies, see John G. Peristiany (ed.), *Honour and Shame: The Values of Mediterranean Society* (London: Weidenfeld and Nicolson, 1965); Raymond Verdier (ed.), *Vengeance: le face-à-face victime/aggresseur* (Paris: Autrement, 2004), pp. 10, 18–19.

34. Nello Zagnoli, 'S'arracher la haine', in Verdier, *Vengeance*, p. 119.

35. See ch. 3 below.

36. Norbert Elias, *The Civilizing Process* [1939], trans. E. Jephcott (Oxford: Blackwell, 1978); Norbert Elias, *The Court Society* [1969], trans. E. Jephcott (Oxford: Blackwell, 1983).

37. Elias, *The Civilizing Process*; and the discussion in Manuel Eisner, 'Long-term historical trends in violent crime', pp. 123–5.

38. Peter Schuster, *Eine Stadt vor Gericht: Recht und Alltag im spätmittelalterlichen Konstanz* (Paderborn: Schöning, 2000).

39. Dag Lindström, 'Interpersonal violence in Scandinavia: interpretation of long-term trends', paper presented at the third GERN Seminar, 'Violence in history: long-term trends and the role of wars', Brussels, 3–4 December 2004, pp. 12–14; Heikki Ylikangas, 'What happened to violence? An analysis of the development of violence from medieval times to the early modern era based on Finnish source material', in Heikki Ylikangas, Petri Karonen and

Martti Lehti (eds), *Five Centuries of Violence in Finland and the Baltic Area* (Columbus: Ohio State University Press, 2001), pp. 78–83.

40. Ylikangas, 'What happened to violence?'.
41. Gerd Schwerhoff, *Köln im Kreuzverhör: Kriminalität, Herrschaft und Gesellschaft in einer frühneuzeitlichen Stadt* (Bonn: Bouvier, 1991), p. 61.
42. Randolph Roth, 'Homicide in Early Modern England, 1549–1800: the need for a quantitative synthesis', *Crime, Histoire et Sociétés/ Crime, History and Societies*, 5, 2 (2001), p. 55; Peter Blastenbrei, *Kriminalität in Rom, 1560–1585* (Tübingen: Niemeyer, 1995), p. 284.
43. Max Weber, *The Protestant Ethic and the Spirit of Capitalism* [1904–5], trans. Talcott Parsons (Oxford: Blackwell, 2002).
44. John H. Langbein, *Torture and the Law of Proof: Europe and England in the Ancien Régime* (Chicago: University of Chicago Press, 1977).
45. Muchembled, 'Fils de Caïn, enfants de Médée', p. 1079.
46. Xavier Rousseaux, 'From case to crime: homicide regulation in medieval and modern Europe', in Dietmar Willoweit (ed.), *Die Entstehung des öffentliche Strafrechts: Bestandsaufnahme eines europäischen Forschungsproblem* (Cologne: Böhlau, 1999), p. 157.
47. See, among others, Heinz Schilling, *Religion, Political Culture and the Emergence of Early Modern Society* (Leiden: Brill, 1992).
48. Gerhard Oestreich, *Neostoicism and the Early Modern State* (Cambridge: Cambridge University Press, 1982); Robert Muchembled, *Popular Culture and Elite Culture in France, 1400–1750*, trans. Lydia Cochrane (Baton Rouge and London: Louisiana State University Press, 1985), pp. 167–70, on the prohibitions affecting young people in the Catholic Low Countries.
49. Robert Muchembled, *La Société policée: politique et politesse en France du XVIe au XXe siècle* (Paris: Seuil, 1998), pp. 77–122.
50. Emile Durkheim, *Suicide: A Study in Sociology* [1897], trans. John A. Spaulding and George Simpson (Glencoe, IL: Free Press, 1951; London: Routledge and Kegan Paul, 1952; repr. London: Routledge, 1989). See also Petit-Dutaillis, *Documents nouveaux sur les moeurs populaires*; Helmut Thome, 'Explaining long-term trends in violent crime', *Crime, Histoire et Sociétés/Crime, History and Societies*, 5, 2 (2001), pp. 69–87.
51. Robert Muchembled, *Le Temps des supplices: de l'obéissance sous les rois absolus, XVe–XVIIIe siècle* (Paris: Armand Colin, 1992; repr. Agora, 2006), p. 57; Lindström, 'Interpersonal violence in

Scandinavia'; Eva Osterberg, 'Criminality, social control and the early modern state: evidence and interpretations in Scandinavian historiography', *Social Science History*, 16 (1992), pp. 76–84; John Braithwaite, *Crime, Shame, and Reintegration* (Cambridge: Cambridge University Press, 1989).

52. Osterberg, 'Criminality, social control and the early modern state', pp. 91–3; Lindström, 'Interpersonal violence in Scandinavia', who refers to the works of Erling Sandmo for Norway after 1600 and those of Jens C. V. Johansen for seventeenth-century Denmark.

53. François Billacois and Hugues Neveux (eds), 'Porter plainte: stratégies villageoises et justice en Ile-de-France', *Droit et culture*, 19 (1990), pp. 5–148.

54. Lindström, 'Interpersonal violence in Scandinavia', p. 13, quoting the works of Hans Henrik Appel and Jens C. V. Johansen.

55. Ibid., p. 14, quoting the works of Lars Geschwind.

CHAPTER 2

1. See ch. 4 below.

2. See chs 5 and 7 below.

3. Bernard Guenée, *Tribunaux et gens de justice dans le bailliage de Senlis à la fin du Moyen Age* (Strasbourg: Publications de la Faculté des Lettres, 1963), pp. 277–94.

4. Claude Gauvard, *'De grace especial': crime, État et société en France à la fin du Moyen Age* (Paris: Publications de la Sorbonne, 1991), vol. 1, pp. 61–2, 65. The *rémissions* are in Series JJ of the Archives Nationales in Paris.

5. Delphine Brihat, 'La criminalité pardonnée dans le ressort du parlement de Paris en 1525', mémoire de maîtrise (under the supervision of Robert Muchembled), University of Paris-Nord, 1999, p. 172.

6. Jacques Dupâquier (ed.), *Histoire de la population française*, vol. 2: *De la Renaissance à 1789* (Paris: PUF, 1988), for a classic description of the French model.

7. Jean-Louis Flandrin, *Les Amours paysannes: amour et sexualité dans les campagnes de l'ancienne France (XVIe–XIXe siècles)* (Paris: Gallimard-Julliard, 1975). The question is summarized in Robert Muchembled, *Orgasm and the West: A History of Pleasure from the Sixteenth Century to the Present*, trans. Jean Birrell (Cambridge: Polity, 2008), pp. 25–7.

8. Rudy Chaulet, 'La violence en Castile au XVIIe siècle d'après les *Indultos de Viernes Santo* (1623–1699)', *Crime, Histoire et Sociétés/ Crime, History and Societies*, 1, 2 (1997), pp. 7, 17.
9. Robert Muchembled, *La Violence au village (XVe–XVIIe siècle): comportements populaires et mentalités en Artois* (Turnhout: Brepols, 1989), pp. 11, 16, 19–20.
10. Robert Muchembled, 'Violence et société: comportements et mentalités populaires en Artois (1400–1660)', thèse de doctorat d'état (under the supervision of Pierre Goubert), University of Paris I, 3 vols, 1985 (copy deposited in the library of the Sorbonne), vol. 1, table on p. 132 and graph on pp. 168–9.
11. Ibid., pp. 190–200.
12. Ibid., pp. 248–59.
13. See ch. 3 below.
14. Robert Muchembled, *Le Temps des supplices: de l'obéissance sous les rois absolus, XVe–XVIIIe siècle* (Paris: Armand Colin, 1992; repr. Agora, 2006), pp. 129–37.
15. Muchembled, 'Violence et société', vol. 1, pp. 192, 196–7.
16. For urban privileges, see ch. 4 below.
17. Muchembled, *Le Temps des supplices*, pp. 134–42.
18. Pieter Spierenburg, 'Long-term trends in homicide: theoretical reflections and Dutch evidence, fifteenth to twentieth centuries', in Eric A. Johnson and Eric H. Monkkonen (eds), *The Civilization of Crime: Violence in Town and Country since the Middle Ages* (Urbana: University of Illinois Press, 1996), p. 80.
19. Eric H. Monkkonen, 'New standards for historical homicide research', *Crime, Histoire et Sociétés/Crime, History and Societies*, 5, 2 (2001), pp. 7–26.
20. Ted Robert Gurr, 'Historical trends in violent crime: a critical review of the evidence', in Michael Tonry and Norval Morris (eds), *Crime and Justice: An Annual Review of Research,* vol. 3 (Chicago: University of Chicago Press, 1981), pp. 295–353. His curve (p. 313) was taken up by many scholars, including Lawrence Stone, 'Interpersonal violence in English society, 1300–1800', *Past and Present*, 101 (1983), pp. 22–33, and provoked fierce debate in England.
21. Gurr, 'Historical trends in violent crime', p. 295.
22. James S. Cockburn, 'Patterns of violence in English society: homicide in Kent 1560–1985', *Past and Present*, 130 (1991), pp. 70–106; for Amsterdam, Spierenburg, 'Long-term trends in homicide'.
23. Manuel Eisner, 'Long-term historical trends in violent crime', *Crime and Justice: A Review of Research*, 30 (2003), pp. 83–142, esp. pp. 95–8.

24. Randolph Roth, 'Homicide in Early Modern England, 1550–1800: the need for a quantitative synthesis', *Crime, Histoire et Sociétés/ Crime, History and Societies*, 5, 2 (2001), pp. 33–67.

25. Max Weber, *The Protestant Ethic and the Spirit of Capitalism* [1904–5], trans. Talcott Parsons (Oxford: Blackwell, 2002).

26. Eric H. Monkkonen, *Crime, Justice, History* (Columbus: Ohio State University Press, 2002), figures 10.1, 10.2.

27. Eisner, 'Long-term historical trends in violent crime', pp. 109–12 for women and pp. 112–15 for age groups. One of the few books to have taken account of this criterion for an earlier period is: Peter King, *Crime, Justice and Discretion in England, 1740–1820* (Oxford: Oxford University Press, 2000), p. 169.

28. Eisner, 'Long-term historical trends in violent crime', p. 117; Pieter Spierenburg, 'Knife fighting and popular codes of honor in early modern Amsterdam', in Pieter Spierenburg (ed.), *Men and Violence: Gender, Honor, and Rituals in Modern Europe and America* (Columbus: Ohio State University Press, 1998), pp. 103–27; James A. Sharpe, *Crime in Early Modern England, 1550–1750* (London: Longman, 1984), p. 95.

29. See ch. 4 below.

30. Robert Muchembled, 'Fils de Caïn, enfants de Médée: homicide et infanticide devant le parlement de Paris (1575–1604)', *Annales Histoire, Sciences Sociales*, 72 (2007), pp. 1063–94; Heikki Ylikangas, 'What happened to violence? An analysis of the development of violence from medieval times to the early modern era based on Finnish source material', in Heikki Ylikangas, Petri Karonen and Martti Lehti (eds), *Five Centuries of Violence in Finland and the Baltic Area* (Columbus: Ohio State University Press, 2001), pp. 46–7.

31. Norbert Elias, *The Civilizing Process* [1939], trans. E. Jephcott (Oxford: Blackwell, 1978).

32. Eisner, 'Long-term historical trends in violent crime', for European comparisons.

33. Ibid., p. 121; Spierenburg, 'Knife fighting and popular codes of honor'; Ylikangas, 'What happened to violence?', pp. 64–5.

34. Manuel Eisner, 'Crime, problem drinking, and drug use: patterns of problem behavior in cross-national perspective', *Annals of the American Academy of Political and Social Science*, 580 (2002), pp. 201–25.

35. Petri Karonen, 'A life for a life versus Christian reconciliation: violence and the process of civilization in the kingdom of Sweden, 1540–1700', in Ylikangas et al., *Five Centuries of Violence in Finland and the Baltic Area*, pp. 85–132.

CHAPTER 3

1. Xavier Rousseaux, 'La répression de l'homicide en Europe occidentale (Moyen Age et Temps modernes)', *Genèses: Sciences sociales et histoire*, 19 (April 1995), pp. 122–47, for an overview of this subject.

2. Bronislaw Geremek, 'Criminalité, vagabondage, paupérisme: la marginalité à l'aube des temps modernes', *Revue d'histoire moderne et contemporaine*, 21 (1974), pp. 339–40.

3. Archives départementales, Arras, A 870, 7 March 1328 (n. st.) to 12 December 1328; my thanks to Bernard Delmaire for drawing my attention to this.

4. Georges Espinas, *Recueil de documents relatifs à l'histoire du droit municipal en France des origines à la Révolution: Artois* (Paris: Recueil Sirey, 1934), vol. 1, no. 106 (*keure* of Arques granted by the abbot of Saint-Bertin, Guillaume Fillastre, lord of Arques, 6 January 1469).

5. James Buchanan Given, *Society and Homicide in Thirteenth-Century England* (Stanford, CA: Stanford University Press, 1977), pp. 12–14.

6. Ibid., pp. 92–3.

7. Rousseaux, 'La répression de l'homicide en Europe occidentale', p. 130.

8. Given, *Society and Homicide in Thirteenth-Century England*, pp. 41–3, 56–7, 62–3.

9. Ibid., pp. 136–7, 144–5.

10. Ibid., pp. 174–5.

11. Ibid., pp. 188–9, 198–9, 213.

12. Mikhaïl Bakhtin, *Rabelais and his World*, trans. Helen Iswolsky (Cambridge, MA: MIT Press, 1968; repr. Bloomington: Indiana University Press, 1984).

13. Robert Muchembled, *Société, cultures et mentalités dans la France moderne: XVIe–XVIIIe siècle* (Paris: Armand Colin, 1994; rev. and corrected edn, 2003), pp. 94–103 (see, in particular, the calendar, p. 103); Julius R. Ruff, *Violence in Early Modern Europe, 1500–1800* (Cambridge: Cambridge University Press, 2001) (pp. 163–6 for European comparisons).

14. Muchembled, *Société, cultures et mentalités*, pp. 46–56 (marriage and sexuality), 87–93 (kingdoms of youth).

15. Robert Muchembled, *Orgasm and the West: A History of Pleasure from the Sixteenth Century to the Present*, trans. Jean Birrell (Cambridge: Polity, 2008). See also Jean-Louis Flandrin, *Les Amours paysannes: amour et sexualité dans les campagnes de*

l'ancienne France (XVIe–XIXe siècles) (Paris: Gallimard-Julliard, 1975) and, for England, Geoffrey Robert Quaife, *Wanton Wenches and Wayward Wives: Peasants and Illicit Sex in Early Seventeenth-Century England* (London: Croom Helm, 1979).

16. Natalie Zemon Davis, *Society and Culture in Early Modern France: Eight Essays* (London: Duckworth, 1975; Stanford, CA: Stanford University Press, 1975; repr. Cambridge: Polity, 1987), 'The Reasons of Misrule', pp. 97–123.

17. Ignace de Coussemaker, *Cartulaire de l'abbaye de Cysoing et de ses dépendances* (Lille: Imprimerie Saint-Augustin, 1884), pp. 554–6.

18. François Lebrun, *La Vie conjugale sous l'Ancien Régime* (Paris: Armand Colin, 1975), pp. 9–55 (for information about marriage).

19. Robert Muchembled, *La Violence au village (XVe–XVIIe siècle): comportements populaires et mentalités en Artois* (Turnhout: Brepols, 1989), esp. pp. 60–105 for the following paragraphs.

20. Stuart Carroll, *Blood and Violence in Early Modern France* (Oxford and New York: Oxford University Press, 2006), pp. 121–4.

21. Muchembled, *La Violence au village*, pp. 200–21 for the inn and drinking habits.

22. Pierre de Vaissière, *Gentilshommes campagnards de l'ancienne France: étude sur les conditions, l'état social et les moeurs de la noblesse de province du XVIe au XVIIIe siècle* (Paris: Perrin, 1903), pp. 114, 117, 126–7, 129–30 (the author ignores both the precise dates and the ages of those concerned).

23. Clifford Geertz, *The Interpretation of Culture: Selected Essays* (New York: Basic Books, 1973), 'Deep Play', pp. 412–53. See also Ruff, *Violence in Early Modern Europe*, pp. 160–83, in particular on the violent European games with animals.

24. Robert C. Davis, *The War of the Fists: Popular Culture and Public Violence in Late Renaissance Venice* (Oxford and New York: Oxford University Press, 1994). See also Edward Muir, *Ritual in Early Modern Europe* (Cambridge: Cambridge University Press, 1997).

25. Timothy Mitchell, *Blood Sport: A Social History of Spanish Bull-fighting* (Philadelphia: University of Pennsylvania Press, 1991).

26. Muchembled, *La Violence au village*, esp. pp. 300–1.

27. Abbé C. Dehaisnes, *Inventaire sommaire des archives départementales antérieures à 1789. Nord. Archives civiles, série B. Chambre des comptes de Lille, no 1681 à 1841*, vol. 3 (Lille: Danel, 1877), pp. 254–5.

28. Ibid., pp. 244–5, 304.

29. Paul Griffiths, *Youth and Authority: Formative Experiences in England, 1560–1640* (Oxford: Clarendon Press, 1996), pp. 34–7, quoting English authors of the period and Pierre Charron.

30. Dehaisnes, *Inventaire sommaire des archives départementales antérieures à 1789*, pp. 176, 180, 181, 187, 196.
31. See ch. 2 above for an introduction to the *lettres de rémission*, and the case of Artois. The following examples are taken from Muchembled, 'Violence et société', vol. 1.
32. Martine Segalen, 'Avoir sa part: sibling relations in partible inheritance Brittany', in Hans Medick and David Sabean (eds), *Interest and Emotion: Essays on the Study of Family and Kinship* (Cambridge: Cambridge University Press, 1984), pp. 129–44.
33. See ch. 6 below.
34. Chris Vandenbroeke, 'Het seksuel gedrag der jongeren in Vlaanderen sinds de late 16de eeuw', *Bijdragen tot de geschiedenis*, 72 (1979), pp. 212, 214.
35. Dehaisnes, *Inventaire sommaire des archives départementales antérieures à 1789*, p. 255.
36. Muchembled, *La Violence au village*, pp. 167–83.
37. See ch. 2 above.
38. Robert Muchembled, 'Fils de Caïn, enfants de Médée: homicide et infanticide devant le parlement de Paris (1575–1604)', *Annales Histoire, Sciences Sociales*, 72 (2007), pp. 1063–94.
39. Delphine Brihat, 'La criminalité pardonnée dans le ressort du parlement de Paris en 1525', mémoire de maîtrise (under the supervision of Robert Muchembled), University of Paris-Nord, 1999, esp. pp. 40–3, 61, 142, 249, 263, 282, 290.
40. Isabelle Paresys, *Aux marges du royaume: violence, justice et société en Picardie sous François Ier* (Paris: Publications de la Sorbonne, 1998), p. 42; Gregory Hanlon, 'Les rituels de l'agression en Aquitaine au XVIIe siècle', *Annales ESC*, 40 (1985), p. 246.

CHAPTER 4

1. Robert Muchembled, *Le Temps des supplices: de l'obéissance sous les rois absolus, XVe–XVIIIe siècle* (Paris: Armand Colin, 1992; repr. Agora, 2006), pp. 27–31.
2. Gérard Jugnot, 'Les pèlerinages expiatoires et judiciaires au Moyen Age', in *La Faute, la Répression et le Pardon*, Actes du 107e congrès national des sociétés savantes, Brest, 1982, Section de philologie et d'histoire jusqu'à 1610, vol. 1 (Paris, CTHS, 1984), pp. 413–20. See also Xavier Rousseaux, 'La répression de l'homicide en Europe occidentale (Moyen Age et temps modernes)', *Genèses: Sciences sociales et histoire*, 19 (April 1995), pp. 132–3.

3. Charles Petit-Dutaillis, *Documents nouveaux sur les moeurs populaires et le droit de vengeance dans les Pays-Bas au XVe siècle: lettres de rémission de Philippe le Bon* (Paris: Champion, 1908), pp. 54–9; Claude Gauvard, *'De grace especial': crime, Etat et société en France à la fin du Moyen Age* (Paris: Publications de la Sorbonne, 1991), vol. 2, p. 779; Nicole Gonthier, *Cris de haine et rites d'unité: la violence dans les villes, XIIIe–XVIe siècle* (Turnhout: Brepols, 1992), p. 160.

4. J. A. Goris, 'Zeden en criminaliteit te Antwerpen in de tweede helft van de XIVe eeuw, naar de rekeningen der schouten van 1358 tot 1387', *Revue belge de philologie et d'histoire*, 5 (1926), pp. 871–86; 6 (1927), pp. 181–205. For comparisons, see Gonthier, *Cris de haine et rites d'unité*.

5. David M. Nicholas, 'Crime and punishment in fourteenth-century Ghent', *Revue belge de philologie et d'histoire*, 48 (1970), pp. 289–334, 1141–76.

6. Esther Cohen, ' "To die a criminal for the public good": the execution ritual in late medieval Paris', in Bernard S. Bachrach and David Nicholas (eds), *Law, Custom, and the Social Fabric in Medieval Europe: Essays in Honor of Bryce Lyon* (Kalamazoo: Medieval Institute Publications, Western Michigan University, 1990), pp. 298–9.

7. Yvonne Lanhers, 'Crimes et criminels au XIVe siècle', *Revue historique*, 240 (1968), pp. 325–38.

8. Archives Municipales of Arras, BB 38 (1405–1495), BB 39 (1423–1449), town police ordinances.

9. Muchembled, *Le Temps des supplices*, pp. 151–7.

10. Archives Municipales of Arras, BB 38, fols 101r, 114r, 136v; BB 39, fols 1r, 24v–25r.

11. Bronislaw Geremek, 'Criminalité, vagabondage, paupérisme: la marginalité à l'aube des temps modernes', *Revue d'histoire moderne et contemporaine*, 21 (1974) , pp. 337–75; Bronislaw Geremek, *Truands et misérables dans l'Europe moderne (1350–1600)* (Paris: Gallimard-Julilard, 1980); Jean-Pierre Gutton, *La Société et les pauvres en Europe (XVIe–XVIIIe siècle)* (Paris: PUF, 1974).

12. Norbert Elias, *The Civilizing Process* [1939], trans. E. Jephcott (Oxford: Blackwell, 1978); Norbert Elias, *La Dynamique de l'Occident* (Paris: Calmann-Lévy, 1975); Norbert Elias, *The Court Society* [1969], trans. E. Jephcott (Oxford: Blackwell, 1983).

13. Max Weber, *The Protestant Ethic and the Spirit of Capitalism* [1904–5], trans. Talcott Parsons (Oxford: Blackwell, 2002).

14. Erasmus, *On Good Manners for Boys/De civilitate morum puerilium*, trans. Brian McGregor, in *Collected Works of Erasmus*, ed. J. K. Sowards (Toronto and London: University of Toronto Press, 1985), ch. 1.

15. Daniela Romagnoli (ed.), *La Ville et la Cour: des bonnes et des mauvaises manières* (Paris: Fayard, 1995), 'La courtoisie dans la ville', pp. 58–9, 74–5.

16. Robert Muchembled, *Orgasm and the West: A History of Pleasure from the Sixteenth Century to the Present*, trans. Jean Birrell (Cambridge: Polity, 2008), for the sublimation of the erotic desires as hidden motor of Western dynamism.

17. Marc Boone, ' "Le tres fort, vilain et detestable criesme et pechié de zodomie": homosexualité et répression à Bruges pendant la période bourguignonne (fin XIVe–début XVIe siècle)', in Hugo Soly and René Vermeir (eds), *Belied en bestuur in de oude Nederlanden: Liber Amicorum Prof. Dr. M. Baelde* (Ghent: Vakgroep Nieuwe Geschiedenis UG, 1993), pp. 2–17.

18. Michael Roecke, *Forbidden Friendships: Homosexuality and Male Culture in Renaissance Florence* (Oxford: Oxford University Press, 1996).

19. Jacques Rossiaud, *La Prostitution médiévale* (Paris: Flammarion, 1988), pp. 26–7, 33–6; Jacques Rossiaud, 'Fraternités de jeunesse et niveaux de culture dans les villes du Sud-Est à la fin du Moyen Age', *Cahiers d'histoire*, 21 (1976), pp. 67–102.

20. Rossiaud, 'Fraternités de jeunesse et niveaux de culture', pp. 87, 90, 101.

21. Natalie Zemon Davis, *Society and Culture in Early Modern France: Eight Essays* (London: Duckworth, 1975; Stanford, CA: Stanford University Press, 1975; repr. Cambridge: Polity, 1987), 'The Reasons of Misrule', pp. 97–123. See also Jean-Baptiste Lucotte Du Tilliot, *Mémoires pour servir à l'histoire de la fête des foux* (Lausanne and Geneva: 1751), especially on the 'Mother Fool' of Dijon, pp. 80–181; Julius R. Ruff, *Violence in Early Modern Europe, 1500–1800* (Cambridge: Cambridge University Press, 2001), pp. 178–9.

22. Archives Municipales of Arras, fiches Guesnon: police morals, theatrical games (including copies of lost documents for 1533–4) and BB 38, fols 144r-145r, 5 February 1494 (n. st.).

23. Valérie Delay, 'Les fêtes à Lille au XVIe siècle', mémoire de maîtrise (under the supervision of Robert Muchembled), University of Lille III, 1984, pp. 161–2. The following information about Lille is also taken from this excellent study.

24. Ibid., p. 253.

25. See below, 'Violence costs dear'.
26. Delay, 'Les fêtes à Lille au XVIe siècle', p. 150.
27. Ibid., esp. 'Men and the festival', pp. 49–87.
28. Petit-Dutaillis, *Documents nouveaux sur les moeurs populaires*, pp. 59, 90–1.
29. Muchembled, *Le Temps des supplices*, pp. 79–91 for Jacques du Clercq.
30. Ibid., pp. 34–57, 357–61 for the fines, pp. 58–68 for the Arras prison.
31. For the years 1401–11, 1415–19, 1424–36, 1441–6, 1451–4, 1461–75, 1494–7 and 1498–1500.
32. Muchembled, *Le Temps des supplices*, pp. 37–8; see also Xavier Rousseaux, 'Taxer ou châtier? L'émergence du pénal: enquête sur la justice nivelloise (1400–1660)', unpublished thesis, University of Louvain-la-Neuve, 1990.
33. Michel Mollat and Philippe Wolff, *The Popular Revolutions of the Late Middle Ages*, trans. A. L. Lytton-Sells (London: Allen and Unwin, 1973).

CHAPTER 5

1. See ch. 3 above.
2. See chs 7 and 9 below.
3. Stefan Brakensiek, 'Peut-on parler d'absolutisme dans l'Allemagne moderne? Une domination désireuse d'être acceptée (*Akzeptanz-orientierte Herrschaft*)', *Bulletin d'information de la Mission historique française en Allemagne*, 42 (2006), pp. 255–6.
4. Michel Foucault, *Discipline and Punish: The Birth of the Prison*, trans. Alan Sheridan (New York: Vintage, 1977).
5. Brakensiek, 'Peut-on parler d'absolutisme dans l'Allemagne moderne?', pp. 257–63.
6. See ch. 4 above.
7. Bernard Schnapper, *Voies nouvelles en histoire du droit: la justice, la famille, la répression pénale (XVIe–XXe siècle)* (Paris: PUF, 1991), 'La répression pénale au XVIe siècle: l'exemple du parlement de Bordeaux (1510–1565)', p. 74.
8. Emile Durkheim, *Leçons de sociologie: physique des moeurs et du droit* (Paris: PUF, 1950), pp. 143, 147.
9. There is a good summary of this question in Xavier Rousseaux, 'La répression de l'homicide en Europe occidentale (Moyen Age et temps modernes)', *Genèses: Sciences sociales et histoire*, 19 (April 1995). See also James S. Cockburn, 'Patterns of violence in

English society: homicide in Kent 1560–1985', *Past and Present*, 130 (1991), p. 90.

10. Schnapper, *Voies nouvelles en histoire du droit*, pp. 63, 90–3, 100, 105.

11. Robert Muchembled, 'Fils de Caïn, enfants de Médée: homicide et infanticide devant le parlement de Paris (1575–1604)', *Annales Histoire, Sciences Sociales*, 72 (2007), pp. 1063–94.

12. Petri Karonen, 'A life for a life versus Christian reconciliation: violence and the process of civilization in the kingdom of Sweden, 1540–1700', in Heikki Ylikangas, Petri Karonen and Martti Lehti (eds), *Five Centuries of Violence in Finland and the Baltic Area* (Columbus: Ohio State University Press, 2001), pp. 85–132; Heikki Ylikangas, 'What happened to violence? An analysis of the development of violence from medieval times to the early modern era based on Finnish source material', in Ylikangas et al., *Five Centuries of Violence in Finland and the Baltic Area*, pp. 78–83. For upper-class violence, see ch. 6 below.

13. Tomas A. Mantecón, 'Long-term trend of crime in Early Modern Castile', paper presented at the third GERN seminar, 'Violence in history: long-term trends and the role of wars', Brussels, 3–4 December 2004, p. 137.

14. Rousseaux, 'La répression de l'homicide en Europe occidentale', p. 137.

15. See François Billacois and Hugues Neveux (eds), 'Porter plainte: stratégies villageoises et justice en Ile-de-France', *Droit et culture*, 19 (1990), pp. 5–148.

16. Alfred Soman, *Sorcellerie et justice criminelle: le parlement de Paris, XVIe–XVIIIe siècle* (Aldershot: Variorum, 1992), 'Pathologie historique: le témoignage des procès de bestialité aux XVIe–XVIIe siècles', pp. 149–61.

17. Bronislaw Geremek, 'Criminalité, vagabondage, paupérisme: la marginalité à l'aube des temps modernes', *Revue d'histoire moderne et contemporaine*, 21 (1974), pp. 337–75.

18. See ch. 6 below.

19. Julius R. Ruff, *Violence in Early Modern Europe, 1500–1800* (Cambridge: Cambridge University Press, 2001), pp. 84–5; Julius R. Ruff, *Crime, Justice, and Public Order in Old Regime France: The Sénéchaussées of Libourne and Bazas, 1696–1789* (London: Croom Helm, 1984); Billacois and Neveux, 'Porter plainte', p. 8.

20. Ruff, *Violence in Early Modern Europe*, pp. 86–7; Robert Muchembled, *La Sorcière au village (XVe–XVIIIe siècle)* (Paris: Gallimard-Julliard, 1975; new edn Gallimard, 1991), pp. 246–56,

for the pressures exerted on justice to act against local witches by the 'better part' of the village communities.

21. Ruff, *Violence in Early Modern Europe*, pp. 87–92; Alan Williams, *The Police of Paris, 1718–1789* (Baton Rouge: Louisiana State University Press, 1979); Elaine Reynolds, *Before the Bobbies: The Night Watch and Police Reform in Metropolitan London, 1720–1830* (Stanford, CA: Stanford University Press, 1998).

22. John H. Langbein, *Torture and the Law of Proof: Europe and England in the Ancien Régime* (Chicago: University of Chicago Press, 1977).

23. Bernard Schnapper, *Les Peines arbitraires du XIIIe au XVIIIe siècle (doctrines savantes et usages français)* (Paris: LGDJ, 1974).

24. Lisa Silverman, *Tortured Subjects: Pain, Truth, and the Body in Early Modern France* (Chicago: University of Chicago Press, 2001).

25. Schnapper, *Voies nouvelles en histoire du droit*, 'La justice criminelle rendue par le parlement de Paris sous la règne de François Ier', pp. 115–16.

26. Soman, *Sorcellerie et justice criminelle*, 'La justice criminelle aux XVIe et XVIIe siècles: le parlement de Paris et les sièges subalternes', pp. 43–4.

27. Ruff, *Violence in Early Modern Europe*, pp. 94–5 century. For Toulouse, see Silverman, *Tortured Subjects*.

28. Robert Muchembled, *Le Temps des supplices: de l'obéissance sous les rois absolus, XVe–XVIIIe siècle* (Paris: Armand Colin, 1992; repr. Agora, 2006).

29. Albéric Allard, *Histoire de la justice criminelle au XVIe siècle* (Ghent: 1868, repub. Aalen: Scienta, 1970), p. 383. See also Adhémar Esmein, *Histoire de la procédure criminelle en France* (Paris: Larose et Farcel, 1882).

30. Richard van Dülmen, *Theatre of Horror: Crime and Punishment in Early Modern Germany* (Cambridge: Polity, 1990); James A. Sharpe, *Crime in Early Modern England, 1550–1750* (London: Longman, 1984); Pieter Spierenburg, *The Spectacle of Suffering: Executions and the Evolution of Repression: From a Preindustrial Metropolis to the European Experience* (Cambridge: Cambridge University Press, 1984), pp. 43, 82, 200–203, 214; Ylikangas, 'What happened to violence?', pp. 33, 46, 51.

31. Claude Le Brun de la Rochette, *Le Procès civil et criminel* (Lyon: 1609), cited in the Rouen edn of François Vaultier of 1661.

32. Maurice Lever, *Canards sanglants: naissance du fait divers* (Paris: Fayard, 1993); Jean-Pierre Seguin, *L'Information en France avant*

le périodique: 517 canards imprimés entre 1529 et 1631 (Paris: Maisonneuve et Larose, 1964).

33. Sergio Poli, *Histoire(s) tragique(s): anthologie/typologie d'un genre littéraire* (Bari: Schena, 1991; Paris: Nizet, 1991); Robert Muchembled, *A History of the Devil from the Middle Ages to the Present*, trans. Jean Birrell (Cambridge: Polity, 2003), ch. 4. See also the anthology edited by Christian Biet, *Théâtre de la cruauté et récits sanglants en France (XVIe–XVIIe siècles)* (Paris: Robert Laffont, 2006), esp. pp. 221–9 on Camus.

34. V. A. C. Gatrell, *The Hanging Tree: Execution and the English People, 1770–1868* (Oxford: Oxford University Press, 1994).

35. Karl Wegert, *Popular Culture, Crime, and Social Control in Eighteenth-Century Württemberg* (Stuttgart: Franz Steiner, 1994), esp. pp. 99–110.

36. Useful summary in Ruff, *Violence in Early Modern Europe*, pp. 102–5; for the Low Countries see Muchembled, *Le Temps des supplices*, pp. 166–76.

37. James A. Sharpe, ' "Last dying speeches": religion, ideology and public execution in seventeenth-century England', *Past and Present*, 107 (1985), pp. 144–67.

38. Robert Muchembled, *Passions de femmes au temps de la Reine Margot, 1553–1615* (Paris: Seuil, 2003), pp. 224–6.

39. Douglas Hay, Peter Linebaugh, John G. Rule, E. P. Thompson and Carl Winslow, *Albion's Fatal Tree: Crime and Society in Eighteenth-Century England* (London: Allen Lane, 1975; repr. Harmondsworth: Penguin, 1977), pp. 112–16.

40. Pascal Bastien, *L'Exécution publique à Paris au XVIIIe siècle: une histoire des rituels judiciares* (Seysel: Champ Vallon, 2006), pp. 144–63.

41. Hay et al., *Albion's Fatal Tree*, p. 117.

42. Muchembled, *Passions de femmes*, pp. 98–101, drawing on Pierre de l'Estoile and the legal documents.

43. Ruff, *Violence in Early Modern Europe*, p. 108.

44. Michel de Montaigne, *The Complete Essays*, trans. M. A. Screech (Harmondsworth: Penguin, 1991), pp. 483–4.

45. Muchembled, *Le Temps des supplices*, pp. 172–6.

46. Schnapper, *Voies nouvelles en histoire du droit*, pp. 92–3, n. 139 and p. 96.

47. Arlette Lebigre, *Les Grand Jours d'Auvergne: désordres et répression au XVIIe siècle* (Paris: Hachette, 1976), especially pp. 134, 139, 153–5. See also Malcolm Greenshields, *An Economy of Violence in Early Modern France: Crime and Justice in the Haute Auvergne, 1587–1664* (University Park: Penn State University

Press, 1994), pp. 219, 229 for the violence of the nobility and p. 241 for death sentences for homicide.

48. François Ploux, *Guerres paysannes en Quercy: violences, concilia-tions et répression pénale dans les campagnes du Lot (1810–1860)* (Paris: La Boutique de l'Histoire, 2002).

49. Mantecón, 'Long-term trend of crime in Early Modern Castile'.

50. Ylikangas, 'What happened to violence?', pp. 58, 65–6; Eva Osterberg, 'Criminality, social control and the early modern state: evidence and interpretations in Scandinavian historiography', *Social Science History*, 16, 1 (1992), pp. 67–98, repr. in Eric A. Johnson and Eric H. Monkkonen (eds), *The Civilization of Crime: Violence in Town and Country since the Middle Ages* (Urbana: University of Illinois Press, 1996), pp. 42, 50–1.

51. Pierre Clément, *La Police de Louis XIV* (Paris: Didier, 2nd edn 1866), pp. 70–1.

52. Ruff, *Violence in Early Modern Europe*, p. 107.

53. See ch. 2 above.

54. Muchembled, *Le Temps des supplices*, pp. 137–42.

55. Pieter Spierenburg, 'Long-term trends in homicide: theoretical reflections and Dutch evidence, fifteenth to twentieth centuries', in Johnson and Monkkonen, *The Civilization of Crime*, p. 159.

56. Hay et al., *Albion's Fatal Tree*, p. 116.

57. Ruff, *Violence in Early Modern Europe*, p. 234.

58. Muchembled, 'Fils de Caïn, enfants de Médée'; see also the last part of the present chapter.

59. Muchembled, 'Fils de Caïn, enfants de Médée', p. 1078; Schnapper, *Voies nouvelles en histoire du droit*, p. 117, for the abandonment of bodily mutilation, already visible by 1545.

60. Schnapper, *Voies nouvelles en histoire du droit*, n. 63, p. 73.

61. Ruff, *Violence in Early Modern Europe*, pp. 110–11.

62. Vanessa McMahon, *Murder in Shakespeare's England* (Hambledon and London: Palgrave Macmillan, 2004), pp. xx–xxii, 71, 109, 181.

63. Muchembled, 'Fils de Caïn, enfants de Médée'.

64. McMahon, *Murder in Shakespeare's England*, p. xx; Ulinka Rublack, *The Crimes of Women in Early Modern Germany* (Oxford: Oxford University Press, 1999), p. 81.

65. Muchembled, 'Fils de Caïn, enfants de Médée'.

66. Ruff, *Violence in Early Modern Europe*, pp. 151–2.

67. Alfred Soman, 'Sorcellerie, justice criminelle et société dans la France moderne: l'ego-histoire d'un Américain à Paris', *Histoire, Économie et Société* (1993), pp. 207–10.

68. Muchembled, 'Fils de Caïn, enfants de Médée'.

69. James R. Farr, *Authority and Sexuality in Early Modern Burgundy (1550–1730)* (Oxford: Oxford University Press, 1995).

70. James A. Sharpe, *Crime in Seventeenth-Century England: A County Study* (Cambridge: Cambridge University Press, 1983), p. 136.

71. Muchembled, 'Fils de Caïn, enfants de Médée'; Farr, *Authority and Sexuality in Early Modern Burgundy*, p. 133 for Burgundy; Annick Tillier, *Des criminelles au village: femmes infanticides en Bretagne (1825–1865)* (Rennes: Presses Universitaires de Rennes, 2001), pp. 122–3, 154, 202, 400.

72. Mark Jackson, *New-Born Child Murder: Women, Illegitimacy and the Courts in Eighteenth-Century England* (Manchester: Manchester University Press, 1996), p. 49.

73. Peter C. Hoffer and N. E. H. Hull, *Murdering Mothers: Infanticide in England and New England, 1558–1803* (New York: New York University Press, 1981), pp. 18–19, 96–7; McMahon, *Murder in Shakespeare's England*, p. 127.

74. Ruff, *Violence in Early Modern Europe*, p. 153; Tillier, *Des criminelles au village*, p. 404.

75. McMahon, *Murder in Shakespeare's England*, p. 130.

76. Hoffer and Hull, *Murdering Mothers*, pp. 28–31, 96–7; Ruff, *Violence in Early Modern Europe*, p. 153.

77. Geoffrey Robert Quaife, *Wanton Wenches and Wayward Wives: Peasants and Illicit Sex in Early Seventeenth-Century England* (London: Croom Helm, 1979), pp. 119–21, 146–58, 171–2.

78. Ibid., pp. 181–3, 186, 249.

79. Biet, *Théâtre de la cruauté et récits sanglants*, 'Médée, caméléon sanglant', pp. 452–8, and for the texts of the stories and *canards* quoted below, pp. 458–505.

80. Ibid., pp. 494–505. See also Lever, *Canards sanglants*; Seguin, *L'Information en France avant le périodique*.

81. Sara F. Matthews-Grieco, *Ange ou diablesse: la représentation de la femme au XVIe siècle* (Paris: Flammarion, 1991).

82. Soman, 'Sorcellerie, justice criminelle et société dans la France moderne', p. 209.

83. Robert Muchembled, *La Société policée: politique et politesse en France du XVIe au XXe siècle* (Paris: Seuil, 1998), pp. 77–122.

84. See ch. 6 below.

85. Ruff, *Violence in Early Modern Europe*, pp. 153–4.

86. Rublack, *The Crimes of Women in Early Modern Germany*, pp. 58–9, 165. For the truth expressed by the body under torture, see Silverman, *Tortured Subjects*.

87. Hoffer and Hull, *Murdering Mothers*, pp. 76–9.

88. Ibid., pp. 86–7; Jackson, *New-Born Child Murder*, p. 273; Soman, 'Sorcellerie, justice criminelle et société dans la France moderne', pp. 207, 210.
89. Tillier, *Des criminelles au village*, pp. 9, 121–2.
90. Gatrell, *The Hanging Tree*, p. 24.

CHAPTER 6

1. See the works of Norbert Elias, especially *La Dynamique de l'Occident* (Paris: Calmann-Lévy, 1975).
2. Lawrence Stone, *The Crisis of the Aristocracy (1558–1641)* (Oxford: Clarendon Press, 1965).
3. Steve Hindle, *The State and Social Change in Early Modern England, c. 1550–1640* (Basingstoke: Palgrave, 2000), pp. 119, 142.
4. See ch. 4 above.
5. By studying only noble violence, isolated from that of the rest of the population, Stuart Carroll, in his *Blood and Violence in Early Modern France* (Oxford and New York: Oxford University Press, 2006), loses the possibility of a correct understanding of the phenomenon. He is taken in by a mythical aristocratic conception of the point of honour, even though it is frequently contradicted by the brutal savagery of the many confrontations he describes.
6. Geoffrey Parker, *The Military Revolution: Military Innovation and the Rise of the West, 1500–1800* (Cambridge: Cambridge University Press, 2nd edn, 1996).
7. See ch. 5 above.
8. André Devyver, *Le Sang épuré: les préjugés de race chez les gentilshommes français de l'Ancien Régime, 1570–1720* (Brussels: Editions de l'Université de Bruxelles, 1973).
9. Carroll, *Blood and Violence in Early Modern France*, pp. 46, 172, 179. He gives a very large number of examples of similar ferocious murderous violence. See also p. 207 for the rarity of executions of noble duellists.
10. See ch. 3 above.
11. François Billacois perfectly captures this French specificity in his *Le Duel dans la société française des XVIe–XVIIe siècles: essai de psychologie historique* (Paris: EHESS, 1986), pp. 31–82 (pp. 21–56 of the English edn). See also Micheline Cuénin, *Le Duel sous l'Ancien Régime* (Paris: Presses de la Renaissance, 1982);

Victor Gordon Kiernan, *The Duel in European History: Honour and the Reign of Aristocracy* (Oxford: Oxford University Press, 1988).

12. Billacois, *Le Duel*, pp. 79–80 (pp. 40–6 of the English edn).
13. Ibid., p. 62 (p. 35 of the English edn).
14. Bibliothèque municipale de Lille, Ms. 510, copy of 'Remarques... de Pierre Desmasures' on the custom of Artois, vol. 6, fols 2564r–2571v.
15. Billacois, *Le Duel*, pp. 42–9, 406 (pp. 21–6 of English edn).
16. Ute Frevert, *Das Duell in der bürgerlichen Gesellschaft* (Munich: Beck, 1996).
17. Heikki Ylikangas, 'What happened to violence? An analysis of the development of violence from medieval times to the early modern era based on Finnish source material', in Heikki Ylikangas, Petri Karonen and Martti Lehti (eds), *Five Centuries of Violence in Finland and the Baltic Area* (Columbus: Ohio State University Press, 2001), pp. 1–83.
18. Billacois, *Le Duel*, pp. 49–59, 407 (pp. 26–33, 407 of English edn).
19. Ibid., p. 56 (p. 27 of English edn).
20. Ibid., p. 83 (p. 49 of English edn).
21. Ibid., p. 115.
22. Carroll, *Blood and Violence in Early Modern France*, p. 259.
23. Billacois, *Le Duel*, pp. 122, 130–5.
24. Ibid., p. 135.
25. Ibid., pp. 247–74 for this very well-documented case (pp. 144–62 of English edn).
26. Ibid., pp. 247, 262–5, 269, 274, 386, 418.
27. Ibid., pp. 348, 351, 386–7, 389, 394–8, for the author's interpretations of the phenomenon.
28. Arlette Jouanna, *Le Devoir de révolte: la noblesse française et la gestation de l'état moderne, 1559–1661* (Paris: Fayard, 1989).
29. Billacois, *Le Duel*, pp. 273, 299, 305, 315.
30. Ibid., pp. 126, 321–2.
31. Quoted in Pascal Brioist, Hervé Drévillon and Pierre Serna, *Croiser le fer: violence et culture de l'épée dans la France moderne, XVIe–XVIIIe siècle* (Seyssel: Champ Vallon, 2002), p. 12. The new use of the rapier to kill is discussed on pp. 53ff.
32. Ibid., pp. 36–7.
33. See ch. 3 above.
34. Isabelle Paresys, *Aux marges du royaume: violence, justice et société en Picardie sous François Ier* (Paris: Publications de la Sorbonne, 1998).
35. Quoted in Brioist et al., *Croiser le fer*, p. 126.

36. Coustard de Massy, *Histoire du duel en France* (London: Elmsly, 1768).

37. Ibid., p. 279.

38. François Billacois, 'Duel', in Lucien Bély (ed.), *Dictionnaire de l'Ancien Régime* (Paris: PUF, 1996).

39. Brioist et al., *Croiser le fer*, pp. 306, 309, 323, 343–9. The authors note either 333 (p. 322) or 325 court cases (p. 362).

40. Ibid., pp. 362–8. The interpretations regarding 'civil' duels and protagonists 'in the prime of life' before thirty are not wholly convincing.

41. Franck Obert, '160 querelles d'honneur devant le tribunal des Maréchaux de France (1774–1789)', mémoire de maîtrise (under the supervision of Robert Muchembled), University of Paris-Nord, 1998, pp. 27, 34, 62, 73, 79, 98, 125.

42. Robert A. Nye, *Masculinity and Male Codes of Honor in Modern France* (Oxford and New York: Oxford University Press, 1993); Jean-Noël Jeanneney, *Le Duel: une passion française (1789–1914)* (Paris: Seuil, 2004), for the bourgeois duel in the nineteenth century.

43. Brioist et al., *Croiser le fer*, pp. 439, 463, 467.

44. Boris Porchnev, *Les Soulèvements populaires en France de 1623 à 1648* (Paris: SEVPEN, 1963, repr. Flammarion, 1972), p. 44.

45. Roland Mousnier, *Peasant Uprisings in Seventeenth-Century France, Russia, and China*, trans. Brian Pearce (New York: Harper and Row, 1970; London: Allen and Unwin, 1971).

46. Robert Mandrou, 'Vingt ans après...: les révoltes populaires en France au XVIIe siècle', *Revue historique*, 242 (1969), pp. 29–40; Robert Mandrou, *Classes et luttes de classes en France au début du XVIIe siècle* (Messina and Florence: D'Anna, 1965), esp. pp. 63–78.

47. Among many works: George Rudé, *The Crowd in History: A Study of Popular Disturbances in France and England, 1730–1848* (New York: John Wiley and Sons, 1964); Yves-Marie Bercé, *Croquants et Nu-pieds: les soulèvements paysans en France du XVIe au XIXe siècle* (Paris: Gallimard-Julliard, 1974); Peter Blickle, *The Revolution of 1525: The German Peasants' War from a New Perspective* (Baltimore, MD: Johns Hopkins University Press, 1981); David Underdown, *Revel, Riot and Rebellion: Popular Politics and Culture in England, 1603–1660* (Oxford: Oxford University Press, 1985); Charles Tilly, *The Contentious French: Four Centuries of Popular Struggle* (Cambridge, MA: Harvard University Press, 1986); Michael Mullett, *Popular Culture and Popular Protest in Late Medieval and Early Modern Europe* (London: Croom Helm, 1987); William Beik, *Urban Protest in Seventeenth-Century France:*

The Culture of Retribution (Cambridge: Cambridge University Press, 1997); Jean Nicolas, *La Rébellion française: mouvements populaires et conscience social, 1661–1789* (Paris: Seuil, 2002).

48. This is true of Julius R. Ruff (*Violence in Early Modern Europe, 1500–1800* [Cambridge: Cambridge University Press, 2001]), who devotes two successive well-informed chapters to 'Ritual group violence', including that of the young (pp. 160–83), and 'Popular protest' (pp. 184–215), without really trying to establish connections between the two phenomena.
49. Bercé, *Croquants et Nu-pieds*, pp. 50–5.
50. Ruff, *Violence in Early Modern Europe*, pp. 204–7.
51. See ch. 3 above.
52. Emmanuel Le Roy Ladurie, *Carnival: A People's Uprising at Romans 1579–1580*, trans. Mary Feeney (London: Scolar Press, 1980; Harmondsworth: Penguin, 1981).
53. Ruff, *Violence in Early Modern Europe*, pp. 196–7, 200.
54. Natalie Zemon Davis, *Society and Culture in Early Modern France: Eight Essays* (London: Duckworth, 1975; Stanford, CA: Stanford University Press, 1975; repr. Cambridge: Polity, 1987). See also Bercé, *Croquants et Nu-pieds*, p. 73.
55. Yves-Marie Bercé, *Fête et révolte: des mentalités populaires du XVIe au XVIIIe siècle* (Paris: Hachette, 1976; repub. Hachette, 'Pluriel', 1994), pp. 66–70; Ruff, *Violence in Early Modern Europe*, pp. 166–73.
56. Bercé, *Fête et révolte*, pp. 84–6, 150–2, 158, 174, 187.
57. Ibid., pp. 80–1 for the Bordeaux Carnival of 1651.
58. Mullett, *Popular Culture and Popular Protest*, pp. 96–9 for the relationship between rebels and Carnival. See also Edward Muir, *Ritual in Early Modern Europe* (Cambridge: Cambridge University Press, 1997), pp. 104–5 for violent youth rituals.
59. Muir, *Ritual in Early Modern Europe*, pp. 104–5, 138, 141.
60. Ibid., pp. 104–7; Edward Muir, *Mad Blood Stirring: Vendetta and Factions in Friuli during the Renaissance* (Baltimore, MD: Johns Hopkins University Press, 1993). See also ch. 3 above.
61. Muir, *Ritual in Early Modern Europe*, p. 138.
62. Ibid., p. 106; see also François Ploux, *Guerres paysannes en Quercy: violences, conciliations et répression pénale dans les campagnes du Lot (1810–1860)* (Paris: La Boutique de l'Histoire, 2002).
63. Jean Yver, *Egalité entre héritiers et exclusion des enfants dotés: essai de géographie coutumière* (Paris: Sirey, 1996).
64. Robert Muchembled, Hervé Bennezon and Marie-José Michel, *Histoire du Grand Paris de la Renaissance à la Révolution* (Paris: Perrin, 2008).

65. Nicolas, *La Rébellion française*, esp. pp. 29, 34 and ch. 11, pp. 443ff.
66. Ruff, *Violence in Early Modern Europe*, pp. 192, 204.
67. Robert Muchembled, *La Société policée: politique et politesse en France du XVIe au XXe siècle* (Paris: Seuil, 1998).
68. Nicolas, *La Rébellion française*, p. 363.
69. Arlette Farge and Jacques Revel, *Logiques de la foule: l'affaire des enlèvements d'enfants: Paris 1750* (Paris: Hachette, 1988).
70. Mikhaïl Bakhtin, *Rabelais and his World*, trans. Helen Iswolsky (Cambridge, MA: MIT Press, 1968; repr. Bloomington: Indiana University Press, 1984).

CHAPTER 7

1. Norbert Elias, *The Civilizing Process* [1939], trans. E. Jephcott (Oxford: Blackwell, 1978); Michel Foucault, *Discipline and Punish: The Birth of the Prison*, trans. Alan Sheridan (New York: Vintage, 1977).
2. Howard Zehr, *Crime and the Development of Modern Society: Patterns of Criminality in Nineteenth-Century Germany and France* (London: Croom Helm, 1976), pp. 114–17, 133, 135.
3. Dag Lindström, 'Interpersonal violence in Scandinavia: interpretation of long-term trends', paper presented at the third GERN seminar, 'Violence in history: long-term trends and the role of wars', Brussels, 3–4 December 2004; Eva Osterberg, 'Criminality, social control and the early modern state: evidence and interpretations in Scandinavian historiography', *Social Science History*, 16, 1 (1992), pp. 67–98, repr. in Eric A. Johnson and Eric H. Monkkonen (eds.), *The Civilization of Crime: Violence in Town and Country since the Middle Ages* (Urbana: University of Illinois Press, 1996), pp. 35–62.
4. V. A. C. Gatrell, 'The decline of theft and violence in Victorian and Edwardian England', in V. A. C. Gatrell, Bruce Lenman and Geoffrey Parker (eds), *Crime and the Law: The Social History of Crime in Western Europe since 1500* (London: Europa, 1980), pp. 286–9.
5. David Philips, *Crime and Authority in Victorian England: The Black Country 1835–1860* (London: Croom Helm, 1977), pp. 160–3, 260–1, 267, 284–5.
6. Benjamin F. Martin, *Crime and Criminal Justice under the Third Republic: The Shame of Marianne* (Baton Rouge: Louisiana State University Press, 1990), pp. 10–17.

7. Ibid., pp. 10, 37.
8. See ch. 6 above; Louis Gruel, *Pardons et châtiments: les jurés français face aux violences criminelles* (Paris: Nathan, 1991). See also Annick Tillier, *Des criminelles au village: femmes infanticides en Bretagne (1825–1865)* (Rennes: Presses Universitaires de Rennes, 2001).
9. Anna Clark, *Women's Silence, Men's Violence: Sexual Assault in England 1770–1845* (London: Pandora, 1987), pp. 40–1.
10. Ann-Louise Shapiro, *Breaking the Codes: Female Criminality in Fin-de-Siècle Paris* (Stanford, CA: Stanford University Press, 1996), p. 14.
11. Louise A. Jackson, *Child Sexual Abuse in Victorian England* (London: Routledge, 2000), pp. 4–5, 18–19, 120, 134.
12. Martin J. Wiener, *Men of Blood: Violence, Manliness, and Criminal Justice in Victorian England* (Cambridge: Cambridge University Press, 2004), pp. 12–13.
13. Ibid., pp. 74, 133. For France, see Gruel, *Pardons et châtiments*, pp. 57–9.
14. Nancy L. Green, 'La construction de la délinquance féminine', in Cécile Dauphin and Arlette Farge (eds), *De la violence et des femmes* (Paris: Pocket, 1999), p. 104.
15. Wiener, *Men of Blood*, pp. 140–1, 148–9.
16. See ch. 2 above.
17. Clive Emsley, *Crime and Society in England, 1750–1900* (London: Longman, 2nd edn, 1996), p. 275.
18. Wiener, *Men of Blood*, pp. 235, 238–9, 256, 288–9.
19. Gruel, *Pardons et châtiments*, pp. 47, 67.
20. Jean-Claude Chesnais, *Histoire de la violence en Occident de 1800 à nos jours*, rev. and expanded edn (Paris: Hachette, 1982), pp. 140–3.
21. Ibid., pp. 50–1, 145–50.
22. Ibid., pp. 156–7, 162, 164.
23. Falk Bretschneider, 'Toujours une histoire à part? L'état actuel de l'historiographie allemande sur l'enfermement aux XVIIIe et XIXe siècles', *Crime, Histoire et Sociétés/Crime, History and Societies*, 8, 2 (2004), pp. 141–62.
24. Martin (*Crime and Criminal Justice under the Third Republic*, p. 5, n. 9) gives a longer list of titles with a number of errors of detail.
25. Chesnais, *Histoire de la violence en Occident*, pp. 56–7, 61–3, 174, 222, 277, 313, 397.
26. The idea is developed in Robert Muchembled, *Orgasm and the West: A History of Pleasure from the Sixteenth Century to the Present*, trans. Jean Birrell (Cambridge: Polity, 2008).

27. Pierre Clément, *La Police de Louis XIV* (Paris: Didier, 2nd edn 1866).
28. Chesnais, *Histoire de la violence en Occident*, p. 100.
29. See ch. 4 above.
30. Aline Logette, 'La peine capitale devant la cour souveraine de Lorraine et Barrois à la fin du règne de Louis XIV', *XVIIe siècle*, 126 (1980), pp. 10–13.
31. Dominique Vié, 'La criminalité à Bordeaux de 1768 à 1777 d'après les plaintes et informations de la cour des Jurats', *Positions des thèses de l'Ecole des Chartes* (Paris, 1971), pp. 193–9.
32. Frances E. Dolan, *Dangerous Familiars: Representations of Domestic Crime in England, 1550–1700* (Ithaca, NY: Cornell University Press, 1994), p. 25.
33. André Abbiateci, François Billacois, Yves Castan, Porphyre Petrovinitch, Yvonne Bongert and Nicole Castan (eds), *Crimes et criminalité en France: XVIIe–XVIIIe siècles* (Paris: Armand Colin, 1971).
34. Pieter Spierenburg, *The Spectacle of Suffering: Executions and the Evolution of Repression: From a Preindustrial Metropolis to the European Experience* (Cambridge: Cambridge University Press, 1984), pp. 138–9; Pieter Spierenburg, 'Knife fighting and popular codes of honor in early modern Amsterdam', in Pieter Spierenburg (ed.), *Men and Violence: Gender, Honor, and Rituals in Modern Europe and America* (Columbus: Ohio State University Press, 1998), pp. 106–7.
35. British Museum, London.
36. Robert B. Shoemaker, *The London Mob: Violence and Disorder in Eighteenth-Century England* (London: Palgrave Macmillan, 2004), pp. 168, 170–5, 178–9.
37. Jennine Hurl-Eamon, *Gender and Petty Violence in London, 1680–1720* (Columbus: Ohio State University Press, 2005), pp. 32–3, 40–1, 46–7.
38. Graham J. Barker-Benfield, *The Culture of Sensibility: Sex and Society in Eighteenth-Century Britain* (Chicago and London: University of Chicago Press, 1992, repr. 1996).
39. Shoemaker, *The London Mob*, pp. 292–7.
40. Ibid., pp. 169–70, 298.
41. Hurl-Eamon, *Gender and Petty Violence in London*, pp. 32–3, 61.
42. Robert Muchembled, *La Société policée: politique et politesse en France du XVIe au XXe siècle* (Paris: Seuil, 1998), pp. 77–122.
43. Edward Twitchell Hall, *The Hidden Dimension: Man's Use of Space in Public and Private* (New York: Anchor Books, Doubleday, 1969).

44. Arlette Farge, *Vivre dans la rue à Paris au XVIIIe siècle* (Paris: Gallimard-Julliard, 1979), esp. pp. 242–4. See also Arlette Farge, *La Vie fragile: violence, pouvoirs et solidarités à Paris au XVIIIe siècle* (Paris: Seuil, 1986); Arlette Farge and André Zysberg, 'Les théâtres de la violence à Paris au XVIIIe siècle', *Annales ESC*, 34 (1979), pp. 984–1015. For the subsequent period, see Louis Chevalier, *Classes laborieuses et classes dangereuses à Paris pendant la première moitié du XIXe siècle* (Paris: Plon, 1958).

45. I deal with these questions in ch. 9 below.

46. For the duel, see ch. 6 above.

47. Heikki Ylikangas, 'What happened to violence? An analysis of the development of violence from medieval times to the early modern era based on Finnish source material', in Heikki Ylikangas, Petri Karonen and Martti Lehti (eds), *Five Centuries of Violence in Finland and the Baltic Area* (Columbus: Ohio State University Press, 2001), pp. 78–83.

48. Chesnais, *Histoire de la violence en Occident*, pp. 78–9.

49. Shani D'Cruze (ed.), *Everyday Violence in Britain 1850–1950* (London: Longman, 2000), pp. 43–6, 70–5, 78, 82.

50. Chesnais, *Histoire de la violence en Occident*, pp. 156–69.

51. Daniele Boschi, 'Homicide and knife fighting in Rome, 1845–1914', in Spierenburg, *Men and Violence*, pp. 132–3.

52. Frédéric Chauvaud, *De Pierre Rivière à Landru: la violence apprivoisée au XIXe siècle* (Turnhout: Brepols, 1991), pp. 161, 168, 184, 187, 190, 197.

53. Fanny Mayet, 'Violence et société à Gonesse, 1620–1700', mémoire de maîtrise (under the supervision of Robert Muchembled), University of Paris-Nord, 1999. For the earlier situation in the countryside, see ch. 3 above.

54. The situation was the same in the next century: see Adeline Cardoso, 'Criminalité et stratégies judiciaires à Gonesse, 1720–1789', mémoire de maîtrise (under the supervision of Robert Muchembled), University of Paris-Nord, 2007.

55. Olivier Jouneaux, 'Villageois et autorités', in François Billacois and Hugues Neveux (eds), 'Porter plainte: stratégies villageoises et justice en Ile-de-France', *Droit et culture*, 19 (1990), pp. 101–18; Cardoso reaches similar conclusions for Gonesse in the eighteenth century: 'Criminalité et stratégies judiciaires à Gonesse'.

56. Archives Départementales du Nord, J 19, 86–87, 'royaume' of Les Timeaux or Estimaux of Fâches-Thumesnil.

57. Julius R. Ruff, *Crime, Justice, and Public Order in Old Regime France: The Sénéchaussées of Libourne and Bazas, 1696–1789* (London: Croom Helm, 1984), pp. 90–1, 132–3.

58. Chauvaud, *De Pierre Rivière à Landru*, pp. 65–92, esp. p. 69.
59. Ibid., pp. 83–4, 93–114.
60. François Ploux, *Guerres paysannes en Quercy: violences, conciliations et répression pénale dans les campagnes du Lot (1810–1860)* (Paris: La Boutique de l'Histoire, 2002). See also Elisabeth Claverie and Pierre Lamaison, *L'Impossible mariage: violence et parenté en Gévaudan, XVIIe, XVIIIe, XIXe siècles* (Paris: Hachette, 1982).
61. Sylvie Lapalus, *La Mort du vieux? Le parricide au XIXe siècle* (Paris: Tallandier, 2004).
62. Chauvaud, *De Pierre Rivière à Landru*, pp. 248–51.
63. Antoine Garapon, *L'Ane portant des reliques: essai sur le rituel judiciaire* (Paris: Le Centurion, 1985), pp. 100, 143–5, 159. See also Antoine Garapon, Frédéric Gros and Rémy Pech, *Et ce sera justice: punir en démocratie* (Paris: Odile Jacob, 2001).
64. Noëlie Vialles, *Le Sang et la Chair: les abattoirs des pays de l'Adour* (Paris: Editions de la Maison des Sciences de l'Homme, 1987).
65. Chauvaud, *De Pierre Rivière à Landru*, pp. 234–9, 244, 245.

CHAPTER 8

1. Alfred Fouillée, *Psychologie du peuple français* (Paris: Félix Alcan, 1898).
2. Pierre Boaistuau, *Le Théâtre du monde* [1558], ed. Michel Simonin (Geneva: Droz, 1981).
3. Pierre Boaistuau, *Histoires tragiques extraictes des oeuvres italiennes de Bandel, et mises en nostre langue françoise par P. Boaistuau, surnommé Launay, natif de Bretaigne* (Paris: Sertenas, 1559).
4. Boaistuau, *Histoires tragiques*, ed. Richard A. Carr (Paris: Champion, 1997); Jean Céard, *La Nature et les Prodiges: l'insolite au XVIe siècle en France* (Geneva: Droz, 1977), p. 253.
5. Sergio Poli, *Histoire(s) tragique(s): anthologie/typologie d'un genre littéraire* (Bari: Schena, 1991; Paris: Nizet, 1991), list of titles on pp. 15–17; Raymond Picard and Jean Lafond (eds), *Nouvelles du XVIIe siècle* (Paris: Gallimard, 1997), pp. xx–xxiv.
6. Picard and Lafond, *Nouvelles du XVIIe siècle*, p. xxii; Poli, *Histoire(s) tragique(s)*, p. 34. See also François de Rosset, *Les Histoires tragiques de notre temps*, pref. René Godenne (Geneva: Slatkine Reprints, 1980), pp. vii–ix for Rosset.
7. Rosset, *Les Histoires tragiques de notre temps*, pp. xiii–xvi, 128, 362–3.
8. Robert Mandrou, 'Le baroque européen: mentalité pathétique et révolution sociale', *Annales ESC*, 15 (1960), pp. 898–914.

9. Jean Descrains, *Essais sur Jean-Pierre Camus* (Paris: Klincksieck, 1992); Jean Descrains, *La Culture d'un évêque humaniste: Jean-Pierre Camus et ses 'Diversités'* (Paris: Nizet, 1985); Max Vernet, *Jean-Pierre Camus: théories de la contre-littérature* (Paris: Nizet, 1995). The most important re-editions of his works are: Jean-Pierre Camus, *Les Spectacles d'horreur* [1630 edn], ed. René Godenne (Geneva: Slatkine Reprints, 1973); Jean-Pierre Camus, *Trente nouvelles*, ed. René Favret (Paris: Vrin, 1977). See also Picard and Lafond, *Nouvelles du XVIIe siècle*.

10. The works are listed by René Godenne in his edition of Camus, *Les Spectacles d'horreur*, p. xxiv.

11. Alain Viala, *Naissance de l'ecrivain: sociologie de la littérature à l'âge classique* (Paris: Minuit, 1985), pp. 132–3.

12. Picard and Lafond, *Nouvelles du XVIIe siècle*, pp. xxv–xxxix, liii.

13. Robert Muchembled, *La Société policée: politique et politesse en France du XVIe au XXe siècle* (Paris: Seuil, 1998).

14. See the introduction by René Favret (pp. 12–31) to Camus, *Trente nouvelles*.

15. Camus, *Les Spectacles d'horreur*, esp. pp. xviii–xix, 27 and the stories in question.

16. Jean-Pierre Seguin, *L'Information en France avant le périodique: 517 canards imprimés entre 1529 et 1631* (Paris: Maisonneuve et Larose, 1964), pp. 14–15.

17. Ibid., pp. 21, 30, 38–45.

18. Maurice Lever, 'De l'information à la nouvelle: les "canards" et les "histoires tragiques" de François de Rosset', *Revue d'histoire littéraire de la France* (1979), pp. 577–93. See also Maurice Lever, *Canards sanglants: naissance du fait divers* (Paris: Fayard, 1993), pp. 28–30 (on Rosset, Camus and the canards).

19. Muchembled, *La Société policée*, ch. 3.

20. Anne de Vaucher Gravili, *Loi et transgression: les histoires tragiques du XVIIe siècle* (Lecce: Milella, 1982), p. 21; see also Poli, *Histoire(s) tragique(s)*, p. 167.

21. Vaucher Gravili, *Loi et transgression*, pp. 25–44; Poli, *Histoire(s) tragique(s)*, p. 170.

22. Vaucher Gravili, *Loi et transgression*, pp. 54–5; Poli, *Histoire(s) tragique(s)*, p. 509.

23. Vaucher Gravili, *Loi et transgression*, pp. 80–3.

24. Robert Muchembled, *Passions de femmes au temps de la Reine Margot, 1553–1615* (Paris: Seuil, 2003), pp. 224–6, and see ch. 5 above. For England, see James A. Sharpe, ' "Last dying speeches": religion, ideology and public execution in seventeenth-century England', *Past and Present*, 107 (1985), pp. 144–67.

25. Françoise du Sorbier, 'De la potence à la biographie, ou les avatars du criminel et de son image en Angleterre (1680–1740)', *Etudes anglaises* (1979), pp. 257–71; Françoise du Sorbier, *Récits de gueuserie et biographies criminelles de Head à Defoe* (Paris: Didier Erudition, 1984).
26. Ibid., pp. 266–71.
27. Julius R. Ruff, *Violence in Early Modern Europe, 1500–1800* (Cambridge: Cambridge University Press, 2001), pp. 219, 234, 236.
28. Ibid., p. 217. The interpretation of Eric Hobsbawm is no longer generally accepted: *Bandits*, rev. edn (New York: Pantheon Books, 1981).
29. See ch. 7 above for the details. See also Jennine Hurl-Eamon, *Gender and Petty Violence in London, 1680–1720* (Columbus: Ohio State University Press, 2005), pp. 32–3, 40–1, 46–7.
30. Florike Egmond, 'The noble bandit and the ignoble bandit: changing literary representations of west-European robbers', *Ethnologia Europaea*, 17 (1987), pp. 140–2.
31. Ibid., pp. 144–5.
32. Ibid., pp. 145–53. See also Ruff, *Violence in Early Modern Europe*, pp. 220–3, 229.
33. Mónika Màtay and György Csepeli, 'The multiple lives of the Hungarian highwayman', in Amy Gilman Srebnick and René Lévy (eds), *Crime and Culture: An Historical Perspective* (Aldershot: Ashgate, 2005), pp. 183–97.
34. Anton Blok, *De Bokkerijders: Roversbenden en geheime genootschappen in de landen van Overmaas (1730–1774)* (Amsterdam: Prometheus, 1991).
35. Lincoln B. Faller, *Turned to Account: The Forms and Functions of Criminal Biography in Late Seventeenth- and Early Eighteenth-Century England* (Cambridge: Cambridge University Press, 1987), pp. x–xi.
36. Ibid., p. 201; Lincoln B. Faller, *Crime and Defoe: A New Kind of Writing* (Cambridge: Cambridge University Press, 1993), pp. 8, 70–1.
37. Ibid., pp. 211–15, 225.
38. Ibid., pp. 6–8.
39. Ruff, *Violence in Early Modern Europe*, p. 226.
40. Frédéric Chauvaud, *De Pierre Rivière à Landru: la violence apprivoisée au XIXe siècle* (Turnhout: Brepols, 1991), esp. pp. 206–27; Dominique Kalifa, *L'Encre et le Sang: récits de crimes et société à la Belle Époque* (Paris: Fayard, 1995), p. 124.
41. For what follows on crime fiction I have drawn heavily on Stefano Benvenuti, Gianni Rizzoni and Michel Lebrun, *Le Roman criminel:*

histoire, auteurs, personnages (pref. Jean-Patrick Manchette) (Paris: L'Atalante, 1982), an excellent descriptive study, although it says little about the evolution of the readership or the relationship between homicide and youth.

42. Kalifa, *L'Encre et le Sang*, p. 270.
43. Chauvaud, *De Pierre Rivière à Landru*, pp. 213, 221.
44. Kalifa, *L'Encre et le Sang*, pp. 156–63.
45. The African light infantry battalions (*bataillons d'infanterie légère d'Afrique*, or '*Bat' d'Af*') were not, strictly speaking, penal units, but they accepted men convicted in civilian and military courts. Discipline was much stricter than in the rest of the army.
46. Kalifa, *L'Encre et le Sang*, pp. 238, 241, 248.
47. Benvenuti et al., *Le Roman criminel*, pp. 131–6.

CHAPTER 9

1. Robert Muchembled, *Orgasm and the West: A History of Pleasure from the Sixteenth Century to the Present*, trans. Jean Birrell (Cambridge: Polity, 2008), pp. 169–77.
2. Jean-Claude Chesnais, 'Les morts violentes dans le monde', *Population et Sociétés*, 395 (2003), pp. 2–7.
3. Ibid., and fig. 1: 'Variations according to age and sex in France in 1999'.
4. Emile Durkheim, *Suicide: A Study in Sociology* [1897], trans. John A. Spaulding and George Simpson (Glencoe, IL: Free Press, 1951; London: Routledge and Kegan Paul, 1952; repr. London: Routledge, 1989).
5. See ch. 8 above.
6. Fiona Brookman, *Understanding Homicide* (London: Sage, 2005), pp. 31, 34–5, 309–10.
7. Shani D'Cruze, Sandra Walklate and Samantha Pegg, *Murder: Social and Historical Approaches to Understanding Murder and Murderers* (Cullompton: Willan, 2006), pp. 15–17, 41, 79, 149, 157–8.
8. David Garland, *The Culture of Control: Crime and Social Order in Contemporary Society* (Chicago: University of Chicago Press, 2001), pp. 90–1.
9. Ibid., pp. x–xi, 10.
10. Eric H. Monkkonen, *Crime, Justice, History* (Columbus: Ohio State University Press, 2002), table 10.1 and figure 10.2, a synthesis of the research published in Eric H. Monkkonen, *Murder in New York City* (Berkeley: University of California Press, 2001).

11. David F. Greenberg, 'The historical variability of the age–crime relationship', *Journal of Quantitative Criminology*, 10 (1994), pp. 370, n. 13, 372.

12. Monkkonen, *Crime, Justice, History*, conclusion of 'The origins of American and European violence differences'.

13. Philippe Robert, *Les Comptes du crime: les délinquances en France et leurs mesures* (Paris: Le Sycomore, 1985), p. 134.

14. Martti Lehti, 'Long-term trends in homicidal crime in Finland 1750–2000', paper presented at the third GERN seminar, 'Violence in history: long-term trends and the role of wars', Brussels, 3–4 December 2004; see also Heikki Ylikangas, Petri Karonen and Martti Lehti (eds), *Five Centuries of Violence in Finland and the Baltic Area* (Columbus: Ohio State University Press, 2001).

15. Paul Griffiths, *Youth and Authority: Formative Experiences in England, 1560–1640* (Oxford: Clarendon Press, 1996), pp. 34–7.

16. Ibid., pp. 128–9 for the controversy among English-speaking historians.

17. See above, esp. ch 7.

18. Pamela Cox and Heather Shore (eds), *Becoming Delinquent: British and European Youth, 1650–1950* (Aldershot: Ashgate, 2002), pp. 8–10, 153–4.

19. Heather Shore, 'The trouble with boys: gender and the "invention" of the juvenile offender in early-nineteenth-century Britain', in Margaret L. Arnot and Cornelie Usborne (eds), *Gender and Crime in Modern Europe* (London: UCL Press, 1999), pp. 75–92.

20. See ch. 8 above.

21. See esp. Andrew Davies, 'Youth gangs, gender and violence, 1870–1900', in Shani D'Cruze (ed.), *Everyday Violence in Britain 1850–1950* (London: Longman, 2000), pp. 70–84.

22. Ibid., pp. 78–82.

23. Ibid., p. 78.

24. Ibid., p. 79.

25. Maria Kaspersson, ' "The great murder mystery" or explaining declining homicide rates', in Barry S. Godfrey, Clive Emsley and Graeme Dunstall (eds), *Comparative Histories of Crime* (Cullompton: Willan, 2003), pp. 72–88.

26. François Marty (ed.), *L'Illégitime violence: la violence et son dépassement à l'adolescence* (Paris: Erès, 1997), pp. 17, 100.

27. Michel Fize, *Les Bandes: l'"entre-soi' adolescent* (Paris: Desclée de Brouwer, 1993), pp. 28–9.

28. Ibid., pp. 32–3.

29. Ibid., pp. 36–41.

30. See ch. 3 above.

31. Fize, *Les Bandes*, pp. 50–1, 63.
32. Norbert Elias, *The Civilizing Process* [1939], trans. E. Jephcott (Oxford: Blackwell, 1978).
33. Fize, *Les Bandes*, pp. 69, 78–9, 85, 114–15.
34. Ibid., pp. 128–9, 138–9, 146.
35. Thomas Sauvadet, *Le Capital guerrier: concurrence et solidarité entre jeunes de cités* (Paris: Armand Colin, 2006).
36. See ch. 4 above.
37. Gérard Mauger, *L'Emeute de novembre 2005: une révolte protopolitique* (Bellecombe-en-Bauges: Editions du Croquant, 2006); Gérard Mauger, *Les Bandes, le milieu et la Bohème populaire: étude de sociologie de la déviance des jeunes des classes populaires, 1975–2005* (Paris: Belin, 2006).
38. Sébastian Roché, *Le Frisson de l'émeute: violence urbaines et banlieues* (Paris: Seuil, 2006).
39. Luc Bronner, 'Le témoignage d'un "hooligan pur", violent pour le plaisir', *Le Monde*, 29 November 2006, p. 12.

IS THE END OF VIOLENCE POSSIBLE?

1. Norbert Elias, *The Civilizing Process* [1939], trans. E. Jephcott (Oxford: Blackwell, 1978); Norbert Elias, *The Court Society* [1969], trans. E. Jephcott (Oxford: Blackwell, 1983).
2. Adnan Houbballah, Roland Gori and Christian Hoffmann (eds), *Pourquoi la violence des adolescents? Voix croisées entre Occident et Orient* (Paris: Erès, 2001), pp. 32–3.
3. Nello Zagnoli, 'S'arracher la haine', in Raymond Verdier (ed.), *Vengeance: le face-à-face victime/aggresseur* (Paris: Autrement, 2004), p. 120.
4. Ibid., p. 119, on contemporary Calabria.
5. Ibid., pp. 19, 124.

SELECT BIBLIOGRAPHY

Abbiateci, André, François Billacois, Yves Castan, Porphyre Petrovinitch, Yvonne Bongert and Nicole Castan (eds), *Crimes et criminalité en France: XVIIe–XVIIIe siècles* (Paris: Armand Colin, 1971).

Allard, Albéric, *Histoire de la justice criminelle au XVIe siècle* (Ghent: 1868; repub. Aalen: Scienta, 1970).

Anglo, Sydney, *The Martial Arts of Renaissance Europe* (Yale: Yale University Press, 2000).

Antoine, Michel, Henri-François Buffet, Suzanne Clémencet, Ferréol de Ferry, Monique Langlois, Yvonne Lanhers, Jean-Paul Laurent and Jacques Meurgey de Tupigny, *Guide des recherches dans les fonds judiciaries de l'Ancien Régime* (Paris: Imprimerie nationale, 1958).

Ariès, Philippe, *L'Enfant et la Vie familiale sous l'Ancien Régime* (Paris: Plon, 1960).

Ariès, Philippe and Georges Duby (eds), *Histoire de la vie privée*, vols 2 and 3 (Paris: Seuil, 1985–7).

Arnot, Margaret L. and Cornelie Usborne (eds), *Gender and Crime in Modern Europe* (London: UCL Press, 1999).

Artaud, Antonin, *Les Tarahumaras* (Paris: Gallimard, 1987).

Astarita, Tommaso, *Village Justice: Community, Family and Popular Culture in Early Modern Italy* (Baltimore, MD: Johns Hopkins University Press, 1999).

Baird, Bruce, 'The social origins of dueling in Virginia', in Michael A. Bellesiles (ed.), *The Lethal Imagination: Violence and Brutality in American History* (New York: New York University Press, 1999), pp. 87–112.

Bakhtin, Mikhaïl, *Rabelais and his World*, trans. Helen Iswolsky (Cambridge, MA: MIT Press, 1968; repr. Bloomington: Indiana University Press, 1984).

Barker-Benfield, Graham J., *The Culture of Sensibility: Sex and Society in Eighteenth-Century Britain* (Chicago and London: University of Chicago Press, 1992, repr. 1996).

Bastien, Pascal, *L'Exécution publique à Paris au XVIIIe siècle: une histoire des rituels judiciares* (Seysel: Champ Vallon, 2006).

339

Bauer, Alain, *Géographie de la France criminelle* (Paris: Odile Jacob, 2006).

Beattie, John M., *Crime and the Courts in England, 1660–1800* (Princeton, NJ: Princeton University Press, 1986).

Béguin, Katia, *Les Princes de Condé: rebelles, courtisans et mécenes dans la France du Grand Siècle* (Seyssel: Champ Vallon, 1999).

Beier, Alexander L., 'Vagrants and the social order in Elizabethan England', *Past and Present*, 64 (1974), pp. 3–29.

Beik, William, *Urban Protest in Seventeenth-Century France: The Culture of Retribution* (Cambridge: Cambridge University Press, 1997).

Benvenuti, Stefano, Gianni Rizzoni and Michel Lebrun, *Le Roman criminel: histoire, auteurs, personnages* (pref. Jean-Patrick Manchette) (Paris: L'Atalante, 1982).

Bercé, Yves-Marie, *Croquants et Nu-pieds: les soulèvements paysans en France du XVIe au XIXe siècle* (Paris: Gallimard-Julliard, 1974).

Bercé, Yves-Marie, *Fête et révolte: des mentalités populaires du XVIe au XVIIIe siècle* (Paris: Hachette, 1976; repub. Hachette, 'Pluriel', 1994).

Bercé, Yves-Marie and Yves Castan (eds), *Les Archives du délit: empreintes de société* (Toulouse: Editions Universitaires du Sud, 1990).

Berkowitz, Alan D., 'The social norms approach to violence prevention', article on the author's website (www.alanberkowitz.com).

Berriot-Salvadore, Evelyne, *Les Femmes dans la société française de la Renaissance* (Geneva: Droz, 1990).

Berriot-Salvadore, Evelyne, *Un corps, un destin: la femme dans la médecine de la Renaissance* (Paris: Champion, 1993).

Biet, Christian (ed.), *Théâtre de la cruauté et récits sanglants en France (XVIe–XVIIe siècles)* (Paris: Robert Laffont, 2006).

Billacois, François, *Le Duel dans la société française des XVIe–XVIIe siècles: essai de psychologie historique* (Paris: EHESS, 1986); see also the substantially condensed version, ed. and trans. Trista Selous, *The Duel: Its Rise and Fall in Early Modern France* (London: Yale University Press, 1990).

Billacois, François, 'Duel', in Lucien Bély (ed.), *Dictionnaire de l'Ancien Régime* (Paris: PUF, 1996).

Billacois, François and Hugues Neveux (eds), 'Porter plainte: stratégies villageoises et justice en Ile-de-France', *Droit et culture*, 19 (1990), pp. 5–148.

Bimbenet-Privat, Michèle, *Ecrous de la justice de Saint-Germain-des-Prés au XVIe siècle: inventaire analytique des registres Z²3393, 3318, 3394, 3395 (années 1537 à 1579)* (Paris: Archives Nationales, 1995).

Blastenbrei, Peter, *Kriminalität in Rom, 1560–1585* (Tübingen: Niemeyer, 1995).

Blickle, Peter, *The Revolution of 1525: The German Peasants' War from a New Perspective* (Baltimore, MD: Johns Hopkins University Press, 1981).

Blickle, Peter, *Resistance, Representation, and Community* (Oxford: Oxford University Press, 1997).

Blok, Anton, *De Bokkerijders: Roversbenden en geheime genootschappen in de landen van Overmaas (1730–1774)* (Amsterdam: Prometheus, 1991).

Boaistuau, Pierre, *Histoires tragiques extraictes des oeuvres italiennes de Bandel, et mises en nostre langue françoise par P. Boaistuau, surnommé Launay, natif de Bretaigne* (Paris: Sertenas, 1559).

Boaistuau, Pierre, *Le Théâtre du monde* [1558], ed. Michel Simonin (Geneva: Droz, 1981).

Boaistuau, Pierre, *Histoires tragiques*, ed. Richard A. Carr (Paris: Champion, 1997).

Boone, Marc, ' "Le tres fort, vilain et detestable criesme et pechié de zodomie": homosexualité et répression à Bruges pendant la période bourguignonne (fin XIVe–début XVIe siècle)', in Hugo Soly and René Vermeir (eds), *Belied en bestuur in de oude Nederlanden: Liber Amicorum Prof. Dr. M. Baelde* (Ghent: Vakgroep Nieuwe Geschiedenis UG, 1993), pp. 2–17.

Boschi, Daniele, 'Homicide and knife fighting in Rome, 1845–1914', in Spierenburg, *Men and Violence*, pp. 128–58.

Boutelet, Bernadette, 'Etude par sondage de la criminalité dans le bailliage de Pont-de-l'Arche (XVIIe–XVIIIe siècles): de la violence au vol, en marche vers l'escroquerie', *Annales de Normandie*, 12 (1962), pp. 235–62.

Braithwaite, John, *Crime, Shame, and Reintegration* (Cambridge: Cambridge University Press, 1989).

Brakensiek, Stefan, 'Peut-on parler d'absolutisme dans l'Allemagne moderne? Une domination désireuse d'être acceptée (*Akzeptanzorientierte Herrschaft*)', *Bulletin d'information de la Mission historique française en Allemagne*, 42 (2006), pp. 249–63.

Bretschneider, Falk, 'Toujours une histoire à part? L'état actuel de l'historiographie allemande sur l'enfermement aux XVIIIe et XIXe siècles', *Crime, Histoire et Sociétés/Crime, History and Societies*, 8, 2 (2004), pp. 141–62.

Briggs, Robin, *Communities of Belief: Cultural and Social Tensions in Early Modern France* (Oxford: Clarendon Press, 1989).

Briggs, Robin, *Witches and Neighbours: The Social and Cultural Context of European Witchcraft* (London: HarperCollins, 1996).

Brihat, Delphine, 'La criminalité pardonnée dans le ressort du parlement de Paris en 1525', mémoire de maîtrise (under the supervision of Robert Muchembled), University of Paris-Nord, 1999.

Brioist, Pascal, Hervé Drévillon and Pierre Serna, *Croiser le fer: violence et culture de l'épée dans la France moderne, XVIe–XVIIIe siècle* (Seyssel: Champ Vallon, 2002).

Bronner, Luc, 'Le témoignage d'un "hooligan pur", violent pour le plaisir', *Le Monde*, 29 November 2006, p. 12.

Brookman, Fiona, *Understanding Homicide* (London: Sage, 2005).

Broomhall, Susan, 'Poverty, gender and incarceration in sixteenth-century Paris', *French History*, 18 (2004), pp. 1–24.

Burke, Peter, *Popular Culture in Early Modern Europe* (New York: New York University Press, 1978).

Cameron, Iain, *Crime and Repression in the Auvergne and the Guyenne, 1720–1790* (Cambridge: Cambridge University Press, 1981).

Camus, Jean-Pierre, *Les Spectacles d'horreur* [1630 edn], ed. René Godenne (Geneva: Slatkine Reprints, 1973).

Camus, Jean-Pierre, *Trente nouvelles*, ed. René Favret (Paris: Vrin, 1977).

Cardini, Franco, *La Culture de la guerre, Xe–XVIIIe siècle* (Paris: Gallimard, 1992).

Cardoso, Adeline, 'Criminalité et stratégies judiciaires à Gonesse, 1720–1789', mémoire de maîtrise (under the supervision of Robert Muchembled), University of Paris-Nord, 2007.

Carroll, Stuart, *Blood and Violence in Early Modern France* (Oxford and New York: Oxford University Press, 2006).

Castan, Nicole, *Justice et répression en Languedoc à l'époque des Lumières* (Paris: Flammarion, 1980).

Castan, Nicole and Yves Castan, *Vivre ensemble: ordre et désordre en Languedoc (XVIIe–XVIIIe siècles)* (Paris: Gallimard-Julliard, 1981).

Céard, Jean, *La nature et les prodiges: l'insolite au XVIe siècle en France* (Geneva: Droz, 1977).

Chartier, Roger, Marie-Madeleine Compère and Dominique Julia, *L'Education en France du XVIe au XVIIIe siècle* (Paris: SEDES, 1976).

Chauchadis, Claude, *La Loi du duel: le code du point d'honneur dans l'Espagne des XVIe au XVIIe siècles* (Toulouse: Presses Universitaires du Mirail, 1997).

Chaulet, Rudy, 'La violence en Castile au XVIIe siècle d'après les *Indultos de Viernes Santo* (1623–1699)', *Crime, Histoire et Sociétés/Crime, History and Societies*, 1, 2 (1997), pp. 5–27.

Chauvaud, Frédéric, *De Pierre Rivière à Landru: la violence apprivoisée au XIXe siècle* (Turnhout: Brepols, 1991).

Chesnais, Jean-Claude, *Histoire de la violence en Occident de 1800 à nos jours*, rev. and expanded edn (Paris: Hachette, 1982).

Chesnais, Jean-Claude, 'Les morts violentes dans le monde', *Population et Sociétés*, 395 (2003), pp. 2–7.

Chevalier, Bernard, *Les Bonnes Villes de France du XIVe au XVIe siècle* (Paris: Aubier, 1982).

Chevalier, Louis, *Classes laborieuses et classes dangereuses à Paris pendant la première moitié du XIXe siècle* (Paris: Plon, 1958).

Clark, Anna, *Women's Silence, Men's Violence: Sexual Assault in England 1770–1845* (London: Pandora, 1987).

Claverie, Elisabeth and Pierre Lamaison, *L'Impossible mariage: violence et parenté en Gévaudan, XVIIe, XVIIIe, XIXe siècles* (Paris: Hachette, 1982).

Clément, Pierre, *La Police de Louis XIV* (Paris: Didier, 2nd edn, 1866).

Cockburn, James S., 'Patterns of violence in English society: homicide in Kent 1560–1985', *Past and Present*, 130 (1991), pp. 70–106.

Cohen, Esther, ' "To die a criminal for the public good": the execution ritual in late medieval Paris', in Bernard S. Bachrach and David Nicholas (eds), *Law, Custom, and the Social Fabric in Medieval Europe: Essays in Honor of Bryce Lyon* (Kalamazoo: Medieval Institute Publications, Western Michigan University, 1990), pp. 285–304.

Compère, Marie-Madeleine, *Du collège au lycée (1500–1850)* (Paris: Gallimard-Julliard, 1985).

Coussemaker, Ignace de, *Cartulaire de l'abbaye de Cysoing et de ses dépendances* (Lille: Imprimerie Saint-Augustin, 1884).

Coustard de Massy, *Histoire du duel en France* (London: Elmsly, 1768).

Cox, Pamela and Heather Shore (eds), *Becoming Delinquent: British and European Youth, 1650–1950* (Aldershot: Ashgate, 2002).

Crouzet, Denis, *Les Guerriers de Dieu: la violence au temps des troubles de religion, vers 1525–vers 1610* (Seysel: Champ Vallon, 2006).

Cuénin, Micheline, *Le Duel sous l'Ancien Régime* (Paris: Presses de la Renaissance, 1982).

Cyrulnik, Boris, *Mémoire de singe et parole d'homme* (Paris: Hachette, 1983).

Cyrulnik, Boris, *La Naissance du sens* (Paris: Hachette, 1995).

Dauphin, Cécile and Arlette Farge (eds), *De la violence et des femmes* (Paris: Pocket, 1999).

Davies, Andrew, 'Youth gangs, gender and violence, 1870–1900', in D'Cruze, *Everyday Violence in Britain*, pp. 70–84.

Davis, Natalie Zemon, *Society and Culture in Early Modern France: Eight Essays* (London: Duckworth, 1975; Stanford, CA: Stanford University Press, 1975; repr. Cambridge: Polity, 1987).

Davis, Natalie Zemon, *Fiction in the Archives: Pardon Tales and their Tellers in Sixteenth-Century France* (Stanford, CA: Stanford University Press, 1987; repr. Cambridge: Polity, 1987).

Davis, Robert C., *The War of the Fists: Popular Culture and Public Violence in Late Renaissance Venice* (Oxford and New York: Oxford University Press, 1994).

D'Cruze, Shani (ed.), *Everyday Violence in Britain 1850–1950* (London: Longman, 2000).

D'Cruze, Shani, Sandra Walklate and Samantha Pegg, *Murder: Social and Historical Approaches to Understanding Murder and Murderers* (Cullompton: Willan, 2006).

Dean, Trevor and K. J. P. Lowe (eds), *Crime, Society, and the Law in Renaissance Italy* (Cambridge: Cambridge University Press, 1994).

Dehaisnes, Abbé C., *Inventaire sommaire des archives départementales antérieures à 1789. Nord. Archives civiles, série B. Chambre des comptes de Lille, no 1681 à 1841*, vol. 3 (Lille: Danel, 1877).

Delay, Valérie, 'Les fêtes à Lille au XVIe siècle', mémoire de maîtrise (under the supervision of Robert Muchembled), University of Lille III, 1984.

Descrains, Jean, *La culture d'un évêque humaniste: Jean-Pierre Camus et ses 'Diversités'* (Paris: Nizet, 1985).

Descrains, Jean, *Essais sur Jean-Pierre Camus* (Paris: Klincksieck, 1992).

Devyver, André, *Le sang épuré: les préjugés de race chez les gentilshommes français de l'Ancien Régime, 1570–1720* (Brussels: Editions de l'Université de Bruxelles, 1973).

Deyon, Pierre, *Le temps des prisons: essai sur l'histoire de la délinquance et les origines du système pénitentiaire* (Lille: Presses Universitaires de Lille, 1975).

D'Hollander, Paul (ed.), *Violences en Limousin à travers les siècles* (Limoges: PULIM, 1998).

Diederiks, Herman, 'Patterns of criminality and law enforcement during the Ancien Regime: the Dutch case', *Criminal Justice History*, 1 (1980), pp. 157–74.

Diederiks, Herman, 'Criminality and its repression in the past: quantitative approaches: a survey', *Economic and Social History in the Netherlands*, 1 (1989), pp. 67–86.

Diederiks, Herman, 'Quality and quantity in historical research in criminality and criminal justice.: the case of Leiden in the 17th and 18th centuries', *Historical Social* Research, 15 (1990), pp. 57–76.

Dolan, Frances E., *Dangerous Familiars: Representations of Domestic Crime in England, 1550–1700* (Ithaca, NY: Cornell University Press, 1994).

Duby, Georges and Michelle Perrot (eds), *Histoire des femmes en Occident*, vol. 3: *XVIe–XVIIIe siècle*, eds Natalie Zemon Davis and Arlette Farge (Paris: Plon, 1991).

Dülmen, Richard van, *Theatre of Horror: Crime and Punishment in Early Modern Germany* (Cambridge: Polity, 1990).

Dupâquier, Jacques (ed.), *Histoire de la population française*, vol. 2: *De la Renaissance à 1789* (Paris: PUF, 1988).

Durkheim, Emile, *Suicide: A Study in Sociology* [1897], trans. John A. Spaulding and George Simpson (Glencoe, IL: Free Press, 1951; London: Routledge and Kegan Paul, 1952; repr. London: Routledge, 1989).

Durkheim, Emile, 'Deux lois de l'évolution penale', *Année sociologique*, 6 (1901), pp. 65–95.

Durkheim, Emile, *Leçons de sociologie: physique des moeurs et du droit* (Paris: PUF, 1950).

Du Tilliot, Jean-Baptiste Lucotte, *Mémoires pour servir à l'histoire de la fête des foux*... (Lausanne and Geneva: 1751).

Eckberg, Douglas Lee, 'Estimates of early twentieth-century U.S. homicide rates: an econometric forecasting approach', *Demography*, 32 (1995), pp. 1–16.

Egmond, Florike, 'The noble bandit and the ignoble bandit: changing literary representations of west-European robbers', *Ethnologia Europaea*, 17 (1987), pp. 139–56.

Egmond, Florike, *Underworlds: Organized Crime in the Netherlands, 1650–1800* (Cambridge: Polity, 1993).

Eisner, Manuel, 'Modernization, self-control, and lethal violence: the long-term dynamics of European homicide rates in theoretical perspective', *British Journal of Criminology*, 41 (2001), pp. 618–38.

Eisner, Manuel, 'Crime, problem drinking, and drug use: patterns of problem behavior in cross-national perspective', *Annals of the American Academy of Political and Social Science*, 580 (2002), pp. 201–25.

Eisner, Manuel, 'Long-term historical trends in violent crime', *Crime and Justice: A Review of Research*, 30 (2003), pp. 83–142.

Elias, Norbert, *The Civilizing Process* [1939], trans. E. Jephcott (Oxford: Blackwell, 1978).

Elias, Norbert, *The Court Society* [1969], trans. E. Jephcott (Oxford: Blackwell, 1983).

Elias, Norbert, *La Dynamique de l'Occident* (Paris: Calmann-Lévy, 1975).

El Kenz, David, *Les Bûchers du roi: la culture protestante des martyrs (1523–1572)* (Seysel: Champ Vallon, 1997).

Elliott, John H., *The Revolt of the Catalans: A Study in the Decline of Spain (1598–1640)* (Cambridge: Cambridge University Press, 1963).

Emsley, Clive, *Crime and Society in England, 1750–1900* (London: Longman, 2nd edn, 1996).

Emsley, Clive, *Hard Men: The English and Violence since 1750* (London: Palgrave Macmillan, 2005).

Erasmus, *On Good Manners for Boys/De civilitate morum puerilium*, trans. Brian McGregor, in *Collected Works of Erasmus*, ed. J. K. Sowards (Toronto and London: University of Toronto Press, 1985), pp. 269–89.

Esmein, Adhémar, *Histoire de la procédure criminelle en France* (Paris: Larose et Farcel, 1882).

Espinas, Georges, *Recueil de documents relatifs à l'histoire du droit municipal en France des origines à la Révolution: Artois*, vol. 1 (Paris: Recueil Sirey, 1934).

Estoile, Pierre de l', *Journal de Henri IV*, vol. 7 *(1595–1601)* (Paris: Alphone Lemerre, 1876).

Estoile, Pierre de l', *Registre-journal du règne de Henri III*, vol. 5 *(1585–1587)*, eds Madeleine Lazard and Gilbert Schrenck (Geneva: Droz, 2001).

Evans, Richard, *Rituals of Retribution: Capital Punishment in Germany, 1600–1987* (Oxford: Oxford University Press, 1996).

Faller, Lincoln B., *Turned to Account: The Forms and Functions of Criminal Biography in Late Seventeenth- and Early Eighteenth-Century England* (Cambridge: Cambridge University Press, 1987).

Faller, Lincoln B., *Crime and Defoe: A New Kind of Writing* (Cambridge: Cambridge University Press, 1993).

Farge, Arlette, *Vivre dans la rue à Paris au XVIIIe siècle* (Paris: Gallimard-Julliard, 1979).

Farge, Arlette, *La Vie fragile: violence, pouvoirs et solidarités à Paris au XVIIIe siècle* (Paris: Seuil, 1986).

Farge, Arlette and Jacques Revel, *Logiques de la foule: l'affaire des enlèvements d'enfants: Paris 1750* (Paris: Hachette, 1988).

Farge, Arlette and André Zysberg, 'Les théâtres de la violence à Paris au XVIIIe siècle', *Annales ESC*, 34 (1979), pp. 984–1015.

Farr, James R., *Authority and Sexuality in Early Modern Burgundy (1550–1730)* (Oxford: Oxford University Press, 1995).

Farr, James R., *A Tale of Two Murders: Passion and Power in Seventeenth-Century France* (Durham, NC: Duke University Press, 2005).

La Faute, le Répression et le Pardon, Actes du 107e Congrès National des sociétés Savantes, Brest, 1982, Section de Philologie et d'Histoire jusqu'à 1610, vol. 1 (Paris: CTHS, 1984).

Fize, Michel, *Les Bandes: l'"entre-soi" adolescent* (Paris: Desclée de Brouwer, 1993).

Flandrin, Jean-Louis, *Les Amours paysannes: amour et sexualité dans les campagnes de l'ancienne France (XVIe–XIXe siècles)* (Paris: Gallimard-Julliard, 1975).

Flandrin, Jean-Louis, *Familles: parenté, maison, sexualité dans l'ancienne France* (Paris: Hachette, 1976).

Fletcher, Jonathan, *Violence and Civilization: An Introduction to the Work of Norbert Elias* (Cambridge: Polity, 1997).

Foucault, Michel, *Surveiller et punir: naissance de la prison* (Paris: Gallimard, 1975), trans. Alan Sheridan as *Discipline and Punish: The Birth of the Prison* (New York: Vintage, 1977).

Fouillée, Alfred, *Psychologie du peuple français* (Paris: Félix Alcan, 1898).

Freud, Sigmund, *Civilization and its Discontents*, trans. Joan Rivière, new edn James Strachey (London: Hogarth Press and Institute of Psychoanalysis, 1963).

Frevert, Ute, *Das Duell in der bürgerlichen Gesellschaft* (Munich: Beck, 1996).

Fróis, *see Traité de Luís Fróis*.

Fromm, Erich, *The Anatomy of Human Destructiveness* (London: Cape, 1974; Harmondsworth: Penguin, 1977).

Fromm, Erich, *The Heart of Man: Its Genius for Good and Evil* (New York and London: Harper and Row, 1980).

Furet, François and Jacques Ozouf, *Lire et écrire: l'alphabétisation des français de Calvin à Jules Ferry* (Paris: Minuit, 1977), trans. as *Reading and Writing: Literacy in France from Calvin to Jules Ferry* (Cambridge: Cambridge University Press, 1982).

Garapon, Antoine, *L'Ane portant des reliques: essai sur le rituel judiciaire* (Paris: Le Centurion, 1985).

Garapon, Antoine, Frédéric Gros and Rémy Pech, *Et ce sera justice: punir en démocratie* (Paris: Odile Jacob, 2001).

Garin, Eugenio (ed.), *L'Homme de la Renaissance* (Paris: Seuil, 1990).

Garland, David, *The Culture of Control: Crime and Social Order in Contemporary Society* (Chicago: University of Chicago Press, 2001).

Garnot, Benoît (ed.), *Histoire et criminalité de l'antiquité au XXe siècle: nouvelles approches* (Dijon: Editions Universitaires de Dijon, 1992).

Garnot, Benoît, *Un crime conjugal au XVIIIe siècle: l'affaire Boiveau* (Paris: Imago, 1993).

Garnot, Benoît, *La Justice en France de l'an mil à 1914* (Paris: Nathan, 1993).

Garnot, Benoît (ed.), *Ordre moral et délinquance de l'antiquité au XXe siècle* (Dijon: Editions Universitaires de Dijon, 1994).

Garnot, Benoît, *Vivre en prison au XVIIIe siècle: lettres de Pantaléon Gougis, vigneron chartrain (1758–1762)* (Paris: Publisud, 1994).

Garnot, Benoît (ed.), *Le Clergé délinquant (XIIIe–XVIIIe siècle)* (Dijon: Editions Universitaires de Dijon, 1995).

Garnot, Benoît, *Le Diable au couvent: les possédées d'Auxonne (1558–1663)* (Paris: Imago, 1995).

Garnot, Benoît (ed.), *L'Infrajudiciaire du Moyen Age à l'époque contemporaine* (Dijon: Editions Universitaires de Dijon, 1996).

Garnot, Benoît (ed.), *Juges, notaires et policiers délinquants: XIVe–XXe siècle* (Dijon: Editions Universitaires de Dijon, 1997).

Garnot, Benoît, *La Petite Délinquance du Moyen Age à l'époque contemporaine* (Dijon: Editions Universitaires de Dijon, 1998).

Garnot, Benoît (ed.), *De la déviance à la délinquance: XVe–XXe siècle* (Dijon: Editions Universitaires de Dijon, 1999).

Garnot, Benoît, *Crime et justice en France au XVIIe et XVIIIe siècles* (Paris: Imago, 2000).

Garnot, Benoît, *Justice et société en France au XVIe, XVIIe et XVIIIe siècles* (Paris: Ophrys, 2000).

Garnot, Benoît (ed.), *Les Victimes, des oubliées de l'histoire?* (Rennes: Presses Universitaires de Rennes, 2000).

Garnot, Benoît (ed.), *Les Témoins devant la justice: une histoire des statuts et des comportements* (Rennes: Presses Universitaires de Rennes, 2003).

Garnot, Benoît (ed.), *L'Erreur judiciaire: de Jeanne d'Arc à Roland Agret* (Paris: Imago, 2004).

Garnot, Benoît, *Intime conviction et erreur judiciaire? Un magistrat assassin au XVIIe siècle* (Dijon: Editions Universitaires de Dijon, 2004).

Garnot, Benoît (ed.), *Les Juristes et l'Argent: le coût de la justice et l'argent des juges du XIVe au XIXe siècle* (Dijon: Editions Universitaires de Dijon, 2005).

Garnot, Benoît (ed.), *Justice et argent: les crimes et les peines pécuniaires du XIIIe au XXIe siècle* (Dijon: Editions Universitaires de Dijon, 2005).

Garnot, Benoît (ed.), *La Justice et l'Histoire: sources judiciaires à l'époque moderne (XVIe, XVIIe et XVIIIe siècles)* (Paris: Bréal, 2006).

Garnot, Benoît, *Questions de justice: 1667–1789* (Paris: Belin, 2006).

Gatrell, V. A. C., *The Hanging Tree: Execution and the English People, 1770–1868* (Oxford: Oxford University Press, 1994).

Gatrell, V. A. C., Bruce Lenman and Geoffrey Parker (eds), *Crime and the Law: The Social History of Crime in Western Europe since 1500* (London: Europa, 1980).

Gauvard, Claude, *'De grace especial': crime, Etat et société en France à la fin du Moyen Age* (Paris: Publications de la Sorbonne, 1991).

Geertz, Clifford, *The Interpretation of Culture: Selected Essays* (New York: Basic Books, 1973).

Geremek, Bronislaw, 'Criminalité, vagabondage, paupérisme: la marginalité à l'aube des temps modernes', *Revue d'histoire moderne et contemporaine*, 21 (1974), pp. 337–75.

Geremek, Bronislaw, *Truands et misérables dans l'Europe moderne (1350–1600)* (Paris: Gallimard-Julliard, 1980).

Geremek, Bronislaw, *The Margins of Society in Late Medieval Paris* [1971], trans. Jean Birrell (Cambridge: Cambridge University Press, 1987).

Gillis, A. R., 'So long as they both shall live: marital dissolution and the decline of domestic homicide in France, 1852–1909', *American Journal of Sociology*, 101 (1996), pp. 1273–1305.

Girard, René, *Violence and the Sacred*, trans. Patrick Gregory (Baltimore, MD: Johns Hopkins University Press, 1977).

Given, James Buchanan, *Society and Homicide in Thirteenth-Century England* (Stanford, CA: Stanford University Press, 1977).

Godfrey, Barry S., Clive Emsley and Graeme Dunstall (eds), *Comparative Histories of Crime* (Cullompton: Willan, 2003).

Godins de Souhesmes, Raymond des, *Etude sur la criminalité en Lorraine d'après les lettres de rémission* (Paris: Berger-Levrault, 1903).

Goffman, Erving, *The Presentation of Self in Everyday Life* (New York: Doubleday, 1959; London: Allen Lane, 1969; London: Penguin, 1990).

Goldstein, Robert J., *Political Repression in Nineteenth Century Europe* (London: Croom Helm, 1983).

Gonthier, Nicole, 'Délinquance, justice et société en Lyonnais (fin XIIIe siècle–début XVIe siècle)', thèse d'état, University of Lyon, 1988.

Gonthier, Nicole, *Cris de haine et rites d'unité: la violence dans les villes, XIIIe–XVIe siècle* (Turnhout: Brepols, 1992).

Goris, J. A., 'Zeden en criminaliteit te Antwerpen in de tweede helft van de XIVe eeuw, naar de rekeningen der schouten van 1358 tot 1387', *Revue belge de philologie et d'histoire*, 5 (1926), pp. 871–86; 6 (1927), pp. 181–205.

Gowing, Laura, *Domestic Dangers: Women, Words, and Sex in Early Modern London* (Oxford: Oxford University Press, 1996).

Green, Nancy L., 'La construction de la délinquance féminine', in Dauphin and Farge, *De la violence et des femmes*.

Greenberg, David F., 'The historical variability of the age–crime relationship', *Journal of Quantitative Criminology*, 10 (1994), pp. 361–73.

Greenshields, Malcolm, *An Economy of Violence in Early Modern France: Crime and Justice in the Haute Auvergne, 1587–1664* (University Park: Penn State University Press, 1994).

Griffiths, Paul, *Youth and Authority: Formative Experiences in England, 1560–1640* (Oxford: Clarendon Press, 1996).

Gruel, Louis, *Pardons et châtiments: les jurés français face aux violences criminelles* (Paris: Nathan, 1991).

Guenée, Bernard, *Tribunaux et gens de justice dans le bailliage de Senlis à la fin du Moyen Age* (Strasbourg: Publications de la Faculté des Lettres, 1963).

Gurr, Ted Robert, 'Historical trends in violent crime: a critical review of the evidence', in Michael Tonry and Norval Morris (eds), *Crime and Justice: An Annual Review of Research*, vol. 3 (Chicago: University of Chicago Press, 1981), pp. 295–353.

Gutton, Jean-Pierre, *La Société et les Pauvres en Europe (XVIe– XVIIIe siècle)* (Paris: PUF, 1974).

Hall, Edward Twitchell, *The Hidden Dimension: Man's Use of Space in Public and Private* (New York: Anchor Books, Doubleday, 1969).

Hammer, C. I., Jr, 'Patterns of homicide in a medieval university town: fourteenth-century Oxford', *Past and Present*, 78 (1978), pp. 3–23.

Hanawalt, Barbara, *Crime and Conflict in English Communities, 1300–1348* (Cambridge, MA: Harvard University Press, 1979).

Handman, Marie-Elizabeth, 'L'Enfer et le Paradis? Violence et tyrannie douce en Grèce contemporaine', in Dauphin and Farge, *De la violence et des femmes*, pp. 120–42.

Hanlon, Gregory, 'Les rituels de l'agression en Aquitaine au XVIIe siècle', *Annales ESC*, 40 (1985), pp. 244–68.

Hay, Douglas, Peter Linebaugh, John G. Rule, E. P. Thompson and Carl Winslow, *Albion's Fatal Tree: Crime and Society in Eighteenth-Century England* (London: Allen Lane, 1975; repr. Harmondsworth: Penguin, 1977).

Heers, Jacques, *Fêtes, jeux et joutes dans les sociétés d'Occident à la fin du Moyen Age* (Paris and Montréal: Conférences Albert le Grand, 1971).

Henry, Philippe, *Crime, justice et société dans la principauté de Neuchâtel au XVIIIe siècle* (Neuchâtel: Editions de la Baconnière, 1984).

Hindle, Steve, *The State and Social Change in Early Modern England, c. 1550–1640* (Basingstoke: Palgrave, 2000).

Hobsbawm, Eric J., *Bandits*, rev. edn (New York: Pantheon Books, 1981).

Hoffer, Peter C. and N. E. H. Hull, *Murdering Mothers: Infanticide in England and New England, 1558–1803* (New York: New York University Press, 1981).

Hogarth, William, *Catalogue de l'exposition du Louvre* (Paris: Hazan and Musée du Louvre Editions, 2006).

Houbballah, Adnan, Roland Gori and Christian Hoffmann (eds), *Pourquoi la violence des adolescents? Voix croisées entre Occident et Orient* (Paris: Erès, 2001).

Humphries, Stephen, *Hooligans or Rebels? An Oral History of Working-Class Childhood and Youth 1889–1939* (Oxford: Blackwell, 1983).

Hurl-Eamon, Jennine, *Gender and Petty Violence in London, 1680–1720* (Columbus: Ohio State University Press, 2005).

Jackson, Louise A., *Child Sexual Abuse in Victorian England* (London: Routledge, 2000).

Jackson, Mark, *New-Born Child Murder: Women, Illegitimacy and the Courts in Eighteenth-Century England* (Manchester: Manchester University Press, 1996).

Jansson, Arne, *From Swords to Sorrow: Homicide and Suicide in Early Modern Stockholm* (Stockholm: Almqvist and Wiksell, 1998).

Jeanneney, Jean-Noël, *Le Duel: une passion française (1789–1914)* (Paris: Seuil, 2004).

Johansen, Jens C. V. and Henrik Stevnsborg, 'Hasard ou myopie: réflexions autour de deux théories de l'histoire du droit', *Annales ESC*, 41 (1986), pp. 601–24.

Johnson, Eric A., *Urbanization and Crime: Germany, 1871–1914* (Cambridge: Cambridge University Press, 1995).

Johnson, Eric A. and Eric H. Monkkonen (eds), *The Civilization of Crime: Violence in Town and Country since the Middle Ages* (Urbana: University of Illinois Press, 1996).

Jouanna, Arlette, *Le Devoir de révolte: la noblesse française et la gestation de l'état moderne, 1559–1661* (Paris: Fayard, 1989).

Jouneaux, Olivier, 'Villageois et autorités', in Billacois and Neveux, 'Porter plainte', pp. 101–18.

Jugnot, Gérard, 'Les pèlerinages expiatoires et judiciaires au Moyen Age', in *La Faute, la Répression et le Pardon*, Actes du 107e congrès national des sociétes savantes, Brest, 1982, Section de philologie et d'histoire jusqu'à 1610, vol. 1 (Paris, CTHS, 1984), pp. 413–20.

Kaeuper, Richard W., *Chivalry and Violence in Medieval Europe* (Oxford: Oxford University Press, 1999).

Kalifa, Dominique, *L'Encre et le Sang: récits de crimes et société à la Belle Epoque* (Paris: Fayard, 1995).

Karonen, Petri, 'A life for a life versus Christian reconciliation: violence and the process of civilization in the kingdom of Sweden, 1540–1700', in Ylikangas et al., *Five Centuries of Violence in Finland and the Baltic Area*, pp. 85–132.

Kaspersson, Maria, ' "The great murder mystery" or explaining declining homicide rates', in Godfrey et al., *Comparative Histories of Crime*, pp. 72–88.

Kiernan, Victor Gordon, *The Duel in European History: Honour and the Reign of Aristocracy* (Oxford: Oxford University Press, 1988).

King, Peter, *Crime, Justice and Discretion in England, 1740–1820* (Oxford: Oxford University Press, 2000).

Laborit, Henri, *L'Agressivité détourné: introduction à une biologie du comportement social* (Paris: Union Génerale d'Editions, 1970).

Langbein, John H., *Torture and the Law of Proof: Europe and England in the Ancien Régime* (Chicago: University of Chicago Press, 1977).

Lanhers, Yvonne, 'Crimes et criminels au XIVe siècle', *Revue historique*, 240 (1968), pp. 325–38.

Lapalus, Sylvie, *La Mort du vieux? Le parricide au XIXe siècle* (Paris: Tallandier, 2004).

Lappalainen, Mirkka and Pckka Hirvonen (eds), *Crime and Control in Europe from the Past to the Present* (Helsinki: Hakapaino, 1999).

Lauwaert, Françoise, *Le Meurtre en famille: parricide et infanticide en Chine (XVIIIe–XIXe siècles)* (Paris: Odile Jacob, 1999).

Lebigre, Arlette, *Les Grand Jours d'Auvergne: désordres et répression au XVIIe siècle* (Paris: Hachette, 1976).

Le Bon, Gustave, *Psychologie des foules* [1895] (Paris: PUF, 1988), trans. as *The Crowd: A Study of the Popular Mind* (London: Ernest Benn, 20th edn, 1952).

Lebrun, François, *La Vie conjugale sous l'Ancien Régime* (Paris: Armand Colin, 1975).

Le Brun de la Rochette, Claude, *Le Procès civil et criminel* (Lyon: 1609; repr. Rouen: François Vaultier, 1661).

Lee, James, 'Homicide et peine capitale en Chine à la fin de l'Empire: analyse statistique préliminaire des données', *Etudes chinoises*, 10, 1–2 (1991), pp. 113–33.

Le Goaziou, Véronique, *La Violence* (Paris: Le Cavalier Bleu, 2004).

Lehti, Martti, 'Long-term trends in homicidal crime in Finland in 1750–2000', paper presented at the third GERN seminar, 'Violence in history: long-term trends and the role of wars', Brussels, 3–4 December 2004.

Le Roy Ladurie, Emmanuel, *Le Carnaval de Romans: de la Chandeleur au mercredi des Cendres, 1579–1580* (Paris: Gallimard, 1979), trans. Mary Feeney as *Carnival: A People's Uprising at Romans 1579–1580* (London: Scolar Press, 1980; Harmondsworth: Penguin, 1981).

Lever, Maurice, 'De l'information à la nouvelle: les "canards" et les "histoires tragiques" de François de Rosset', *Revue d'histoire littéraire de la France* (1979), pp. 577–93.

Lever, Maurice, *Canards sanglants: naissance du fait divers* (Paris: Fayard, 1993).

Libert, Christelle, 'Les appels au parlement de Paris à la fin du XVIe siècle', mémoire de DEA (under the supervision of Robert Muchembled), University of Paris-Nord, 1995.

Lindström, Dag, 'Interpersonal violence in Scandinavia: interpretation of long-term trends', paper presented at the third GERN seminar, 'Violence in history: long-term trends and the role of wars', Brussels, 3–4 December 2004.

Lizet, Pierre, *Pratique judiciaire pour l'instruction et décision des causes criminelles et civiles* [1557], with additions by L. Charondas Le Caron (Paris: Veuve Claude de Monstr'oeil, 1613).

Logette, Aline, 'La peine capitale devant la cour souveraine de Lorraine et Barrois à la fin du règne de Louis XIV', *XVIIe siècle*, 126 (1980), pp. 7–19.

Lorenz, Konrad, *On Aggression*, trans. Marjorie Latzke (London: Methuen, 1966; rev. edn London: Routledge, 1996).

Mac Lynn, Frank, *Crime and Punishment in Eighteenth-Century England* (Oxford: Oxford University Press, 1991).

Mandrou, Robert, 'Le baroque européen: mentalité pathétique et révolution sociale', *Annales ESC*, 15 (1960), pp. 898–914.

Mandrou, Robert, *Introduction à la France moderne: essai de psychologie historique, 1500–1640* (Paris: Albin Michel, 1961).

Mandrou, Robert, *Classes et luttes de classes en France au début du XVIIe siècle* (Messina and Florence: D'Anna, 1965).

Mandrou, Robert, *Magistrats et sorciers en France au XVIIe siècle: une analyse de psychologie historique* (Paris: Plon, 1968).

Mandrou, Robert, 'Vingt ans après... les révoltes populaires en France au XVIIe siècle', *Revue historique*, 242 (1969), pp. 29–40.

Mandrou, Robert, *Possession et sorcellerie au XVIIe siècle: textes inédits* (Paris: Fayard, 1979).

Mantecón, Tomas A., 'Long-term trend of crime in early modern Castile', paper presented at the third GERN seminar, 'Violence in history: long-term trends and the role of wars', Brussels, 3–4 December 2004.

Martin, Benjamin F., *Crime and Criminal Justice under the Third Republic: The Shame of Marianne* (Baton Rouge: Louisiana State University Press, 1990).

Marty, François (ed.), *L'Illégitime violence: la violence et son dépassement à l'adolescence* (Paris: Erès, 1997).

Màtay, Mónika and György Csepeli, 'The multiple lives of the Hungarian highwayman', in Srebnick and Lévy, *Crime and Culture*, pp. 183–97.

Matthews-Grieco, Sara F., *Ange ou diablesse: la représentation de la femme au XVIe siècle* (Paris: Flammarion, 1991).

Mauger, Gérard, *Les Bandes, le Milieu et la Bohème populaire: étude de sociologie de la déviance des jeunes des classes populaires, 1975–2005* (Paris: Belin, 2006).

Mauger, Gérard, *L'Emeute de novembre 2005: une révolte protopolitique* (Bellecombe-en-Bauges: Editions du Croquant, 2006).

Mayet, Fanny, 'Violence et société à Gonesse, 1620–1700', mémoire de maîtrise (under the supervision of Robert Muchembled), University of Paris-Nord, 1999.

McMahon, Vanessa, *Murder in Shakespeare's England* (Hambledon and London: Palgrave Macmillan, 2004).

Medick, Hans and David Sabean (eds), *Interest and Emotion: Essays on the Study of Family and Kinship* (Cambridge: Cambridge University Press, 1984).

Michaud, Yves, *La Violence* (Paris: PUF, 1986).

Michaud, Yves, *Changements dans la violence: essai sur la bienveillance universelle et la peur* (Paris: Odile Jacob, 2002).

351

Mitchell, Timothy, *Blood Sport: A Social History of Spanish Bull-Fighting* (Philadelphia: University of Pennsylvania Press, 1991).

Mollat, Michel and Philippe Wolff, *Ongle Bleues, Jacques et Ciompi: les révolutions populaires en Europe aux XIVe et XVe siècles* (Paris: Calmann-Lévy, 1970), trans. A. L. Lytton-Sells as *The Popular Revolutions of the Late Middle Ages* (London: Allen and Unwin, 1973).

Monkkonen, Eric H., *Murder in New York City* (Berkeley: University of California Press, 2001).

Monkkonen, Eric H., 'New standards for historical homicide research', *Crime, Histoire et Sociétés/Crime, History and Societies*, 5, 2 (2001), pp. 7–26.

Monkkonen, Eric H., *Crime, Justice, History* (Columbus: Ohio State University Press, 2002).

Monter, E. William, *Judging the French Reformation: Heresy Trials in Sixteenth-Century Parliaments* (Cambridge, MA: Harvard University Press, 1999).

Morris, Desmond, *The Human Sexes: A Natural History of Man and Woman* (London: Network Books, 1997).

Motley, Mark, *Becoming a French Aristocrat: The Education of the Court Nobility, 1580–1715* (Princeton, NJ: Princeton University Press, 1990).

Mousnier, Roland, *Fureurs paysannes: les paysans dans les révoltes du XVIIe siècle (France, Russie, Chine)* (Paris: Calmann-Lévy, 1967), trans. Brian Pearce as *Peasant Uprisings in Seventeenth-Century France, Russia, and China* (New York: Harper and Row, 1970; London: Allen and Unwin, 1971).

Moxey, Keith, *Peasants, Warriors, and Wives: Popular Imagery in the Reformation* (Chicago: University of Chicago Press, 1989).

Mucchielli, Laurent, *Violences et insécurité: fantasmes et réalités dans le débat français* (Paris: La Découverte, 2001; new edn 2002).

Muchembled, Robert, *La Sorcière au village (XVe–XVIIIe siècle)* (Paris: Gallimard-Julliard, 1975; new edn Gallimard, 1991).

Muchembled, Robert, *Culture populaire et culture des élites dans la France moderne (XVe–XVIIIe siècle): essai* (Paris: Flammarion, 1978; rev. edn with new introduction, 'Champs', 1991), trans. Lydia Cochrane as *Popular Culture and Elite Culture in France, 1400–1750* (Baton Rouge and London: Louisiana State University Press, 1985).

Muchembled, Robert, *Les Derniers Bûchers: un village de Flandre et ses sorcières sous Louis XIV* (Paris: Ramsay, 1981).

Muchembled, Robert, 'Crime et société urbaine: Arras au temps de Charles Quint (1528–1549)', in *La France d'Ancien Régime: études réunies en l'honneur de Pierre Goubert* (Toulouse: Privat, 1984), vol. 2, pp. 481–90.

Muchembled, Robert, 'Violence et société: comportements et mentalités populaires en Artois, 1400–1660', thèse de doctorat d'état (under the supervision of Pierre Goubert), University of Paris I, 3 vols, 1985 (copy deposited in the library of the Sorbonne).

Muchembled, Robert, 'Anthropologie de la violence dans la France moderne (XVe–XVIIIe siècle)', *Revue de synthèse*, 108, gen. ser. (1987), pp. 31–55.

Muchembled, Robert, *Sorcières, justice et société aux XVIe et XVIIe siècles* (Paris: Imago, 1987).

Muchembled, Robert, *L'Invention de l'homme moderne: culture et sensibilités en France du XVe au XVIIIe siècle* (Paris: Fayard, 1988; repr. Hachette, 1994).

Muchembled, Robert, *La Violence au village (XVe–XVIIe siècle): comportements populaires et mentalités en Artois* (Turnhout: Brepols, 1989).

Muchembled, Robert, *Le Temps des supplices: de l'obéissance sous les rois absolus, XVe–XVIIIe siècle* (Paris: Armand Colin, 1992; repr. Agora, 2006).

Muchembled, Robert, *Le Roi et la Sorcière: l'Europe des bûchers, XVe–XVIIIe siècle* (Paris: Desclée, 1993).

Muchembled, Robert (ed.), *Magie et sorcellerie en Europe du Moyen Age à nos jours* (Paris: Armand Colin, 1994).

Muchembled, Robert, *Société, cultures et mentalités dans la France moderne: XVIe–XVIIIe siècle* (Paris: Armand Colin, 1994; rev. and corrected edn, 2003).

Muchembled, Robert, *La Société policée: politique et politesse en France du XVIe au XXe siècle* (Paris: Seuil, 1998).

Muchembled, Robert, 'Les théâtres du crime: villes et campagnes face à la justice (XVIe–XVIIIe siècle)', in d'Hollander, *Violences en Limousin à travers les siècles*, pp. 91–111.

Muchembled, Robert, *Une histoire du diable, XIIe–XXe siècle* (Paris: Seuil, 2000), trans. Jean Birrell as *A History of the Devil from the Middle Ages to the Present* (Cambridge: Polity, 2003).

Muchembled, Robert, *Passions de femmes au temps de la reine Margot, 1553–1615* (Paris: Seuil, 2003).

Muchembled, Robert, *L'Orgasme et l'Occident: une histoire du plaisir du XVIe siècle à nos jours* (Paris: Seuil, 2005), trans. Jean Birrell as *Orgasm and the West: A History of Pleasure from the Sixteenth Century to the Present* (Cambridge: Polity, 2008).

Muchembled, Robert (ed.), *Cultural Exchange in Early Modern Europe*, 4 vols (Cambridge: Cambridge University Press, 2007), vol. 1: *Religion*; vol. 2: *Cities*; vol. 3: *Correspondence*; vol. 4: *Forging European Identities*.

Muchembled, Robert, 'Fils de Caïn, enfants de Médée: homicide et infanticide devant le parlement de Paris (1575–1604)', *Annales Histoire, Sciences Sociales*, 72 (2007), pp. 1063–94.

Muchembled, Robert and Gérard Sivery (eds), *Nos ancêtres les paysans: aspects du monde rural dans le Nord-Pas-de-Calais des origines à nos jours* (Lille: CRDP, 1983).

Muir, Edward, *Mad Blood Stirring: Vendetta and Factions in Friuli during the Renaissance* (Baltimore, MD: Johns Hopkins University Press, 1993).

Muir, Edward, *Ritual in Early Modern Europe* (Cambridge: Cambridge University Press, 1997).

Mullett, Michael, *Popular Culture and Popular Protest in Late Medieval and Early Modern Europe* (London: Croom Helm, 1987).

Newman, Graeme (ed.), *Global Report on Crime and Justice* (New York: Oxford University Press for the *United Nations Office for Drug Control and Crime Prevention, Centre for International Crime Prevention*, 1999).

Nicholas, David M., 'Crime and punishment in fourteenth-century Ghent', *Revue belge de philologie et d'histoire*, 48 (1970), pp. 289–334, 1141–76.

Nicolas, Jean, *La Rébellion française: mouvements populaires et conscience social, 1661–1789* (Paris: Seuil, 2002).

Nye, Robert A., *Masculinity and Male Codes of Honor in Modern France* (Oxford and New York: Oxford University Press, 1993).

Obert, Franck, '160 querelles d'honneur devant le tribunal des Maréchaux de France (1774–1789)', mémoire de maîtrise (under the supervision of Robert Muchembled), University of Paris-Nord, 1998.

O'Donnell, Ian, 'Lethal violence in Ireland, 1841–2003: famine, celibacy and parental pacification', *British Journal of Criminology*, 45 (2005), pp. 671–95.

Oestreich, Gerhard, *Neostoicism and the Early Modern State* (Cambridge: Cambridge University Press, 1982).

Osterberg, Eva, 'Criminality, social control and the early modern state: evidence and interpretations in Scandinavian historiography', *Social Science History*, 16, 1 (1992), pp. 67–98, repr. in Johnson and Monkkonen, *The Civilization of Crime*, pp. 35–62.

Osterberg, Eva and Dag Lindström, *Crime and Social Control in Medieval and Early Modern Swedish Towns* (Uppsala: Academia Upsaliensis, 1988).

Parella, Anne, 'Violence in northern France: a social historical analysis of murder, 1815–1909', unpublished PhD thesis, University of Virginia, 1983.

Parella, Anne, 'Industrialization and murder: northern France, 1815–1904', *Journal of Interdisciplinary History*, 22 (1992), pp. 627–54.

Paresys, Isabelle, *Aux marges du royaume: violence, justice et société en Picardie sous François Ier* (Paris: Publications de la Sorbonne, 1998).

Parker, Geoffrey, *The Military Revolution: Military Innovation and the Rise of the West, 1500–1800* (Cambridge: Cambridge University Press, 2nd edn, 1996).

Pellegrin, Nicole, *Les Bachelleries: organisations et fêtes de la jeunesse dans le Centre-Ouest, XVe–XVIIIe siècle* (Poitiers: Mémoires de la Société des Antiquaires de l'Ouest, 1982).

Peristiany, Jean G. (ed.), *Honour and Shame: The Values of Mediterranean Society* (London: Weidenfeld and Nicolson, 1965).

Perry, Mary Elizabeth, *Crime and Society in Early Modern Seville* (Hanover, NH: University Press of New England, 1980).

Perry, Mary Elizabeth, *Gender and Disorder in Early Modern Seville* (Princeton, NJ: Princeton University Press, 1990).

Peterson del Mar, David, *Beaten Down: A History of Interpersonal Violence in the West* (Seattle: University of Washington Press, 2002).

Petit, Jacques-Guy (ed.), *Histoire des galères, bagnes et prisons* (Toulouse: Privat, 1991).

Petit-Dutaillis, Charles, *Documents nouveaux sur les moeurs populaires et le droit de vengeance dans les Pays-Bas au XVe siècle: lettres de rémission de Philippe le Bon* (Paris: Champion, 1908).

Petkov, Kiril, *The Kiss of Peace: Ritual, Self and Society in the High and Late Medieval West* (Leiden: Brill, 2003).

Philips, David, *Crime and Authority in Victorian England: The Black Country 1835–1860* (London: Croom Helm, 1977).

Picard, Raymond and Jean Lafond (eds), *Nouvelles du XVIIe siècle* (Paris: Gallimard, 1997).

Pierquin, Hubert, *La Juridiction du point d'honneur sous l'Ancien Régime* (Paris: Picard, 1904).

Ploux, François, *Guerres paysannes en Quercy: violences, conciliations et répression pénale dans les campagnes du Lot (1810–1860)* (Paris: La Boutique de l'Histoire, 2002).

Poli, Sergio, *Histoire(s) tragique(s): anthologie/typologie d'un genre littéraire* (Bari: Schena, 1991; Paris: Nizet, 1991).

Porchnev, Boris, *Les Soulèvements populaires en France de 1623 à 1648* (Paris: SEVPEN, 1963, repr. Flammarion, 1972).

Quaife, Geoffrey Robert, *Wanton Wenches and Wayward Wives: Peasants and Illicit Sex in Early Seventeenth-Century England* (London: Croom Helm, 1979).

Rauch, André, *Boxe, violence au XXe siècle* (Paris: Aubier, 1992).

Rawlings, Philip, *Policing: A Short History* (London: Willan, 2002).

Reinhardt, Steven G., *Justice in the Sarladais, 1770–1790* (Baton Rouge: Louisiana State University Press, 1991).

Rey, Roselyne, *Histoire de la douleur* (Paris: La Découverte, 1993).

Reynolds, Bryan, *Becoming Criminal: Transversal Performance and Cultural Dissidence in Early Modern England* (Cambridge: Cambridge University Press, 2002).

Reynolds, Elaine, *Before the Bobbies: The Night Watch and Police Reform in Metropolitan London, 1720–1830* (Stanford, CA: Stanford University Press, 1998).

Riches, David, *The Anthropology of Violence* (Oxford: Blackwell, 1986).

Robert, Philippe, *Les Comptes du crime: les délinquances en France et leurs mesures* (Paris: Le Sycomore, 1985).

Roché, Sébastian, *Le Frisson de l'émeute: violences urbaines et banlieues* (Paris: Seuil, 2006).

Rochelandet, Brigitte, *Sorcières, diables et bûchers en Franche-Comté aux XVIe et XVIIe siècles* (Besançon: Cêtre, 1997).

Roecke, Michael, *Forbidden Friendships: Homosexuality and Male Culture in Renaissance Florence* (Oxford: Oxford University Press, 1996).

Romagnoli, Daniela (ed.), *La Ville et la Cour: des bonnes et des mauvaises manières* (Paris: Fayard, 1995).

Rosset, François de, *Les Histoires tragiques de notre temps*, pref. René Godenne (Geneva: Slatkine Reprints, 1980).

Rossiaud, Jacques, 'Fraternités de jeunesse et niveaux de culture dans les villes du Sud-Est à la fin du Moyen Age', *Cahiers d'histoire*, 21 (1976), pp. 67–102.

Rossiaud, Jacques, *La Prostitution médiévale* (Paris: Flammarion, 1988).

Roth, Randolph, 'Spousal murder in Northern New England, 1776–1865', in C. Daniels and M. V. Kennedy (eds), *Over the Threshold: Intimate Violence in Early America* (New York: Routledge, 1999), pp. 65–93.

Roth, Randolph, 'Child murder in New England', *Social Science History*, 25 (2001), pp. 100–47.

Roth, Randolph, 'Homicide in Early Modern England, 1549–1800: the need for a quantitative synthesis', *Crime, Histoire et Sociétés/Crime, History and Societies*, 5, 2 (2001), pp. 33–67.

Roth, Randolph, 'Guns, gun culture and homicide: the relationship between firearms, the uses of firearms, and interpersonal violence', *William and Mary Quarterly*, 3rd ser., 49 (2002), pp. 223–40.

Roth, Randolph, 'Twin evils: the relationship between slavery and homicide in New England, the Chesapeake, and the Shenandoah Valley, 1677–1800', in S. Mintz and J. Stauffer (eds), *The Problem of Evil: Slavery, Freedom, and the Ambiguities of American Reform* (Amherst: University of Massachusetts Press, 2006).

Rousseaux, Xavier, 'Ordre et violence: criminalité et répression dans une ville brabançonne, Nivelles (1646–1695)', *Revue de droit pénal et de criminologie*, 66 (1986), pp. 649–92.

Rousseaux, Xavier, 'Taxer ou châtier? L'émergence du pénal: enquête sur la justice nivelloise (1400–1660)', unpublished thesis, University of Louvain-la-Neuve, 1990.

Rousseaux, Xavier, 'La répression de l'homicide en Europe occidentale (Moyen Age et temps modernes)', *Genèses: Sciences sociales et histoire*, 19 (April 1995), pp. 122–47.

Rousseaux, Xavier, 'From case to crime: homicide regulation in medieval and modern Europe', in Dietmar Willoweit (ed.), *Die Entstehung des öffentliche Strafrechts: Bestandsaufnahme eines europäischen Forschungsproblem* (Cologne: Böhlau, 1999).

Rousseaux, Xavier, Frédéric Vesentini and Antoon Vrints, 'Statistics of homicide in Belgium: a preliminary analysis', paper presented at the third GERN seminar, 'Violence in history: long-term trends and the role of wars', Brussels, 3–4 December 2004.

Rublack, Ulinka, *The Crimes of Women in Early Modern Germany* (Oxford: Oxford University Press, 1999).

Rudé, George, *The Crowd in History: A Study of Popular Disturbances in France and England, 1730–1848* (New York: John Wiley and Sons, 1964).

Ruff, Julius R., *Crime, Justice, and Public Order in Old Regime France: The Sénéchaussées of Libourne and Bazas, 1696–1789* (London: Croom Helm, 1984).

Ruff, Julius R., *Violence in Early Modern Europe, 1500–1800* (Cambridge: Cambridge University Press, 2001).

Ruggiero, Guido, *Violence in Early Renaissance Venice* (New Brunswick, NJ: Rutgers University Press, 1980).

Ruggiero, Guido, *The Boundaries of Eros: Sex Crime and Sexuality in Renaissance Venice* (Oxford: Oxford University Press, 1985).

Sauvadet, Thomas, *Le Capital guerrier: concurrence et solidarité entre jeunes de cités* (Paris: Armand Colin, 2006).

Schalk, Ellery, *From Valor to Pedigree: Ideas of Nobility in France in the Sixteenth and Seventeenth Centuries* (Princeton, NJ: Princeton University Press, 1986).

Schilling, Heinz, *Religion, Political Culture and the Emergence of Early Modern Society* (Leiden: Brill, 1992).

Schnapper, Bernard, *Les Peines arbitraires du XIIIe au XVIIIe siècle (doctrines savantes et usages français)* (Paris: LGDJ, 1974).

Schnapper, Bernard, *Voies nouvelles en histoire du droit: la justice, la famille, la répression pénale (XVIe–XXe siècle)* (Paris: PUF, 1991), esp. 'La répression pénale au XVIe siècle: l'exemple du parlement de Bordeaux (1510–1565)', pp. 53–105; 'La justice criminelle rendue par le parlement de Paris sous la règne de François Ier', pp. 108–33; 'A propos de la procédure criminelle du parlement de Paris au temps de François Ier', pp. 135–44.

Schuster, Peter, *Eine Stadt vor Gericht: Recht und Alltag im spätmittelalterlichen Konstanz* (Paderborn: Schöning, 2000).

Schwerhoff, Gerd, *Köln im Kreuzverhör: Kriminalität, Herrschaft und Gesellschaft in einer frühneuzeitlichen Stadt* (Bonn: Bouvier, 1991).

Schwerhoff, Gerd, 'Criminalized violence and the civilising process: a reappraisal', *Crime, Histoire et Sociétés/Crime, History and Societies*, 6 (2002), pp. 103–26.

Schwerhoff, Gerd, 'Justice et honneur: interpréter la violence à Cologne (XVe–XVIIIe siècle)', *Annales Histoire, Sciences Sociales*, 72 (2007), pp. 1031–61.

Segalen, Martine, 'Avoir sa part: sibling relations in partible inheritance in Brittany', in Medick and Sabean, *Interest and Emotion*, pp. 129–44.

Seguin, Jean-Pierre, *L'Information en France avant le périodique: 517 canards imprimés entre 1529 et 1631* (Paris: Maisonneuve et Larose, 1964).

Shapiro, Ann-Louise, *Breaking the Codes: Female Criminality in Fin-de-Siècle Paris* (Stanford, CA: Stanford University Press, 1996).

Sharpe, James A., *Crime in Seventeenth-Century England: A County Study* (Cambridge: Cambridge University Press, 1983).

Sharpe, James A., *Crime in Early Modern England, 1550–1750* (London: Longman, 1984).

Sharpe, James A., ' "Last dying speeches": religion, ideology and public execution in seventeenth-century England', *Past and Present*, 107 (1985), pp. 144–67.

Sharpe, James A., 'Crime in England: long-term trends and the problem of modernization', in Johnson and Monkkonen, *The Civilization of Crime*.

Shoemaker, Robert B., *The London Mob: Violence and Disorder in Eighteenth-Century England* (London: Palgrave Macmillan, 2004).

Shore, Heather, 'The trouble with boys: gender and the "invention" of the juvenile offender in early-nineteenth-century Britain', in Arnot and Usborne, *Gender and Crime in Modern Europe*, pp. 75–92.

Sibony, Daniel, *Violence* (Paris: Seuil, 1998).

Silverman, Lisa, *Tortured Subjects: Pain, Truth, and the Body in Early Modern France* (Chicago: University of Chicago Press, 2001).

Smith, M. Dwayne and Margaret A. Zahn (eds), *Homicide: A Source-Book of Social Research* (Thousand Oaks, CA: Sage, 1999).

Snyders, Georges, *La Pédagogie en France aux XVIIe et XVIIIe siècles* (Paris: PUF, 1965).

Soman, Alfred, *Sorcellerie et justice criminelle: le Parlement de Paris, XVIe–XVIIIe siècle* (Aldershot: Variorum, 1992), esp. 'La justice criminelle aux XVIe et XVIIe siècles: le parlement de Paris et les sièges subalternes', pp. 15–52; 'Pathologie historique: le témoignage des procès de bestialité aux XVIe–XVIIe siècles', pp. 149–61.

Soman, Alfred, 'Sorcellerie, justice criminelle et société dans la France moderne: l'ego-histoire d'un Américain à Paris', *Histoire, Economie et Société* (1993), pp. 177–217.

Sorbier, Françoise du, 'De la potence à la biographie, ou les avatars du criminel et de son image en Angleterre (1680–1740)', *Etudes anglaises* (1979), pp. 257–71.

Sorbier, Françoise du, *Récits de gueuserie et biographies criminelles de Head à Defoe* (Paris: Didier Erudition, 1984).

Spierenburg, Pieter, *The Spectacle of Suffering: Executions and the Evolution of Repression: From a Preindustrial Metropolis to the European Experience* (Cambridge: Cambridge University Press, 1984).

Spierenburg, Pieter, 'Faces of violence: homicide trends and cultural meanings: Amsterdam, 1431–1816', *Journal of Social History*, 27 (1994), pp. 701–16.

Spierenburg, Pieter, 'Long-term trends in homicide: theoretical reflections and Dutch evidence, fifteenth to twentieth centuries', in Johnson and Monkkonen, *The Civilization of Crime*, pp. 63–105.

Spierenburg, Pieter, 'Knife fighting and popular codes of honor in early modern Amsterdam', in Spierenburg, *Men and Violence*, pp. 103–27.

Spierenburg, Pieter (ed.), *Men and Violence: Gender, Honor, and Rituals in Modern Europe and America* (Columbus: Ohio State University Press, 1998).

Srebnick, Amy Gilman and René Lévy (eds), *Crime and Culture: An Historical Perspective* (Aldershot: Ashgate, 2005).

Stone, Lawrence, *The Crisis of the Aristocracy (1558–1641)* (Oxford: Clarendon Press, 1965).

Stone, Lawrence, 'Interpersonal violence in English society, 1300–1800', *Past and Present*, 101 (1983), pp. 22–33.

Sueur, Philippe, *Histoire du droit public français, XVe–XVIIIe siècle* (Paris: PUF, 1989).

Thome, Helmut, 'Explaining long-term trends in violent crime', *Crime, Histoire et Sociétés/Crime, History and Societies*, 5, 2 (2001), pp. 69–87.

Tillier, Annick, *Des criminelles au village: femmes infanticides en Bretagne (1825–1865)* (Rennes: Presses Universitaires de Rennes, 2001).

Tilly, Charles, *The Contentious French: Four Centuries of Popular Struggle* (Cambridge, MA: Harvard University Press, 1986).

Tilly, Charles, *Coercion, Capital, and European States, AD 900–1990* (Malden, MA: Blackwell, 1990).

Traité de Luís Fróis, s.j. (1585) sur les contradictions de moeurs entre Européens et Japonais, trans. from Portuguese by Xavier de Castro (Paris: Editions Chandeigne, 1993). (English translation: Robin D. Gill, *Topsy-Turvy 1585: The Short Version: A Full Translation, Explication and Essay of Luis Frois by S.J.'s famous treatise (Tratado) listing 611 ways Europeans & Japanese differ* (Florida: Paraverse Press, 2004).)

Underdown, David, *Revel, Riot and Rebellion: Popular Politics and Culture in England, 1603–1660* (Oxford: Oxford University Press, 1985).

United Nations (1970–), 'United Nations survey of crime trends and operations of criminal justice systems'.

Vaissière, Pierre de, *Gentilshommes campagnards de l'Ancienne France: étude sur les conditions, l'état social et les moeurs de la noblesse de province du XVIe au XVIIIe siècle* (Paris: Perrin, 1903).

Vaissière, Pierre de, *De quelques assassins* (Paris: Emile-Paul, 1912).

Vandenbroeke, Chris, 'Het seksuel gedrag der jongeren in Vlaanderen sinds de late 16de eeuw', *Bijdragen tot de geschiedenis*, 72 (1979), pp. 193–230.

Vaucher Gravili, Anne de, *Loi et transgression: les histoires tragiques du XVIIe siècle* (Lecce: Milella, 1982).

Verdier, Raymond (ed.), *Vengeance: le face-à-face victime/aggresseur* (Paris: Autrement, 2004).

Verdier, Raymond and Jean-Pierre Poly (eds), *La Vengeance: études d'ethnologie, d'histoire et de philosophie*, 4 vols (Paris: Cujas, 1980–6).

Vernet, Alain and Franck Henry, with Cyril Boutet and Abdeenour Chalal, 'Contribution à la compréhension des comportements agressifs et violents', *Le Journal des Psychologues*, 241 (Oct. 2006), pp. 59–63.

Vernet, Max, *Jean-Pierre Camus: théories de la contre-littérature* (Paris: Nizet, 1995).

Viala, Alain, *Naissance de l'ecrivain: sociologie de la littérature à l'âge classique* (Paris: Minuit, 1985).

Vialles, Noëlie, *Le Sang et la Chair: les abattoirs des pays de l'Adour* (Paris: Editions de la Maison des Sciences de l'Homme, 1987).

Vié, Dominique, 'La criminalité à Bordeaux de 1768 à 1777 d'après les plaintes et informations de la cour des Jurats', *Positions des thèses de l'Ecole des Chartes* (Paris, 1971), pp. 193–9.

Vigarello, Georges, *Histoire du viol: XVIe–XXe siècle* (Paris: Seuil, 1998), trans. Jean Birrell as *A History of Rape: Sexual Violence in France from the 16th to the 20th Century* (Cambridge: Polity, 2001).

Weber, Max, *The Protestant Ethic and the Spirit of Capitalism* [1904–5], trans. Talcott Parsons (Oxford: Blackwell, 2002).

Wegert, Karl, *Popular Culture, Crime, and Social Control in Eighteenth-Century Württemberg* (Stuttgart: Franz Steiner, 1994).

Wiener, Martin J., 'The Victorian criminalization of men', in Spierenburg, *Men and Violence*.

Wiener, Martin J., *Men of Blood: Violence, Manliness, and Criminal Justice in Victorian England* (Cambridge: Cambridge University Press, 2004).

Wikström, Per-Olof H., *Everyday Violence in Contemporary Sweden: Situational and Ecological Aspects* (Stockholm: National Council for Crime Prevention, 1985).

Williams, Alan, *The Police of Paris, 1718–1789* (Baton Rouge: Louisiana State University Press, 1979).

Wilson, Stephen, *Feuding, Conflict, and Banditry in Nineteenth-Century Corsica* (Cambridge: Cambridge University Press, 1988).

Ylikangas, Heikki, 'What happened to violence? An analysis of the development of violence from medieval times to the early modern era based on Finnish source material', in Ylikangas et al., *Five Centuries of Violence in Finland and the Baltic Area*, pp. 1–83.

Ylikangas, Heikki, Petri Karonen and Martti Lehti (eds), *Five Centuries of Violence in Finland and the Baltic Area* (Columbus: Ohio State University Press, 2001).

Yver, Jean, *Egalité entre héritiers et exclusion des enfants dotés: essai de géographie coutumière* (Paris: Sirey, 1996).

Zagnoli, Nello, 'S'arracher la haine', in Verdier, *Vengeance*, pp. 115–24.

Zehr, Howard, *Crime and the Development of Modern Society: Patterns of Criminality in Nineteenth-Century Germany and France* (London: Croom Helm, 1976).

Zimring, Franklin E. and Gordon Hawkings, *Crime Is Not the Problem: Lethal Violence in America* (New York: Oxford University Press, 1997).

Zmora, Hillay, *State and Nobility in Early Modern Germany: The Knightly Feud in Franconia, 1460–1567* (Cambridge: Cambridge University Press, 1996).

INDEX

'abbeys' or 'kingdoms' of youth, 29,
    55–8, 61, 65, 93–4, 95, 134,
    187, 260–1, 270, 290–1, 293
abortion, 205
adolescence, 6, 41, 100
    attitudes towards, 283
    demands of, 221–2
    emergence of youth crime, 284
    ideal masculine, 275
    invention of, 2, 17, 29–30, 122
    literary representations of, 255
    as source of anxiety, 126
    in urban areas, 224
Advent, 52, 105
age of offenders, 40–1, 74, 79,
    201–2, 236
    decrease in, 280–1
    in duels, 178, 179–80
    in Gonesse, 227
    of thieves, 144, 237
aggression, 1–2
    channelled into sport, 209
    ethological theories, 10–11
    management of male, 19, 22–3,
        109, 122, 301–2
    in modern adolescents, 288
    municipalization of, 5
    positive value of, 16
    redirected to external enemies, 182
    in rural areas, 302

territorial, 11–12
    distinguished from violence, 10
alcohol, 71, 81, 207, 279
All Saints' Day, 53, 54, 86
Allain, Marcel, 267
Ambrus, Attila, 259–60
American Graffiti (film), 292
Amiens, 98, 102, 143
Amsterdam
    age of male murderers in, 41
    city-state model, 162
    correction houses in, 159
    crime figures for, 38, 39
    decline in violence in, 224
    knife fights in, 28, 43
    public executions in, 132, 146
    rural migration to, 240
    thieves in, 144, 215
ancien régime, 8, 9, 20, 41, 127, 141,
    188
Andalusia, 65
animal fighting, 67, 169, 204
Antwerp, 84, 89, 91, 118, 143, 159,
    162
Apaches, 19, 43, 175, 220, 222, 224,
    243, 269–70, 275, 278, 285,
    291
apaiseurs, 84
Applebee, John, 253
aristocracy see nobles

Arques, in Artois, 47–8
Arras, 33, 35, 86–7, 101
  banishment from, 116, 117
  festivals in, 95, 98
  municipal dog-killer in, 90
  murder rate in, 36–7
  prison in, 105
  prostitutes, 89
  punishments, 27, 47, 88, 103–4,
    107, 115, 143
  sodomy, 102
Artois, 4, 39, 47, 70, 71–2, 77, 81,
    101
  crime figures, 33–7
  duels, 171
  festivals, 53, 61
  insults, 64
  knife fights, 43, 80
  lettres de rémission, 78
  marriage, 57, 103
  pardons, 109, ,
  punishments, 88
  ritual battles, 75
  swords, 175
  taverns, 63
  youth violence, 78
asseurement, 84
Austria, 147, 210
Aztecs, 136, 168

bachelor gangs, 17, 21–2, 34
Bakelandt, Lodewijk, 258, 259
Balzac, Honoré de, 264
banishment, 36, 103, 104, 116–17,
    144, 179, 230
banlieues, 4, 19, 23, 64, 263, 288,
    292–300
bare-knuckle fighting, 169, 199, 222,
    226, 233
Baroque, 134, 135, 155, 160, 173, 191
bastardy, 36, 153
begging, 90, 125–6, 263
Belgium
  gangs, 289
  juvenile delinquency, 284
  murder rate, 210

Belleforest, François de, 154, 245
Benedek, Laslo, 289
bestiality, 55, 102, 124–5
Béthune, 37, 71, 96, 98, 117, 144
Birmingham, 67, 201, 285
Blake, Blueskin, 253
'blood peace', 16
Bloody Code, 206, 213, 241
Boaistuau, Pierre, 244–5
Bordeaux, 124, 214
  age of offenders, 236
  Carnival, 188
  murders in, 221
  petty crime, 213
  public executions, 146
  rural migration to, 240
  torture, 130
Bouteville affair, 171–4
boxing, 66, 169, 190, 195, 222
branding, 143, 146
Brandons, feast of, 66
Bridewell, 159
Brittany
  infanticide, 150
  inheritance law, 71
  judicial system, 123
  rebellion in, 185
  soule, 66
  torture, 130–1
'broken window' theory, 115
brothels, 89
Bruegel the Elder, Pieter, 53, 62, 76
Bruges, 92–3, 117, 143
Brussels, 39, 89, 106, 143, 146, 159
buffes (slaps), 107, 108, 111, 112,
    113, 114–15
bullfighting, 67, 190
Burgundy
  court of, 91
  festivals, 94, 95, 97, 98
  infanticide, 150
  judicial system, 123
  punishments, 103
  social pact, 116
  urban cohesion, 97
burning at the stake, 135, 140, 147

Cain and Abel, 134, 145, 154
Calabria, 21, 304
Calvinism, 35, 91, 101, 161, 184
Cambrai, 95, 96, 98, 144
Camus, Jean-Pierre, 134, 154, 155, 156, 245, 246–51
canards, 134, 155, 169, 243, 249–50, 251
capitalism, 24, 91, 92, 122, 240
Carleton, Mary, 253
Carné, Marcel, 289, 290
Carnival, 53, 54, 66, 72, 97–8, 105, 187
  bloodshed at, 186, 191
  Paris, 79
  revolts linked to, 188–9
Cartouche, 30, 144, 243–4, 253, 256–7, 259–60, 262, 264, 266, 268, 270
Castiglione, Baldassare, 302
Castile, 45, 124, 141
Catholicism, 24, 28, 45, 53, 154, 165
  confession, 187
  educational structures, 100
  'matrimonial purgatory', 34
  moral supervision, 25, 128, 145
  religious riots, 186
  suppression of festivals, 187
  upsurge of, 134
cemeteries, 61–2
charivaris, 65, 94, 186, 193
Charles the Rash, Duke of Burgundy, 88, 97, 102, 117, 162
children
  corporal punishment, 20
  crimes against, 16
  cruelty to, 240
  culture of violence, 21
  innocence, 23, 284
  juvenile delinquency, 284–5
  sexual abuse of, 202–4
  'social discipline', 25–6
  see also infanticide
China, 13–14

Christianity, 7, 10, 16, 29, 52, 65, 170
  burning at the stake, 135
  commandment against murder, 133–4
  message of peace, 132
  modern state, 120
  moral supervision, 128
  public executions, 136, 137, 140, 141
  sacrifices forbidden by, 67
  sin, 283
  see also Catholicism; Protestantism
churches, 61–2
cities *see* urban areas
city-states, 162, 165
'civilizing process', 2, 22–4, 42, 81, 91, 111–12, 122, 127, 176, 194, 198, 217, 226, 248, 292, 302
  in England, 206
  resistance, non-adaptation to, 199, 288
  and *A Clockwork Orange* (film), 292
Cologne, 43
Colombia, 276, 277, 278
colonialism, 8, 30
compensation, 26–7, 46, 47, 84, 104, 108, 232, 235
Conan Doyle, Arthur, 266–7
confession, 129, 130, 187
'confessionalization', 126
confraternities, 67, 68, 93
conquistadors, 8, 163, 168
Coquillards of Dijon, 87
corporal punishment, 20, 51, 103, 116, 120, 131, 140–1
corpses, display of, 140
correction, houses of, 159
Corsica, 192, 200, 238, 303–4
Counter-Reformation, 34, 65, 72, 77, 245, 247
'court of miracles', 87, 90
courts *see* criminal justice system; lawsuits

crafts, trades, 28, 99, 107, 113–14,
213, 234
crime fiction, 256–7, 262–72
crime figures, 31–44, 240
criminal justice system, 5, 27, 32,
198–9
court mechanism, 142
'judicial revolution', 120, 121–31,
240
criminality, 16
criminology, 41, 269
culture of violence, 8, 21, 41, 44, 45,
46–52, 58, 75, 302
Cureau de la Chambre, Martin, 176
'curialization', 22, 42, 117, 302
Cyrulnik, Boris, 10
Czechoslovakia, 210

Damhouder, Josse de, 123, 133–4
'dangerous classes', 221–2, 225,
240–1, 264, 269, 281, 291,
296, 299, 302
see also working class
death penalty, 5, 14, 18, 25, 45, 51,
122
abolition of, 7, 16, 208
Antwerp, 84
Artois, 88
for bestiality, 125
decline in use of, 146, 147, 208
for duels, 171–2, 174
England, 49, 162–3
European comparisons, 207–8
for firearm use, 76
Gonesse, 229
increased use of, 15, 42, 43, 78
infanticide, 149, 151, 159
in Madrid, 124
Nordic kingdom, 169
Paris, 85
public executions, 27, 121, 129,
131–47, 160, 190, 191, 195,
251–2, 262
sodomy, 92–3
theft, 102, 215–16
urban areas, 102
women, 50, 120–1

and see burning at the stake,
decapitation
decapitation, 135, 137, 146, 148
'de-civilizing process', 3
Defoe, Daniel, 253, 254, 261, 262
delinquency, 125–6, 201, 202, 236,
282
female, 214
imprisonment, 198
juvenile, 283–8
physiognomy, 269
urban areas, 211
Denmark, 27, 137, 149, 208
Desmoulins, Camille, 180
devil, 246, 248, 249, 250–1, 261, 262
Dickens, Charles, 285
Dijon, 87, 94, 95, 149, 296
domestic violence, 31–2, 51, 147,
205–6, 239
Artois law, 48
increase in, 209, 212
law of silence, 50
legal cases, 218–19
Douai, 96, 98, 101
Drillon, Paul, 209
drunkenness, 71, 81, 207, 279
duels, 3, 5, 9, 21, 42–3, 61, 161,
163–82, 194–5
botte secrète (secret thrust), 170
invention of, 22, 29
loss of prestige, 221
Dumas, Alexandre, 169–70, 175,
180, 245, 265, 268, 272
Duprat, G.-L., 210
Durkheim, Emile, 121–2, 210, 277–8,
280

education, 2, 51, 100, 302
civic, 109
moral supervision, 128, 145
upper classes, 9
Elias, Norbert, 2, 23–4, 28, 42, 91,
92, 176, 198–9, 292
England
age of offenders, 144, 201
animal fighting, 67
Bloody Code, 206, 213, 241

boxing, 195, 222
characteristics of murders, 18,
  278–9
class divide, 196
'culture of sensibility', 19
culture of violence, 48–9, 50
death penalty, 207–8
decline in homicide, 8, 24, 28, 201
domestic violence, 147, 205, 206
duels, 169, 171, 221
fear of youth violence, 285
festivals, 52, 187
games, 66, 190
gangs,
  'scuttlers', 223, 285–7
  Teddy boys, 289
infanticide, 149, 150–1, 158, 214
'judicial revolution', 123, 127, 129
judicial system, 25
juries, 127, 129
juvenile delinquency, 284
knife fights, 43
literature, 243, 253–5, 261
manslaughter, 45
moral supervision, 128
murder rates, 38–9, 40, 49, 278
offences against the person, 204,
  206–7, 224
'Peaceable Kingdom' of, 198
penal system reform, 159
property crime, 15, 162–3, 206,
  208, 241
public executions, 27, 132, 137,
  138, 146, 147, 252
rape, 210
religious riots, 161, 186
revolts, 184, 188
risk of being murdered, 276
'rough music', 65
witchcraft, 152
women offenders, 148
Enlightenment, 10, 24, 137, 146, 262
  Age of, 8, 15, 28, 41, 177, 212,
    213, 251, 274, 284
  penal system reform, 159
  philosophes of the, 11, 130, 131,
    135

Erasmus of Rotterdam, 81, 91–2,
  219, 302
ethics, 40
ethnic minorities, 293
ethology, 10–11, 302
European Union (EU), 7
executioners, 105, 136–8
  see also death penalty

face, losing, 26, 69, 111
'fair fights', 222, 223, 226, 228, 298
fait divers, 249, 250, 263, 269,
  270–1
family, 31–2, 49–50, 75
  see also domestic violence
famine, 185, 188, 290
Fantômas, 6, 243, 264, 265, 267–8,
  270, 271, 272, 278
Feast of Fools, 52, 94, 97, 98, 187
Fellini, Federico, 289
femininity, 218
fencing, 167, 176
fertility rites, 65, 67
Festival of the Boy Bishop, 52
festivals, 5, 46, 52–67, 102, 236
  riots related to, 186, 187, 189, 193
  rural areas, 237, 238
  seasonality of violence, 72
  suppression of, 81, 187–8
  urban areas, 94–100
Féval, Paul, 263, 265, 268
films, 289–90, 292
fines, 3, 32, 37, 47
  Artois, 88
  duels, 179
  fullers, 114
  Ghent, 85
  Gonesse, 229–30
  paix à partie, 27
  unpaid, 115–16, 117
  urban areas, 5, 83, 103–4, 106–13,
    115–16
Finland
  duels, 169
  judges, 42
  knife fights, 43, 221, 282
  murder rate, 210, 282

Finland (cont.)
  public executions, 132
  repression, 124
firearms, 76, 80, 222, 227, 278, 282,
    301
First World War, 208, 210, 225, 241,
    269, 272
Flanders, 36, 71, 75, 78, 117
  high level of lethal violence, 83
  political system, 100
  rebellion in, 193
  revolts, 114
  witch hunts, 72
Flandrin, Jean-Louis, 34
Florence, 66, 93, 127, 146
football fans, 6, 298
Foucault, Michel, 15, 120, 129, 147,
    159, 198–9, 209
fourjurement, 84
Franc, Martin, 98
France
  'abbeys of youth', 93–4
  age of offenders, 41, 201–2, 280
  animal sacrifices, 67
  Apaches, 19, 43, 175, 220, 222,
    224, 243, 269–70, 275, 278,
    285, 291
  banlieues, 263, 292–300
  begging, 90
  'brutalization' of French society,
    177
  centralized state, 46, 162
  'civilizing process', 194
  class divide, 196
  codes of politeness, 26
  court leniency, 207
  criminal stereotypes, 209
  criminalization of violence, 78
  'curialization', 22
  death penalty, 207, 208
  decline in homicide, 8, 24, 28, 200
  disarmament, 142–3, 165
  duels, 29, 42–3, 61, 161, 164,
    166–7, 169, 170–82, 194–5,
    221
  English criticism of, 207
  extreme murder cases, 45

festivals, 52, 94–6
French Revolution, 30, 131, 180,
    212, 260
games, 66, 190
gangs, 289, 292–300
infanticide, 145, 148–9, 151,
    154–6, 158–9, 205
judges, 42
'judicial revolution', 123–4, 127,
    129
judicial system, 25
juvenile delinquency, 284, 285
'kingdoms of youth', 55
knife fights, 43
lettres de rémission, 32–3, 70
literature, 160, 169, 243, 244–51,
    262–9
marginal populations, 281
marriage age, 291
murder rates, 39, 40, 200, 210
nobles, 64–5
offences against the person, 204,
    224
organized banditry, 256
paedophilia, 14
'Peaceable Kingdom' ideal, 198
police, 27, 88, 128
public executions, 136, 138–9,
    141, 145, 146, 252
rape, 210
regicide, 15
revolts, 182–3, 184, 185, 188–9,
    192, 193–4
risk of being murdered, 276
robbery, 15, 144
rural areas, 225, 226–38, 239
strikers, 224
suicide, 277
'sworn bands', 99–100
times of peace, 4, 275
torture, 130–1, 146
vendettas, 192
village assemblies, 127
women criminals, 13, 203
youth violence, 67–70, 284
Francis I, King of France, 33, 78, 79,
    88, 117, 128, 175, 187

Frankfurt, 146
French Revolution, 30, 131, 180, 212, 260
Freud, Sigmund, 10, 225, 269, 302
Fróis, Luís, 12–13, 16
Fromm, Erich, 10, 302
fullers, 114

Gaboriau, Emile, 263, 265
gallows literature, 251–5, 260, 261
Galois, Evariste, 180
Gambetta, Léon, 180
games, 62, 66–7, 86, 87, 190, 192
  soule, 66, 189
gangs, 6, 12, 102, 181, 256, 260, 283
  Apaches, 19, 43, 175, 220, 222, 224, 243, 269–70, 275, 278, 285, 291
  bachelor, 17, 21–2, 34
  modern, 22, 282, 288–300
  New York, 43
Geertz, Clifford, 66
gender
  changing gender roles, 19–20, 275
  differing perceptions of violence, 147
  see also women
Genoa, 117, 162
genocide, 10
Germany
  age of male murderers, 41
  'books of the devil', 160
  decline in homicide, 200
  'elders', 127
  festivals, 52, 187
  infanticide, 149
  juvenile delinquency, 284–5
  Katzenmusik, 65
  'kingdoms of youth', 55
  military heroes, 180
  murder rates, 39, 200, 210
  offences against the person, 224
  'Peaceable Kingdom' ideal, 198
  peasant revolts, 126, 161, 164, 184
  Protestant urban leagues, 162

public executions, 132, 135, 137, 146
rape, 210
risk of being murdered, 276
suicide, 277, 278
Teufelbücher, 135
torture, 130, 131
women offenders, 148
see also Prussia
Ghent, 85, 102, 118
Giuliani, Albert, 210
Glasgow, 285
'Goatriders', 260–1
Gonesse, 226–34, 235
good manners, see politeness
Granier, Camille, 225
Great Discoveries, 4, 8
Greece, 20, 21, 210
Grenaille, F. de, 247
Grosmolard, J., 209
Gurr, Ted Robert, 38, 39

Habanc, Vérité, 245
La haine (film), 292
Haton, Claude, 174
Henri IV, King of France, 15, 25, 133, 145, 161, 170–1, 172
highwaymen, 30, 88, 261
Hitchcock, Alfred, 273
Hobbes, Thomas, 11, 24
Hogarth, William, 216, 255
Holmes, Sherlock, 266–7
Holy Roman Empire
  centralized state, 46
  duels, 167
  festivals, 187
  Free Cities, 162
  infanticide, 148, 149
  'judicial revolution', 129
  murder rates, 39
  public executions, 139, 146
  revolts, 184–5
  Thirty Years War, 161
  witches, 144
homicide see murder
homosexuals, 15, 93, 102, 119, 285

honour, 9, 21, 30, 42, 69, 303–4
  codes of, 157, 239
  court mechanism, 142
  culture of violence, 8
  defence of, 26, 81, 125, 200
  devaluation of, 30
  duels, 3, 29, 166, 170, 176, 177
  inner-city gangs, 22
  insults, 232
  Italy, 167
  knife fights, 43
  law of, 22
  masculine, 2, 46
  norms of, 61
  paix à partie, 26
  right to kill, 190
  rural areas, 219, 238
  urban trades, 28
hooliganism, 285, 289
Hugh of Saint Victor, 92
Hugo, Victor, 180, 264
Hundred Years War, 169, 191
Hungary, 55, 210, 259–60, 277

I vitelloni (film), 289
Iceland, 192
imprisonment, 104–6, 198, 209
  duels, 179
  Gonesse, 229, 230
  infanticide, 159
  United States, 281
incest, 14, 202, 204, 206, 210,
  240
infanticide, 9, 20, 102, 148–59, 201,
  205
  age of offenders, 202
  female servants, 203, 214
  focus of criminal justice system, 5,
    125
  'judicial revolution', 120, 126
  law of silence, 32
  Lorraine, 212
  as most serious offence, 14, 15,
    121, 122
  public executions, 132, 145
  rarity, 49–50
  trend towards leniency, 158–9

inheritance law, 36, 71, 192–3
injuries, types of, 228–9, 233
insanity, 16, 241–2
insults, 64, 179, 213–14, 236–7
  Gonesse, 226, 229–30, 231–2
  women's suffering of, 218
intergenerational relations, 18–19,
  126, 238, 260, 283, 291
Islam, 7
Italy
  centralized state, 46
  'civilizing process', 91
  duels, 167
  games, 66–7
  gangs, 289
  good manners, 92
  high level of lethal violence, 83
  'kingdoms of youth', 55
  knife fights, 43
  mattinata, 65
  metropolitan regulation, 117
  murder rates, 39–40, 208, 210
  political system, 100
  public executions, 146
  rape, 210
  revolts, 114
  rural areas, 238
  urban renaissance, 82

Jack the Ripper, 241, 244, 286
Jacques du Clercq, 101–3, 107, 114
Japan, 12–13, 16, 276
Jesuits, 145
Johnson, Charles, 254
jousting, 102
judges
  assassination of, 133
  death sentences, 42
  torture, 129
  view of women, 156–7
  see also magistrates
'judicial revolution', 120, 121–31,
  240
juvenile delinquency, 283–8

Kassovitz, Mathieu, 292
'kingdoms of youth', see 'abbeys'

knife fights, 75–6, 80, 167, 174–5, 221
  Apaches, 19, 222
  culture of, 43
  decline in, 28
  England, 222–3
  Finland, 282
  Gonesse, 227
  juvenile delinquency, 284
  masculine honour, 21, 51
  repression of, 224
  urban areas, 215
Kubrick, Stanley, 292
Kuwait, 277

Lamartine, Alphonse de, 180
Latvia, 276, 277
Le Bon, Gustave, 12
Le Breton, Auguste, 272
Le Brun de la Rochette, Claude, 133
LeBlanc, Maurice, 266, 267, 268
Lehti, Martti, 282–3
Leroux, Gaston, 266, 267
Leroy, Raoul, 209–10
lese-majesty, 15
lettres de rémission, 32–7, 40–1, 46, 68, 70, 75, 78, 82, 123–4
  duels, 170–1, 178
Leturcq, David, 67–8
Lichte, Jan de, 258, 259
Lille, 69, 143, 144, 187
  beggars, 90
  festivals, 94, 96, 97–9
  prostitutes, 89
literature, 6, 134–5, 156, 160, 243–73
  canards, 134, 155, 169, 243, 249–50, 251
  crime fiction, 255–6, 262–72
  gallows literature, 251–5, 260, 261
  social bandits, 256–7, 258, 262
  swashbuckler novels, 181–2, 269
  tragic stories, 154–5, 244–9, 250–1Lithuania, 149
Liverpool, 222, 224, 285

London, 162, 216–19
  Bridewell Palace, 159
  crime figures, 38
  culture of violence, 28
  decline in violence, 224
  disarmament, 220
  fear of subversion, 255
  fear of youth violence, 285
  festivals, 95
  literature, 264
  Mohocks affair, 216–17, 224, 257
  murder rate, 50
  police, 129
  property crime, 15, 122
  public executions, 27, 140, 191, 262
  punishments, 27
  rural migration to, 240
  Tyburn, 27, 132, 191, 216, 262
Lorenz, Konrad, 10–11, 302
Lorraine, 123, 212–13
Louis XI, King of France, 102
Louis XIII, King of France, 134, 175, 185, 219, 246, 247–8
Louis XIV, King of France, 22, 27, 33, 42, 117, 128, 159, 164–5, 167, 177, 185, 211, 235, 302
Low Countries
  apaiseurs, 84
  centralized state, 46
  confraternities, 68
  criminalization of homicide, 123
  decline in homicide, 8, 28
  extreme murder cases, 45
  festivals, 95, 187
  'judicial revolution', 130
  judicial system, 25
  knife fights, 174
  lettres de rémission, 34, 70
  mounted police, 88
  murder rates, 39
  pacification, 42, 91
  'Peaceable Kingdom' ideal, 198
  police, 128
  princely leniency, 81
  public executions, 140, 146
  religious riots, 161

Low Countries (cont.)
  revolts, 184
  urban cohesion, 96–7
  village assemblies, 127
  witchcraft, 151–2
Lucas, George, 292
Lupin, Arsène, 265, 266–7, 268, 272
Luther, Martin, 126
Lyon, 82, 94, 118, 143, 159, 221, 249

Madrid, 124
Manchester, 222–3, 285–7
Mandrin, 30, 135, 144, 146, 244,
  256
Mandrou, Robert, 183
manliness, 12–23, 45, 51, 122, 190,
  194
  ambiguity of, 147
  cult of, 304
  culture of violence, 8, 75
  defence of honour, 26
  festive confrontations, 46
  football fans, 298
  glorification of, 296
  head as symbolic centre of, 77, 79
  see also masculinity
manslaughter, 45, 123, 201, 206
Mantua, 39, 41, 174
maréchaussée, 88, 128, 165, 194,
  263
market economy, 23–4
marriage, 53, 54, 57–8, 103
  age of, 33–4, 55, 72, 126, 178,
    193, 291
  competition for women, 59
  marital status of offenders, 74–5
  sexual relations outside, 153
  weddings, 99
Marseille, 221
masculinity, 2, 8, 12–23, 218, 304
  changes in meaning, 221
  dual model of, 197
  hegemonic, 19, 279
  modern gangs, 297, 299
  urban areas, 220
  working-class, 286
  see also manliness

mass murderers, 241–2, 278
Massacre of the Innocents, 52
masturbation, 34, 55, 274–5
materialism, 299–300
matricide, 49–50
Medea, 121, 145, 154–5
media, 18, 280, 290, 292, 295, 300
medicine, 233, 241
Mediterranean countries, 24, 141
  honour, 21
  law of vengeance, 127
  organized banditry, 257
  penal system reform, 159
  vendettas, 27, 195
Mercier, Louis-Sébastien, 158–9
Mexico, 210, 277, 303
Middle Ages, 3, 4, 8, 303
  crime figures, 32
  culture of violence, 21, 46–52
  infanticide, 148
  judicial system, 123
  knife fights, 43
  murder rates, 39
  peasant revolts, 71
middle class, 217, 284, 287, 289–90
Mohocks affair, 216–17, 224, 257
molestation of girls, 202–4, 240
Un monde sans pitié (film), 292
Montaigne, Michel de, 139–40
Mousnier, Roland, 182–3, 184
murder
  age of offenders, 202
  Bruges, 92–3
  characteristics of murderers, 1, 9
  classification of, 9
  contemporary era, 275–6
  crime figures, 31, 32–8, 39–40, 41
  criminalization of, 78, 81, 113,
    123–4, 163, 199, 208
  culture of violence, 46–52
  decrease in, 1, 2, 8, 15, 17, 28–30,
    38–44, 199–201, 204, 301
  domestic, 239
  duels, 170–1
  fear of, 101
  focus of criminal justice system, 5,
    125

glorification of, 6
Gonesse, 227
Japan, 12–13
'judicial revolution', 120, 123, 126
justifications for pardons, 70–1
London, 216, 217
Lorraine, 212
male aggression, 12–23
as most serious offence, 14, 121, 122, 133
new definition of, 142
normality of, 82
Paris, 221
prosecution of cases, 45
public executions, 132, 141
punishment of, 46–7, 48–9
repression of, 134
seasonal variations, 72, 79
as social construction, 18
of spouses, 205, 207
as taboo, 3, 5, 7, 44, 141, 181, 246
taverns, 72–3
three forms of, 25
torture of murderers, 130
as transgression of cultural norms, 11
mutilation, 15, 84, 89–90, 143–4, 146

New England, 24
New York, 41, 43, 101, 280, 281
newspapers, 263
Nicolas, Jean, 193
Nivet, Philippe, 256
nobles, 5, 17, 73, 74, 220
    contempt for lower classes, 196
    duels, 3, 22, 163–4, 166–7, 170–82, 194–5
    honour, 42
    manly ethic of violence, 42
    pacification of, 178, 302
    participation in festivals, 64–5
    retreat of lethal violence, 28–9
    right to kill, 3, 120, 190, 198
Normandy, 66, 71, 179, 185

norms, 2–3, 11, 65, 145
    bourgeois, 220
    failure to assimilate, 202
    gender roles, 20
    of honour, 61
    'judicial revolution', 127
    Puritan, 189
    rural areas, 234
    taverns, 63
Norway, 208, 284
Nuremburg, 138

Oedipus complex, 10, 225, 269
oil, boiling alive in, 146

pacification, 83, 112, 115, 116–17, 164, 196, 304
    due to self-interest, 235–6
    everyday behaviour, 198, 208
    fictional violence, 244
    intergenerational relations, 18–19
    London, 216
    Low Countries, 91
    noble behaviour, 178, 302
    private space, 241
    public/collective space, 9, 204
    resistance to, 301
    swashbuckler novels, 181
    threshold of, 298
    urban areas, 199, 223
paedophilia, 14, 210, 240
paix à partie, 26–7, 46, 47
pardons, 32–7, 70–1, 74–5, 109
    duels, 166, 168, 170–1
    England, 49
    increase in, 123
    infanticide, 148
    public executions, 139
    see also lettres de rémission
Paris, 82–3, 117, 143, 220–1
    animal sacrifices, 67
    Apaches, 43, 224, 243, 269–70, 285
    canards, 134, 155, 243, 249
    Carnival, 79
    codes of politeness, 219

Paris (cont.)
  criminal register, 85
  decline in violence, 224
  disarmament, 142–3
  duels, 177, 179
  executions, 125
  foundling hospitals, 158
  infanticide, 149, 151, 155–6
  literature, 264
  modern gangs, 23, 293, 294, 298
  murder rates, 221Paris Saint-
    Germain, 298
  penal system reform, 159
  police, 128–9, 211
  property crime, 15, 122, 215
  public executions, 132, 136,
    138–9, 141, 145, 191, 252,
    262
  riots, 195
  rural migration to, 240
  torture, 130, 146
  women offenders, 148
Parival, Jean-Nicolas de, 247
parricide, 13–14, 15, 49–50, 133
  death penalty, 45
  financial motives for, 239
  literary representations, 154
  Lorraine, 212
peasants, 3, 5, 17, 29, 73–4, 234–5
  Camus on, 248
  customs, 52
  festive violence, 164
  manly ethic of violence, 42
  migration to urban areas, 90
  resistance to change, 20
  revolts, 8, 71, 126, 161, 164,
    182–94, 297
  women, 152–3
  see also rural areas
Philip II, King of Spain, 34–6, 76,
    123, 130, 161, 162, 167–8,
    174
Picardy, 66, 67, 79, 101, 103, 143,
    175, 229
Pierre de l'Estoile, 138–9, 170, 249
Poe, Edgar Allan, 264

Poissenot, Bénigne, 245
Poland, 210, 289
police, 27, 87–8, 128–9, 211, 237
politeness, 2–3, 24, 62, 92,198, 297
  codes of, 26, 219, 302
  taverns, 63
Ponson du Terrail, Vicomte, 263, 265
population growth, 35, 36
Porchnev, Boris, 182, 184
Portugal, 12, 123, 210
poverty, 125–6, 186, 213, 240, 263,
    275
property crime, 15, 162–3, 199, 206,
    208, 211–12, 235, 241
  see also robbery; theft
prostitutes, 110–13, 115, 255, 275
  Apaches, 270
  Arras, 86–7, 89
  children, 285
  Gonesse, 229
  tolerance for, 214
Protestantism, 24, 28, 35, 45, 165
  educational structures, 100
  moral supervision, 25, 128, 145
  murder rates, 40
  reformers, 118
  religious riots/revolts, 184, 186
  suppression of festivals, 187
  urban leagues, 162
  Westphalia treaty, 197
Proudhon, Pierre-Joseph, 180
Prussia
  alleviation of sentences, 147
  death penalty, 207
  duels, 43, 168
  murder rate, 221
  see also Germany
psychoanalysis, 10, 288
psychology, 10, 12
public squares, 60–1, 62, 83
punishments, 3, 14, 19, 45
  Artois, 47–8, 88
  duels, 179
  Gonesse, 229–30
  infanticide, 150
  'judicial revolution', 124

Paris, 85
property crime, 37, 102, 162–3
regicide, 15
responsibility for, 126
United States, 280
urban areas, 83, 84–5
see also death penalty; fines;
  imprisonment
Puritans, 187, 189

quarrels, 62, 64, 69, 213, 231, 278

rape, 102, 124–5, 202, 203–4
acquittals, 218
Bruges, 93
criminalization of, 210
gang, 94, 293, 296
in Gonesse, 229
increase in, 240
rapiers, 173, 174, 175–6Ravaillac,
  François, 15
Ray, Nicholas, 289
Rebel Without a Cause (film), 289,
  290
Reformation, 65, 187
regicide, 15, 119, 121, 133, 146
religion, 4, 7, 11, 302
festivals, 97
public executions, 136, 140
religious riots, 184, 186
sexual repression, 75
'social discipline', 25
supervision of the population, 35
see also Catholicism; Christianity;
  Protestantism
Renaissance, 24, 81, 91, 122, 148,
  160, 191, 219
repeat offenders, 108–9, 110, 114
Restif de la Bretonne, 54
revolts, 3, 8, 71, 182–94
France, 141
fullers, 114
Germany, 126, 164
Ghent, 102
relationship to duels, 161
see also riots

Richelieu, Cardinal, 172, 174
riots, 3, 186–7, 193, 195, 276
banlieues, 19, 263, 288, 293,
  295–6, 297–8
see also revolts
robbery, 15, 87–8, 144, 214, 240
age of offenders, 202
fear of, 160
modern gangs, 293, 299
severity of punishment, 121
social bandits, 256–60, 262, 266,
  268
see also property crime; theft
Rochant, Eric, 292
Romania, 55, 135, 210
Rome
animal sacrifices, 67
festivals, 94
murder rate, 39, 224
public executions, 139
Rosset, François de, 134, 154, 156,
  245–6, 250
Rouletabille, 265–6, 272
Rousseau, Jean-Jacques, 11, 263,
  284
rural areas, 27, 73, 195, 219–20,
  225–40, 302
culture of violence, 50
decline in rural violence, 199–200
festivals, 187
homicides in, 71
revolts, 193
see also peasants
Russia
gangs, 289
homicidal violence, 23
infanticide, 149
murder rates, 1
risk of being murdered, 276
suicide, 277
Ryckére, Raymond de, 203

Saint-Omer, 33, 37, 47, 71, 72, 77,
  98, 102, 117
Saint-Pol, 96, 102–3, 144
Sazie, Léon, 267

Scandinavia
  decline in homicide, 28
  fines, 27
  murder rates, 39, 40, 210
Schinderhannes, 257–8, 259, 262
Scotland, 45, 149, 192, 278
self-control, 199, 216, 274
  English, 207
  increase in, 41, 233
  internalization of, 198
  lack of, 68–9
  rural areas, 81
  training and socialization of youth,
    209
  urban areas, 91, 92, 100, 103, 112,
    117
self-defence, 71, 123, 130, 198, 281
self-esteem, 12, 111, 142
sexual abuse, 202–4, 206, 218,
    240
sexual activity, 34, 55, 65, 75, 126,
    275, 285
sexual power, 21, 66, 303
sexuality, 46, 152, 294
Shakespeare, William, 147, 173, 283
shame, 26, 190, 303
  'reintegrative', 27
Sheppard, John (Jack), 253
Shipman, Harold, 278
Sibony, Daniel, 10
Sicily, 208
Smith, Adam, 24
Smith, Alexander, 254
smugglers, 30
Sobri, Jóska, 259
social bandits, 256–60, 262, 266,
    268
social class, 9, 10
  see also middle class; nobles;
    peasants; working class
social control, 18, 39, 41, 119, 120,
    122, 228
'social discipline', 25–6, 65
sodomy, 92–3, 102
soldiers, 28, 73, 74, 163, 165
  duels, 168–9, 177–8, 179
  Gonesse, 227–8

Souvestre, Paul, 267
Spain
  bullfighting, 67, 190
  duels, 167–8
  festivals, 52
  'judicial revolution', 127,
    129–30
  judicial system, 25
  'kingdoms of youth', 55
  murder rate, 210
  penal system reform, 159
  police, 128
  public executions, 136
  robbers, 144
spectacle of punishment, 121,
    122, 129, 131, 135, 137, 190,
    191
sport, 66–7, 190, 192, 209, 298,
    304
St John's Night, 53, 54, 86, 188
state, 25, 82, 119–20, 122, 160
  centralized, 46, 162
  city-states, 162
  'civilizing process', 23–4, 91
  fear instilled by the, 129
  monopoly of violence, 3, 18, 24,
    198, 304, 471
strangers, fear of, 86, 88–9, 237
strikes, 186, 192, 221, 224
students, 28, 193
Sue, Eugène, 265
suicide, 210, 211, 275–6, 277–8
Sweden
  abolition of death penalty, 208
  decline in homicide, 8, 24, 201
  duels, 169
  fights and murders, 287
  gangs, 289
  infanticide, 149
  juvenile delinquency, 284
  knife fights, 43
  murder rates, 39, 44
  penal system reform, 159
  rape, 210
  repression, 124
  risk of being murdered, 276
  student violence, 28

Switzerland
  'kingdoms of youth', 55
  murder rates, 39
  public executions, 135
  suppression of festivals, 187
swords, 80, 174–5, 301

taboo, 3, 7, 18, 23, 29, 44, 141, 211, 274
  acceptance of blood taboo, 5, 8, 181, 195
  cultural construction of, 303
  homosexuality, 93
  law of silence, 50
  literature, 246
  patricide, 13–14
  rural areas, 225–6
Tarahumaras Indians, 303, 304
taverns, 62–4, 72–3, 83, 231
theft, 37, 64, 68, 122, 143, 236
  age of offenders, 144, 237
  Antwerp, 84
  Bruges, 93
  contempt for, 47
  cycle of poverty, 126
  execution of thieves, 27, 102
  fines, 106
  Gonesse, 226, 228–9
  leniency towards, 125
  Lorraine, 212, 213
  mutilation of thieves, 89–90
  torture of thieves, 130
  urban areas, 211–12, 214, 215–16
  women, 148
  see also property crime; robbery
Thirty Years War, 25, 161, 168, 169, 171, 195, 197
Three Musketeers, 181–2
torture, 15, 25, 117, 129, 130–1
  decline in use of, 146, 159–60
  public, 83, 119, 132
see also wheel, breaking on, oil,boiling alive in
Tournai, 70, 96, 98, 144
towns see urban areas
trades, see crafts

trêves, 84, 86
Les tricheurs (film), 289, 290

Ukraine, 276
unemployment, 6, 125–6, 299, 304
United Kingdom, 204, 216, 276, 278
United Provinces
  Calvinism, 161, 184
  cities, 162
  decline in homicide, 24, 28
  festivals, 187
  French invasion of, 165
  French loss of, 33
  infanticide, 149
  murder rates, 39, 40
  penal system reform, 159
  public executions, 146
  robbers, 144
  towns, 117–18
United States
  age of male murderers, 41
  conquest of America, 8
  homicidal violence, 23
  increase in crime rates, 279
  influence of American mass culture, 300
  murder rates, 210, 280, 301
  risk of being murdered, 276
  western frontier, 13
  young murderers, 280, 281, 288
urban areas, 3, 73, 82–118, 211–25, 240–1
  'civilizing process', 91
  containment of violence, 50
  control of the young, 93–100
  crime figures, 37
  gangs, 290
  inner-city brutality, 6
  municipalization of aggression, 5
  pacification, 3, 199
  prohibitions and ordinances, 86–7
  prostitutes, 89
  punishments, 84–5, 88, 89–90
  revolts, 193
  sodomy, 92–3
  see also banlieues
d'Urfé, Honoré, 245

Vacher, Jacques, 241
vagrants, 86, 89, 117, 159, 211, 219, 263
values, 16, 125
  chauvinist, 294, 300
  honour, 26
  manly, 288
vendettas, 27, 85, 192, 195
vengeance, 3, 21, 30, 46, 81, 84, 102–3, 190
  English writers, 169
  law of, 22, 109, 125, 127, 303–4
  motives for crimes, 230
  prevention of, 111
  replaced by personal interest, 107
  right of, 100
  as sacred obligation, 26
  towns' use of private, 116
Venice, 53, 67, 117, 132, 162, 190
Vidocq, Eugène François, 264, 272
violence
  culture of, 8, 21, 41, 44, 45, 46–52, 58, 75, 302
  definitions of, 7, 10
  innateness, 9–12
  seasonal variations, 72, 79, 105, 231
Vouglans, Muyart de, 123, 131, 141
Vulpius, Christian August, 259

Wales, 188, 278
war, 2, 11, 40, 164–5
  calming effect of, 23
  'culture of', 8
  'just', 4, 7, 18, 143, 163, 165, 197, 240, 274, 304
Wars of Religion, 14, 25, 29, 124, 161
weapons, 8, 18, 75–6, 81, 110, 301
  Artois law, 47–8
  bachelor gangs, 17
  disarmament, 142–3, 165, 220
  Gonesse, 227
  prohibition on carrying, 86
  and see firearms, rapiers, swords
Weber, Max, 40

weddings, 99
Westphalia, peace of (1648), 160, 197
wheel, breaking on the, 135, 144, 146
Wild, Jonathan, 253, 261
The Wild One (film), 289
witches, 121, 151–2, 153
  decline in persecution of, 156
  execution of, 15, 135–6, 140, 144–5
  Germany, 148
  punished by men, 158
  torture of, 119
women, 2, 147–59, 198–9
  bourgeois norms, 220
  changing gender roles, 19–20
  criminal girls, 285
  docile wife role, 153–4, 156
  domestic violence, 205–6
  duels, 179
  English law, 207
  execution of, 120–1, 144–5
  feminine norms, 218
  fines, 106, 109, 110, 111
  gangs, 290
  'gentle' nature of, 23
  imprisonment of, 105
  insults by, 232
  juvenile delinquency, 287
  'kidnapping by seduction', 214
  leniency towards, 5, 204–5
  literary representations, 154–5, 244, 255
  male competition for, 59
  model of weak woman, 8, 46
  modern gang attitudes towards, 294–5
  molestation of girls, 202–4
  as murder victims, 51, 279
  murderers, 1, 13, 14, 40, 50
  purity of, 26, 238, 303
  riots, 186, 187
  scuttler gangs, 286
  seditious role of, 183
  tutelage of girls, 55–6

violence against, 74, 218–19, 228–9, 234
violence by, 20–1, 50, 203
see also infanticide
working class, 9, 20, 192, 208–9, 275
Apaches, 270
'civilizing process', 217
fear of subversion, 255
fear of the, 222
juvenile delinquency, 284, 285
macho traditions, 300
mass literature, 264–5
modern gangs, 294, 295
pacification, 302
scuttler gangs, 223, 285–7
see also 'dangerous classes'

xenophobia, 58, 83, 97, 188, 196

youth, 'kingdoms' or 'abbeys' of, see abbeys of
Ypres, 67, 90, 117, 143, 144

Zévaco, Michel, 268, 272